THE POLITICS OF
THE CRIMINAL JUSTICE
SYSTEM

POLITICAL SCIENCE

A Comprehensive Publication Program

Executive Editor

KENNETH FRIEDMAN

U. S. Department of Energy
Office of the Assistant Secretary
for Conservation and Solar Application
Washington, D.C.

Publications in Political Science

1. Public Administration as a Developing Discipline (in two parts)
   by Robert T. Golembiewski
2. Comparative National Policies on Health Care
   by Milton I. Roemer, M.D.
3. Exclusionary Injustice: The Problem of Illegally Obtained Evidence
   by Steven R. Schlesinger
4. From Contract to Community: Political Theory at the Crossroads
   edited by Fred R. Dallmayr
5. Liberalism and the Modern Polity: Essays in Contemporary Political Theory
   edited by Michael J. Gargas McGrath
6. The Politics of the Criminal Justice System: An Organizational Analysis
   by Ralph A. Rossum

Other volumes in preparation

Developmental Editors

Robert Agranoff
Northern Illinois University

Keith G. Baker
California State University at Long Beach

Carl J. Bellone
California State University at Hayward

Thad L. Beyle
University of North Carolina

Howard Bucknell, III
The Ohio State University

C. Gregory Buntz
University of the Pacific

James A. Caporaso
Northwestern University

James D. Carroll
Syracuse University

Raymond D. Duvall
University of Minnesota

William B. Eddy
The University of Missouri - Kansas City

Richard A. Eribes
Arizona State University

Victor Ferkiss
Georgetown University

H. George Frederickson
Eastern Washington University

Robert T. Golembiewski
University of Georgia

Muriel Greenhill
Medgar Evers College

John Stuart Hall
Arizona State University

Ferrel Heady
University of New Mexico

Charles H. Levine
University of Maryland

Fremont J. Lyden
University of Washington

Jerry L. McCaffery
Indiana University

Michael J. Gargas McGrath
Brown University

Vincent L. Marando
University of Maryland

J. Donald Moon
Wesleyan University

Elizabethann O'Sullivan
Arizona State University

Ralph A. Rossum
Memphis State University

Steven R. Schlesinger
Rutgers University
The Catholic University of America

William R. Shaffer
Purdue University

Mulford Q. Sibley
Duke University

Michael S. Stohl
Purdue University

Frank J. Thompson
University of Georgia

Bruce Vladeck
Columbia University

David Vogel
University of California, Berkeley

Gary L. Wamsley
Virginia Polytechnic Institute

Ronald E. Weber
Indiana University

THE POLITICS OF THE CRIMINAL JUSTICE SYSTEM

AN ORGANIZATIONAL ANALYSIS

Ralph A. Rossum
Department of Political Science
Memphis State University
Memphis, Tennessee

MARCEL DEKKER, INC.   New York and Basel

Library of Congress Cataloging in Publication Data

Rossum, Ralph A   [Date]
   The politics of the criminal justice system.

   (Political science ; 6)
   Includes index.
   1. Criminal justice, Administration of--United
States. 2. Interorganizational relations--United
States. I. Title. II. Series: Political science
(New York) ; 6.
HV8138.R7   364'.973   78-18519
ISBN 0-8247-6707-1

COPYRIGHT © 1978 by MARCEL DEKKER, INC. ALL RIGHTS RESERVED

Neither this book nor any part may be reproduced or transmitted in any form or by any means, electronic or mechanical, including photocopying, microfilming, and recording, or by any information storage and retrieval system, without permission in writing from the publisher.

MARCEL DEKKER, INC.
270 Madison Avenue, New York, New York 10016

Current printing (last digit):
10 9 8 7 6 5 4 3 2 1

PRINTED IN THE UNITED STATES OF AMERICA

To Constance

FOREWORD

Professor Ralph A. Rossum has written an outstanding textbook in the field of criminal justice. His primary tool, compliance analysis, is highly successful in probing for the major flaws in American criminal justice and in suggesting avenues for reform.

Professor Rossum evinces a thorough grasp of the vast literature on criminal justice, both empirical and more traditional. He provides a penetrating analysis of the alternatives for reform as well as a profound understanding of those aspects of the American regime which limit the possibilities for such reform.

This is a timely book, coming as it does when so many Americans are justifiably skeptical about the government's ability to protect them from crime. While this book will certainly not calm their fears, it will provide them with a clear-headed analysis of the nature, scope, and causes of the problem. Certainly, it will candidly inform them of the promise, assets and liabilities, of each of the major options for reform.

This book deserves the widest readership among students of criminal justice and concerned citizens.

Steven R. Schlesinger

PREFACE

Considered either individually or in conjunction with one another, police, courts, and corrections are failing to accomplish the goals which society has assigned to them. This volume introduces the reader to these major components of the criminal justice system and to the problems that each of them confronts. Utilizing a form of compliance analysis adapted from Amatai Etzioni's *A Comparative Analysis of Complex Organizations,* it considers the criminal justice system from an organizational perspective, explores the interrelationship or interface problems that exist among these components, and attempts to explain that failure on the basis of this internal politics and conflict.

Compliance analysis provides an excellent and heretofore unused framework of considerable organizational and heuristic power for the study of the criminal justice system. In particular, it helps to provide a realistic appraisal of the criminal justice system and the prospects for reform of each of its components. With it, for example, the on-going discussion in the literature over police role—i.e., over the proper function of the police in democratic society—can be at once evaluated and approached afresh; so, too, can the various proposals for enhancing police-community relations. Compliance analysis also serves to inject a much needed dosage of political realism into the discussion of the other components of the criminal justice system and their possible reform. Thus, when applied to the lower courts, it can be used to highlight the difficulties involved in attempting to bring about an end of plea bargaining, and when applied to correctional agencies, it can help to explain the growing disenchantment with the rehabilitative ideal and the increased respectability now attached to the notion of simple punishment.

The reader will quickly note that the volume gives particular attention to the manifold problems that presently confront the criminal justice system and that limit the prospects for its reform. This is not done out of a sense of pessimism and despair, but out of the hope that the public will come to appreciate that there are inherent limits to what can be accomplished by large hierarchical organizations, including the components of the criminal justice system.* If these limits are recognized, the public may well lower its often grandiose expectations concerning what the police, courts, and corrections are to achieve and may come instead to a more realistic assessment of what is possible.

I would like to acknowledge my debt to those who helped make this book possible. I am grateful to Lloyd Rudolph of the University of Chicago for introducing me to possible applications of Professor Etzioni's work; to James Q. Wilson of Harvard University for his many writings and the influence they have had on my thought; to William R. Marty of Memphis State University for reading and criticizing sections of the manuscript; to Steven R. Schlesinger of Catholic University for his encouragement throughout the preparation of the entire manuscript and for his suggestions for revision; to my wife, Constance Rossum, for suggestions of both style and substance; and to Laura Ingram, for her diligent and good-natured typing of the manuscript.

Ralph A. Rossum

---

*In this regard, the volume continues and elaborates upon the arguments of James Q. Wilson in "The Bureaucracy Problem," *The Public Interest*, no. 6 (Winter 1967): 3-9; and Jeffrey L. Pressman and Aaron B. Wildavsky, *Implementation* (Berkeley: University of California Press, 1973).

CONTENTS

Foreword					*v*

Preface					*vii*

1. **An Overview of the Criminal Justice System**		1

    Crime in America				5
    The Steps in the Criminal Process			24
    Notes					38
    Bibliography				46

2. **The Nonsystem of Criminal Justice**			48

    Interface Problems in the Criminal Justice System		49
    Compliance Analysis and the Criminal Justice System		56
    Notes					61
    Bibliography				66

3. **The Police**				67

    Problems in the Definition of Police Role		69
    Contradictory Perceptions of the Police Role		74
    Proposed Improvements in Police-Community Relations		80
    The Problematic Nature of Police-Community Relations		99
    Notes					101
    Bibliography				113

4. The Supreme Court, the Constitution, and Criminal Procedure — 116

    The Constitution and Criminal Procedure — 117
    The Fourteenth Amendment and the Bill of Rights — 118
    The Law of Search and Seizure — 124
    The Privilege Against Self-Incrimination and Coerced Confessions — 134
    The Right to Counsel — 139
    The Protection Against Double Jeopardy — 144
    The Right to a Fair Trial — 147
    The Protection Against Cruel and Unusual Punishments — 151
    Posttrial Procedures — 156
    Retroactive Application of Criminal Procedural Guarantees — 159
    Basic Themes — 162
    Notes — 163
    Bibliography — 178

5. The Lower Courts and the Administration of "Justice" — 181

    The Limited Normative Power of the Supreme Court — 181
    Two Models of the Criminal Process — 183
    The Performance of the Lower Courts — 186
    The Prospects for Judicial Reform — 201
    An End to Plea Bargaining? — 213
    Notes — 214
    Bibliography — 222

6. Corrections — 224

    The Purpose of Criminal Sanctions — 224
    Correctional Programs — 234
    Corrections: The Need for a New Definition — 252
    Notes — 253
    Bibliography — 262

7. Criminal Justice in the American "Commercial" Republic: An Assessment — 264

    America: The Commercial Republic — 266
    The Need for Realism — 267
    Notes — 270
    Bibliography — 272

Case Index — 275

Index — 281

THE POLITICS OF
THE CRIMINAL JUSTICE
SYSTEM

1
AN OVERVIEW OF THE CRIMINAL JUSTICE SYSTEM

The criminal justice system has as its goal the prevention of crime, or, barring that, the successful apprehension, conviction, and correction of the offender. Presently, however, it is failing to accomplish either. As rapidly rising crime rates serve to illustrate, the criminal justice system has been singularly unsuccessful in preventing crime. During the 1960s, the number of serious crimes committed in the United States increased 196.9 percent from 2,019,000 offenses to 5,995,200 offenses. This increase much more than kept pace with the growth in population. The rate of offenses per 100,000 inhabitants jumped from 1,126.2 to 2,906.7, an increase of 158.1 percent.[1] These figures, of course, include only those crimes brought to the attention of the police. A 1974 Law Enforcement Assistance Administration (LEAA) study of the nation's five largest cities reveals that actual rates of victimization are two to five times greater than the number of crimes reported to the police.[2]

Statistics compiled by the Federal Bureau of Investigation (FBI) also reveal that the criminal justice system has failed in its efforts to apprehend, convict, and correct the offender. The data for 1974 are representative. In that year, there were 10,192,000 major, or index, crimes reported to the police, but only 1,698,000 suspects were arrested, only 613,400 were convicted, and only 241,600 were sentenced to prison[3] (see Figure 1.1).

All three components of the criminal justice system are in part to blame. Thus, the police in 1974 cleared by arrest only 21.3 percent of the 7,226,079 known offenses that occurred in metropolitan areas that year.[4] However, even that low clearance rate has been sufficient to inundate the judiciary. As a consequence, the courts are compelled to tolerate and even encourage the use of plea bargaining, so much so that it is now employed in approximately 90 percent of all criminal cases in the United States.

In plea bargaining, the defendant agrees to plead guilty in return for a reduced charge or sentence. But in so doing, he* waives an entire array of con-

---

*Masculine forms are used where actual gender is indefinite.

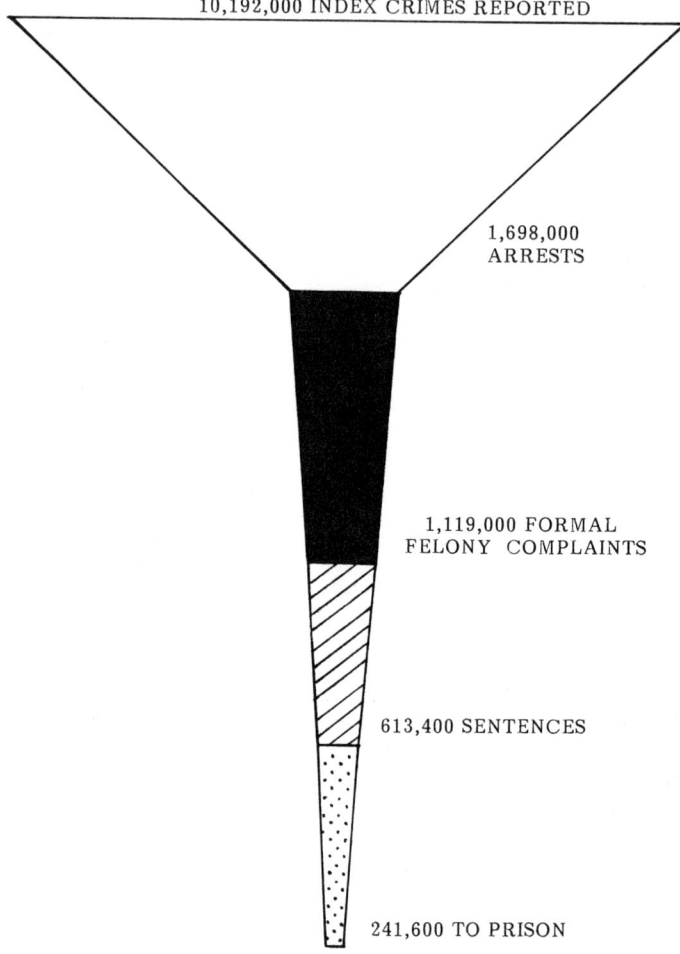

Figure 1.1 Funneling effect from reported crimes through prison sentence.

stitutional rights designed to protect him against unjustified conviction, including the right to remain silent, the right to confront witnesses against him, the right to trial by jury, and the right to be proved guilty beyond a reasonable doubt. It is efficient in that it spares the criminal justice system the need for a trial. As a result, it is favored by the entire court organization, from the judge who is anxious to clear his docket, to the prosecutor who is eager to achieve a high rate of conviction (even if it is for lesser offenses), to the clearly guilty defendant who seeks to minimize the punitive sanctions that can be imposed on him, to the defense attorney (or public defender) who wants to get the best deal for his client. Despite these advantages, however, plea bargaining comes at a high cost. To begin with, clearly innocent defendants find themselves enmeshed in an operation where defendants are presumed to be guilty—after all, over 90 percent of all defendants ultimately enter guilty pleas. Once enmeshed, there is little opportunity to escape unscathed. As Abraham Blumberg has pointed out, "It would appear at least tentatively that once one is caught up in the system as an accused (indicted) individual, there is little chance of escaping conviction."[5]

The cost of plea bargaining is also borne by society as a whole. Thus a common result of plea bargaining is that defendants (especially professional criminals) are not dealt with as severely as might be appropriate. This leniency reduces the deterrent impact of the law. Likewise, plea bargaining also endangers society's interests in protection and security by making the correctional task of rehabilitation more difficult. It reinforces the defendant's belief that he can manipulate the criminal justice system, and, as a result, it minimizes his motivation to participate in correctional programs. As Jonathan D. Casper perceptively observes:

> The situation the defendant faces in the period preceding his eventual plea is, in many respects, an extension of his life in the streets. You scuffle around, trying to accumulate a little wealth or power; you con others and are conned by them; you exploit those you can and are exploited by those who are more powerful; you use people for your own ends and are, in turn, used by others. You lie, you cheat, you care little about abstract moral principles. How you make out on the street depends upon what you've got and how you use it. In addition, luck and fate are crucial elements of life in the streets .... These same characteristics seem to the defendants to characterize their experience within the legal system. Their initial arrest is often simply the product of bad luck: they are arrested for an activity that they have been engaging in frequently. Something goes wrong, and they get caught. They then must attempt to make the best of their situation and use the techniques that they already know well in order to attempt to ameliorate their plight. The other participants in the system seem to be doing the same things. They are going about their jobs in fashions that seem to the defendants quite similar to the hypocritical and manipulative ways which they themselves treat people. And they are probably correct.[6]

If the courts have failed to convict and sentence as they should, correctional agencies have failed to correct as they should. Recent statistics from the FBI's *Uniform Crime Reports* reveal that 65 percent of those persons arrested during the period from 1970 to 1972 (184,809 of a total of 228,032) had been arrested before. "The 228,032 offenders had a total of 867,000 documented charges during their criminal careers, with 244,239 reporting convictions and

87,358 imprisonments of six months or more."[7] Figure 1.2 indicates the percentage of persons arrested from 1970 to 1974 who were repeaters (recidivists).

Clearly, the criminal justice system is failing to achieve its goals. This book explores the causes of its failure while acquainting the reader with its various functions, components and procedures. It considers the criminal justice system from an organizational perspective, explores the interrelationship or interface problems that exist among its various components—the police, the courts, and corrections—and offers an explanation for its failure on the basis of this internal politics. It begins with a rather straightforward yet comprehensive overview of the way in which a case moves through the criminal justice system—from the

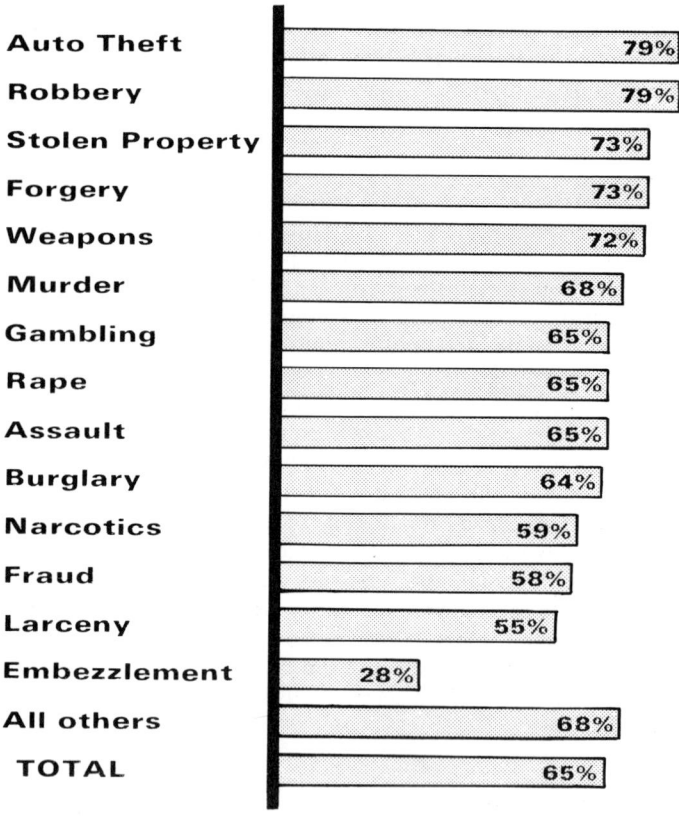

Figure 1.2 Percent repeaters by type of crime. Persons arrested 1970-1974. [Source: *Crime in the United States—Uniform Crime Reports—1974*, U. S. Department of Justice (Washington, D. C.: Government Printing Office, 1975), p. 49.]

OVERVIEW OF THE CRIMINAL JUSTICE SYSTEM

commission of the offense to the arrest, the initial judicial appearance, the preliminary hearing, the formal criminal charge, the arraignment, the trial, the appeals process, the collateral attack, and on through such correctional practices as incarceration, parole, probation, or pretrial diversion. Against this background, this book attempts to provide a sustained theoretical explanation for the failure the system is experiencing.

Crime in America

Crime may be defined as antisocial behavior so dangerous that perpetrators are threatened with punishment legitimately imposed by the government. This behavior may consist of actions, words, thoughts, or intentions.[8] This definition, however, is so broad as to be of limited utility. As the President's Commission on Law Enforcement and Administration of Justice points out:

> A skid-row drunk lying in a gutter is crime [sic]. So is the killing of an unfaithful wife. A Cosa Nostra conspiracy to bribe public officials is crime. So is a strong-arm robbery by a fifteen-year-old boy. The embezzlement of a corporation's funds by an executive is crime. So is the possession of marijuana cigarettes by a student.[9]

These crimes can be no more appropriately lumped together for purposes of analysis than can "measles and schizophrenia, or lung cancer and a broken ankle."[10] To be properly understood and evaluated, each class of crime must be considered separately. Accordingly, this chapter will take up and explore in turn three classes of crime: index crimes, white-collar crimes, and "victimless" crimes. It will also address, if briefly, what are commonly attributed to be the various causes of these crimes.

Index Crimes

There are more than 2,800 federal crimes on the statute books, and a much larger number of state and local ones. Some involve serious bodily harm, some stealing, some public order and public morals, some regulation of the economy, some government revenues, and some the creation of hazardous conditions. Some are perpetrated in a ruthless and systematic fashion; others are committed spontaneously.[11] Of this large array of crimes, however, only seven are reported by the FBI in its *Uniform Crime Reports*—the basic source of information on the nationwide crime situation[12] (see Table 1.1). These seven crimes include four crimes of violence—murder and nonnegligent manslaughter, forcible rape, robbery, and aggravated assault—and three property crimes—burglary, larceny-theft, and

Table 1.1 Index of Crime, United States, 1960-1974

Population	Total crime index	Violent crime[a]	Property crime[a]	Murder and nonnegligent manslaughter
Number of offenses:				
1960–179,323,000	3,363,700	286,890	3,076,800	9,060
1961–182,992,000	3,466,800	287,800	3,179,000	8,690
1962–185,771,000	3,729,500	299,860	3,429,600	8,480
1963–188,483,000	4,084,400	315,230	3,769,200	8,590
1964–191,141,000	4,537,100	362,210	4,174,800	9,310
1965–193,526,000	4,710,800	385,260	4,325,500	9,910
1966–195,576,000	5,192,000	427,840	4,764,100	10,808
1967–197,457,000	5,868,100	497,290	5,370,800	12,170
1968–199,399,000	6,680,300	591,080	6,088,300	13,730
1969–201,385,000	7,366,900	685,530	6,708,300	14,680
1970–203,235,000	8,049,900	735,160	7,314,700	15,910
1971–206,212,000	8,537,100	812,480	7,724,600	17,680
1972–208,230,000	8,199,700	830,690	7,369,000	18,570
1973–209,851,000	8,666,200	871,450	7,794,800	19,530
1974–211,392,000	10,192,000	969,820	9,222,200	20,600
% change 1960-1974[b]	+203.0	+238.0	+199.7	+127.4
Rate per 100,000 inhabitants:				
1960	1,875.8	160.0	1,715.8	5.1
1961	1,894.5	157.3	1,737.2	4.7
1962	2,007.6	161.4	1846.2	4.6
1963	2,167.0	167.2	1,999.8	4.6
1964	2,373.7	189.5	2,184.2	4.9
1965	2,434.2	199.1	2,235.1	5.1
1966	2,654.7	218.8	2,435.9	5.6
1967	2,971.8	251.8	2,720.0	6.2
1968	3,350.2	269.9	3,053.3	6.9
1969	3,658.1	327.0	3,331.1	7.3
1970	3,960.9	361.7	3,599.1	7.8
1971	4,140.0	394.0	3,746.0	8.6
1972	3,937.8	398.9	3,538.9	8.9
1973	4,129.7	415.3	3,714.4	9.3
1974	4,821.4	458.8	4,362.6	9.7
% change 1960-1974	+157.0	+186.8	+154.3	+90.2

[a]Violent crime is offenses of murder, forcible rape, robbery, and aggravated assault. Property crime is offenses of burglary, larceny-theft, and auto theft.

[b]Percent change and crime rates calculated prior to rounding number of offenses. Revised estimates and rates based on changes in reporting practices.

OVERVIEW OF THE CRIMINAL JUSTICE SYSTEM

Forcible rape	Robbery	Aggravated assault	Burglary	Larceny-theft	Auto theft
17,130	107,570	153,140	906,600	1,843,100	327,100
17,160	106,400	155,560	943,800	1,900,300	334,900
17,490	110,580	163,310	988,300	2,075,800	365,600
17,590	116,180	172,880	1,079,800	2,282,600	406,900
21,350	130,060	201,500	1,205,800	2,497,800	471,200
23,330	138,340	213,680	1,274,700	2,555,600	495,200
25,730	157,590	233,530	1,401,500	2,803,300	559,300
27,530	202,400	255,190	1,622,200	3,091,000	657,600
31,560	262,180	284,510	1,847,600	3,459,700	781,000
37,050	298,100	308,710	1,969,900	3,862,900	875,600
37,860	348,980	332,410	2,191,600	4,197,900	925,300
42,120	386,730	365,940	2,384,700	4,394,900	945,000
46,690	375,350	390,080	2,361,100	4,123,700	884,200
51,230	383,260	417,430	2,549,900	4,319,100	925,700
55,210	441,290	452,720	3,020,700	5,227,700	973,800
+222.4	+310.2	+195.6	+233.2	+183.6	+197.7
9.5	60.0	85.4	505.6	1,027.8	182.4
9.4	58.1	85.0	515.7	1,038.5	183.0
9.4	59.5	87.9	532.0	1,117.4	196.8
9.3	61.6	91.7	572.9	1,211.0	215.9
11.2	68.0	105.4	630.9	1,306.8	246.5
12.1	71.5	110.4	658.7	1,320.5	255.9
13.2	80.6	119.4	716.6	1,433.4	286.0
13.9	102.5	129.2	829.5	1,565.4	333.0
15.8	131.5	142.7	926.6	1,735.1	391.7
18.4	148.0	153.3	978.2	1,918.2	434.8
18.6	171.7	163.6	1,078.4	2,065.5	455.3
20.4	187.5	177.5	1,156.4	2,131.3	458.3
22.4	180.3	187.3	1,133.9	1,980.4	424.6
24.4	182.6	198.9	1,215.1	2,058.2	441.1
26.1	208.8	214.2	1,429.0	2,473.0	460.6
+174.7	+248.0	+150.8	+182.6	+140.6	+152.5

Source: *Crime in the United States—Uniform Crime Reports—1974,* U.S. Department of Justice (Washington, D.C.: Government Printing Office, 1975), p. 55.

and auto theft. These seven crimes have been selected by the FBI to be included in the crime index—composed of the simple sum of the number of known crimes in each of these constituent crime categories—because "they represent the most common local crime problem. They are all serious crimes, either by their very nature or due to the volume in which they occur."[13] Table 1.1 reveals the total number of offenses known to the police, by offense, in the United States from 1960 to 1974. It also shows the rate of the index crimes per 100,000 inhabitants. These seven index crimes, because of their "seriousness, frequency of occurrence, and likelihood of being reported to the police" deserve additional attention.[14] Each will be considered in turn.

Murder

Murder and nonnegligent manslaughter is defined in the *Uniform Crime Reports* as the willful killing of another. Deaths caused by negligence, suicide, accident, or justifiable homicide are not included in this offense classification. Neither are attempts to murder or assaults to murder, which are scored as aggravated assaults and not as murder. In 1974, there were an estimated 20,600 murders committed in the United States. This figure, however, represents only 2 percent of all violent crime committed in the United States and less than one-half of 1 percent of the total of seven crime index offenses. In that same year, there were 9.7 murder victims for every 100,000 inhabitants in the nation. It must be noted, however, that the murder rate varies significantly according to the population groupings. Thus, in cities of 250,000 or more inhabitants, the murder rate averages approximately 21 victims per 100,000 inhabitants; in suburban areas, the rate is a low 5 per 100,000 inhabitants; and in rural areas, the rate averages about 7.5 per 100,000 inhabitants. Approximately 75 percent of murder victims are male. In 1974, 48 percent were white, 50 percent were black, and 2 percent were other. A full 30 percent of all victims were between the ages of 20 and 29.

A firearm is the most frequently employed murder weapon. In 1974, firearms were employed in 68 percent of all homicides, whereas cutting and stabbing weapons were used in 18 percent, other weapons (clubs, poison, and so forth) were utilized in 7 percent, and personal weapons (hands, fists, feet) were employed in 8 percent. These figures have remained virtually unchanged over the past decade (see Figure 1.3).

The circumstances that result in murder range from murder within the family (which accounts for approximately 25 percent of all murder offenses) to felony murder—those killings resulting from robbery, burglary, sex crimes, gangland and institutional slaying, and all other felonious activities (which accounts for another 28 percent of all homicides). Romantic triangles, lovers' quarrels, and other arguments account for the bulk of the remainder. Given these figures, it should be apparent that criminal homicide is largely a societal problem that is beyond the control of police.[15]

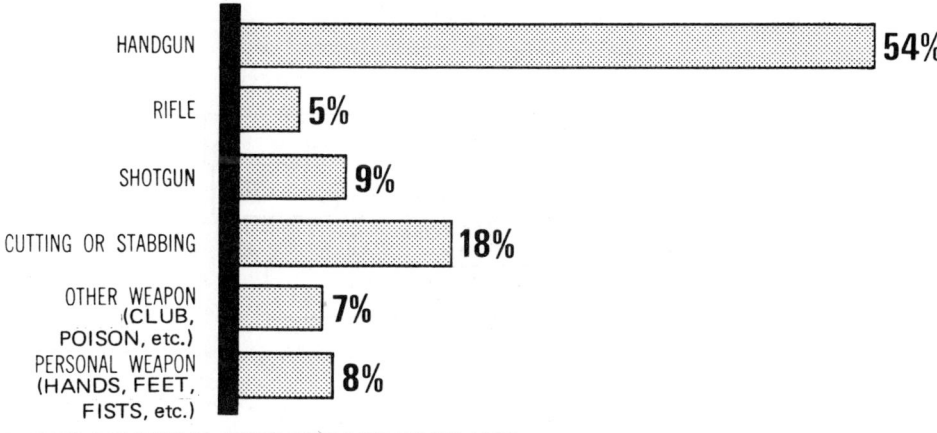

Figure 1.3 Murder by type of weapon used—1974. [Source: *Crime in the United States—Uniform Crime Reports—1974*, U. S. Department of Justice (Washington, D. C.: Government Printing Office, 1975), p. 17.]

Nationally, the police are able to clear or solve by arrest more homicides than any other index crime (see Figure 1.4, which contrasts the clearance rate for murder with the other index crimes). In 1974, 80 percent of all homicides were cleared by arrest. Of those persons arrested for murder, 10 percent were under 18, 45 percent were under 25, and 57 percent were black. Ultimately, 54 percent of these persons were prosecuted, and of those prosecuted, 45 percent were found guilty as charged, 21 percent were convicted of a lesser charge, 9 percent were juveniles whose cases were referred to juvenile court, and the remaining 25 percent won release by acquittal or dismissal of the charges against them.

Aggravated Assault

The *Uniform Crime Reports* defines aggravated assault as "an unlawful attack by one person upon another for the purpose of inflicting severe bodily injury usually accompanied by the use of a weapon or other means likely to produce death or serious bodily harm."[16] In 1974, there were an estimated 452,720 aggravated assaults in the United States, up 8 percent over 1973 and 47 percent over 1969. This corresponds to an aggravated assault rate of 214 victims per 100,000 inhabitants.[17] In many respects, murder and aggravated assault are alike—the only real difference is that in the former, the assault proves to be

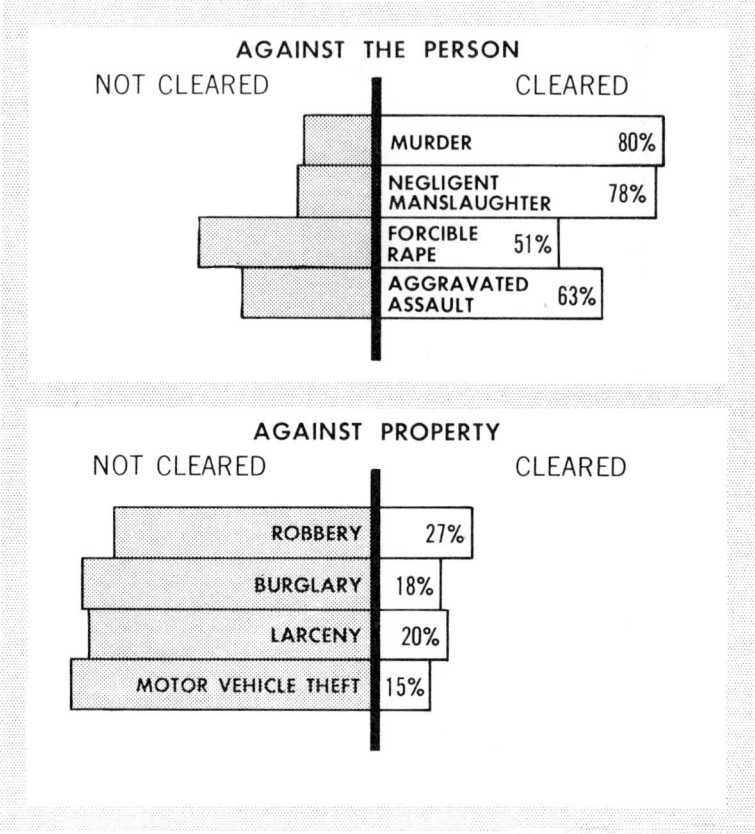

Figure 1.4 Crimes cleared by arrest—1974. [Source: *Crime in the United States — Uniform Crime Reports—1974*, U. S. Department of Justice (Washington, D. C.: Government Printing Office, 1975), p. 43.]

fatal, whereas in the latter, it does not. This similarity is apparent in the victim-offender relationship (most aggravated assaults also occur within the family unit or among neighbors and acquaintances) as well as in the nature of the attack (the same type of weapons are typically employed in both offenses). Also as in murder, the clearance rate for aggravated assault is high. Sixty-three percent of all such crimes were solved by law enforcement agencies in 1974.[18] Clearance rates are much lower, however. Because of the close family or other relationship that typically exists between victims and assailants, many victims are unwilling to testify for the prosecution. As a result, 43 percent of all prosecutions end in acquittals or dismissals, whereas 26 percent result in convictions for the original offense, 14 percent in convictions for lesser charges, and 17 percent in referral to juvenile courts.

OVERVIEW OF THE CRIMINAL JUSTICE SYSTEM

Forcible Rape

Forcible rape is the carnal knowledge of a female through the use of force or the threat of force. This offense classification also includes assaults to commit forcible rape; however, it does not include statutory rape (carnal knowledge without force of a female below the age of consent). During 1974, there were an estimated 55,210 forcible rapes in the United States, up 8 percent over 1973. These figures translate into a forcible rape rate of approximately 51 rapes per 100,000 females in this country. These figures are generally regarded as unrealistically low, however. Of all the *Uniform Crime Reports* offenses, this offense is considered the most underrecorded. This is in large part due to fear and/or embarrassment on the part of the victims. If many rapes go unreported to the police, many also are unsolved by the police; only about 50 percent are ever cleared by arrest. Of those persons ultimately brought to trial, 49 percent win acquittals or dismissals, and only 35 percent are found guilty as charged. Another 16 percent are found guilty of lesser offenses, and the remainder are referred to juvenile courts.

Robbery

Robbery takes place in the presence of the victim and involves the stealing of anything of value from the care, custody, and control of the victim by force, violence, or the threat of force or violence. It includes armed robbery (where any weapon is used), strong-arm robbery (where no weapon other than a personal weapon is used), assaults to rob, and attempts to rob. Robberies account for almost one-half of all crimes of violence. Thus, in 1974, there were 441,290 robbery offenses committed in the United States. The resulting robbery rate was 209 per 100,000 inhabitants. *Uniform Crime Reports* figures further disclose that most robberies are committed in the streets (50 percent) of cities with over 250,000 inhabitants (67 percent). In 66 percent of these robberies, the perpetrator was armed (most often with a firearm, 63 percent). Although the object of robbery is money or physical property, many victims suffer serious personal injury during the commission of this crime. As a consequence, the cost of this violent crime to the victim cannot be completely measured in terms of dollar loss alone. Nonetheless, during 1974, the average value loss in each robbery incident was $321, with a total nationwide loss of $142 million. Few robberies are ever cleared by arrest—in 1974, only 27 percent were. When arrests were made, 77 percent of the persons arrested were under 25 years of age; 93 percent were male; and 62 percent were black. Of those eventually prosecuted, 35 percent were referred to juvenile courts, 30 percent were convicted of the original charges, 10 percent were convicted of lesser charges, and a full 25 percent won release by acquittal or dismissal.

Burglary

Burglary consist of the unlawful entry of a structure to commit a felony or theft. It includes forcible entry, unlawful entry where no force is used, and attempted forcible entry. In 1974, there were an estimated 3,020,700 burglaries committed in the United States, translating to a burglary rate of 1,429 per 100,000 inhabitants. The dollar loss suffered by the victims of this crime was $1.2 billion. Because burglary is a crime of stealth, detection of the perpetrator is low, and less than 20 percent of all burglaries are cleared by arrest. Those persons arrested for this crime tend to be young, with about 85 percent being under 25 years of age. Of those prosecuted during 1974, 22 percent were found guilty as charged, 7 percent were convicted of lesser offenses, 13 percent were released through acquittal or dismissal, and 58 percent were referred to juvenile courts.

Larceny-Theft

Larceny-theft is defined as the unlawful taking or stealing of property or articles without the use of force, violence, or fraud. It includes such crimes as shoplifting, pocket-picking, purse-snatching, thefts from autos, thefts of auto parts and accessories, and bicycle thefts. It does not include auto theft (which is a separate crime index offense), embezzlement, "con" games, forgery, or the writing of worthless checks. In 1974, there were an estimated 5,227,700 offenses of larceny-theft. This large number constituted 51 percent of all the crime index total. Larceny rates also run high—2,473 offenses per 100,000 inhabitants in 1974. The total dollar loss from this crime was $816 million. Larceny is for the most part a crime of opportunity; as a consequence, less than 20 percent of larceny offenses are cleared by arrest. Of those arrested in 1974, 49 percent were under 18 years of age and 67 percent were under 21. Thirty-one percent of the arrestees were female, making larceny the crime index offense with the highest proportion of female violators. Of those prosecuted in 1974, 43 percent were convicted as charged, 4 percent were convicted of lesser offenses, 15 percent were released by acquittal or dismissal, and 38 percent were transferred to juvenile court.

Auto Theft

Auto theft is defined by *Uniform Crime Reports* as the unlawful taking or stealing of a motor vehicle, including attempts to do so. In 1974, 973,800 motor vehicles were reported stolen in the United States. This translates into an auto theft rate of 461 offenses per 100,000 inhabitants, or to use a more pertinent statistic, into the theft of one out of every 129 registered automobiles in the United States (see Figure 1.5, which indicates the locations from which most motor vehicles are stolen). Only 15 percent of all auto thefts are cleared by

OVERVIEW OF THE CRIMINAL JUSTICE SYSTEM

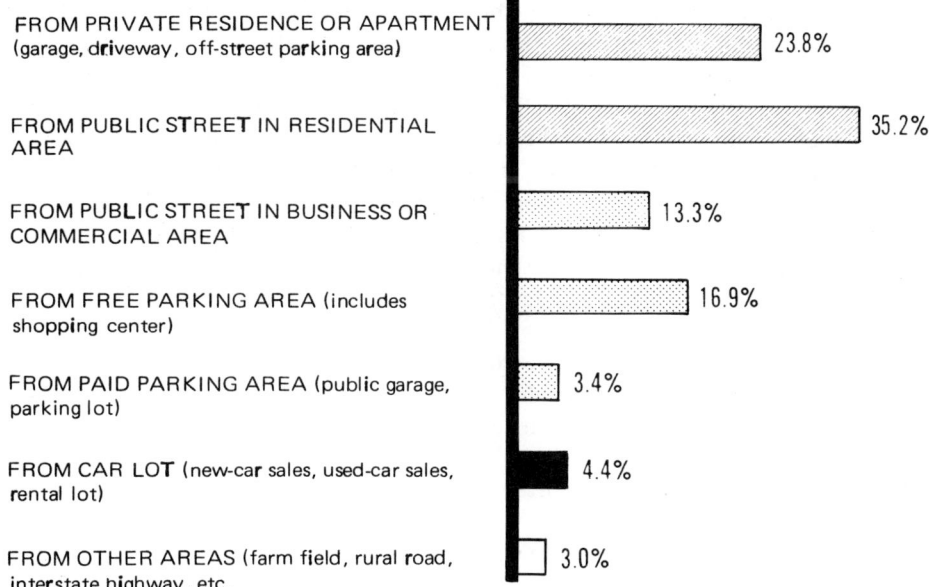

Figure 1.5 Motor vehicle theft by location—September-October, 1974. [Source: *Crime in the United States—Uniform Crime Reports—1974*, U. S. Department of Justice (Washington, D. C.: Government Printing Office, 1975), p. 39.]

arrests, the smallest percentage for all crime index offenses. Of those arrested in 1974, 55 percent were under 18 years of age, and 74 percent were under 21. As a consequence, of those ultimately prosecuted in 1974, 64 percent were referred to juvenile courts, 17 percent were found guilty as charged, 5 percent were convicted of lesser offenses, and 14 percent were released by dismissal or acquittal.

The figures presented in Table 1.1 and discussed in the text are for those index crimes actually known to the police. It should be emphasized, however, that these figures in no way indicate the total number of these offenses. Studies have established that a great deal of crime, even serious crime, is never reported to the police. Thus, in 1967, the National Opinion Research Center (NORC) of the University of Chicago surveyed 10,000 households, asking whether the person questioned, or any member of his or her household, had been the victim of a crime during the past year, whether the crime had been reported to the police, and if not, the reasons for not reporting. This study, sponsored by the President's Commission on Law Enforcement and Administration of Justice, disclosed that the amount of crime in the United States is several times that reported in the *Uniform Crime Reports*.[19] The amount of violent crime reported to NORC was almost twice the *Uniform Crime Reports* rates, and the amount of property crime was more than twice the *Uniform Crime Reports* figures.

NORC found the number of forcible rapes to be about three and one-half times the reported rates, burglaries three times, aggravated assaults and larcenies more than double, and robbery 50 percent greater than the reported rates.[20] The NORC study was dramatically confirmed by a 1974 Law Enforcement Assistance Administration (LEAA) study based on interviews with 22,000 residents and 2,000 business firms in each of the nation's five largest cities—New York, Los Angeles, Chicago, Detroit, and Philadelphia. It revealed that in Philadelphia, the actual crime rate was five times higher than the reported rate, and in the other cities, it was two to three times higher. The reasons given by the respondents for not reporting criminal acts to the police were as follows:[21]

1. Victim felt nothing could be done about it   34%
2. Not important enough   28
3. Police would not want to be bothered   8
4. Too inconvenient   5
5. Private, personal matter   4
6. Afraid of reprisal   2
7. Reported to someone else   7
8. Other reasons   12

These figures are of considerable importance for appreciating the present plight of the criminal justice system. Seventy percent of all unrecorded crime goes unreported because the public does not believe that the police—the most visible component of the criminal justice system—will be interested in their problems or effective in resolving them. As Donald Santarelli, former LEAA administrator, notes, "The crime survey results demonstrate in an astounding number of instances that Americans simply do not think it is worthwhile to report to public authorities that they have been the victims of criminal acts." He concludes, "In my judgment the data transmit a strong message of public apathy toward its criminal justice institutions bordering on contempt."[22] This contempt obviously stems, in part, from the failure the criminal justice system is experiencing in its efforts either to prevent crime or to deal with its effects. Hence, the need to explore the reasons for this failure grows all the more important.

White-Collar Crime

Although public attention naturally focuses on such index crimes as murder, robbery, and burglary, other crime, often unknown and unseen, erodes American society. It is white-collar crime. White-collar crime may be defined as "an illegal act or series of illegal acts committed by nonphysical means and by concealment or guile, to obtain money or property, to avoid the payment or loss of money or property, or to obtain business or personal advantage."[23] It may be divided into four categories. The first deals with crimes by persons acting alone in a nonbusiness context; it includes such offenses as loan and credit card frauds and income tax violations. The second pertains to crimes by persons against their employer; embezzlement, conflict of interest, bribery, and kickbacks are examples of this category. The third category involves crimes that further business operations but are apart from the central purpose of the business; it includes short-weighing, antitrust violations, housing code violations, kickbacks, stock theft and manipulation, and fraud. Finally, the fourth category focuses on crimes that constitute the central purpose of the business or activity, such as phony contests or home improvement schemes and charity, insurance, and school frauds.[24]

The incidence and cost of white-collar crime perpetrated in the United States each year is extremely difficult to ascertain. The victims of many white-collar crimes, such as short-weighing and charity frauds, never know they have been victimized. The use of computers to manipulate and conceal records of fraudulent dealings likewise poses an increasingly difficult problem. Occasionally, studies shed some light on the magnitude of this problem in certain industries. Thus, a recent investigation revealed that business fraud runs rampant in automobile repair shops. Investigators disconnected an electric wire on an automobile—an easily diagnosed problem—and then took the car to 347 garages in 48 states. Of the garages surveyed, 218 overcharged, did unnecessary work, or inserted unnecessary parts. Only 37 percent correctly diagnosed the problem and charged either nothing or a nominal fee for their work.[25] Such investigations, however, are not systematic. Like the highly publicized electrical industry price-fixing trials of the early 1960s and the Billie Sol Estes and Bobby Baker scandals, they serve more to attract the public's attention to the existence of white-color crime than they do to reveal its parameters and significance. As a consequence, statistics on the extent of white-collar crime remain woefully incomplete. All that is available are arrest data, which, for 1974, show 60,600 arrests for forgery and counterfeiting and 161,600 arrests for fraud and embezzlement.[26] These figures, of course, reflect only unsuccessful white-collar crime and in no way reveal the magnitude of that which is successful. Statistics on the cost of white-collar crime are equally incomplete. Nonetheless, a report of the Bureau of National Affairs presently estimates the annual cost of white-collar crime to be in excess of $40 billion—four times greater than the cost of all other crimes combined[27] (see Table 1.2). However staggering these dollar losses may be, they in no way represent the entire cost of white-collar crime. Other losses, of an economic, political, social, and moral nature, are also incurred. Of all of these, perhaps the moral costs are the most tragic. As the President's Commission observed:

Table 1.2 The Annual Cost of Selected White-Collar Crimes in the United States (Billions of Dollars)

Bankruptcy, fraud		$ .08
Bribery, kickbacks, payoffs		3.00
Computer-related crime		.10
Consumer fraud, illegal competition, deceptive practices		21.00
Consumer victims	$ 5.50	
Business victims	3.50	
Government revenue loss	12.00	
Credit card and check fraud		1.10
Credit card	$ .10	
Check	1.00	
Embezzlement and pilferage		7.00
Embezzlement	$ 3.00	
Pilferage	4.00	
Insurance fraud		2.00
Insurer victims	1.50	
Policyholder victims	.50	
Receiving stolen property		3.50
Securities theft and fraud		4.00
	TOTAL:	$41.78

Source: Bureau of National Affairs, "White Collar Justice," *Criminal Law Reporter 19*, no. 2 (1976): 3.

> Serious erosion of morals accompanies violations of this nature. It is reasonable to assume that prestigious companies that flout the law set an example for other businesses and influence individuals, particularly young people, to commit other kinds of crime on the ground that everyone is taking what he can get. If businessmen who are respected as leaders of the community can do such things as break the anti-trust laws or rent dilapidated houses to the poor at high rents, it is hard to convince the young that they should be honest.[28]

"Victimless" Crimes

Most people are in fundamental agreement concerning the legitimacy and propriety of imposing criminal sanctions against those who engage in index and white-collar crimes. However, there presently exists a third category of criminal offenses about which considerable debate rages concerning the appropriateness

OVERVIEW OF THE CRIMINAL JUSTICE SYSTEM

and even the constitutionality of the imposition of such criminal sanctions. The category includes drunkenness, narcotics and drug abuse, gambling, disorderly conduct, vagrancy, prostitution, homosexuality, pornography—in general, the whole range of what are often referred to as "crimes without victims." Many students of the criminal justice system propose the decriminalization of such activities; they do so on the basis of a number of arguments. To begin with, "victimless" crimes[29] seriously deplete much of the time, energy, and manpower available to the criminal justice system. Statistics from the FBI's *Uniform Crime Reports* reveal that there were 9,270,700 arrests in the United States in 1973, of which 3,890,600 (43.1 percent) were for "victimless" crimes. Table 1.3 itemizes the number and percent of arrests by particular "victimless" crime.

The number of arrests for "victimless" crimes is more than twice the number of arrests for the seven most serious index offenses (1,833,300 or 20.3 percent). Proponents of decriminalization contend that if the criminal justice system were relieved of the responsibility for dealing with these "victimless" crimes, it could more effectively and efficiently control the burgeoning increase in crimes against persons and property. They point to the criminal justice system's efforts to handle the offenses of public drunkenness and deviant sexual behavior to illustrate their point. In 1973, there were approximately 1,600,000 arrests in the United States for drunkenness.[30] This great volume of arrests places an enormous burden on the operation of the criminal justice system; it overloads the police, clogs the courts, and crowds correctional facilities.[31] Moreover, it is extremely costly. It is estimated that the cost of handling each drunkenness case is about $50 per arrest.[32] Thus, a conservative estimate of the annual expenditure

Table 1.3 Number and Percent of Arrests for "Victimless" Crimes in 1973

Crime	Number	Percent
Drunkenness	1,599,000	17.7
Disorderly conduct	720,400	8.0
Narcotic drug laws	628,900	7.0
Liquor laws	272,000	3.0
Runaways	265,600	2.9
Curfew and loitering law violations	151,200	1.7
Gambling	68,300	.8
Suspicion	67,100	.7
Vagrancy	62,300	.7
Prostitution and commercialized vice	55,800	.6
Total known "victimless" crimes arrests	3,890,600	43.1

Source: Crime in the United States—Uniform Crime Reports—1973, U. S. Department of Justice (Washington, D. C.: Government Printing Office, 1974), p. 121.

for the handling of drunkenness offenders is $75 million. Proponents of decriminalization observe that all these problems arise when criminal sanctions are employed to handle what are essentially social problems.

Offenses involving deviant consensual sexual relations pose a very different set of problems but likewise lead many to advocate their decriminalization. They advance a number of arguments for not invoking the criminal sanction in the case of such behavior.[33] To begin with, no secular harm can be shown to come from such conduct. Second, the moral sense of the community no longer strongly demands the use of the criminal sanction. Third, no utilitarian goal of criminal punishment is substantially advanced by proscribing such conduct. Fourth, widespread knowledge that the law is violated with impunity creates disrespect for law generally both in those who violate it and in the public at large. Fifth, the rarity of enforcement of such laws creates a problem of arbitrary police and prosecutorial discretion.[34] Sixth, the extreme difficulty of detecting such conduct often leads to undesirable police practices. As John Kaplan notes, "The police, in order to enforce such laws, to a large extent must depend upon the use of informers, entrapment, eavesdropping, searches, and a whole variety of intrusive methods of police investigation. Even where these methods are not illegal, they impinge strongly on the privacy of the citizen, and are resented by those who fall under suspicion."[35] Seventh, and most importantly, imposition of the criminal sanction upon such behavior is criminogenic—it is likely to contribute to the very crime problem it is intended to alleviate. The criminogenic effect of legislation concerning drunkenness, narcotics, gambling, and sexual behavior occurs in a number of different ways. To begin with, the proscription of certain behavior (for example, prostitution, drug addiction, homosexuality) by the criminal law tends to create an extensive criminal subculture that is subversive to the social order generally. Moreover, laws regulating "victimless" crimes operate as "crime tariffs." They make the supply of such goods and services as narcotics, gambling, and prostitution profitable for the criminal by driving up prices and by discouraging competition from those who might enter the market were it legal. As Morris and Hawkins observe, this easily leads to the development of "large-scale organized criminal groups which, as in the field of legitimate business, tend to extend and diversify their operations, thus financing and promoting other criminal activity."[36] The high prices that criminal prohibition and law enforcement maintain in turn have a secondary criminogenic effect in that persons (for example, the narcotics addict) often have to resort to crime in order to obtain the money to pay these prices. Still another criminogenic effect results from attempts by the criminal justice system to enforce statutes relating to sexual behavior, drug abuse, gambling, and other matters of private morality. These efforts seriously deplete the time, energy, and manpower available for dealing with crimes against persons and property. This particular allocation of resources contributes to the failure to deal adequately with current serious crime and, because of the increased chances of impunity, encourages further crime as well. Finally, and perhaps most distressing, because these "victimless" crimes lack complainants seeking the protection of the criminal law, it is extremely difficult for the police to enforce the law. This creates a situation in which extortion and, on occasion, police corruption may take place.

The arguments presented thus far for decriminalization of these offenses have been largely of a pragmatic nature—enforcement of these criminal proscriptions is expensive, unsuccessful, and counterproductive. However, many proponents of decriminalization base their arguments on theoretical or constitutional considerations as well. Thus, many express sentiments in keeping with the famous words of John Stuart Mill in his essay "On Liberty":

> The sole end for which mankind are warranted, individually or collectively, in interfering with the liberty of action of any of their number, is self-protection. The only purpose for which power can be rightfully exercised over any member of a civilized community, against his will, is to prevent harm to others. His own good, either physical or moral, is not a sufficient warrant. He cannot rightfully be compelled to do or forbear because it will be better for him to do so, because it will make him happier, because in the opinion of others, to do so would be wise, or even right.[37]

This view that "over his own body and mind, the individual is sovereign," now has received constitutional support. The Fifth and Fourteenth Amendments to the U. S. Constitution ensure that no person shall be deprived of life, liberty, or property without due process of law. In the 1973 Supreme Court decision of *Roe* v. *Wade,* Justice Blackmun declared for the Court majority that state criminal abortion laws that restrict too narrowly the liberty of a woman to control her own body—including her liberty to have an abortion—are unconstitutional. "A state criminal abortion statute . . . that excepts from criminality only a lifesaving procedure on behalf of the mother, without regard to pregnancy stage and without recognition of the other interests involved, is violative of the Due Process Clause of the Fourteenth Amendment."[38]

The arguments of the proponents of decriminalization have had an impact. Thus, the President's Commission on Law Enforcement and Administration of Justice recommended that "drunkenness should not itself be a criminal offense."[39] The recent National Advisory Commission on Criminal Justice Standards and Goals concurs; it recommends that "drunkenness in and of itself should not continue to be treated as a crime."[40] Instead, it recommends that all states give "serious consideration to enacting the Uniform Alcoholism and Intoxication Act." This act, already adopted by nine states and the District of Columbia, authorizes police officers to take intoxicated persons into protective custody rather than arrest them. It also provides for a comprehensive program for treatment of alcoholics and intoxicated persons, including emergency, inpatient, intermediate, outpatient, and follow-up treatment, and authorizes appropriate facilities for such treatment. The National Advisory Commission goes even further, however, and "recommends that states re-evaluate their laws on gambling, marijuana use and possession for use, pornography, prostitution, and sexual acts between consenting adults in private."[41] At a minimum, it recommends that "each state should remove incarceration as a penalty for these offenses, except in the case of persistent and repeated offenses by an individual, when incarceration for a limited period may be warranted."[42]

The National Advisory Commission stopped short of advocating outright decriminalization of these offenses, perhaps aware of the compelling arguments that also can be adduced on the other side. Those who wish to see laws against "victimless" crimes remain in force and who insist on the importance of a public morality observe that throughout the greater part of recorded history, thoughtful and philosophic men have been of the opinion that republican government requires the greatest self-imposed restraints whereas tyrannies and other decadent regimes can often afford the greatest individual liberties.[43] Republican and constitutional government depends, for its vitality as well as its survival, upon the character of its citizens. Because it relies so heavily upon their responsibility and judgment, it cannot be utterly indifferent to the ways in which its citizens publicly entertain themselves. Irving Kristol has perceptively stated this issue: "Bear-baiting and cockfighting are prohibited only in part out of compassion for the suffering animals; the main reason they were abolished was because it was felt that they debased and brutalized the citizenry who flocked to witness such spectacles."[44] Neither can it dispense with laws that foster self-discipline and promote mutual respect.[45] As Walter Berns has noted, "To live together requires rules and a governing of the passions, and those who are without shame will be unruly and unrulable; having lost the ability to restrain themselves by observing the rules they collectively give themselves, they will have to be ruled by others. Tyranny is the mode of government for the shameless and the self-indulgent who have carried liberty beyond any restraint, natural or conventional."[46]

Laws proscribing pornography, prostitution, homosexuality, drug abuse, and gambling are seen as contributing to that crucially important self-discipline. As Harry M. Clor points out:

> They affirm that the society has a standard of decency and indecency—a public morality. The majority of us usually require some guidance from communal standards. And it would seem that no community of men can do without a public morality. By means of [these] laws . . . we are reminded, and we remind ourselves, that "We the People" have an ethical order and moral limits. The individual is made aware that the community in which he lives regards some things as beyond the pale of civility. The educative function of . . . [these] laws is ultimately more significant than their coercive function.[47]

Professor Clor emphasizes the fact that "'We the People' have an ethical order and moral limits." Those in favor of retaining laws against "victimless" crimes enlarge upon this theme and argue that the purpose of republican government cannot possible be the "endless functioning of its own political machinery." The purpose of any political order is to achieve some version of the good life and the good society. Laws regulating public morality can help to give meaning or definition to these objectives. Without them, it is not at all difficult to imagine a perfectly functioning republican government that "answers all questions except one—namely, why should anyone of intelligence and spirit care a fig for it?"[48]

These arguments take on all the more force, their advocates contend, in a richly diverse heterogeneous society like the United States. In certain fairly homogeneous European nations—Scandinavia, for example—a legally enforced public morality may not be necessary to ensure or preserve the society. After all, everyone in Denmark is a blue-eyed, blond-haired, Lutheran Dane. In the United States, however, it is quite a different matter. Here, perhaps the only bond—the only cement—holding the nation together as one society, one community, is its public morality.[49] Thus, they argue, extreme caution and reflection should precede any attempt to loosen this bond, for fear that it will reduce us to mere aggregates of individuals. As a consequence, the debate over "victimless" crimes continues, and the criminal justice system, appropriately or inappropriately, is obliged to deal with this difficult, emotional, and frustrating set of offenses.

The Causes of Crime

What accounts for these different kinds of crimes and their substantial increase in number? Various theories of crime causation have been advanced in answer to this question. Most of these (at least most of the ones propounded by the "sociological" school of criminology[50]) focus on the environment and its effect on the individual. Ramsey Clark captures the concerns of those who make these arguments: "Most crime in America is born in environments saturated in poverty and its consequences: illness, ignorance, idleness, ugly surroundings, hopelessness. Crime incubates in places where thousands have no jobs, and those who do have the poorest jobs; where houses are old, dirty and dangerous; where people have no rights." Eliminate these conditions, Clark asserts, and most crime will be abolished as well:

> Every major city in America demonstrates the relationship between crime and poor education, unemployment, bad health and inadequate housing. When we understand this, we take much of the mystery out

of crime. We may prefer the mystery. If so, we are condemned to live with crime we could prevent.[51]

To these general environmental factors, others add the impact of "broken" homes; they view discord, absence of affection and consistent discipline, and improper moral instruction as contributing especially to juvenile delinquency and youth crime.[52] Alternatively, others stress unemployment and the frustration brought on by the lack of opportunity. They point out that if legitimate opportunities for work were available, those who might otherwise be induced to engage in crime would be able to earn by socially acceptable means the material and psychic rewards that society declares to be the indispensable marks of success.[53] Still others place blame on the effects of alienation or anomie brought on by the forces of modernization. As Peter L. Berger has observed, "The capitalish market economy, the centralized bureaucratic state, the new technology let loose by industrialism, the consequent rapid population growth in urbanization, and finally the mass media of communication . . . have caused havoc to all the social and cultural formations in which human beings used to be at home, creating a radically new context for human life."[54] Crime and other social dislocations are seen as inevitable consequences.

But, whatever the specifics, the answer for those who attribute the causes of crime to the environment is simple.[55] The President's Commission on Law Enforcement and Administration of Justice perhaps stated it most succinctly: "Warring on poverty, inadequate housing and unemployment, is warring on crime. A civil rights law is a law against crime. Money for schools is money against crime. More broadly and more importantly every effort to improve life in America's 'inner cities' is an effort against crime."[56]

There are certain problems with these theories of criminal causation, however. To begin with, they lack the power to explain why, under similar circumstances, one individual does, and another does not, commit a particular crime. After all, as Ramsey Clark himself admits, "most who live in poverty never commit a serious crime."[57] More importantly, however, recent research also indicates that these theories are unable to account for even long-term fluctuations in the rate of crime. Thus, James Q. Wilson has found that the "great increase in English crime rates" cannot be explained by reference to "poverty, drug abuse, relative deprivation, social or political frustration, rising unemployment, or the absence of legitimate opportunities. Such factors simply cannot account for the crime increase in England."[58] Neither can they account for the steadily declining crime rates of Japan. As David H. Bayley notes, the number of crimes committed annually in Japan in recent years is actually lower than 25 years ago, despite its increasingly modern industrial and economic base, its population congestion, and its violent traditions.[59]

Wilson's and Bayley's findings are significant, for not only do they challenge the established theories of the causes of crime and its increase, but they also point to common alternative explanations. Thus, Wilson attributes rising crime rates to "the growth of urbanization and affluence; the spread, especially among the young, of the cult of personal liberation and unfettered self-expression; and the change in attitudes of the young toward authority, schooling, and the family."[60] Bayley likewise suggests that the rising "levels of criminal behavior that Americans find so disturbing may be the inevitable consequence of aspects of national life that Americans prize—individualism, mobility, privacy, autonomy, suspicion of authority, and separation between public and private roles, between government and community."[61] These factors are altogether consistent with Edward C. Banfield's more general formulations in *The Unheavenly City Revisited*.[62]

Banfield argues that crime is the result of the operation of two sets of variables. The first set determines an individual's "propensity" to crime. It is comprised of five principal elements. The first involves the way in which an individual conceptualizes right and wrong (his type of morality): Does he understand a "right" action to be one that serves his purposes and that can be gotten away with (preconventional morality), to be doing one's duty or what those in authority require (conventional morality), or to be in accord with some universal principle that he considers worthy of choice (postconventional morality)? The second element refers to the individual's ability to manage his impulses, to postpone present gratifications, and to adhere to and act on his intentions (his ego strength). The third element concerns the individual's future orientation—his ability to anticipate and take account of consequences that lie in the future (his time horizon). The fourth involves the individual's fondness for risk (his taste for risk), and the fifth refers to his willingness to do bodily harm to specifiable individuals (his willingness to inflict injury).[63]

The second set of variables determines the individual's inducement. It relates to situational factors that may provide him with the necessary incentive to commit a crime. As Banfield points out, "Situational factors are often decisive even with persons who have little propensity toward crime. One who would 'never think of stealing' steals when the temptation becomes great enough; that is, when the situation promises great enough benefits at small enough cost."[64]

As is apparent, both of these variables are very much affected by the various factors identified by Wilson and Bayley. Individualism, personal liberation, mobility, privacy, and suspicion of authority are all likely to influence not only an individual's propensity but also situational factors and, therefore, incentive. Thus, this brief analysis suggests that crime may result in large part from the presence and operation of values that at once define and characterize a free society. It also suggests that crime is not likely to be abolished or even dramatically reduced so long as a society remains fundamentally committed to those values. The eradication of crime would necessarily and inexorably involve the destruction of liberty, and as *Federalist* No. 10 has observed, "It could never be more truly said of . . . [this] remedy, that it is worse than the disease."[65]

Of more immediate relevance, this analysis further suggests that the American criminal justice system must be content to pursue a rather modest program of crime prevention and must be willing to devote most of its energies to responding to crime that has already been committed.

The Steps in the Criminal Process

Once a crime is committed, it is up to the criminal justice system to respond. This response will vary somewhat from state to state and even from locality to locality within a state—practices followed in urban areas are often different from those utilized in rural or semirural communities.[66] Nonetheless, the basic procedural steps remain largely the same and are set forth in simplified form in Figure 1.6. These basic steps in the criminal process must be elaborated upon so that the operation of the criminal justice system, along with the problems that it confronts, will be better appreciated.

The Police

The Arrest

At the very beginning of the criminal process is the police decision to arrest. Arrest refers to the decision to take a suspect into custody (that is, transporting him to the station) for the purpose of charging him with a crime.[67] Arrests can be made either with or without a warrant. In an arrest made pursuant to a warrant, a police officer or some other person will have submitted evidence against the accused to a judicial officer—typically a local magistrate—who determines whether the evidence is sufficient to justify an arrest. Warrants are generally obtained in cases in which the identity of the accused is known to the police but his likely whereabouts are unknown, or the nature of the case suggests prosecutorial review before any action is taken (for example, a statutory rape charge).[68] Most arrests, however, are made without a warrant. They are based on the individual police officer's evaluation that there is sufficient basis for believing that a crime has been committed by the accused.

Police and the Exercise of Discretion—The Decision to Arrest

The arresting officer commonly exercises considerable discretion in determining whether or not to make an arrest. As the President's Commission flatly acknowledged:

> Law enforcement policy is made by the policeman.[69] For policemen cannot and do not arrest all the offenders they encounter. It is doubtful

that they arrest most of them. A criminal code, in practice, is not a set of specific instructions to policemen but a more or less rough map of the territory in which policemen work. How an individual moves around that territory depends largely on his personal discretion.[70]

A number of factors account for this discretion. To begin with, there are definitional problems. For example, the police officer must determine how much noise or profanity makes conduct "disorderly" within the meaning of the law. He must likewise determine what makes a brawl a criminal assault: Is it the first threat, the first shove, the first blow, after blood is drawn, or when serious injury is inflicted? His problems are no less difficult when he must judge if certain actions by an accused are sufficiently suspicious to constitute probable cause, the constitutional basis for an arrest. Clearly, as the President's Commission observed, "Crime does not look the same on the street as it does in the legislative chamber."[71]

A second reason for the exercise of police discretion stems from an entirely proper conviction by police officers that the invocation of criminal sanctions may be too drastic a response to many offenses. This is especially true when dealing with juveniles. Although a boy throwing rocks through a school's windows is committing the statutory offense of vandalism, the police officer must decide whether he can better serve the interests of the community and of the boy by taking him home to his parents or by arresting him. The proper disposition of this question requires judgment and discretion based on the answers to another set of questions: Who are the boy's parents? Can they control him? Is he a repeat offender who has responded badly to leniency? Is vandalism so prevalent in the neighborhood that he should be made a deterrent example?[72]

Finally, a third reason for the exercise of personal discretion arises from the massive extent to which police work is influenced by practical matters. For example, is the available evidence admissible in court? Is the victim willing to press charges, and are witnesses willing to testify? Is the victim more likely to get restitution without the arrest? Is the victim at fault for inciting the crime? Is the statute unenforced but nonetheless unrepealed? Is the crime common within the subcultural group? What is the temper of the community? How much time, manpower, and information are at the police department's disposal? These and other policy problems must be resolved by the police as they consider the question of arrest.

Although the police exercise considerable discretion in the performance of their duties, it is by no means unlimited. It is fundamentally affected by at least four factors.[73] The first factor involves the nature of the crime. Thus, police have less freedom to ignore serious crimes such as murder than they do trivial ones such as petty theft. Likewise, they have less discretion in handling crimes that occur in full public view than they do in dealing with crimes that occur in private.

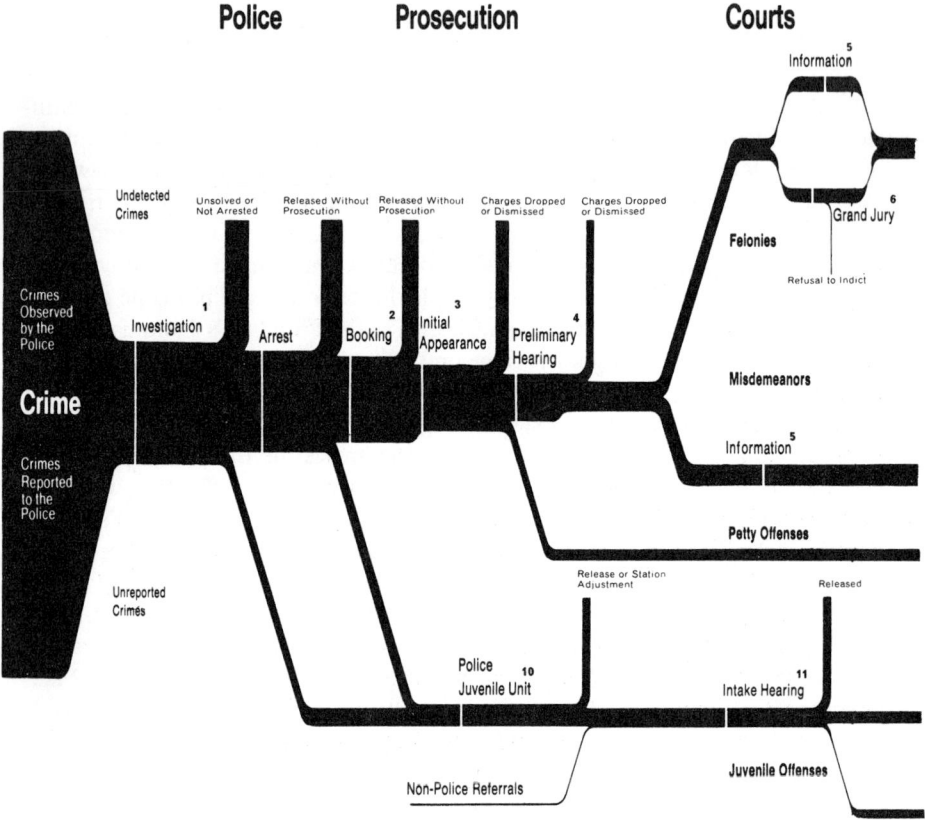

1. May continue until trial.
2. Administrative record of arrest. First step at which temporary release on bail may be available.
3. Before magistrate, commissioner, or justice of peace. Formal notice of charge, advice of rights. Bail set. Summary trials for petty offenses usually conducted here without further processing.
4. Preliminary testing of evidence against defendant. Charge may be reduced. No separate preliminary hearing for misdemeanors in some systems.
5. Charge filed by prosecutor on basis of information submitted by police or citizens. Alternative to grand jury indictment; often used in felonies, almost always in misdemeanors.
6. Reviews whether Government evidence sufficient to justify trial. Some States have no grand jury system; others seldom use it.

Figure 1.6 A general view of the criminal justice system. This chart seeks to present a simple yet comprehensive view of the movement of cases through the criminal justice system. Procedures in individual jurisdictions may vary from the pattern shown here. The differing weights of line indicate the relative volumes of cases disposed of at various points in the system, but this is only suggestive because no nationwide data of this sort exists. [Source: The President's Commission on Law Enforcement and Administration of Justice, *The Challenge of Crime in a Free Society* (Washington, D. C.: Government Printing Office, 1967), pp. 8-9.]

OVERVIEW OF THE CRIMINAL JUSTICE SYSTEM

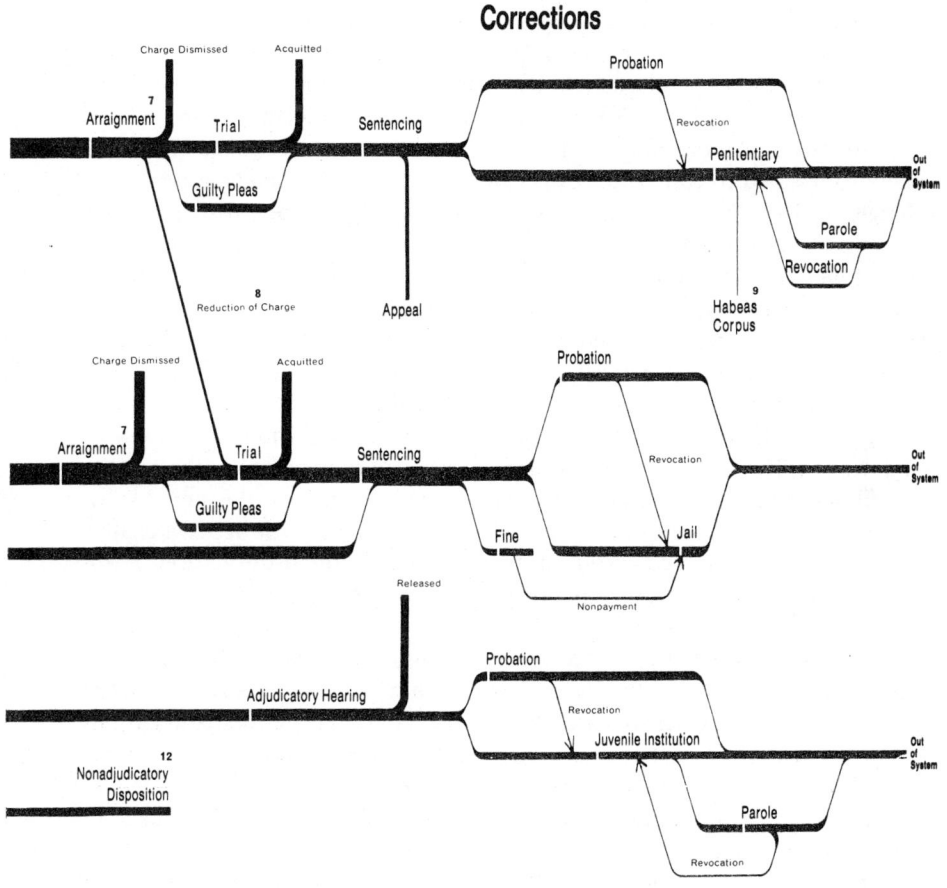

7 Appearance for plea; defendant elects trial by judge or jury (if available); counsel for indigent usually appointed here in felonies. Often not at all in other cases.

8 Charge may be reduced at any time prior to trial in return for plea of guilty or for other reasons.

9 Challenge on constitutional grounds to legality of detention. May be sought at any point in process.

10 Police often hold informal hearings, dismiss or adjust many cases without further processing.

11 Probation officer decides desirability of further court action.

12 Welfare agency, social services, counselling, medical care, etc., for cases where adjudicatory handling not needed.

A second factor involves the relationship between the alleged criminal and the victim. The closer the relationship, the more likely the use of police discretion. Thus, for example, police are reluctant to make arrests in calls involving domestic quarrels. Not only are these calls extremely dangerous—22 percent of all police fatalities occur during investigations of altercations between husband and wife or parent and child[74]—but they also seem to defy proper legal resolution. Police are justifiably wary of risking their lives and safety by placing a participant in a domestic quarrel under arrest, only to discover the next day that the victim is willing to forgive the spouse and is reluctant to press charges.

Where the victim and alleged criminal are strangers, however, the police are likely to behave with greater constancy. In such a case, there are fewer extenuating circumstances that may call for the use of police discretion.

A third factor is the relationship between the police officer on the one hand and the victim or alleged criminal on the other. Thus, a complainant who is deferential to the officer is more likely to have his complaint taken seriously than one who is antagonistic.[75] In much the same manner, police are more likely to respond to complaints of persons of the upper or middle class than to charges made by persons of lower-class status. Finally, the police are more inclined to label particular behavior as criminal if the complainant is insistent than if he is himself dubious about its criminal character.[76] Because most police behavior is reactive (in response to citizen complaints) as opposed to proactive (initiated by the police themselves), these elements are significant in affecting the way in which police exercise their discretionary powers to define behavior as criminal or to dismiss it as merely private conflict.

The relationship between the police and the alleged wrongdoer is also of importance. The more antagonistic and threatening the accused is, the greater the amount of force the police will apply to ensure order and the more likely an arrest will follow. On the other hand, the more deferential the accused is, the less likely it is that the police will arrest him. In addition, if the accused is working as a police informant, the discretion of the police in their dealings with him will be restricted.

Finally, a fourth factor that somewhat influences the way in which police exercise discretion is the "political culture" in which they operate. James Q. Wilson has directed particular attention to this factor. He defines political culture as "those widely shared expectations as to how issues will be raised, governmental objectives determined, and power for their attainment assembled; it is an understanding of what makes a government legitimate."[77] The prevailing political culture of a community creates "zones of indifference" within which the police are free to act as they please. Wilson identifies three basic political cultures, each of which promotes a certain style of police behavior. The first political culture, typically found in predominantly working-class and lower-middle-class "unreformed" cities, encourages the watchman style. It leads police officers to emphasize order maintenance over law enforcement. Arrests are made only when an incident threatens to become uncontrollable; otherwise, police officers are likely to dismiss the offender with a warning. The second political culture, typically found in wealthy, suburban, highly professional, city governments, fosters the legalistic style of police behavior. Police are expected to enforce the law, even when the public order is not threatened. As Wilson writes:

> The legalistic style does mean that, on the whole, the department will produce many arrests and citations, especially with respect to those matters in which the police and not the public invoke the law; even when the po-

lice are called by the public to intervene, they are likely to intervene formally, by making an arrest or urging the signing of a complaint, rather than informally, as through conciliation or by delaying an arrest in hopes that the situation will take care of itself.[78]

Obviously, this style imposes much more stringent control over the use of police discretion than does the watchman style. Between these two extremes, there is the service style, promoted by a third political culture, which is typically found in fairly homogeneous, middle-class communities. Service style departments respond to citizen complaints as legalistic departments do but avoid arrests and attempt to handle situations informally through warnings and lectures in much the same way that watchman style departments do. Police discretion is less restricted than in legalistic departments and is checked primarily by the department's commitment to service and good public relations.

Booking

Once supects are arrested and transported to the precinct or district station, they will be "booked." This is essentially a clerical process, involving little more than an entry on the police blotter of the suspect's name, time of arrest, and alleged offense. If the offense is serious, the suspect will be fingerprinted and photographed. Once the suspect is booked, a report of the offense, based on the officer's arrest report, is made to a member of the prosecutor's staff. It is this person's responsibility to review the discretion exercised by the arresting officer and to decide whether or not the suspect should be charged with an offense. This decision will be based on a number of considerations, including the weight of the evidence, the nature of the crime, the personal history of the defendant, and the availability of alternative remedies (for example, pretrial diversion).[79] A substantial percentage of arrested persons (often running as high as 40 percent) are released without the filing of charges. A large proportion of these cases involve arrestees charged with minor offenses (such as public drunkenness) or misdemeanors. Although the police themselves initiate many of these releases, most evidence indicates that the decision of whether or not to prosecute rests primarily with the prosecutors.[80] Once the prosecutor decides that a case has been made and that the suspect should be prosecuted, he prepares a complaint that identifies the defendant and specifies the charges against him. This complaint will then be presented at the defendant's initial appearance.

Courts

The Initial Judicial Appearance

In all jurisdictions, the police officer or other person making an arrest must bring the arrested person before a judge without unreasonable delay. In most major cities, the length of delay will depend upon a number of factors, including the timing of the arrest (was the arrest made at a time when neither prosecutors nor judges are readily available—for example, Sunday), the desire of the stationhouse detectives to interrogate the suspect, and the number of arrested persons being processed. In most urban centers, a suspect arrested on a felony charge in the afternoon or evening will not be brought before a judge until the next day and if arrested on a weekend will not be presented until the following Monday.[81]

It is at this initial appearance that most suspects have their first contact with the courts. This initial appearance is usually before a lower court—a magistrate or a justice of the peace.[82] Consequently, in prosecutions for serious offenses, the initial appearance occurs in a court that does not have jurisdiction to determine the guilt or innocence of the accused. By this time, the prosecution will have typically prepared a complaint, a formal document charging the defendant with a specific crime.

At the initial appearance, the magistrate informs the defendant of the charges against him, usually by means of the complaint. The magistrate also informs the defendant of his constitutional rights, including the protection against self-incrimination. He will generally inform the felony defendant of his right to a preliminary hearing and to representation by counsel at that hearing. If the defendant is indigent and wishes a court-appointed attorney, the magistrate will begin the mechanical process of assigning counsel. Finally, unless the defendant is convicted of an offense at this juncture, the magistrate will make arrangements for the release of the defendant as he awaits further proceedings. This may take the traditional form of setting bail. Bail is a procedure for releasing arrested persons on financial or other conditions to ensure their return for trial. Typically, this involves an amount of security the defendant himself or a professional bondsman whom he may hire must deposit with the court to ensure that the defendant will appear for later proceedings. Frequently, the amount of security is determined by a set schedule and varies in amount according to the crime charged. Ordinarily, the felony defendant will not post the security himself but rather will obtain a bond from a bail bondsman at a cost of approximately 10 percent of the face value of the bond. Alternatives to bail are now becoming more popular, however. In several jurisdictions, including the federal and Illinois courts, the defendent is permitted to obtain his release by paying 10 percent of the total amount to the court, almost all of which will be returned to him upon his subsequent appearance.[83] In other jurisdictions, pretrial release may take the form of an ROR (release on recognizance) program, whereby selected defendants are released simply upon their promise to appear at a later time.[84]

The matters discussed thus far have all been collateral to the issue of guilt; however, the initial appearance also begins the judicial inquiry into the actual merits of the case. Thus, if the charge is minor and is one that the lower

OVERVIEW OF THE CRIMINAL JUSTICE SYSTEM

court has authority to try, the defendant may be asked how he pleads. If he pleads guilty, he may be convicted at this point. Approximately 75 to 85 percent of all misdemeanor defendants plead guilty at this point.[85]

Preliminary Hearing

The preliminary hearing typically occurs in the same lower court before which the defendant has had his initial appearance. It is designed to protect felony defendants from unwarranted prosecutions. At this proceeding, the prosecutor must produce sufficient evidence to satisfy the magistrate that there is probable cause to warrant holding the defendant for trial. He does not have to convince the court of the defendant's guilt beyond a reasonable doubt; rather, he need only establish that he has sufficient evidence from which a jury could conclude that the defendant is guilty as charged.

At this hearing, the defendant may cross-examine witnesses and introduce evidence on his own behalf. If the court finds at the end of the preliminary hearing that probable cause does exist, the magistrate will then "bind over" the defendant for trial on the charge before a court of general jursidiction.[86] However, if the court finds that probable cause does not exist, the magistrate will dismiss the complaint and release the defendant.

In addition to protecting felony defendants from unwarranted prosecutions, the preliminary hearing also serves another valuable function for the defendant. It serves as an informal discovery device. It gives the defendant and his attorney a look at the case the prosecution will produce at trial. It provides the defense attorney with the opportunity to cross-examine witnesses he will later have to confront in court. As the National Advisory Commission on Criminal Justice Standards and Goals points out: "This informal previewing function may be more valuable to defendants than the theoretical function of the preliminary hearing."[87]

The Formal Criminal Charge

Following the decision by the magistrate that probable cause exists, a formal criminal charge against the defendant is made in the court that will hear the case if it goes to trial. In about half the states, this is a relatively simply procedure. The prosecutor merely files with the court a document called an information, which specifies the formal charges against the defendant. In other jurisdictions, however, use of the grand jury is necessary. The prosecutor must go before this body, ordinarily consisting of sixteen to twenty-three citizens, and present his evidence again. Unlike the preliminary hearing, the defendant is not present and has no right to be heard or to present evidence of his own. If a majority of the grand jurors find that the prosecutor has established probable cause, the grand jury will issue an indictment—a written accusation, prepared by the prosecutor and signed by the grand jury foreman, charging the defendant with the commission of a specified crime. If the grand jury determines that there is no probable cause, it takes no action and the prosecution of the defendant is terminated. This occurs, however, only in about 10 percent of the cases.[88]

Once a formal charge has been filed with the trial court, either by information or indictment, a whole array of legal questions may arise that require resolution. To begin with, a question may arise concerning the competency of the defendant to stand trial. If the defendant is adjudged by the court to be too impaired mentally to participate meaningfully in his own defense, the trial will have to be postponed until he retains his competency. Another issue may focus on the validity of the formal charge itself. The defendant may challenge the legitimacy of the grand jury, claiming that it was selected in a manner contrary to state or federal law and asserting that the indictment is, therefore, invalid. Or he may challenge the admissibility of certain evidence, claiming violation of the U. S. Constitution's Fourth Amendment protections against unreasonable searches and seizures and its Fifth Amendment protections against self-incrimination. Still another issue that the defendant may raise is his right to access to the evidence of the prosecution. Increasingly, the courts are abandoning the traditional approach that neither side is entitled to know what evidence the other side is going to produce until it actually presents it in court and instead are routinely granting defendants greater access to witnesses' statements and physical evidence, such as fingerprints, that may be inculpatory. Some courts are even requiring defendants to grant limited disclosure to the prosecution.

Arraignment

Because of the great complexity of these pretrial issues, a great deal of significant activity in the criminal prosecution may already have occurred prior to the defendant's first formal appearance before the court in which he is to be tried. This appearance is called the arraignment. At the arraignment, the defendant is informed of the charges against him and is asked to plead to them. The defendant can respond in one of four ways. He can decline to plead, in which case the judge automatically enters for him a plea of not guilty. He can plead not guilty, in which case the judge will schedule the case for trial and put in motion the full adversary process. If the defendant pleads not guilty, he may at this time make a variety of pretrial motions, seeking discovery of evidence, suppression of evidence, change of venue, or outright dismissal of the charges for want of probable cause. All of these issues may well have been the subject of previous discussions.[89] The defendant can plead guilty, as between 70 and 85 percent of all felony defendants do. The law requires that certain precautions be taken to ensure that this plea is made voluntarily. Consequently, the trial judge accepting the plea must question the defendant to determine whether he is knowingly, willingly, and intelligently waiving such constitutional protections as the right to trial by jury, the right to confrontation of witnesses, and the protection against self-incrimination and whether he understands the charges against him and the penalties that may be imposed. To establish further the validity of the guilty plea, the judge may also require the prosecution to present some of its evidence. Finally, the defendant can plead *nolo contendere* or no contest. This plea has the same legal effect as a plea of guilty insofar as the proceedings at hand are concerned. However, it cannot be used as an admission elsewhere, as in any subsequent civil litigation for damages.

The Trial

If the defendant pleads not guilty at his arraignment, it is then incumbent upon the prosecution in full trial to establish his guilt beyond a reasonable doubt to a jury or a judge. Unless both the defendant and the prosecution voluntarily waive a jury trial, a jury is selected. The jury selection process, or *voir dire,* is frequently time-consuming and arduous. The prospective jurors are closely questioned in an attempt to ascertain whether they might be biased. Both the prosecuting and defense attorneys have the right to reject potential jurors on that ground. In addition, both sides have a limited number of peremptory challenges that they can employ to reject potential jurors without cause. Once the jury has been empaneled, both sides make opening statements outlining the points they intend to prove or disprove in the course of the trial.

Because the prosecution must bear the burden of proof, it presents its evidence first. Once all the evidence is in, the defense attorney will typically move to dismiss, asserting that the prosecution's case is so weak that no jury could conclude beyond a reasonable doubt that the defendant is in fact guilty. If the judge grants the motion, this not only results in a dismissal of the prosecution but also prevents the prosecution from bringing another charge for the same crime.[90] The prosecution is unlikely to bring such a weak case to trial, however, and typically the judge will reject this motion, leaving the defendant with two options: He can make no case and simply rely on the prosecution's inability to establish in the minds of the jurors guilt beyond a reasonable doubt, or he can present evidence and witnesses of his own tending to disprove the prosecution's case or tending to prove additional facts constituting a defense under applicable law.

After all the evidence is in and all defense motions have been disposed of, the judge typically instructs the jury on the applicable law. This is followed by the prosecuting and defense attorneys' closing arguments to the jury.[91] Armed with the evidence and instructed on the applicable law, the jury retires for its deliberations. Typically, the jury may return only one of two verdicts: not guilty or guilty. If the defendant is found not guilty, the charge against him is dismissed and, under the constitutional proscription against double jeopardy, the prosecution is prevented from bringing another charge against him for the same crime.[92] This verdict is unusual, however; the acquittal rate for all felonies is under 20 percent. Generally, the defendant is found guilty, and the court formally enters a judgment of conviction against him unless there is a legally sufficient reason for not doing so. On rare occasions, a jury may become hopelessly deadlocked and unable to reach a verdict. When such a hung jury occurs, the judge may dismiss it and call for a new trial.[93]

The defendant may attack the court's judgment of conviction, typically through a motion to set aside the verdict and order a new trial. He may base his attack on a claim that unconstitutionally seized evidence was improperly admitted during the trial; that the evidence was so weak that no reasonable jury could find that it established guilt beyond a reasonable doubt; or that he has uncovered new evidence that, had it been available at the time of the trial, would have led to an acquittal. Typically, these motions are rather perfunctorily dismissed by the court, and even on those occasions where they are granted, the common practice is not to acquit the defendant but rather to require the holding of a new trial.

Sentencing

The next step in the criminal process is sentencing. (If the defendant has engaged in plea bargaining, this step immediately follows acceptance of the plea.) This step is, as Federal District Court Judge Marvin E. Frankel observes, "probably the most critical point in our system of administering criminal justice."[94] Frankel's words merely underscore the conclusions of the President's Commission on Law Enforcement and Administration of Justice:

> There is no decision in the criminal process that is as complicated and difficult as the one made by the sentencing judge. A sentence prescribes punishment, but it also should be the foundation of an attempt to rehabilitate the offender to ensure that he does not endanger the community, and to deter others from similar crimes in the future. Often these objectives are mutually inconsistent, and the sentencing judge must choose one at the expense of the others.[95]

Of course, the judge receives some guidance from statutory provisions that establish the range of sentencing alternatives, but, his discretion remains, for the most part, "unbounded."[96] To assist the judge further in fashioning appropriate sentences, an increasing number of jurisdictions now require the preparation of a presentence investigation report by professional probation officers. This report includes an investigation of the offense, the offender and his background, and any other matters of potential value to the sentencing judge. Armed with this report, the judge is then in a better position to impose the sentencing alternative most appropriate to the offender: incarceration, probation, or fine.[97]

Appeal

Following the conclusion of the proceedings in the trial court, the next step in the criminal process involves the appellate courts. In most jurisdictions, a defendant convicted of a minor offense in a court of limited jurisdiction has the right to a new trial (trial *de nova*) in a higher court. However, in all cases involving serious offenses, the right of appeal is limited to an appellate court examination for error of the record of the trial proceedings. If harmless error (that is, error committed in the progress of the trial but that is not prejudicial to the rights of the defendant) is found, the appellate court will not reverse the conviction. However, if prejudicial error is established, the appellate court may order that the prosecution be dismissed. It may also set aside the conviction and remand the case for a new trial, thereby giving the prosecution the opportunity to obtain a valid conviction. Generally, a time limit is placed upon the period in which an appeal may be made.

Collateral Attack

Once a conviction is finalized (that is, once a convicted defendant has exhausted his appeal rights or has declined to exercise them within the appropriate time limits), further relief is available to the defendant only by means of a collateral attack upon his conviction. For the most part, such collateral relief is sought by applying in either the state or federal courts for a writ of habeas corpus on the grounds that the conviction under which the applicant is held is invalid. This remedy is rarely successful, but it is frequently utilized; approximately one-sixth of the federal district courts' civil dockets are taken up with petitions from state and federal prisoners alleging constitutional violations.[98] These collateral attacks not only place a burden on the federal judiciary, they have also become increasingly a point of friction in federal-state relations. The federal courts have, for the most part, offered a more sympathetic forum for assertions that federal constitutional rights have been violated during state court prosecutions, and state judges and prosecutors have come to resent federal court interventions that have reversed convictions for reasons unpersuasive to the state courts.[99]

Corrections

Once a defendant has been duly convicted and sentenced, he enters the correctional stage of the criminal justice system. This stage is often hidden from the public by thick walls, locked doors, physical remoteness, and legal procedures,[100] but it is nevertheless extremely important. As Robert O. Dawson writes:

> The corrections segment of the criminal justice system is a decision-making process for determining what to do with the convicted offender—whether to commit him to prison or to permit him to live in the community under probation supervision; if he is permitted to live in the community, what kinds of controls to impose upon him, for how long, and how to determine whether community living should be terminated in favor of commitment to prison; if committed to prison, to determine how long he should be incarcerated and whether he should be released unconditionally or under supervision; and if he is released under supervision, for how long, under what conditions, and subject to recommitment for what conduct.[101]

The very safety and security of the community depend upon the answers given to these questions.[102] Four principal correctional alternatives are most commonly employed by the criminal justice system: imprisonment, probation, parole, and pretrial diversion.

Imprisonment

Imprisonment is, of course, incarceration in a penal institution—either a jail or a prison. It constitutes the "hard-core base of the correctional process."[103] Imprisonment as a means of punishment or correction is also a relatively modern practice. "Before the 18th century, prisons were not used to punish but to detain the accused until the debtor paid his debt, the rapist was castrated, the thief's hands were cut off, or the perjuror's tongue was torn out."[104] Although imprisonment arose out of a spirit of reform and humanitarianism, it has for the most part failed as an instrument of reform. Imprisonment is seen as atrophying the offender's capacity to live successfully in the free world. It brutalizes attitudes and destroys self-confidence. Prisons and jails have come to be regarded as little more than "schools of crime."[105] For these and other reasons (to be discussed in Chapter 5) the National Advisory Commission has adopted the philosophy that the criminal justice system should "incarcerate only when nothing less will do, and then incarcerate as briefly as possible."[106] It has joined with the National Council on Crime and Delinquency (NCCD) in suggesting that imprisonment must be understood as the exception and community-based corrections as the rule: "Imprisonment must be viewed as an alternative to community treatment."[107] In brief, the commission has recommended that the criminal justice system place increasingly greater emphasis on the correctional alternatives of probation, parole, and pretrial diversion.

Probation

Probation may be defined as a sentence that does not involve confinement but that instead places the offender under supervision in the community subject to the authority of the sentencing court. Probation consists of two basic

OVERVIEW OF THE CRIMINAL JUSTICE SYSTEM

operations: the presentence investigation, conducted to determine which offenders will receive the sentence of probation, and supervision of probationers. It is considered by many to be perhaps "the most successful phase of the correctional process."[108] Studies of probation effectiveness have generally indicated success rates of from 60 to 90 percent.[109] As a consequence, approximately 75 percent of all convictions today result in probation.[110] Because probation is often a one-time disposition whereas institutional case loads are often cumulative, the actual count of those on probation at any given time drops to about 53 percent.[111]

Parole

Parole and probation are often confused. They are, in fact, quite similar in that they both provide the defendant with a degree of liberty in the community, under supervision, and both involve a threat of incarceration by a summary proceeding far short of a trial for violation of the conditions of liberty. Parole, however, involves the release of one who has already served a portion of his sentence in a correctional or penal institution, and such parole is understood to be a part of his prison term. In contrast, probation is granted prior to incarceration and is understood to be an alternative to imprisonment.[112] According to many, the fact that parole is less treatment-oriented and more punitive than probation accounts for its higher failure rates. Thus, for example, 47 percent of the 7,582 male offenders paroled in California in 1965 had been declared violators by 1966.[113] Likewise, of those men paroled from the Illinois State Penitentiary between 1926 and 1943, 44 percent were violators. And, of the 1,015 inmates released from federal prisons in 1956, 35 percent were classed as failures by 1960.[114] Nonetheless, the use of parole remains widespread. In 1970, 80,043 felons left state prisons; 70.1 percent of them were released by parole.[115]

Pretrial Diversion

Because of the high failure rates of parole and the even higher rates of prisons, correctional alternatives that minimize penetration into the criminal justice system are becoming increasingly prominent. Probation is certainly one such alternative, and so is pretrial diversion, which minimizes penetration even further. Pretrial diversion refers to a decision to halt or suspend formal criminal proceedings against a person before conviction on the condition or assumption that he will do something in return. As the National Advisory Commission describes it:

> Diversion uses the threat or possibility of conviction of a criminal offense to encourage an accused to agree to do something: he may agree to participate in a rehabilitation program designed to change his behavior,

or he simply may agree to make restitution to the victim of the offense. This agreement may not be entirely voluntary, as the accused often agrees to participate in a diversion program only because he fears formal criminal prosecution.[116]

Pretrial diversion can provide many benefits. To begin with, because legislatures have not been able to prescribe in criminal statutes exactly which individuals should or should not be subject to the formal imposition of criminal liability, pretrial diversion allows adjustment for inevitable overcriminalization. Second, it can encourage the offender to make restitution to the victim, thereby serving a valuable penological function by forcing the offender to come to grips with the consequences of his criminal behavior.[117] Third, pretrial diversion is extremely economical. Because it operates at the early stages in the criminal process, it avoids the necessity for some formal proceedings, and the resources that otherwise would have to be used to process the individuals through the criminal justice system can be used for some other purpose. Finally, it broadens the resources that can be used to deal with offenders. It permits dispositions of offenders that would be difficult or impossible under the more traditional sentencing alternatives. Diversion is not without its problems, however. Thus, candidates for diversion must be carefully screened, and most offenders are thereby appropriately excluded. Moreover, diversion's long-term effect on deterrence of criminal activity remains to be determined.[118]

As this analysis of the stages of the criminal process should suggest, the cooperation of the entire criminal justice system is absolutely imperative for its successful operation. Although the components of the system are organizationally separate, they are, nonetheless, functionally interrelated. Neither the police, the courts, nor correctional agencies can perform their tasks without directly affecting the efforts of the others. Although they are in general agreement that the major goal of the criminal justice system is the reduction of crime through the use of criminal procedure consistent with the protection of individual liberties, they are frequently in disagreement on the specific means by which to achieve that goal and on what to do when one set of means conflicts with another. The various and diverse interrelationship or interface problems that afflict the criminal justice system will be taken up next. Chapter 2 will explore, through the use of compliance analysis, the nature and extent of these problems.

Notes

1. Michael J. Hindelang et al., *Sourcebook of Criminal Justice Statistics, 1973,* Law Enforcement Assistance Administration, U.S. Department of Justice (Washington, D.C.: Government Printing Office, 1973), p. 198.

2. *Crime in the Nation's Five Largest Cities,* Law Enforcement Assistance Administration, U.S. Department of Justice (Washington, D.C.: Government Printing Office, 1974), pp. 28-29. See, however, Wesley G. Skogan, "Measurement Problems in Official and Survey Crime Rates," *Journal of Criminal Justice* 3, no. 1 (Spring 1975): 17-31.
3. *Crime in the United States—Uniform Crime Reports—1974,* U.S. Department of Justice (Washington, D.C.: Government Printing Office, 1975). Figures derived from pp. 18-55.
4. Ibid., p. 166.
5. Abraham S. Blumberg, *Criminal Justice* (Chicago: Quadrangle Books, 1970), p. 31.
6. Jonathan D. Casper, *American Criminal Justice: The Defendant's Perspective* (Englewood Cliffs, N.J.: Prentice-Hall, 1972), p. 81.
7. *Crime in the United States—Uniform Crime Reports—1972,* U.S. Department of Justice (Washington, D.C.: Government Printing Office, 1973), p. 36.
8. See Herbert Jacob, *Urban Justice: Law and Order in American Cities* (Englewood Cliffs, N.J.: Prentice-Hall, 1973), p. 16. See also Abraham S. Blumberg, "Crime and the Social Order," in *Current Perspectives on Criminal Behavior: Original Essays on Criminology,* ed. Blumberg (New York: Knopf, 1974), pp. 16-20.
9. President's Commission on Law Enforcement and Administration of Justice, *The Challenge of Crime in a Free Society* (Washington, D.C.: Government Printing Office, 1967), p. 3.
10. Ibid. See Hazel Erskine, "The Polls: Fear of Violence and Crime," *Public Opinion Quarterly* 38, no. 1 (Spring 1974): 131-145; and "The Polls: Causes of Crime," *Political Science Quarterly* 38, no. 2 (Summer 1974): 288-298.
11. *The Challenge of Crime in a Free Society,* p. 18.
12. *The Uniform Crime Reports* brings together reports from approximately 8,000 police agencies covering 92 percent of the population. *The Challenge of Crime in a Free Society,* p. 20. For a discussion of the problems involved in using *Uniform Crime Reports* statistics, see David Seidman and Michael Couzens, "Crime, Criminal Statistics, and the Great American Anti-Crime Crusade: Police Misreporting of Crime and Political Pressure" (paper delivered at the Annual Meeting of the American Political Science Association, Washington, D.C., 1972).
13. *Crime in the United States—Uniform Crime Reports—1971,* U.S. Department of Justice (Washington, D.C.: Government Printing Office, 1972), p. 5.
14. *Crime in the United States—Uniform Crime Reports—1973,* U.S. Department of Justice (Washington, D.C.: Government Printing Office, 1974), p. 50.
15. Ibid., p. 19.
16. Ibid., pp. 19-20.
17. Large core cities with over 250,000 inhabitants recorded a victim rate of 360 aggravated assaults per 100,000 inhabitants.

18. Of those persons arrested, males outnumbered females seven to one.
19. *The Challenge of Crime in a Free Society*, p. 21.
20. Hindelang, *Sourcebook of Criminal Justice Statistics, 1973*, p. 173.
21. *Crime in the Nation's Five Largest Cities*, p. 5.
22. *Memphis Commercial Appeal*, April 15, 1974, p. 1.
23. This definition is from Herbert Edelhertz, *The Nature, Impact, and Prosecution of White-Collar Crime*, Law Enforcement Assistance Administration, U.S. Department of Justice (Washington, D.C.: Government Printing Office, 1970), p.3.
24. *Crime and the Law* (Washington D.C.: Congressional Quarterly, 1971), pp. 19-20. See also Edelhertz, *The Nature, Impact, and Prosecution of White-Collar Crime*, pp. 73-75.
25. *Crime and the Law*, pp. 19-20.
26. *Crime in the United States—Uniform Crime Reports—1974*, p. 179.
27. *Memphis Commercial Appeal*, April 20, 1975, p. 4.
28. *The Challenge of Crime in a Free Society*, p. 48.
29. Throughout this volume, quotation marks will consistently be used wherever reference is made to "victimless" crimes. This practice is being followed to indicate that a question exists as to whether crimes usually labeled as "victimless" really are so. Thus, drunkenness, narcotics and drug abuse, and gambling often rather severely victimize the dependents of those who dissipate their lives and exhaust their financial resources by engaging in these offenses. Prostitution often leads to the robbery of the customer and the further spread of venereal disease. Even pornography and obscenity may have consequences that are of real social concern. After all, as Irving Kristol has pointed out, "if you believe that no one was ever corrupted by a book, you have also to believe that no one was ever improved by a book (or a play or a movie). You have to believe, in other words, that all art is morally trivial and that, consequently, all education is morally irrelevant." Irving Kristol, *On the Democratic Idea in America* (New York: Harper & Row, 1972), p. 32.
30. This number is down somewhat from 1965 when 2,000,000 of the total of approximately 6,000,000 arrests made in the United States that year were for the offense of public drunkenness. *The Challenge of Crime in a Free Society*, p. 233.
31. Ibid.
32. Norval Morris and Gordon Hawkins, *The Honest Politician's Guide to Crime Control* (Chicago: University of Chicago Press, 1970), p. 6.
33. See Herbert L. Packer, *The Limits of the Criminal Sanction* (Stanford, Calif.: Stanford University Press, 1968), pp. 304-306; and Morris and Hawkins, *The Honest Politician's Guide to Crime Control*, pp. 5-6.
34. See Kenneth Culp Davis, *Discretionary Justice* (Baton Rouge: Louisiana State University Press, 1969), pp. 162-180.
35. John Kaplan, *Criminal Justice* (Mineola, N.Y.: The Foundation Press, 1973), p. 682. See also Ben Hardy, "The Traps of Entrapment," *American Journal of Criminal Law* 3, no. 2 (Fall, 1974): 165-204.
36. Morris and Hawkins, *The Honest Politician's Guide to Crime Control*, p. 5.

37. John Stuart Mill, "On Liberty," in *Utilitarianism, On Liberty, and Essay on Bentham,* ed. Mary Warnock (New York: World Publishing, 1962), p. 135. It must be remembered that Mill was speaking of a "civilized" community. See note 46.
38. *Roe* v. *Wade,* 410 U.S. 113, 164 (1973).
39. *The Challenge of Crime in a Free Society,* p. 236. The President's Commission did, however, recommend that "disorderly and other criminal conduct accompanied by drunkenness should remain punishable as separate offenses."
40. National Advisory Commission on Criminal Justice Standards and Goals, *A National Strategy to Reduce Crime* (Washington, D.C.: Government Printing Office, 1973), p. 205.
41. Ibid. p. 203.
42. Ibid.
43. See Allan Bloom's "Introduction" to Jean-Jacques Rousseau, *Politics and the Arts: Letter to M. D'Alembert on the Theatre,* trans. Allan Bloom (Ithaca, N.Y.: Cornell University Press, 1968), p. xi.
44. Kristol, *On the Democratic Idea in America,* p. 33.
45. See Harry M. Clor, "Obscenity and Freedom of Expression," in *Censorship and Freedom of Expression: Essays on Obscenity and the Law,* ed. Clor (Chicago: Rand McNally, 1971), p. 109. See also Harry M. Clor, *Obscenity and Public Morality: Censorship in a Liberal Society* (Chicago: University of Chicago Press, 1969).
46. Walter Berns, "Pornography Versus Democracy: The Case for Censorship," *The Public Interest,* no. 22 (Winter 1971), p. 13. See also in this connection John Stuart Mill's comment that "Despotism is a legitimate mode of government when dealing with barbarians, provided the end be their improvement, and the means justified by actually effecting that end." "On Liberty," p. 136.
47. Clor, "Obscenity and Freedom of Expression," p. 110.
48. Kristol, *On the Democratic Idea in America,* p. 41.
49. See Lord Devlin, *The Enforcement of Morals* (Oxford: Oxford University Press, 1959), p. 13.
50. The "sociological" school of criminology rejects the "classical" theories of crime advanced by such men as Jeremy Bentham and Cesare Beccaria because of their underlying psychological assumption that individuals calculate the pains and pleasures of crime and pursue it if the latter outweighs the former. This "assumes freedom of the will in a manner which gives little or no possibility of further investigation of the causes of crime or of efforts to prevent crime." Moreover, they see these theories and the psychology on which they are based as "too individualistic, intellectualistic, and voluntaristic." Edwin H. Sutherland and Donald R. Cressey, *Principles of Criminology,* 7th ed. rev. (Philadelphia: Lippincott, 1966), p. 53.
51. Ramsey Clark, *Crime in America* (New York: Simon and Schuster, 1970), pp. 56-57.
52. See President's Commission on Law Enforcement and Administration of

Justice, *Task Force Report: Juvenile Delinquency and Youth Crime* (Washington, D.C.: Government Printing Office, 1967), pp. 45-46. See also Barbara Wooten, *Social Science and Social Pathology* (London: George Allen and Unwin, 1959).
53. This, of course, assumes that legitimate opportunities are preferable to criminal ones. For many, however, "this neglects the advantages of a criminal income." As James Q. Wilson observes, "One works at crime at one's convenience, enjoys the esteem of colleagues who think a 'straight' job is stupid and skill at stealing is commendable, looks forward to the occasional 'big score' that may make further work unnecessary for weeks, and relishes the risk and adventure associated with theft. The money value of all these benefits . . . is hard to estimate, but is almost certainly far larger than what either public or private employers could offer to unskilled or semiskilled young workers." James Q. Wilson, *Thinking about Crime* (New York: Basic Books, 1975), pp. 202-203.
54. Peter L. Berger, "The Socialist Myth," *The Public Interest*, no. 44 (Summer 1976), p. 8.
55. For further discussion on the causes of crime, see Kaplan, *Criminal Justice*, pp. 612-658, and Paul W. Tappan, *Crime, Justice and Correction* (New York: McGraw-Hill, 1960).
56. *The Challenge of Crime in a Free Society*, p. 6.
57. Clark, *Crime in America*, pp. 56-57. See James C. Etchison, "Theories of Crime Causation," *Policy Studies Journal* 3, no. 1 (Autumn 1974): 10.
58. James Q. Wilson, "Crime and Punishment in England," *The Public Interest*, no. 43 (Spring 1976), p. 10.
59. David H. Bayley, "Learning About Crime–The Japanese Experience," *The Public Interest*, no. 44 (Summer 1976), pp. 55-61.
60. Wilson, "Crime and Punishment in England," pp. 10-11. For an excellent discussion of the impact of "the cult of personal liberation and unfettered self-expression" and the general change of attitude in American society toward authority, see Edward C. Banfield, "A Critical View of the Urban Crisis," *The Annals of the American Academy of Political and Social Science*, 405 (January 1973): 7-14.
61. Bayley, "Learning About Crime–The Japanese Experience," p. 68.
62. Edward C. Banfield, *The Unheavenly City Revisited* (Boston: Little, Brown, 1974), pp. 179-210.
63. Ibid., pp. 182-183. As Banfield points out, "In general, an individual whose morality is preconventional also has little ego strength, a short time horizon, a fondness for risk, and little distaste for doing bodily harm to specifiable individuals. The opposites of these traits also tend to be found together." Ibid., p. 183.
64. Ibid., p. 182.
65. Alexander Hamilton, James Madison, and John Jay, *The Federalist*, ed. Jacob E. Cooke (New York: World, 1961), p. 58.
66. See, for example, Michael Ginsberg, "Rural Criminal Justice: An Overview,"

American Journal of Criminal Law 3, no. 1 (Summer 1974): 35-52.
67. See Wayne R. LaFave, *Arrest: The Decision to Take a Suspect into Custody* (Boston: Little, Brown, 1965), p. 3. See also Yale Kamisar, Wayne R. LaFave, and Jerold H. Israel, *Basic Criminal Procedure,* 4th ed. (St. Paul: West, 1974), p. 5; and Donald M. McIntyre, *Criminal Justice in the United States* (Chicago: American Bar Foundation, 1974), pp. 8-10.
68. See Kamisar et al., *Basic Criminal Procedure,* p. 6. See *U.S.* v. *Watson,* 423 U.S. 411 (1976), in which Justice White held for a five member majority that the opportunity to obtain a warrant does not invalidate a warrantless felony arrest made with probable cause.
69. See Kenneth Culp Davis' response to this statement in his *Discretionary Justice,* pp. 88-89. See also his *Police Discretion* (St. Paul: West, 1975), pp. 3-7.
70. *The Challenge of Crime in a Free Society,* p. 10.
71. Ibid.
72. See Davis, *Discretionary Justice,* p. 82. See also LaFave, *Arrest,* pp. 125-143.
73. See Jacob, *Urban Justice,* pp. 27-29. See also A. Didrick Castberg, "The Exercise of Discretion in the Administration of Justice" (Paper delivered at the Annual Meeting of the American Political Science Association, Washington, D.C., 1972).
74. Suzanne K. Steinmetz, "The Family Is Cradle of Violence," *Social Science and Modern Society* 10, no. 6 (September-October 1973): 51. Many police officers coming to the aid of a wife who is beaten by her husband have had chairs or bottles thrown at them or have even been stabbed or shot by a wife who suddenly becomes fearful of what is going to happen to her husband and who abruptly transfers her rage from her husband to the police.
75. Donald J. Black, "Reduction of Crime Rates," *American Sociological Review* 35 (1970): 740-747. Black's findings were limited strictly to high-crime precincts in three large cities. Whether or not the same relationships obtain in low-crime areas of large cities or in smaller cities is not yet empirically established.
76. See Jacob, *Urban Justice,* p. 28.
77. James Q. Wilson, *Varieties of Police Behavior: The Management of Law and Order in Eight Communities* (Cambridge, Mass.: Harvard University Press, 1968), p. 233.
78. Ibid., p. 173.
79. See Kamisar et al., *Basic Criminal Procedure,* p. 7. See also *Prosecution of Adult Felony Defendants in Los Angeles County: A Policy Perspective,* Law Enforcement Assistance Administration, U.S. Department of Justice (Washington, D.C.: Government Printing Office, 1973).
80. Kamisar et al., *Basic Criminal Procedure,* p. 8. David W. Neubauer also found this to be the case in his study of Prairie City, Illinois. "The overriding feature of the charging process in Prairie City is the dominance of the prosecutor." Neubauer, *Criminal Justice in Middle America*

(Morristown, N.J.: General Learning Press, 1974), p. 116. See also Frank W. Miller, *Prosecution: The Decision to Charge a Suspect with a Crime* (Boston: Little, Brown, 1969), pp. 11-19.
81. Kamisar et al., *Basic Criminal Procedure*, p. 8. In most jurisdictions, suspects arrested on misdemeanor charges as well as certain felony charges may be released on bail by the police prior to their initial judicial appearance. The amount of such bail is typically regulated by a schedule established by the courts or by statute.
82. National Advisory Commission on Criminal Justice Standards and Goals, *Report on Courts* (Washington, D.C.: Government Printing Office, 1973), p. 12.
83. See Paul Wice and Rita James Simon, "Pre-Trial Release: A Survey of Alternative Practices," *Federal Probation* 34, no. 4 (December 1970): 60-63. See also National Advisory Commission on Criminal Justice Standards and Goals, *Report on Corrections* (Washington, D.C.: Government Printing Office, 1973), pp. 98-110.
84. See Charles E. Ares, Anne Rankin, and Herbert Sturz, "The Manhattan Bail Project: An Interim Report on the Use of Pre-Trial Parole," *New York University Law Review* 38 (1963).
85. Kamisar et al., *Basic Criminal Procedure*, p. 9.
86. If the magistrate finds that probable cause supports only a misdemeanor charge, he will direct the charge to be so reduced.
87. *Report on Courts*, p. 12.
88. Kamisar et al., *Basic Criminal Procedure*, p. 10.
89. Available information suggests that pretrial motions are not very common. They are filed in less than 20 percent of all cases which go to trial. Kamisar et al., *Basic Criminal Procedure*, p. 12.
90. *Report on Courts*, p. 13.
91. In some jurisdictions, however, these closing arguments by the prosecution and defense counsel precede the judge's instructions to the jury.
92. A verdict of not guilty may be misleading; although it may mean that the jury believes that the defendant is innocent of the charges against him, it may also mean that the jury does not believe that the prosecution has established guilt by the criterion the law imposes—guilt beyond a reasonable doubt.
93. Herbert Jacob, *Justice in America: Courts, Lawyers, and the Judicial Process*, 2nd ed. (Boston: Little, Brown, 1972), p. 126.
94. Marvin E. Frankel, *Criminal Sentences: Law Without Order* (New York: Hill & Wang, 1973), p. xii.
95. *The Challenge of Crime in a Free Society*, p. 141. See also President's Commission on Law Enforcement and Administration of Justice, *Task Force Report: The Courts* (Washington D.C.: Government Printing Office, 1967), p. 14.
96. As Judge Frankel writes: "The almost wholly unchecked and sweeping powers we give to judges in the fashioning of sentences are terrible and intolerable for a society that professes devotion to the rule of law." *Criminal Sentences*, p. 5.

97. See Robert O. Dawson, *Sentencing: The Decision as to Type, Length, and Conditions of Sentence* (Boston: Little, Brown, 1969).
98. It is in part to meet this difficulty that the Supreme Court held in *Stone v. Powell,* 428 U.S. 465 (1976) that federal habeas corpus relief can be appropriately limited in Fourth Amendment cases in which the state prisoner has had the opportunity to litigate fairly and fully his claims at the state level. See also *Francis* v. *Henderson,* 425 U.S. 536 (1976).
99. See Ralph A. Rossum, "New Rights and Old Wrongs: The Supreme Court and the Problem of Retroactivity," *Emory Law Journal* 23, no. 2 (Spring 1974): 414-416. See also Stephen L. Wasby, *Continuity and Change: From the Warren Court to the Burger Court* (Pacific Palisades, Calif.: Goodyear, 1976), p. 53, n. 52.
100. As the National Advisory Commission on Criminal Justice Standards and Goals observes: "The correctional system is one of the few public services left today that is characterized by an almost total isolation from the public it serves." *Report on Corrections,* p. 600. See also *The Challenge of Crime in a Free Society,* pp. 11-12.
101. Dawson, *Sentencing,* p. 3.
102. President's Commission on Law Enforcement and Administration of Justice, *Task Force Report: Corrections* (Washington, D.C.: Government Printing Office, 1967), p. 16.
103. Vernon Fox, *Introduction to Corrections* (Englewood Cliffs, N.J.: Prentice-Hall, 1972), p. 124.
104. James S. Campbell, Joseph R. Sahid, and David P. Stang, *Law and Order Reconsidered,* a staff report to the National Commission on the Causes and Prevention of Violence (Washington, D.C.: Government Printing Office, 1969), p. 572.
105. See Daniel Glaser, "Some Notes on Urban Jails," in *Crime in the City,* ed. Glaser (Harper & Row, 1971), p. 241.
106. *Report on Corrections,* p. 223.
107. Ibid., pp. 231-232.
108. Fox, *Introduction to Corrections,* p. 120.
109. See Ralph W. England, Jr., "What is Responsible for Satisfactory Probation and Post-Probation Outcome?" *Journal of Criminal Law, Criminology, and Police Science* 47 (1957): 667-676. See also Frank R. Scarpitti and Richard M. Stephenson, "A Study of Probation Effectiveness," *Journal of Criminal Law, Criminology, and Police Science* 59 (1968): 361-362. For a recent and devastating critique of these studies, however, see Robert Martinson, "What Works?—Questions and Answers About Prison Reform," *The Public Interest,* no. 35 (Spring 1974), pp. 22-54.
110. Fox, *Introduction to Corrections,* p. 104.
111. See *Task Force Report: Corrections,* p. 27.
112. See *Attorney General's Survey of Release Procedures* (Washington, D.C.: Government Printing Office, 1939), vol. 4, p. 4.
113. Edwin H. Sutherland and Donald R. Cressey, *Criminology,* 8th ed. (Philadelphia: Lippincott, 1970, p. 598.

114. Daniel Glaser, *The Effectiveness of a Prison and Parole System* (Indianapolis: Bobbs-Merrill, 1964), pp. 19-20.
115. U.S. Department of Justice, Federal Bureau of Prisons, *National Prisoner Statistics: Prisoners in State and Federal Institutions for Adult Felons, 1968, 1969, 1970* (Washington, D.C.: Government Printing Office, 1971), pp. 22-23.
116. *Report on Courts,* p. 27.
117. See Gerhard O. W. Mueller and H. H. A. Cooper, *The Criminal, Society and the Victim,* U.S. Department of Justice (Washington, D.C.: Government Printing Office ,1973).
118. See Joan Mullen, *The Dilemma of Diversion,* U.S. Department of Justice (Washington, D.C.: Government Printing Office, 1975).

Bibliography

Banfield, Edward C. *The Unheavenly City Revisited.* Boston: Little, Brown, 1974.
Bayley, David H. "Learning About Crime—The Japanese Experience." *The Public Interest,* no. 44 (Summer 1976), pp. 55-68.
Bent, Alan Edward, and Rossum, Ralph A. *Police, Criminal Justice, and the Community.* New York: Harper & Row, 1976.
Berns, Walter. "Pornography Versus Democracy: The Case for Censorship." *The Public Interest,* no. 22 (Winter 1971), pp. 3-24.
Blumberg, Abraham S. *Criminal Justice.* Chicago. Quadrangle Books, 1970.
Bureau of National Affairs. "White Collar Justice." *Criminal Law Reporter* 19, no. 3 (1976).
Campbell, James S., Sahid, Joseph R., and Stang, David P. *Law and Order Reconsidered.* A Staff Report to the National Commission on the Causes and Prevention of Violence. Washington, D.C.: Government Printing Office, 1969.
Casper, Jonathan D. *American Criminal Justice: The Defendant's Perspective.* Englewood Cliffs, N.J.: Prentice-Hall, 1972.
Clor, Harry M., ed. *Censorship and Freedom of Expression: Essays on Obscenity and the Law.* Chicago: Rand McNally, 1971.
Cole, George F., ed. *Criminal Justice: Law and Politics.* 2nd ed. North Scituate, Mass.: Duxbury Press, 1976.
Crime and the Law. Washington, D.C.: Congressional Quarterly, 1971.
Crime in the Nation's Five Largest Cities. U.S. Department of Justice. Washington, D.C.: Government Printing Office, 1974.
Crime in the United States—Uniform Crime Reports. Published annually. U.S. Department of Justice. Washington, D.C.: Government Printing Office.
Davis, Kenneth Culp. *Discretionary Justice.* Baton Rouge: Louisiana State University Press, 1969.
———. *Police Discretion.* St. Paul: West, 1975.
Dawson, Robert O. *Sentencing: The Decision as to Type, Length and Conditions of Sentence.* Boston: Little, Brown, 1969.

Edelhertz, Herbert. *The Nature, Impact, and Prosecution of White Collar Crime.* U.S. Department of Justice. Washington, D.C.: Government Printing Office, 1970.

Fox, Vernon. *Introduction to Corrections.* Englewood Cliffs, N.J.: Prentice-Hall, 1972.

Frankel, Marvin E. *Criminal Sentences: Law Without Order.* New York: Hill & Wang, 1973.

Jacob, Herbert. *Justice in America: Courts, Lawyers and the Judicial Process.* 2nd ed. Boston: Little, Brown, 1972.

———. *Urban Justice: Law and Order in American Cities.* Englewood Cliffs, N.J.: Prentice-Hall, 1973.

Kamisar, Yale, LaFave, Wayne R., and Israel, Jerold H. *Basic Criminal Procedure.* 4th ed. St. Paul: West, 1974.

Kaplan, John. *Criminal Justice.* Mineola, N.Y.: The Foundation Press, 1973.

LaFave, Wayne R. *Arrest: The Decision to Take A Suspect into Custody.* Boston: Little, Brown, 1965.

McIntyre, Donald M. *Criminal Justice in the United States.* Chicago: American Bar Foundation, 1974.

Martinson, Robert. "What Works?—Questions and Answers About Prison Reform." *The Public Interest,* no. 35 (Spring 1974), pp. 22-54.

Morris, Norval, and Hawkins, Gordon. *The Honest Politician's Guide to Crime Control.* Chicago: University of Chicago Press, 1970.

National Advisory Commission on Criminal Justice Standards and Goals. *A National Strategy to Reduce Crime.* Washington, D.C.: Government Printing Office, 1973.

———. *Report on Corrections.* Washington, D.C.: Government Printing Office, 1973.

———. *Report on Courts.* Washington, D.C. Government Printing Office, 1973.

———. *Report on Police.* Washington, D.C.: Government Printing Office, 1973.

Neubauer, David W. *Criminal Justice in Middle America.* Morristown, N.J.: General Learning Press, 1974.

Newman, Donald J. *Introduction to Criminal Justice.* Philadelphia: Lippincott, 1975.

Packer, Herbert L. *The Limits of the Criminal Sanction.* Stanford, Calif.: Stanford Univeristy Press, 1968.

President's Commission on Law Enforcement and Administration of Justice. *The Challenge of Crime in a Free Society.* Washington, D.C.: Government Printing Office, 1967.

Randell, Donald A., and Glickman, Arthur P. *The Great American Auto Repair Robbery.* New York: Charterhouse, 1972.

Sutherland, Edwin H. *White Collar Crime.* New York: Dryden Press, 1949.

Wilson, James Q. "Crime and Punishment in England." *The Public Interest,* no. 43 (Spring 1976), pp. 3-25.

———. *Thinking About Crime.* New York: Basic Books, 1975.

———. *Varieties of Police Behavior: The Management of Law and Order in Eight Communities.* Cambridge, Mass.: Harvard University Press, 1968.

2
THE NONSYSTEM OF CRIMINAL JUSTICE

As the preceding discussion of the steps in the criminal process reveals, the criminal justice system is arranged in such a way as to resemble an "obstacle course." In Herbert L. Packer's words, "each of its successive stages is designed to present formidable impediments to carrying the accused any further along in the process."[1] To overcome these obstacles and to be at all effective in dealing with the crime problem, all of the components of the criminal justice system must cooperate and work together. However, this cooperation is often lacking. In reality, the administration of criminal justice is not the "continuous and coordinated process" it is often thought to be. Rather it suffers from "serious gaps and barriers." As Robert H. Scott has observed:

> Inconsistencies inhibit cooperation; chasms cut communication. The process of criminal justice becomes a series of segments, separated from each other by differences in philosophy, purpose and practice. Moreover, the segments themselves are often characterized by internal conflicts and confusion. The blanket of the administration of justice, when seen at close range, becomes a patchwork quilt.[2]

With such a "patchwork quilt" a "coordinated and consistent response to crime" becomes impossible.[3] The court's heavy reliance on the plea bargaining process—negotiation of a plea of guilty in exchange for a lesser sentence—is a good example. It shows the conflict and hostility that can characterize the interrelationships among the components of the criminal justice system. In many courts across the land, over 90 percent of all criminal cases are disposed by means of a plea bargain. This practice has been strongly defended by Chief Justice Warren Burger:

> There is another factor. It is elementary, historically and statistically, that systems of courts—the number of judges, prosecutors, and of courtrooms—have been based on the premise that approximately 90 percent of

all defendants will plead guilty leaving only 10 percent, more or less, to be tried .... The consequence of what might seem on its face a small percentage change in the rate of guilty pleas can be tremendous. A reduction from 90 percent to 80 percent in guilty pleas requires the assignment of twice the judicial manpower and facilities—judges, court reporters, bailiffs, clerks, jurors, and courtrooms. A reduction to 70 percent trebles this demand.[4]

The President's Commission on Law Enforcement and Administration of Justice concurs: "If a substantial percentage of [criminal cases] were not dropped or carried to negotiated conclusions administratively, justice would not be merely slowed down; it would be stopped."[5] However, neither the police nor correctional agencies share the court's enthusiasm for plea bargaining. The police often view the results of such bargains as unjustified leniency. They condemn this practice as indicative of the prosecution's permissiveness or inefficiency in not being able to try all the cases brought to it by the police.[6] Correctional officers likewise fear that plea bargaining may encourage sentences inconsistent with correctional goals and may reinforce an offender's belief that he can manipulate the criminal justice system, thus minimizing his motivation to participate in rehabilitative programs.

Interface or interrelationship problems are by no means unique to the plea bargaining process; they are found throughout the entire criminal justice system. These problems have, for the most part, gone unstudied.[7] Nonetheless, they must be explored and analyzed as they offer much instruction on why the criminal justice system is failing as it is.

Interface Problems in the Criminal Justice System

The interrelationships among the three components of the criminal justice system are complex: each may interact with the other components, and all may interact with the general public. These interrelationships are often characterized by conflict and even hostility. This is in part the result of competition for attention and funds from outside the system. Thus, for example, if a city were to appropriate $250,000 in additional funds for law enforcement and crime prevention purposes, the various components would likely differ considerably in their recommendations of how these funds should be allocated. The police would probably point out that this money could be used to pay for ten additional police officers for a year's time, including salaries, uniforms, training, equipment, overhead, and fringe benefits. In contrast, the courts might well observe that this same money could provide for eight new prosecutors together with their necessary support services. Finally, correctional personnel would be likely to argue that these funds could be used to buy 3 months of special training in prerelease centers for each of 120 offenders or pay for an entire year of noninstitutional aftercare for 70 people in the system. They might also note that the same money could greatly aid narcotics treatment centers or maintain for a year's time three or four prearrest youth service bureaus.[8] The competition for these funds inevitably leads to a deterioration in relationships among the components of the criminal justice system. But this competition is not the only source of conflict and hostility. Others arise from their differences in "philosophy, purpose and practice." These differences will become more apparent as we examine each of these relationships in turn.

Courts and the Police

The courts, as the middle step in the criminal process, provide the natural focal point for interface conflicts. They play a dual role in the criminal justice system: They are both participants in the criminal process and supervisors of its practice. As participants, they determine the guilt or innocence of those accused of crime and impose sanctions. As supervisors, they act as guardians of the requirements of the Constitution and statutory law. Both roles have generated conflict and hostility between the courts and the other components of the criminal justice system.

Hostility and conflict typically characterize the interrelationships between the police and the courts when the courts function as participants in the criminal justice system. This is true in both the formal and informal aspects of court procedure. Thus, for example, formal trials frequently result in lengthy delays. These delays are often irritating to the police, who see offenders free on bail pending trial and engaged in further criminal activity. Moreover, in practically every criminal case, testimony is needed from police officers who are subpoenaed like other prosecution witnesses. Because cases are often continued or are disposed of by plea bargaining, there is a substantial waste of police resources, as officers must wait hours to testify—if they testify at all.[9] During the trial itself, police officers often observe, and are subjected to, procedural requirements that appear to them to be useless or even detrimental to a determination of the facts. Police may also be critical of the quality of the prosecution. They may witness their efforts rendered meaningless by what they perceive to be a lack of skill or effort on the part of prosecution attorneys. Finally, the disposition of the offender following formal conviction may also be a point of friction. The police may feel that the sentence imposed by the judge was too lenient.

Several informal aspects of court processing also cause interface conflict between police and the courts. One of these, plea bargaining, has already been discussed, but two others also deserve comment: screening and pretrial diversion. Screening generally refers to a discretionary decision to stop, prior to trial or plea, all formal proceedings against a person who has become involved in the criminal justice system.[10] It is often resented by the police as unjustifiably negating their efforts. As with most issues generating interface conflict, it is also of concern to correctional personnel, because it screens individuals from the system and thereby deprives correctional agencies of the opportunity to provide them with the services such agencies can offer. Despite these tensions, however, screening is very widely used: Only about 40 percent of all suspects apprehended for the commission of serious crimes are ever formally charged.[11]

Pretrial diversion generates much the same kind of response. Diversion, as discussed in Chapter 1, involves a decision to encourage a suspect to participate in a noncriminal rehabilitative program by suspending or dismissing formal proceedings. Police are likely to consider such action as unreasonable leniency. Correctional agencies may also resent diversion as an attempt to pressure an individual into participating in a program they may feel is not appropriate for him.

Interface conflict and hostility are likely to become all the more intensified when courts assume a supervisory, as opposed to a participatory, role. When the practices of the criminal justice system, especially as carried out by the police, come into conflict with other values in the society, the courts in their supervisory role must determine which takes precedence over the other. In recent years, the courts—and especially, the U.S. Supreme Court—have determined that those values reflected in the Constitution must take precedence over the efficient administration of criminal justice. Thus, for example, the Supreme Court held in *Mapp* v. *Ohio* that evidence obtained in violation of the Fourth Amendment's guarantees against unreasonable searches and seizures must be excluded from introduction in a criminal trial, however trustworthy, conclusive, or indispensable it may be.[12] By so doing, the court sought to deprive the police of any incentive to violate constitutional rights in their efforts to obtain criminal convictions. As Robert J. Traynor, former Chief Justice of the California State Supreme Court, has observed:

> Granted that the adoption of the exclusionary rule will not prevent all illegal searches and seizures, it will discourage them. Police officers and prosecuting officials are primarily interested in convicting criminals. Given the exclusionary rule and a choice between securing evidence by legal rather than illegal means, officers will be impelled to obey the law themselves since not to do so will jeopardize their objectives.[13]

A great deal of interface conflict and hostility has also emerged from court supervision of police interrogations and confessions. Jerold H. Israel and Wayne R. LaFave are correct in their assessment that "no area of constitutional criminal procedure has provoked more debate over the years than that dealing with police interrogation."[14] Nowhere has this debate received more public attention than in the celebrated decision of *Miranda* v. *Arizona*.[15] In *Miranda,* the Supreme Court expressed serious misgivings over pretrial police custodial interrogation. It found the salient features of this investigative practice to be "incommunicado interrogation of individuals in a police-dominated atmosphere, resulting in self-incriminating statements without full warnings of constitutional rights." The Court reviewed representative samples of interrogation techniques as found in various police manuals and textbooks on criminal investigation and concluded that they were employed

> for no other purpose than to subjugate the individual to the will of his examiner. This atmosphere carries its own badge of intimidation. To be sure, this is not physical intimidation, but it is equally destructive of human dignity. The current practice of incommunicado interrogation is at odds with one of our Nation's cherished principles—that the individual may not be compelled to incriminate himself. Unless adequate protective devices are employed to dispel the compulsion inherent in custodial surroundings, no statement obtained from the defendant can truly be the product of his free choice.

To ensure that all statements made to police interrogators are the product of the defendant's "free choice," the Court spelled out a "stiff code of conduct for police interrogation."[16] These *Miranda* "rights" include the following requirements: (1) a suspect subjected to pretrial police custodial interrogation must be informed of his right to remain silent; (2) he must be warned that anything he says may be used against him in court; (3) he must be given the right to consult with an attorney prior to questioning and may have his attorney present during questioning if he wishes; (4) he must be told that if he wants an attorney, but cannot afford one, an attorney will be provided for him without charge; (5) if, after being told this, the suspect says that he does not want an attorney and is willing to be questioned, he may be, provided that he has reached this decision "knowingly and intelligently"; and (6) if, after being told all his rights, the suspect agrees to be questioned, he can refrain from answering additional questions at any time, whether or not he has an attorney with him.

The police response to this judicial supervision has been predictable. They have accused the courts of handcuffing law enforcement officers and have questioned both the reasonableness and intelligence of such judges, often wondering aloud how such naive and misled men could have risen to such high positions of authority.[17] Jerome Skolnick has observed that there is a police attitude toward judges that is rather akin to that of George Bernard Shaw's quip: "Those who can, do; those who cannot, teach."[18] They tend to be contemptuous and resentful of those judges whose zealous commitment to abstract principles has never been tempered by the "reality" of the world which the police know, live in, and see. The police view criminal procedure with the "administrative bias of a craftsman."[19] They tend to emphasize their own expertise and specialized abilities to distinguish between guilt and innocence and their ability to make judgments concerning what is necessary to apprehend suspects. They see themselves as craftsmen, as masters of their trade; as such, they feel that they ought to be free to employ the techniques of their trade. The courts, however, in their supervisory role, seem to be continually constricting rather than expanding this freedom. Repeated and publicly ventilated court-police hostility has been the result.

Courts and Corrections

The interrelationships between courts and corrections have been almost as stormy. As in the case of the police, problems with corrections arise when the courts act as either participants or supervisors. As participants, the courts cause correctional agencies problems at each step along the criminal process. To begin with, repeated court delays may neutralize the specific deterrent effect that the threat of immediate punishment may provide. Likewise, the technicalities of litigation, like plea bargaining, may complicate rehabilitation by reinforcing the offender's belief that he can manipulate the system. Correctional officials may also feel that justice is perverted by inappropriate defense tactics or an injudicious judge. The court's disposition of the offender following formal conviction may also have an adverse effect. On the one hand, sentencing disparity is often cited as a source of offender resentment that makes the correctional task all the more difficult. On the other hand, however, individual sentencing—that is, making the punishment fit the crime—is also promoted as a desirable correctional objective. Finally, the lengthy and intricate appellate process of the courts is also a cause of friction. Frequent delays during appeal often mean that incarceration is delayed, during which time the offender is given the opportunity to commit additional crimes. Moreover, offenders who spend all their time and effort attempting to invalidate their convictions are unlikely to develop new patterns of behavior and are consequently less susceptible to rehabilitation.[20]

Interface problems between courts and corrections also occur as a result of the courts' supervisory role. Until recently, a convicted offender was deemed to have forfeited virtually all his rights, retaining only such rights as were expressly granted to him by statute or the correctional authority. It was commonly assumed that, short of extreme physical abuse, virtually anything could be done with an offender in the name of "correction" or "punishment."[21] However, beginning with *Coffin* v. *Reichard*,[22] courts have abandoned this "hands-off" policy and have come to accept the premise that a "prisoner retains all of the rights of an ordinary citizen except those expressly or by necessary implication taken from him by law." No longer will courts accept the notion that "upon entering a prison one is entirely bereft of all his civil rights and forfeits every protection of the law."[23] Rather, correctional authorities must now adhere to the "least restrictive means" test. When they restrict the rights of an offender, they must establish to the satisfaction of the courts that this action serves a relevant penological objective "more effectively than some less severe punishment."[24] Additionally, courts have subjected correctional administrators to standards of due process. They require that all facilities and programs be administered with clearly enunciated policies and with established, fair procedures for the resolution of grievances. This increased willingness of the courts to evaluate correctional practices has led to such recent U.S. Supreme Court decisions as *Morrissey* v. *Brewer*,[25] which held that formal procedures are required in order to revoke a person's parole; *Jackson* v. *Indiana*,[26] which held that indefinite commitment of an accused who is not mentally competent to stand trial for a criminal offense violates due process of law; *Wolff* v. *McDonnell*,[27] which held that due process requirements must be employed in prison disciplinary proceedings; and *Procunier* v. *Martinez*,[28] which invalidated California's prison mail-censorship regulations as unduly burdening the First and Fourteenth Amendments.

Various lower federal and state courts have been even more willing to abandon the courts' traditional "hands-off" policy toward problems of correctional administration. Thus, in *Holt* v. *Sarver*,[29] the U.S. District Court for the Eastern District of Arkansas held that imprisonment in the Arkansas State Prison system constituted "cruel and unusual punishment" and gave the state 2 years to correct the situation or release all prisoners then incarcerated in the state's facilities. State claims that they cannot bring their correctional facilities into compliance with constitutional requirements because of inadequate funding have not proved persuasive. Thus, in *Gates* v. *Collier*,[30] the Court of Appeals for the Fifth Circuit held that Mississippi State Penitentiary at Parchman must spend whatever it takes to satisfy constitutional dictates.[31] Vigilant in their efforts to ensure that "no iron curtain [is] drawn between the Constitution and the prisons of this country,"[32] the U.S. District Court for the Western District of North Carolina held that extended solitary confinement for disciplinary purposes in a local jail constitutes cruel and unusual punishment;[33] the Michigan and California Courts of Appeal held that properly established fear of homosexual attacks may be asserted as a justifiable defense to charges of prison escape;[34] and the California State Supreme Court held that inmates must be given written reasons for denial of parole release.[35]

The Police and Corrections

The police and corrections are the two components of the criminal justice system that are the most separated both in the sequence of their operations and in the nature of their tasks. Nonetheless, conflict and hostility are rife even in their interrelationships. These interface problems can likewise be traced to the differences in "philosophy, purpose and practice" between these two components. Thus, the police are primarily concerned with law enforcement and order maintenance and generally view confinement of an offender as an excellent, if temporary, expedient. Correctional personnel, on the other hand, must take a longer view. Because virtually all inmates eventually return to society—less than 1 percent die in prisons[36] —corrections must strive toward the successful reintegration of the offender into the community. This long-range perspective often necessitates the taking of short-run risks; inevitably, the release of an offender either upon completion of his sentence or on parole always involves some uncertainties. These risks, however, are often unacceptable to the police, and interface conflict results. After all, the police are much more intimately involved with the offender's specific criminal behavior than are correctional personnel. They have seen the victim and have had to deal with the havoc the offender has caused. In addition, "they are subjected to and influenced by the emotional reactions of the community."[37] Like the community, the police are inclined to regard retribution and incapacitation rather than rehabilitation and reintegration as the proper objectives of corrections. In contrast, members of the correctional staff are seldom confronted with the victim and the emotions surrounding him.

George L. Kirkham, a professor of criminology who in an effort to broaden his understanding of the entire criminal justice system became temporarily a patrolman in the Jacksonville-Duval County, Florida, police department, provides considerable insight on this matter when he relates how his experiences as a police officer altered some of his ideas about the police, criminals, and the victims of crime. Among other things, he reveals the following:

> I found that there was a world of difference between encountering individuals, as I had, in mental health or correctional settings and facing them as a policeman must: when they are violent, hysterical, desperate. When I put the uniform of a police officer on, I lost the luxury of sitting in an air conditioned office with my pipe and books, calmly discussing with a rapist or armed robber the past problems that had led him into trouble with the law.
>
> Such offenders had seemed so innocent, so harmless in the sterile setting of prison. The often terrible crimes which they had committed were long since past, reduced like their victims to so many printed words on a page.[38]

Correctional personnel, unlike the police, have the opportunity to deal with sanitized defendants. As a consequence, they are willing to take risks that the police are not. Hostility mounts and is heightened by each bad risk, for the correctional staff thus adds an additional burden to already overtaxed police resources. When it is recalled that recidivism rates are presently running at 65 percent, the magnitude of interface problems between police and corrections is dramatically underscored.

The effect of correctional risk taking on the police is great, but so is the impact of various police practices on corrections. The arresting police officer is often the first contact an offender has with the criminal justice system. As such, he becomes a representative or ambassador of the society that the system serves, and, hence, has a substantial influence on the offender's attitude toward the society and its institutions and on his receptivity to rehabilitative measures.

The influence the police have on correctional endeavors is not limited to their initial contact with the offender at the time of arrest. The success of such rehabilitative programs as probation and parole is often fundamentally dependent upon police understanding and cooperation. Offenders in these community-based correctional programs are likely to come in contact with the police, and "the nature of the contact and the police response may directly affect an offender's adjustment."[39] Thus, close surveillance of released felons is both understandable and to be expected; after all, they are a more readily identifiable risk than average citizens. However, when this surveillance becomes too intense, and when police officers make a practice of checking ex-offenders first whenever a crime is committed, the ex-offender may come to believe that, at least insofar as he is concerned, the presumption of innocence has been altered to a presumption of guilt. This may have significantly deleterious effects for correctional programs. Aware of this, the National Advisory Commission has admonished the police to "recognize that the nature of their contact with ex-offenders, as with citizens in general, is critically important in developing respect for law and legal institutions."[40]

Compliance Analysis and the Criminal Justice System

Many of the interface problems that exist among the components of the criminal justice system have now been explored; however, they must also be explained. By employing an adaptation of the analytical framework that Amitai Etzioni provides in his *Comparative Analysis of Complex Organizations*,[41] an explanation for these interrelationship problems emerges.

Etzioni argues that organizations can be productively analyzed on the basis of the compliance mechanisms they employ. Compliance, he argues, "is a relationship consisting of the power employed by superiors to control subordinates and the orientation of the subordinates to this power."[42] Compliance mechanisms can differ from organization to organization. Thus, the power employed by an organization's superiors can be of three different kinds: (1) coercive, resting on the application, or the threat of application, of physical sanctions; (2) remunerative, based on control over material resources and rewards; or (3) normative, dependent on the allocation and manipulation of symbolic rewards and deprivations.[43] Most organizations emphasize one means of power over the others. The reason for this is clear: "When two kinds of power are emphasized at the same time, over the same subject group, they tend to neutralize each other."[44]

The involvement with, or orientation to, this power on the part of the organization's subordinates or lower participants can likewise be of three kinds: (1) alienative, with an intense negative orientation; (2) calculative, with either a negative or positive orientation of low intensity; or (3) moral, with a positive

THE NONSYSTEM OF CRIMINAL JUSTICE

orientation of high intensity.[45] When these three kinds of involvement are combined with the three kinds of power, nine possible compliance relationships result, as shown in Table 2.1. When the kind of involvement that the lower participants have in an organization tends to coincide with the kind of power the organization employs—that is, when an organization's compliance structure falls within one of the three diagonal cases, 1, 5 or 9—the compliance relationship may be said to be congruent. Congruent compliance structures are more likely to occur in practice, because, as Etzioni points out, congruence is more effective, and organizations are under both external and internal pressures to be effective.[46] Thus, for example, normative power requires that the lower participants be highly committed. If they are alienated from the organization, or if they are only mildly committed to it, the application of normative power is likely to be ineffective. Similarly, remuneration is at least partially wasted if the lower participants are either highly alienated, and thereby likely to disobey despite material compensation, or highly committed, and thereby likely to obey with only symbolic or normative rewards. Finally, coercive power is perhaps effective only when dealing with highly alienated lower participants. If it is applied to committed or only mildly alienated lower participants, it is likely to affect morale, recruitment, socialization, and communication and to reduce effectiveness. (However, through the alienation it generates, it is likely to produce a congruent relationship.)

When properly adapted, compliance analysis is of considerable utility in helping to explain the many interface or interrelationship problems that police, courts, and corrections are experiencing. The criminal justice system is characterized by its efforts to employ more than one kind of power. Each of its components has, as Robert H. Scott notes, a different "philosophy, purpose and practice."[47] Each fundamentally relies upon a different kind of power. Thus, the police find the use of coercion indispensable in the performance of their basic functions of law enforcement and order maintenance. Courts, especially in their supervisory role, must rely on normative power to obtain compliance with their understanding of due process (itself a normative concept). Finally, corrections continues to justify (although to what extent is an open question)

Table 2.1 Typology of Compliance Relationships

Kinds of power	Kinds of involvement		
	Alienative	Calculative	Moral
Coercive	1	2	3
Remunerative	4	5	6
Normative	7	8	9

the penal sanctions it invokes on the calculative principle of deterrence.[48] As these different components and different powers interact with one another, it is not strange that conflict should result. The dominant power of one component begins to compete with the dominant power of another, vitiates its strength, and thereby diminishes its ability to meet the challenges before it. Interface problems are inevitable.

In addition to offering an explanation for interface or interrelationship problems, compliance analysis provides an excellent—and heretofore unused[49]—framework of considerable organizational and heuristic power for the study of the entire criminal justice system. Thus, it helps to explain the system's overall failure. Increasingly, each component is being called upon to employ more than one kind of power, thereby neutralizing the potency of each. Again, whereas the police are expected to employ such force or coercion as is necessary to maintain order and enforce the law, increasingly they are also called upon to employ moral suasion, through both the examples they set and the acts of service they provide, in order to encourage public adherence to the law and respect for legal institutions. To the extent that they earnestly try to do both, they are likely to accomplish neither, and even law enforcement and order maintenance are likely to become problematic. Clearly, the contemporary debate concerning the role of the police in democratic society must confront compliance analysis.

The courts are in much the same situation. The more they employ normative power to supervise the criminal justice system and to ensure that due process is accorded each defendant, the more they resort to legal technicalities that cause delay and "system overload" and encourage calculative plea bargaining; the more they contribute to the manipulation of the system by crafty and experienced defendants; the more they minimize the opportunity for a moral rehabilitation of the defendant; and the more they prompt the need for coercive correctional treatment. Correctional systems experience the same dilemma, although perhaps even more intensely. One of the major problems faced by the correctional system in the United States arises from the fact that there is no agreement on an answer to the question, "Why punish crimes?" Three very different justifications for criminal punishment are possible: retrubution, deterrence, and rehabilitation—these, it should be noted, correspond rather closely to coercive, remunerative, and normative compliance relationships. Each of these justifications is in conflict with the others; yet correctional personnel in the United States often attempt to rely on all of them, and, as a result, fail to achieve the objectives of any of them[50] (with the possible exception of retribution—the mere imposition of coercion having the potential, as mentioned above, to generate sufficient alienation in the lower participants to make the compliance relationship congruent.

Compliance analysis also helps to explain why the criminal justice system has come to embrace to the extent that it has what Herbert L. Packer calls the "crime control model" of criminal justice.[51] The intense positive involvement stimulated by the criminal justice system's use of normative power and the intense negative involvement prompted by its contemporaneous reliance on coercive power end up cancelling out each other. The result is an orientation in the lower participants of either low positive or low negative intensity. This, however, is what Etzioni defines as calculative involvement. Thus, criminal justice becomes a business where remunerative power comes to replace normative and coercive power.[52] As a consequence, it is not strange that it should be dominated by plea bargaining and a concern for administrative efficiency. It is altogether appropriate that Packer should characterize it as

> an assembly-line conveyor belt down which moves an endless stream of cases, never stopping, carrying the cases to workers who stand at fixed stations and who perform on each case as it comes by the same small but essential operation that brings it one step closer to being a finished product, or, to exchange the metaphor for the reality, a closed file.[53]

Finally, the use of compliance as a framework for analysis helps to provide a realistic appraisal of the criminal justice system and the prospects for reform of each of its components. Thus, with it the ongoing discussion in the literature over police role—that is, over the proper function of the police in democratic society—can be at once evaluated and approached afresh. For example, although the police are increasingly called upon to employ normative power and to assume social service and "police advocacy"[54] roles in an attempt to generate greater moral involvement on the part of the lower participants, that is, the community, compliance analysis suggests that as long as the police must also employ coercive power in order to perform their traditional law enforcement and order maintenance roles, their attempts to generate increased moral involvement will fail.[55] In fact, their efforts are much more likely to generate alienative involvement; for the community, unable to reconcile the police's simultaneous use of coercive and normative power, is likely to feel betrayed and confused and to regard the police as not only coercive but also hypocritical. Thus, compliance analysis urges caution in efforts to expand the social service role of the police and suggests fundamental problems for police-community relations.

Compliance analysis can also be used to examine the lower courts and the recommendation of the National Advisory Commission on Criminal Justice Standards and Goals that all plea bargaining in the United States be abolished forthwith.[56] The plea bargaining that presently occurs in approximately 90 percent of all criminal cases is in large part a calculative response by the lower courts to the specter of "system overload" brought on by increasingly insurmountable case loads. In these cases, the lower courts effectively dispense with what the U.S. Supreme Court and its normative due process model require and substitute instead the calculative crime-control model. The dual presence of both normative and calculative influences, however, contributes to even greater incongruence and court inefficiency, which in turn impose an ever greater need for plea bargaining. Thus, the use of compliance as an analytical framework suggests that the lower courts are not soon likely to become the "palladiums of liberty" and "citadels of justice" that the Supreme Court would have them be.[57] It suggests that shortcuts will continue to be taken, and that due process as understood by the Supreme Court will continue to be frustrated. After all, there is only so much that the Supreme Court can do. As *Federalist* No. 78 points out, it has neither the power of the sword nor the power of the purse, but only that of judgment.[58] It must rely almost exclusively on normative power to effect its will. Given the calculative involvement of the lower courts and their personnel, there is likely to continue to be, as Theodore L. Becker and Malcolm M. Feeley note, "a rather wide gap between what the Court says *ought* to be done and what, in fact, *is* actually done."[59]

Compliance analysis is also appropriate for approaching the third component of the criminal justice system, corrections. As has already been noted, offenders are presently incarcerated in America's prisons for three very different reasons: retribution, deterrence, and rehabilitation. These three reasons—corresponding as they do with coercive, remunerative, and normative power—end up neutralizing one another, and correctional agencies, now virtually powerless, are left to confront recidivism rates of approximately 65 percent. Until some agreement on the purpose of corrections and the kind of power it is to employ is reached, compliance analysis suggests that such rates can be expected to persist. Efforts will increase to "minimize" the "penetration" of offenders into the correctional system and to subject them through probationary programs and pretrial diversion to only one kind of power—namely, normative rehabilitative power.[60] However, so too will efforts simply to isolate and punish offenders, who through the very acts for which they have been convicted have proved themselves impervious to normative power and amenable only to coercion.[61]

Thus, compliance analysis suggests that the prospects for reform of the criminal justice system are remote and that incongruity and inefficiency will continue. Due process will yield to crime control, and remunerative-calculative compliance relationships will predominate. Paradoxically, however, there is a certain congruence in this incongruity, for the United States is essentially a "commercial" republic. Instead of employing coercion or normative power to govern its citizens, it relies almost exclusively on calculation and on what Tocqueville has called the "principle of self-interest rightly understood."[62] The consequences of such an arrangement on the criminal justice system have been pervasive and profound. To begin with, because the entire American regime is so fundamentally committed to the use of remunerative power, it has all but eliminated the possibility that the criminal justice system will be able to break free from the use of remunerative-calculative compliance structures. Having thus committed the criminal justice system to the use of "commercial" principles, it has also wedded it to both their problems and their promise. Commerce, after all, is a mixed blessing. As Montesquieu observed, it has the tendency to corrupt

THE NONSYSTEM OF CRIMINAL JUSTICE 61

the purest morals and yet refine and polish the most barbarous.[63] Vibrating between purity and barbarity, between an attraction to normative power on the one hand and a necessary embrace of coercion on the other, the criminal justice system, no less than the American regime more generally, has managed to convert even matters of principle (or justice) into matters of interest that are subject to bargaining and negotiation.[64] The criminal justice system is by no means immune to this "commercial" spirit; as a result, plea bargaining and calculation are perhaps inevitable. However reluctant its present critics may be to acknowledge this fact, the criminal justice system may be said to reflect the basic character of the American "commercial" republic. It is not likely to be changed dramatically until the regime itself is.[65] The remaining chapters of this volume explore these themes in a more systematic and comprehensive fashion.

Notes

1. Herbert L. Packer, *The Limits of the Criminal Sanction* (Stanford, Calif.: Stanford University Press, 1968), p. 163.
2. Robert H. Scott, "Problems in Communication and Cooperation in the Administration of Criminal Justice," in *Police and Community Relations: A Sourcebook*, ed. A. F. Brandstatter and Louis A. Radelet (Beverly Hills, Calif.: Glencoe Press, 1968), p. 430. See also Donald M. McIntyre, *Criminal Justice in the United States* (Chicago: American Bar Foundation, 1974): "While all agencies presumably and theoretically work together, their own immediate, distinctive goals set them apart from one another. As a result, the cooperation and coordination of their efforts do not approach the theoretical model that says that the system and all its components work as a coordinated unit toward the general goal of protecting society and insuring justice" (p. 50).
3. National Advisory Commission on Criminal Justice Standards and Goals, *Report on Corrections* (Washington, D.C.: Government Printing Office, 1973), p. 5.
4. Chief Justice Warren Burger, in a speech delivered before the American Bar Association, August 10, 1970. Reprinted in *American Bar Association Journal* 56 (October 1970): p. 931.
5. President's Commission On Law Enforcement and Administration of Justice, *The Challenge of Crime in a Free Society* (Washington, D.C.: Government Printing Office, 1967), p. 130.
6. See, for example, David W. Neubauer, *Criminal Justice in Middle America* (Morristown, N.J.: General Learning Press, 1974), pp. 54-63.
7. As David Neubauer writes: "Unfortunately, the relationships between the principal organizations in criminal justice rarely have been studied." *Criminal Justice in Middle America,* p. 63. See, however, William C. Louthan,

"Relationships among Police, Court, and Correctional Agencies," *Policy Studies Journal* 3, no. 1 (Autumn 1974): 30-37.

8. See National Advisory Commission on Criminal Justice Standards and Goals, *Report on the Criminal Justice System* (Washington, D.C.: Government Printing Office, 1973), pp. 1-3, for a discussion of this problem.
9. See National Advisory Commission on Criminal Justice Standards and Goals, *Report on Police* (Washington, D.C.: Government Printing Office, 1973), pp. 5-7.
10. See Donald M. McIntyre and David Lippman, "Prosecutors and Early Disposition of Felony Cases," *Journal of the American Bar Association* 56 (December 1970): 1154-1155.
11. President's Commission on Law Enforcement and Administration of Justice, *The Challenge of Crime in a Free Society,* p. 262.
12. 361 U.S. 643 (1961). Thus, a study of the police in Rochester, New York, reveals that the solution suggested most often by police officers (31.2 percent) in response to the question, "How could the problems of being a police officer be best taken care of?" was "Get the judges and politicians out of our jobs and off our backs." See David C. Perry and Paula A. Sornoff, "Politics at the Street Level: The Select Case of Police Administration and the Community" (Paper delivered at the Annual Meeting of the American Political Science Association, Washington, D.C. 1972), p. 34.
13. *People* v. *Cahan,* 44 Cal. 2d 434, 488 (1955).
14. Jerold H. Israel and Wayne R. LaFave, *Criminal Procedure: Constitutional Limitations,* 2nd ed. (St. Paul: West, 1975), p. 196.
15. 384 U.S. 436 (1966).
16. C. Herman Pritchett, *The American Constitution,* 2nd ed. (New York: McGraw-Hill, 1968), p. 631.
17. See Jerome Skolnick, *Justice Without Trial: Law Enforcement in Democratic Society* (New York: Wiley, 1966), p. 225. See also Neal Milner, "Some Common Themes in Police Responses to Legal Change," in *Police in Urban Society,* ed. Harlan Hahn (Beverly Hills, Calif.: Sage Publications, 1971), pp. 247-262. See also Robert Graham Caldwell, "The Supreme Court and Law Enforcement," *Journal of Police Science and Administration* 3, no. 2 (June 1975): 222-237, who argues that "what the Court has done in the law enforcement cases is to put the police on trial" (p. 234).
18. Skolnick, *Justice Without Trial,* pp. 196-197.
19. *Ibid.,* p. 196. See also Albert J. Reiss, Jr., *The Police and the Public* (New Haven, Conn.: Yale University Press, 1971): "Paradoxically, in our legal system, matters that the police want defined by rules, the courts want to leave open to discretion. And what the courts want defined by rules, the police want to leave open to discretion. Thus the courts want police procedures to be clear, definite, and unambiguously defined, but they want matters of substance to be left open to argument and decision, and even to

THE NONSYSTEM OF CRIMINAL JUSTICE

new interpretation and precedent. For them, precedent governs but does not rule. The police, on the other hand, want to be left with broad discretion in enforcing the law, obtaining information and determining procedures for handling clients, but they want the courts to make clear how substance is to be applied and what is a bona fide case" (p. 132).

20. *Report on Courts*, p. 7.
21. *Report on Corrections*, p. 18.
22. 143 F. 2d 443 (6th Cir. 1944).
23. Decision of the Michigan Court of Appeals, *People* v. *Harmon*, 15CrL 2425 (1974).
24. *Furman* v. *Georgia*, 408 U.S. 238 (1972). Mr. Justice Brennan concurring.
25. 408 U.S. 471 (1972).
26. 406 U.S. 715 (1972).
27. 418 U.S. 539 (1974). However, see *Baxter* v. *Palmigiano*, 96 S. Ct. 1551 (1976), in which the Supreme Court refused to extend further the due process standards spelled out in *Wolff*.
28. 416 U.S. 396 (1974). See also *Main Road* v. *Aytch*, 17 CrL 2480 (1975), and *K.Q.E.D., Inc.* v. *Houchins*, 18 CrL 2252 (1975).
29. 309 F. Supp. 362 (E.D. Ark. 1970).
30. 16 CrL 2055 (5th Cir. 1974).
31. See also *Rehm* v. *Malcolm*, 14 CrL 1069 (S.D. N. Y., 1974).
32. *Wolff* v. *McDonnell*, 418 U.S. 539 (1974). Mr. Justice White for the Court majority.
33. *Berch* v. *Stahl*, 15 CrL 1022 (W.D. N. C., 1974).
34. As the Michigan Court of Appeals noted: "The time has come when we can no longer close our eyes to the growing problem of institutional gang rapes in our prison systems. Although a person sentenced to serve a period of time in prison for the commission of a crime gives up certain of his rights, 'it has never been held that upon entering a prison one is entirely bereft of all his civil rights and forfeits every protection of the law.'" *People* v. *Harmon*, 15 CrL 2425 (1974). See also the decision of the California Court of Appeals, *People* v. *Lovercamp*, 16 CrL 2375 (1975).
35. *In re Strum*, 15 CrL 1030 (1974). Not every court review of correctional administrative practices has generated interface problems. Thus, the U.S. District Court for Connecticut in *Paka* v. *Manson*, 16 CrL 2256 (1974), upheld the actions of Connecticut correctional officials who refused to allow prisoners to form a prisoner's union. Likewise, the Court of Appeals for the Seventh Circuit in *LeBatt* v. *Twomey*, 16 CrL 2351 (1975), declared that notice and hearings were not required during a 9-day emergency lockup at Illinois State Penitentiary at Stateville.
36. In 1970, only 663 inmates, of an average total prison population in the United States of 196,000, died in prison. U.S. Department of Justice, Federal Bureau of Prisons, *National Prisoner Statistics: Prisoners in State*

and Federal Institutions for Adult Felons, 1968, 1969, 1970 (Washington, D.C.: Government Printing Office, 1971), p. 6.
37. *Report on Corrections,* p. 6.
38. George L. Kirkham, "A Professor's Street Lessons," *FBI Law Enforcement Bulletin,* March 1974, p. 6.
39. *Report on Corrections,* p. 7.
40. *Report on Police,* p. 77.
41. Amitai Etzioni, *A Comparative Analysis of Complex Organizations: On Power, Involvement, and Their Correlates* (New York: The Free Press, 1961). For a discussion of the utility of Etzioni's compliance theory, see Richard H. Hall, J. Eugene Haas, and Norman J. Johnson, "An Examination of the Blau-Scott and Etzioni Typologies," *Administrative Science Quarterly* 12, no. 1 (June 1967): pp. 118-139.
42. Etzioni, *A Comparative Analysis of Complex Organizations,* xv.
43. Ibid., pp. 4-6.
44. Ibid., p. 7.
45. Ibid., pp. 8-11.
46. For a discussion of the importance of effectiveness for organizations, see Chester I. Barnard, *The Functions of the Executive* (Cambridge, Mass.: Harvard University Press, 1938), pp. 82-95.
47. Scott, "Problems in Communication and Cooperation," p. 430.
48. An alternative discussion of the different powers associated with each component of the criminal justice system is possible. Thus, it could be argued, perhaps equally persuasively, that the courts, to the extent that they rely upon plea bargaining, are employing remunerative power and that correctional agencies, to the extent that they stress rehabilitation of the offender, are utilizing normative power. The possibility of alternative understandings of the principal power associated with each component does not, however, undercut the analysis; quite the contrary, it strengthens the overall argument that is about to be made—namely, that each component is being increasingly called upon to employ more than one kind of power, thereby neutralizing the potency of each—and, as a consequence, helps to explain the overall failure the criminal justice system is experiencing.
49. However, see Malcolm M. Feeley, "Coercion and Compliance: A New Look at an Old Problem," *Law and Society Review* 4, no. 4 (May 1970: 505-519.
50. As a result, Ward Elliott observes that "the most advanced known 'California' techniques of rehabilitation—clinical analysis, intensive counseling, group therapy, school and work release, half-way houses, etc.—[do not appear to be] any more rehabilitory than the benighted and savage Arkansas [penal farm] practices, condemned for their failure to rehabilitate." Ward Elliott, "Crime, Punishment, and Professional Paradigms" (Paper de-

livered at the Annual Meeting of the American Political Science Association, Washington, D.C., 1972), p. 7. See also Robert Martinson, "What Works?— Questions and Answers About Prison Reform," *Public Interest*, no. 35 (Spring 1974), pp. 22-54, esp. p. 49.
51. Packer, *The Limits of the Criminal Sanction*, pp. 158-163.
52. The extent to which the criminal justice system has become a business is perhaps nowhere more fully realized than in Memphis, Tennessee, where the attitude of the city fathers toward the city courts is captured in the slogan, "Let the cash registers ring with justice." See Ralph A. Rossum, "Problems of Municipal Court Administration and the Stress of Supreme Court Decisions: A Memphis Case Study," *American Journal of Criminal Law* 3, no. 1 (Summer 1974): 53-84.
53. Packer, *The Limits of the Criminal Sanction*, p. 159.
54. For a fuller discussion of the concept of "police advocacy," see Alan Edward Bent and Ralph A. Rossum, *Police, Criminal Justice, and the Community* (New York: Harper & Row, 1976), pp. 300-301, 309-311.
55. See, for example, Jerome H. Skolnick's discussion of the failure of the San Francisco Police Department's Police-Community Relations Unit in Skolnick's *The Police and the Urban Ghetto* (Chicago: American Bar Foundation, 1968).
56. *Report on Courts*, p. 46.
57. *Illinois* v. *Allen*, 397 U.S. 337, 346-347 (1970).
58. Alexander Hamilton, James Madison, and John Jay, *The Federalist*, ed. Jacob B. Cooke (New York: World, 1961), p. 523.
59. Theodore L. Becker and Malcolm M. Feeley, eds., *The Impact of Supreme Court Decisions*, 2nd ed. (New York: Oxford University Press, 1973), p.3. Emphasis in the original.
60. *Report on Corrections*, p. 73.
61. See James Q. Wilson, *Thinking About Crime* (New York: Basic Books, 1975), pp. 200-201.
62. Alexis de Tocqueville, *Democracy in America*, ed. Phillips Bradley, 2 vols. (New York: Random House, 1945), II: 130.
63. Baron de Montesquieu, *The Spirit of the Laws*, trans. Thomas Nugent (New York: Hafner, 1949), bk. XX, chap. 1. In Montesquieu's words, "Commercial laws, it may be said, improve manners for the same reason that they destroy them. They corrupt the purest morals . . . and we see every day that they polish and refine the most barbarous" (p. 316).
64. See Robert Paul Wolff, "Beyond Tolerance," in Robert Paul Wolff, Barrington Moore, Jr., and Herbert Marcuse, *A Critique of Pure Tolerance* (Boston: Beacon Press, 1969), p. 21.
65. For a further and more complete discussion of the American "commercial" republic and its relation to the criminal justice system, see Chapter 7.

Bibliography

Bent, Alan Edward, and Rossum, Ralph A. *Police, Criminal Justice, and the Community.* New York: Harper & Row, 1976.

Caldwell, Robert Graham. "The Supreme Court and Law Enforcement" *Journal of Police Science and Administration* 3, no. 2 (June 1975): 222-237.

Gardiner, John A., and Mulkey, Michael A. "Symposium on 'Crime and Criminal Justice Policy.'" *Policy Studies Journal* 3, no. 1 (Autumn 1974): 5-96.

Kerper, Hazel B., and Kerper, Janeen, eds. *Legal Rights of the Convicted.* St. Paul: West, 1974.

Kirkham, George L. "A Professor's Street Lessons." *FBI Law Enforcement Bulletin,* March 1974.

McIntyre, Donald M. *Criminal Justice in the United States.* Chicago: American Bar Foundation, 1974.

National Advisory Commission on Criminal Justice Standards and Goals. *Report on Corrections.* Washington, D.C.: Government Printing Office, 1973.

——. *Report on Courts.* Washington, D.C.: Government Printing Office, 1973.

——. *Report on the Criminal Justice System.* Washington, D.C.: Government Printing Office, 1973.

——. *Report on Police.* Washington, D.C.: Government Printing Office, 1973.

Packer, Herbert L. *The Limits of the Criminal Sanction.* Stanford, Calif.: Stanford University Press, 1968.

President's Commission on Law Enforcement and Administration of Justice. *The Challenge of Crime in a Free Society.* Washington, D.C.: Government Printing Office, 1967.

——. *Task Force Report: Corrections.* Washington, D.C.: Government Printing Office, 1967.

——. *Task Force Report: Courts.* Washington, D.C.: Government Printing Office, 1967.

——. *Task Force Report: Police.* Washington, D.C.: Government Printing Office, 1967.

Reiss, Albert J., Jr. *The Police and the Public.* New Haven, Conn.: Yale University Press, 1971.

Rossum, Ralph A. "Compliance Theory and the Criminal Process: Toward an Understanding of Interface Problems in the Criminal Justice System." *Midwest Review of Public Administration* 9, no. 4 (October 1975); 209-222.

Skolnick, Jerome. *Justice Without Trial: Law Enforcement in Democratic Society.* New York: Wiley, 1966.

3

THE POLICE

The police are, quite simply, the most significant of the three components of the criminal justice system. Of the three, the police are the most visible, most conspicuously symbolize the American political system, perform the widest range of functions, and exercise the most discretionary power; and of the three, only the police possess a virtual monopoly on the legitimate use of force.[1]

To begin with, by virtue of their large numbers and distinctive uniforms, the police are the most visible component of the criminal justice system. Police bureaucracies employ approximately 65 percent of all the personnel and expend almost 60 percent of all the financial resources of the criminal justice system.[2] This visibility is enhanced all the more because the police are what Michael Lipsky calls "street-level bureaucrats."[3] As such, they are required to perform their many and varied functions "where all eyes are upon them and the going is roughest, on the street."[4]

Because of their visibility, the police have come to be regarded as the representatives of the entire criminal justice system. Thus, research indicates that the public's attitudes toward the entire criminal justice system are conditioned by their appraisals of the police. As the National Advisory Commission on Civil Disorders has observed: "The policeman in the ghetto is a symbol not only of law, but of the entire system of law enforcement and criminal justice."[5] Thus, negative community attitudes toward the police will also be reflected towards courts and corrections. Reciprocally, however, the police are likely to be blamed for failures elsewhere in the system. Thus, they frequently become "the tangible target for grievances against shortcomings throughout the system: against assembly-line justice in teeming lower courts; against wide disparity in sentences; against antiquated correctional facilities; against the basic inequities imposed by the system on the poor—to whom, for example, the option of bail means only jail."[6]

Not only have the police come to symbolize the whole criminal justice system, they have also come to represent the authority of the entire political system to the average citizen.[7] Like all public bureaucrats in their official capacities at the street level, "they are the people citizens encounter when they seek help from, or are controlled by, the American political system."[8] As such, it is "possible for them not only to influence the allocation of resources, but also to define the public norms of morality and to designate which acts violate them."[9]

Another factor that contributes to the particular significance of the police is the multiplicity of functions they are expected to perform as they interact with the public. In addition to such conventional responsibilities as law enforcement, order maintenance, and crime prevention, police are often called upon to regulate traffic and parking, inspect buildings, issue permits, guard public morals through the censorship of books, movies, and plays, and provide a vast array of social welfare services for the community, especially for its less affluent members.[10] This wide range of responsibilities requires officers having extraordinary skills. Ramsey Clark has attempted to catalog a few of these:

> Law enforcer and lawyer, scientist in the whole range of physical sciences —chemistry, physics, electronics—medic, psychologist, social worker, human relations and race relations expert, marriage counselor, youth advisor, athlete, public servant—these are but a few of the many skills a major police department must exercise daily. Individual policemen must personally possess many of them—and perform them with excellence. Safety, life and property, equal justice, liberty, confidence in government and in the purpose of our laws will depend on it.[11]

The relative significance of the police vis-a-vis the other components in the criminal justice system is further enhanced as a consequence of their vast discretionary authority. They are the gatekeepers of the criminal justice system. It is their discretion—their decisions and their actions—that brings defendants into the system or screens them from it. The average uniformed patrolman in this country is expected to enforce approximately 30,000 federal, state, and local enactments.[12] When this incredible array of laws that the police are expected to enforce is added to the vast number of services they are obliged to perform, exercise of discretion by the police is inevitable.[13] And, unlike almost every other public organization, where the lowest-ranking members perform routinized tasks and where discretion over how these tasks are to be performed increases with rank, in police departments, "discretion increases as one moves *down* the hierarchy."[14] As a consequence, the lowest-ranking police officer—the patrolman on the beat—has the greatest discretion. As Alan E. Bent observes, he "is left to choose the standard of service and behavior for application in his area of responsibility. The patrolman on the beat thus becomes a policy-forming administrator in miniature, 'who operates beyond the scope of the usual devices for control.'"[15]

This vast discretionary authority and lack of administrative control take on even greater significance when it is recalled that these police officers enjoy a virtual monopoly on the legitimate exercise of coercion. The importance of this monopoly on the use of legal force cannot be emphasized sufficiently. To

THE POLICE

begin with, this coercive power of the police supports the normative and remunerative power employed elsewhere in the criminal justice system. It provides the bedrock upon which the other components operate. Albert J. Reiss, Jr., has addressed this consideration; he has explored the way in which the courts' normative compliance structure is fundamentally dependent upon the police's coercive compliance structure:

> No one punishes even minor threats to deference more than judges, who expect everyone, including lawyers, to show deference towards their authority. Cases of lawyers being cited for contempt of judicial authority are not uncommon. Judges, in fact, surround themselves with police of their own. When they cannot secure deference, they summon these police. A judge who cannot maintain order in the court by sheer weight of *his* authority may, for example, first issue orders for silence, and then for contempt. Failing this, he may issue orders to detain or to clear the court, and he fully expects that the bailiffs or police will exercise *their* authority to do so.[16]

The monopoly on the legitimate use of violence that the police enjoy is important for a second reason as well. Police abuse of this trust can arbitrarily and capriciously deprive citizens of their liberties and even their lives; it can render the hope for a government of laws and not of men altogether illusory.[17] The impact that such potential abuse can have on the entire political system, which the police have come so much to symbolize, can be devastating.

Problems in the Definition of Police Role

Given the particular significance of the police in the criminal justice system— their visibility, their symbolic representation of the political system, their multiplicity of roles, their vast discretionary authority, and their monopoly on the exercise of legal coercion—a great deal of attention has been focused on the police. Because the operational discretion of the police is so pervasive and is so intimately intertwined with all other matters affecting or affected by the police, the greatest concern has typically been with devising schemes that can "establish the limits of discretion . . . [and] provide guidelines for its exercise within those limits."[18] To date, however, these efforts have failed, and compliance analysis suggests that future efforts are no more likely to succeed. To limit police discretion and to provide guidelines within those limits for its proper exercise, it is necessary to define what the proper police role is. However, with the rise of positive and expanding government in the United States, it has become increasingly difficult to ascertain just what the proper police role is. Since the New Deal, the American government has been continuously called upon by its citizens to do more and more in the areas of social welfare, economic regulation, and civil rights. As a consequence, its responsibilities and powers commensurate with these responsibilities have expanded tremendously.[19] The police, as the most visible representatives of the government, have undergone a similar metamorphosis. No longer is the police role limited to those law enforcement and order maintenance functions that arise by virtue of the police's monopoly on the legitimate exercise of coercion. Now it has come to embrace a whole range of social service and police advocacy responsibilities as well—based not so much on coercion as on normative and remunerative power. The police are expected to perform a "bewildering hodge-podge of contradictory roles."[20] As Miami Police Chief Bernard L. Garmire writes:

> We may well ask, for example, are the police to be concerned with peace keeping or crime fighting? The blind enforcers of the law or the discretionary agents of a benevolent government? Social workers with guns or gunmen in social work? Facilitators of social change or defenders of the "faith"? The enforcers of criminal law or society's legal trashbin? A social agency of last resort after 5:00 P.M. or mere watchmen for business and industry? Actually, the police are expected to do all of those things and to become all things to all people, at once the confessor and the inquisitor, the friend of all, yet the armed nemesis of some.[21]

A police officer thus represents many things to many people. In these various roles, he becomes, as Arthur Niederhoffer puts it, "a 'Rorschach' in uniform," stimulating fantasies and projections in all with whom he comes in contact.[22] This "role conflict" exists within police departments themselves and extends throughout the ranks. Thus, Richard H. Ward reports that his survey research data reveal that 85 percent of all officers agree with the following statement: "It is difficult to define the role of the police in today's society."[23]

With the use of compliance analysis, the consequences of this debate over the proper police role are fully predictable. With the increase in the number of police functions, and with the increased expectations on the part of policy makers and the public alike that the police should embrace a variety of responsibilities that depend upon normative and remunerative power as much as they do upon coercion, the likelihood of internal incongruence in police compliance structures is heightened. As the police become more incongruent, they in turn are likely to become more ineffective, for the simultaneous presence of coercive, remunerative, and normative power tends to neutralize the potency of each.[24] As they become more ineffective, they are likely to resist any further increases in the nature of their responsibilities and are likely to emphasize those traditional police functions such as law enforcement and order maintenance that are dependent upon coercion in the hopes of reestablishing congruence. To the extent, however, that they fail to reestablish congruence and are rendered ever more ineffective, they are likely to become increasingly dependent upon the judgment and discretion of individual officers—an ironic fate, indeed, for actions

THE POLICE

intended to limit police discretion and to provide guidelines within those limits for its proper exercise.

The efforts to limit police discretion are, thus, necessarily united with efforts to define the police role.[25] Presently, three fundamentally separate and distinct understandings of the police role are competing for hegemony: the law enforcement and order maintenance role, the social service role, and the police advocacy role. Each of these roles will be examined in turn.

The Law Enforcement and Order Maintenance Role

Law enforcement and order maintenance are really two quite separate and distinct functions. As Jerome H. Skolnick has observed, "substantial incompatibilities" can exist between the two.[26] The complete enforcement of the law, including the law of criminal procedure, is likely to result in some disorder; just as the unequivocal maintenance of order, including the suppression of the potentially disruptive rights of speech, press, assembly, and petition, is likely to require some illegality. Law and order are, thus, occasionally oxymoronic.[27] Nonetheless, for purposes of this analysis of the various police roles, these two functions will be considered together. After all, they are both fundamentally dependent upon the monopoly that the police enjoy on the legitimate use of coercive force.[28]

The law enforcement and order maintenance role encompasses a number of primary tasks. Bernard L. Garmire has defined these as "criminal investigation, collection of evidence, interrogation of suspects, arrests of suspects, maintenance of order and safety, combatting organized crime, suppression of disturbances and riots, and, generally the hard-core enforcement of criminal laws."[29] Chief Garmire's catalog of tasks is interesting. It stresses law enforcement and crime fighting to the virtual exclusion of order maintenance. This is in keeping with what psychiatrist Jesse Rubin calls "the lure of crime fighting."[30]

As William A. Westley observes, the apprehension and conviction of a felon constitutes for the police officer the essence of police work.[31] It is tangible evidence of effectiveness and productivity and, hence, is a "source of prestige both within and without police circles." As a consequence, police officers are likely to go to great lengths to pursue the crime fighting role. Thus, on a busy night, a robbery-in-progress call will draw large numbers of patrol cars in addition to those directly ordered to the scene, despite the existence of a backlog of more routine calls such as complaints, accidents, or disturbances.

Despite this emphasis on the "good pinch," however, crime fighting and law enforcement activities make up only a small part of the police role. A variety of recent studies reveals that only between 10 and 20 percent of a police officer's time is spent in such crime prevention and law enforcement activities as stopping a burglary in progress, catching a prowler, making an arrest of a suspect being held by another party, or investigating a suspicious car or an open window.[32] (See Table 3.1, which breaks down citizen complaints radioed to patrol vehicles by type of call in such geographically, economically, and racially diverse cities as Memphis, Tennessee, and Syracuse, New York.) Approximately 30 percent of a police officer's time is spent in more mundane order maintenance activities such as investigating gang disturbances, quelling domestic altercations, or settling disputes—be they public or private, serious or trivial.[33]

Even more significant, however, is the fact that despite the great stress the police place on the "protection of life and property and the preservation of peace," fully 40 percent of their time is spent on service-related activities. Many of these services involve locating missing persons and recovering stolen property, directing traffic, investigating accidents, providing emergency medical aid, checking on the homes of families on vacation, and getting cats out of trees. However, the police are increasingly being called upon to provide a vast array of social services as well. As San Jose, California, Police Chief Ray J. Blackmore has put it:

> The police cannot operate in a vacuum. We can no longer neglect the social problems that are so prevalent in our community. For many years we have just gone along with the tide of social problems. We are finally beginning to realize that the police cannot remain passive bystanders . . . . The police must engage in service work.[34]

This service orientation, it is understood, will gain the approval of the public and thereby foster inproved police-community relations. Dependence by the police on coercion will be replaced with a reliance on normative power and remuneration. Compliance will be achieved through the respect the police win and

Table 3.1 Citizen Complaints Radioed to Patrol Vehicles in Memphis, Tennessee, and Syracuse, New York, by Type of Call

Type of call	Percent	
	Memphis	Syracuse
Information gathering	9.1	22.1
Service	42.9	37.5
Order maintenance	27.5	30.1
Law enforcement	20.5	10.3
Totals	100.0	100.0

Source: Table constructed from data obtained from Alan E. Bent and Ralph A. Rossum, *Police, Criminal Justice, and the Community* (New York: Harper & Row, 1976), p. 7, and James A. Wilson, *Varieties of Police Behavior: The Management of Law and Order in Eight Communities* (Cambridge, Mass.: Harvard University Press, 1968), p. 18.

THE POLICE

the advantages they provide.[35] This new emphasis on community service has stimulated the development of two new police roles: the social service role and the police advocacy role.

The Social Service Role

The social service role involves attempts by the police to "meet the needs of individuals in crises."[36] It includes a whole range of functions, including finding lost children, recovering drowning victims, referring individuals for emergency medical services, and, on occasion, rendering emergency medical or rescue aid, receiving complaints about rubbish, and generally acting as a social agency of last resort—particularly after 5 P.M. and on weekends. Unlike other community agencies, the police provide round-the-clock service. As a consequence, they are likely to be called upon to assist the impoverished, the sick, the old, and the lower socioeconomic classes whose needs are not met by the social service agencies. On those critical occasions when the middle-class member of the community is likely to call on the family physician, clergyman, or attorney for assistance, the lower-status person is likely to call on the police.[37]

The social service role attempts to deal not only with crisis situations when they occur but also to prevent them from arising in the first place. Thus, this role seeks to engage in various types of social welfare activities including police-sponsored recreational programs and athletic leagues, employment assistance, summer camps for children, and alcohol- and narcotics-education projects.[38]

This social service role obviously does not have "the lure of crime fighting"; however, it does have the potential to be of some considerable benefit to law enforcement. Thus, the President's Commission on Law Enforcement and Administration of Justice contends:

> that traffic officers often do deter crimes or solve them by virtue of their presence and availability; that answering service calls stimulates public esteem for and cooperation with the police, helps familiarize policemen with the community and furnishes investigative leads to alert and intelligent officers; that opportunities to be friendly and useful are psychologically valuable to men who spend much of their time dealing with the seamy side of life.[39]

The Police Advocacy Role

Increasingly, police departments are being encouraged to expand their social welfare orientation and to become virtual "ombudsmen for the poor."[40] As the President's Commission on Law Enforcement and the Administration of Justice has observed:

> Policemen are uniquely situated to observe what is happening in the community. They are in constant contact with the conditions associated with crime. They see in minute detail situations that need to be and can be corrected. If a park is being badly maintained, if a school playground is locked when it is needed, if garbage goes uncollected, if a landlord fails to heat or maintain his building, perhaps the police could make it their business to inform the municipal authorities of these derelictions. In this way, police would help to represent the community in securing services to which it is entitled.[41]

In this role, the police are encouraged to dispense with neutrality and to assume the role of the "social activist."[42] As Robert Wasserman and his associates write in their prescriptive package for improving police-community relations, prepared for the Law Enforcement Assistance Administration:

> This can indeed be a legitimate role for the police. Oakland's landlord-tenant unit sees its responsibility as siding with the tenant: advising him of his rights, helping him develop strategies for dealing with his landlord and attempting to make his power equal to that of the landlord. The premise underlying this kind of conflict management is that violence tends to result when disputing parties have unequal power. Disputes can usually be handled peacefully if the power is roughly equal, and the police may have a legitimate role in seeing this is the case—by siding with the weaker party when it is necessary.[43]

Many police departments are reluctant to embrace advocacy policing, however. Not only is it based on a mixture of normative and remunerative powers rather than on coercion and, hence, likely to render police departments more ineffective, but it is also likely to be counterproductive. Instead of generating increased moral and calculative involvement on the part of the community, the use of the police to advocate the needs and demands of segments of the community is much more likely to make the police more vulnerable to attack and even more the target of hostility. As David Bordua admits, there is no assurance that police advocacy will in fact improve the level of city services as they affect the poor. As a consequence, "the police could be held responsible for a wide range of service 'failures' from which they are at least disassociated at present."[44]

Contradictory Perceptions of the Police Role

Police Self-perceptions

The competition for predominance among the law enforcement and order maintenance role, the social service role, and the police advocacy role has led to contradictory perceptions of the police role. Thus, the police have come to

THE POLICE

emphasize the law enforcement and order maintenance role to the virtual exclusion of the others. Many students of the criminal justice system are in fundamental agreement. Thus, noted police authority James Q. Wilson writes that "the crime-prevention and order-maintenance functions of the patrolmen are the essence of his task."[45] Likewise, the National Advisory Commission on Criminal Justice Standards and Goals proposes the following as Standard 1.1 in its *Report on Police:*

> Every police chief executive should acknowledge that the basic purpose of the police is the maintenance of public order and the control of conduct legislatively defined as crime. The basic purpose may not limit the police role but should be central to its full definition.[46]

Those who believe that the police role should focus exclusively on law enforcement and order maintenance advance a number of arguments on behalf of their position. To begin with, after a policeman has been trained to fight crime, use of his time and skills for an unrelated purpose is wasteful, especially in light of the acute manpower shortages many departments suffer.[47] Second, every moment that a police officer spends on service-related duties away from crime fighting is a moment during which a crime that might have been deterred may be committed. Third, a patrolman responding to a service call may be temporarily out of radio communication and hence unable to respond to an emergency call. Fourth, the only way a police officer can establish expertise in crime fighting is by concentrating on it exclusively during every working hour. And fifth, routine performance of trivial or menial functions discourages able men from entering police work, deflates morale, and, as a consequence, helps to drive other able men and women from it.

Other reasons also exist for emphasizing the law enforcement and order maintenance role, although they are less likely to be articulated. Thus, law enforcement and order maintenance functions are much more easily measured. The number of "good pinches" officers make, like the number of traffic tickets they issue, lends itself much more readily to objective measurement than does the amount of goodwill and community service they provide.[48] Because all bureaucracies, police bureaucracies included, are under pressure to be productive and to justify their financial and personnel resources, police departments are likely to stress law enforcement and order maintenance in order to stave off criticisms and to ensure institutional autonomy.[49]

However, compliance analysis suggests that perhaps the paramount reason for the emphasis the police place on law enforcement and order maintenance is that this role depends almost entirely upon the police's coercive powers. It does not introduce remunerative or normative dimensions to the definition of the police role, which might neutralize their coercive power; the entire criminal justice system is fundamentally based on such power, and reducing it might thereby promote police incongruence and ineffectiveness. The introduction of such normative and remunerative elements as delivery of social services and police advocacy makes successful policing considerably more difficult. To begin with, these elements are likely to undercut the police officer's ability to establish his authority in the community. As Reiss points out: "Unlike most professionals, who deal with clients who are prepossessed to accept the authority of the professional when he enters the situation, the police officer must *establish his authority*. The uniform, badge, truncheon, and arms all may play a role in asserting authority."[50]

When such potentially coercive elements as the uniform, badge, truncheon, and arms are downplayed and when the delivery of social services and police advocacy are emphasized instead, the ability of the police officer to establish his authority is jeopardized. As a consequence, the officer may be prompted to engage in unnecessarily aggressive actions in an effort to assert his authority and the fact that the police alone possess a monopoly on the legitimate exercise of coercive force.[51]

The simultaneous presence of coercive power on the one hand and remunerative and normative power on the other also complicates successful policing in another respect. Bernard L. Garmire sets the stage:

> One person simply cannot reasonably be expected to master both roles intellectually and jump psychologically from one to another in an instant's notice.... Here is the kind of thing we expect from today's police officer: at 9 P.M., he responds to a robbery in progress and upon arrival exchanges gunshots with a suspect. At 10 P.M., after he has made a report of the incident, he receives a call of a violent family brawl. He is white, they are black, and the suspect with whom he just exchanged gunfire an hour earlier was black. The officer is expected to handle their marital problems effectively and dispassionately, but he also has to return to radio service quickly because it is Saturday night and two other calls are waiting for him. Need more be said?[52]

The need to employ and rely upon normative and remunerative as well as coercive power subjects the police officer to considerable "role conflict."[53] He ends up living "on the grinding edge of social conflict without a well-defined, well-understood notion of what he is supposed to be doing there."[54] In this exposed position, the individual officer is likely to become increasingly frustrated, cynical, and isolated. The frustration he experiences is likely to result in part from his feeling that he is unable to perform the extensive range of medical, welfare, and social functions as well as he should; in part from a recognition that his frequently risky interventions accomplish little or nothing and are, hence, a waste of time; and in part from a realization that because of severe measurement problems, there are no built-in rewards for good performance in social service and police advocacy. His cynicism develops out of his negative contacts with society, as provided by the radio of his patrol car and as reinforced by his encounters with felons, drunks, and social outcasts of all types. He may mull these negative interactions over and over again in his mind during the boredom of routine patrol until he loses his intellectual capacity to distinguish between those citizens who turn to him for protection and assistance and those who flaunt his authority and break the law.[55]

This frustration and cynicism perhaps inevitably instills in the police officer a sense of isolation and separation from the community he serves, which in turn promotes a spirit of police solidarity and fraternalism. As Gus Plebesly observes in Joseph Wambaugh's *New Centurians:*

> You can't exaggerate the closeness of our dealings with people.... We see them when nobody else sees them, when they're being born and dying and fornicating and drunk.... We see people when they're taking anything of value from other poeple and when they're without shame or very much ashamed and we learn secrets that their husbands and wives don't even know, secrets that they even try to keep from themselves and what the hell, when you learn these things about people who aren't institutionalized, people who're out here where you can see them function every day, well then, you really *know*. Of course you get clannish and associate with others who know. It's only natural.[56]

This sense of isolation and solidarity among police officers has fostered the increased politicization of the police. Convinced that they have suffered a loss of respect and authority in the community,[57] police have sought to compensate for this loss through the establishment of police unions, guilds, and social organizations that have provided the police with a great deal of political power in local politics. "These fraternal organizations have given police departments, as institutions, the power to contend with existing control mechanisms over police operations such as they are, as well as providing policemen, as workers in police institutions, with the political power that has been protective of their autonomy and freedom."[58] This "fraternalistic politics," as Louis A. Radelet terms it, reinforces police isolation and the distinction they draw between "us" and "them." This in turn serves to exacerbate the negative view the police have of the public, so much so that even in such social service programs as Cincinnati's "Community Sector Team Policing Program" (COMSEC), 85 percent of the officers involved believe that chances of being abused by citizens are high.[59]

The Police View of the Public

Because of what they perceive as meddlesome efforts by the community to expand the notion of police role—to weaken their monopolistic hold on the exercise of coercive power through the introduction of remunerative and normative responsibilities—the police are likely to experience a sense of frustration and isolation and, in turn, to develop negative attitudes toward the public.[60] These feelings are reinforced by the lowly "pariah" position contemporary police officers occupy on the status scale.[61] Two surveys, one conducted in 1947 and the second in 1963, place police officers in relatively low status positions on a list of ninety occupations. In the first study, the police were ranked fifty-fifth, ten occupations below the midpoint;[62] in the second study, which replicated the first, their status had improved only slightly to forty-seventh place.[63] This low status is largely attributable to what Richard N. Harris calls "a moral division of labor."[64] Certain jobs such as disposing of garbage, processing rejected or dead persons, and enforcing the law are simply indispensable; however, "respectable" persons in the community are likely to find these tasks distasteful and to believe them better left to those who are not so offended by doing "dirty work."[65] Moreover, in doing these indispensable if unpleasant jobs, the police are well aware that they are serving the public collectively rather than distributively and that, as a result, they are likely to receive no public approval or support. As Harlan Hahn has written:

> Unlike many other government agencies whose programs bestow major benefits upon specific segments of the population that can be depended upon to provide energetic political support for their activities, police officers are unable to develop an identifiable constituency that enjoys the advantages of their services and that will become politically active in promoting the value of their work. In fact, the only distinct clientele that occupies a special relationship to police forces are violators of the law who are essentially hostile to law enforcement officers and who may possess the least political influence of any group in the society.[66]

The pariah status and low public support that police officers experience and the reciprocal animosity and hostility toward the public that they generate are confirmed all the more by wide-scale public efforts to impose greater internal and external controls over the police.[67] These efforts have proved to be most controversial, especially when they propose the establishment of civilian review boards or ombudsmen,[68] charged with the responsibility of investigating citizen complaints of alleged police misconduct and determining their validity. These proposals are regarded by the police as indicative of the suspicion, contempt, and animosity in which they are held by the public.

Public Perceptions of the Police

This view of the public, however, is fundamentally in error. As James Q. Wilson observes: "The single most striking fact about the attitudes of citizens, black and white, toward the police is that in general these attitudes are positive and not negative."[69] Thus, a 1967 study by the National Opinion Research Center

THE POLICE 79

(NORC) for the President's Commission on Law Enforcement and Administration of Justice indicated that of several thousand persons interviewed, 67 percent thought their local police did a good-to-excellent job of enforcing the law, 77 percent believed that they were "very good" or "pretty good" at providing protection to the people in their neighborhood, and 85 percent felt that they were "very good" or "pretty good" at being "respectful to people" like themselves.[70] A Gallup Poll of the same year revealed that 77 percent of the public had a "great deal" of respect for the police.[71] A 1970 Harris Poll disclosed that 64 percent of the public thought that their local law enforcement officers were doing an "excellent" or "pretty good" job.[72] Finally, according to a 1972 Gallup Poll, 83 percent of the public believe that the police are not too coercive at all, but feel rather that they *"should* be tougher than they are now in dealing with crime and lawlessness."[73] The public's concern appears to be with leniency, not with excessive force. Thus, in another 1972 Gallup Poll, the public considered the major causes behind the high crime rate in the United States to be laws that are too lenient and penalties that are not stiff enough.[74] The discrepancy between the public's opinion of the police and the police's perception of that opinion is perhaps best explained by James Q. Wilson: "The average patrolman in a big city is most frequently in contact, not with the 'average' citizen, but with a relatively small number of persons who are heavy users of police services (willingly or unwillingly), and his view of citizen attitudes is strongly influenced by this experience."[75] These "heavy users" include in disproportionate numbers the poor, the black, and the young. These groups are more likely to be involved in criminal activity and breaches of the peace, just as they are more likely to rely on the police for a whole array of social services (for example, quelling domestic quarrels) that middle-class families either do not require or obtain from nonpolice sources. This frequent contact by the police with these heavy users obscures the generally good opinion of the police held by "the majority of all citizens and the vast majority of white citizens"[76] and emphasizes instead the negative perceptions of the few. It exaggerates the criminal deviant's disrespect for, and contempt of, the police, the law, and society as a whole, and at the same time it magnifies the personal and social disorganization of those law-abiding citizens who are fundamentally dependent upon police services. This, in turn, simply reinforces the negative feelings and perceptions of the police toward the community, especially the minority community. The consequences of this negative reinforcement are tragic:

> The police-minority contact situation often becomes a vicious circle perpetuating negative reinforcement of each group by the other. . . . When either can be "read" as manifesting what the other already believes, the situation becomes negative and enhances the possibility of negativism in future contact. Repeated situations may preclude positive contacts of any nature between police and minorities.[77]

The vicious circle of negative reinforcement in the contacts between the police and the heavy users of their services simply confirms the police officers' sense of isolation and underscores their belief in the need for police solidarity and fraternalism—that is, for further politicization of the police. It strengthens their resistance to external control by the community and their opposition to civilian review boards. These perceptions and reactions in turn exacerbate the negative feelings and attitudes toward the police held by the public, especially by its minority members.[78] The claim that the police are there to serve the community as virtual ombudsmen conflicts in their minds with the reality of police aloofness and resistance to community control. The police's monopoly on the legitimate exercise of coercion predominates and offsets the remunerative and normative dimensions of an expanded police role. In the end, the public—especially the heavy users of police services—perceives the police as being both coercive and mendacious.

These perceptions only add to a further deterioration of police effectiveness and community relations. Thus, to begin with, they reduce the extent to which the police can carry out their law enforcement and order maintenance functions. For the most part, policing in the United States is reactive, with the police responding to calls and complaints from citizens.[79] Unless a cooperative public is willing to report crimes to the police and to testify as to the facts in court, the ability of the police to carry out what they regard as their primary function will be severely restricted.[80] Moreover, these negative public perceptions of the police also undercut police effectiveness and community relations by engendering greater police suspicion of the community they serve. These suspicions justify their development of a "perceptual shorthand" by which to identify those members of the community who are most likely to challenge their authority and cause law enforcement or order maintenance problems.[81] Thus, it rationalizes and, hence, validates police "stereotyping" of members of the public.[82] This stereotyping, this identification of "symbolic assailants," serves only to reinforce negative contacts and perceptions all the more; the vicious circle continues, and strained police-community relations are further exacerbated.

Proposed Improvements in Police-Community Relations

A number of solutions have been proposed by which to break this chain of negative reinforcements in the contacts between the police and the public. These proposals include a division within police departments of police functions, selective recruitment of police personnel in an effort to screen out the much-maligned "police personality," and increased police professionalization at both the individual and departmental level. Although each of these proposals possesses considerable merit, all are deficient in one decisive respect—they all tend to overlook the importance and centrality of the use of coercive power in the

THE POLICE

definition of the police role. Each of these proposed solutions to the present problems in police-community relations will be discussed in detail.

Division of Police Functions

One suggested improvement in police-community relations has been offered by Miami Police Chief Bernard L. Garmire:

> The contemporary police organization should be divided into two agencies under one department, one concerned with the law-enforcement function, the other with the community-service function. The community-service agency would operate on a 24-hour basis, and would be staffed by people who are psychologically best suited for this function as well as specifically educated and trained to perform it. There would be no need for them to operate in uniform and, depending on locality, generally no need for them to be armed. They may or may not have full powers of arrest. The law-enforcement agency would function as criminal investigators, thief catchers and so forth, and it likewise would be composed of people psychologically attuned to the law-enforcement role and for it. In essence, they would be performing the police functions of patrol and investigation; they would, of course, be armed and possess full police powers.[83]

Garmire proposes to reorganize police service both structurally and functionally so that police departments can simultaneously provide law enforcement and order maintenance functions, on the one hand, and social service and advocacy policing, on the other, without fear that they will cancel out each other. His insight is keen, his concern justified. The ability of police departments to win the trust and confidence of many members of the public through their community service activities is often adversely affected by the action of officers who are required to employ coercive power in the performance of their law enforcement and order maintenance functions. The fact that many officers must employ more than one kind of power to fulfill the present contradictory understanding of the police role serves only to increase public mistrust and makes the police appear to be hypocritical as well. Garmire's proposal is an attempt to remove this considerable obstacle to successful police-community relations. However, as Garmire himself acknowledges, it "raises more questions than it answers."[84]

To begin with, it is questionable whether Garmire's proposal would in fact render police departments less hypocritical in the eyes of the public. For successful police-community relations to exist, a police department cannot consist of two agencies, "one made up of men who like to knock heads and another of men providing bandages for the cuts and bruises."[85] As long as some police officers must employ force, the whole department is likely to be identified with this force, and its community service activity is likely to be regarded as a sham and as an elaborate public relations snow job. Moreover, what public confidence might be gained through reduced public perception of police hypocrisy will in all probability be lost through greater police ineffectiveness as interface problems flare between the two agencies. Every coercive action by the law enforcement agency will jeopardize fragile community service programs. Furthermore, jurisdictional disputes and budgetary competition will be inevitable. These and other interface problems are likely to result in publicly ventilated conflict that is as demoralizing as it is divisive. Both the law enforcement and community service agencies will be compelled to elicit political support from sympathetic interests in the community, thereby further politicizing the police and eroding public confidence in, and respect for, fair, impartial, and effective criminal justice. Finally, Garmire's proposal merely sidesteps the real problem and makes what is presently a problem for the whole police department into a problem only for the law enforcement agency within the department. Garmire's proposed law enforcement agency will depend fundamentally upon its monopoly on the legitimate exercise of coercion. This reliance on coercion cannot be avoided, at least not so long as there are members of society who violate the law and break the peace. This dependence on coercion, however, renders harmonious police-community relations—or, in Garmire's framework, the relation between the law enforcement agency and the community—altogether problematic. As James Q. Wilson concludes regarding the prospect for positive police-community relations:

> Seeing the police-ghetto problem in the context of the central police mission and its incompatibility with the freedom of all persons to come and go as they please cannot make one optimistic about how much improvement is possible at all in police relations with blacks. As long as crime and disorder are disproportionately to be found among young lower-class males and so long as blacks remain over-represented in (though by no means identical with) such groups, blacks—especially young ones—and the police are going to be adversaries.[86]

Selective Recruitment: Avoidance of the Police Personality

Another proposal for improved police-community relations focuses on more selective recruitment of police personnel in an effort to screen out those possessed of the much touted "authoritarian" police personality. Those who support this reform argue that the principal problems police departments face today—overbroad discretionary authority at the patrolman level, reluctance of the police officer to accept an expanded view of the police role including social service and police advocacy functions, and resulting problems in police-community relations—all stem from the predominance of the authoritarian personality within the police ranks.[87]

Among those students of the police who stress this proposal, there is remarkable agreement on the traits that ostensibly make up the police personality: it is characterized by suspicion, conventionalism, conservatism, cynicism, bigotry, and a fondness for violence.[88] At this juncture, however, the consensus breaks down; there is a considerable division of opinion about how these personality traits are developed. Some believe that authoritarian personalities naturally gravitate toward police work, while others believe that police work itself develops an authoritarian world view.[89]

According to the first point of view, police officers are authoritarian because only individuals already possessing authoritarian characteristics are selected for police work. Three kinds of selection are possible: (1) self-selection, whereby authoritarian individuals may deliberately choose police work because it is compatible with their personalities; (2) the elimination of liberals through a screening process by which the police are able to identify and thereupon weed out applicants whose values are incompatible with those already prevalent in the department, or should liberals overcome that hurdle and actually become policemen, through the police organization's paramilitary bureaucracy, which rewards conformity and discourages innovation; and (3) recruitment from an authoritarian class of people—more specifically, from the working class and the lower middle class, that is, from the "forgotten men" who comprise the insecure and status-anxious "silent majority."[90]

There is considerable support for this explanation. Thus, using a "cell-thermometer" to rate attitudes toward a variety of political, occupational, and ethnic groups, Alan E. Bent found that police officers showed the "warmest feelings" for the American Legion, the National Guard, policemen, the military, and whites, and the coldest feelings for blacks—especially the Black Panthers—liberals, and women's liberation.[91] He attributes this, in part, to a conscious or unconscious perpetuation of existing departmental "mores, attitudes, and opinions."

> The desired values and norms are discernible in the oral interview and attitudinal questionnaire stage. While these methods tend to eliminate unstable and undesirable personalities, they also have the effect of screening out applicants with "incompatible" values such as "liberalism" if the officials doing the screening feel this attitude is inconsistent with the effective police work.[92]

My experience while teaching at the Chicago Police Academy in 1970 and 1971 confirms Bent's findings. Thus, of the approximatley 280 police recruits with whom I had contact during that time, approximately 50 percent had joined the police department because of their penchant for action and their desire for an intense way of life. Most of these men were Vietnam veterans who had seen considerable action as Marines, Green Berets, or paratroopers. Once out of the service, the prospect or the reality of a routine civilian job in an office, warehouse, or factory became most unattractive; as one recruit put it, such work drove him "batty." A career with the police department offered them variety, excitement, and danger.[93] Another 45 percent of the recruits had joined the police department because of their concern for job security. Many had fathers or other close relatives who were police officers or governmental employees; as a consequence, they were aware of the advantages of civil service employment— good salary and fringe benefits, no layoffs, and a secure and generous pension after 25 years. One recruit put it bluntly: "Look, I am 32 years old and have two kids. I've been driving a truck for 10 years, and haven't gotten very far. I want a job where I can have some time at home and where I can earn enough money to keep my kids out of the public schools, have enough free time to get my boat to the lake, and not have to fear the prospect of retirement. Being a cop provides that. Oh sure, it can be dangerous but not if you're careful." Very few, if any, of the recruits exhibited a strong service orientation; the remainder were for the most part disillusioned and frustrated high school teachers who concluded that, because teaching in Chicago's inner city schools involved an unacceptable combination of part-time policing and part-time social work, they might as well engage in one or the other on a full-time basis.

Most of the recruits were veterans of the armed forces who did not chafe at the prospect of discipline or authority and who quickly conformed to police procedures. Approximately 85 percent were Mayor Daley Democrats, regulars who supported fully and faithfully the party's slate and who expected occasional political favors in return. Some had already benefited from this symbiotic relationship and credited their presence at the police academy to such political favors. Others were preserving their reliance on favors for the future—say, the sergeant's examination. This approach to politics was neither applauded nor condemned; rather, it was simply accepted. Moreover, it was in keeping with a tendency exhibited by a vast majority of the recruits to explain all human behavior with the following statement: "He did it for the money." They simply refused to admit the possibility of normative power. Thus, most white recruits—and even many black recruits—rejected the notion that Martin Luther King, Jr., was motivated by a sense of racial justice and brotherhood and held instead to a crude economic interpretation of his actions. The motivations of President John F. Kennedy, Ralph Nader, and Gloria Steinem were similarly explained. Generally, these recruits were imbued with a sense of "conventional morality" and understood "right" action to be doing one's "duty" or doing what those in authority require, although, on occasion—especially at examination time—many succumbed to "pre-conventional morality" and perceived an action to be right if they could get away with it.[94] Finally, many of the white recruits were extremely skeptical of the civil rights movement. They felt that blacks were now using violence and disruption to get an unfair advantage. Their sentiments were well captured in the frequently overheard assertion that blacks "should have to work for what they get like everyone else."

The alternative explanation of police authoritarianism is that it is "an unavoidable by-product of police work, i.e., the formal responsibilities, informal expectations, and everyday experiences of police patrolmen."[95] The centrality of coercion to the police mission, the danger officers face, and the savagery and hypocrisy they experience all combine together to make the police suspicious, cynical, prejudiced, opposed to tender-minded, sympathetic visionaries, fond of violence as a problem-solving technique, and rigidly committed to middle-class values.

Both of these explanations of police authoritarianism, however, are rendered meaningless and irrelevant when police attitudes and psychological traits are compared with those of the public at large. Thus, for example, Bent found in his attitudinal survey of members of the public and the police in Memphis, Tennessee, that "the police and a large number of white civilians sampled share common attitudes about law enforcement practices and the expectations of police 'efficiency' as a law enforcement value."[96] Bayley and Mendelsohn similarly concluded that police officers in Denver, Colorado, are "absolutely average people."[97] Robert W. Balch has reviewed these and other studies and has made this observation:

> Authoritarianism, as a personality syndrome, is widespread in this country, and policemen may not be any more authoritarian than other people from similar socioeconomic backgrounds. Bigotry is hardly unusual in the United States. Nor is conservatism, cynicism, or any other authoritarian trait. From a sociological point of view, the important question is not, "Why are policemen authoritarian?" but "Why are they singled for special attention?"[98]

Balch's question deserves an answer. As he notes, there was once a time when social scientists were attracted to an investigation of the "criminal mind"; subsequent research has revealed, however, that the personality characteristics of criminals are not appreciably different from those of the public generally. Today, the concern is with the "police mind." Yet, evidence here too suggests that police officers "appear to be good representatives of white middle- or working-class America." Thus, why are they singled out for special attention? The answer to Balch's question is perhaps best approached through compliance analysis. The presumption of police authoritarianism may stem from overlooking the essentially coercive nature of the police role. As long as danger exists, as long as police must employ coercion to perform their essential law enforcement and order maintenance functions, police suspicion and cynicism are likely to continue and may in all fairness be more appropriately described as police realism and objectivity.

Professionalization of the Police

Finally, a third proposal for improved police-community relations (and perhaps the most widely touted) is increased police professionalism. It is seen as a means of both gaining public respect and improving the effectiveness of law enforcement. Police professionalization has two aspects: individual professionalization, which stresses improvements in recruitment standards and preservice and inservice training; and departmental professionalization, which entails organizational changes and the adoption of more sophisticated criteria for evaluating delivery of police services. Each of these aspects must be explored in an effort to assess the promise that increased police professionalism holds in store.

Individual Professionalization

Improved recruitment standards   One of the major recommendations for improved police professionalism focuses on the need for improved recruitment standards. As the President's Commission on Law Enforcement and Administration of Justice bluntly stated:

> Existing selection requirements and procedures in a majority of departments . . . do not screen out the unfit. Hence, it is not surprising that far too many of those charged with protecting life and property and rationally enforcing our laws are not respected by their fellow officers and are incompetent, corrupt, or abusive. One incompetent officer can trigger a riot, permanently damage the reputation of a citizen, or alienate a community against a police department. It is essential, therefore, that the requirements to serve in law enforcement reflect the awesome responsibility facing the personnel that is selected.[99]

To meet these requirements, departments are being encouraged to place increasingly greater stress on recruitment standards that will ensure officers who have sound character, emotional stability, and above-average intelligence.

Charles Saunders, Jr., has been especially influential in developing these standards of suitability.[100] Thus, regarding the recruitment of officers with sound character, he advocates, at a minimum, thorough background investigations and personal interviews. Few departments, however, make systematic use of these techniques. Most engage in only perfunctory checks of local police records, FBI files, and references supplied by the applicant. These are generally extremely limited in scope, and investigators seldom probe deeply enough to uncover information needed for a professional evaluation. As a consequence, these departments deprive themselves of a most useful screening device, because municipalities that do make thorough background checks find they produce higher rejection rates.[101]

Emotional stability to withstand the stress of police work is also crucial.

A recent survey, however, by the International Association of Chiefs of Police reveals that only about 25 percent of all departments administer psychiatric examinations. Saunders considers such personality tests as the Minnesota Multiphasic Personal Inventory to be "largely successful in eliminating persons with mental disorders from those whose applications have been accepted."[102] Thus, between 1953 and 1957, of the 760 persons tested by the Los Angeles Police Department for personality disorders, 86 (11.3 percent) were rejected as not meeting acceptable psychological standards. Of those rejected, 51 percent were found to be latent or borderline psychotics, and 22 percent were diagnosed as schizoid personalities.[103] Although there is considerable conflict over the reliability of such tests, Saunders notes that major cities that conduct psychological screening end up with recruits who are better adjusted, more stable, and display better judgment than the general population.[104] Consequently, the need for such a recruitment standard (and the need for greater research to improve it further) would seem to be compelling.

Above-average intelligence is also essential for effective police performance. Most of the standard texts in the field consider an IQ of 110-120—the high-average range for the general population—to be the minimum acceptable score for admission into a police department. Most departments, however, do not administer IQ tests; the International Association of Chiefs of Police reveals that only 55 out of 162 major law enforcement agencies administer such examinations. Nonetheless, educational qualifications can provide an important, if rough, index of intelligence, competence, and capacity for professional training. In keeping with this emphasis on educational qualifications, the President's Commission on Law Enforcement and Administration of Justice recommends as an ultimate goal that "all personnel with general enforcement powers have baccalaureate degrees."[105] The more recent National Advisory Commission has gone even further and urges the establishment of standards that would require as a condition of initial employment by 1975 the completion of at least 2 years of college, by 1978 the completion of at least 3 years of college, and by 1982 the possession of a baccalaureate degree or its equivalent.[106] Two primary reasons can be advanced on behalf of these increased educational requirements. The first reason, and, according to Saunders, the most "compelling," "is the steadily rising educational level of the general population."[107] As the educational attainments of the general public rise, so do entry standards in other occupations, thereby intensifying the competition for that pool of talented manpower which is so desperately needed in law enforcement. After all, many prospective applicants with college degrees will shun police work because they are unwilling to identify themselves with typically low police educational standards. The second reason for raising educational requirements relates to the first. As more and more police departments employ college graduates, the evidence mounts that college-educated persons are better suited for police work. Thus, a 1972 study of the New York Police Department revealed that men with college degrees demonstrated better-than-average on-the-job performance; they were the object of fewer citizen complaints, had a lower incidence of misconduct, and took less sick leave than those without college degrees.[108] This substantiated the findings of a 1968 Chicago study that disclosed that the highest-rated group of tenured police officers were those with significantly higher levels of education.[109] The greater suitability of college-educated persons for police work appears to remain constant, regardless of city or departmental size. Thus, Ventura, California, which in 1966 instituted a policy that police recruits must have a degree from a four-year college, has found fewer personnel complaints against college-educated police officers, a lower rate of personnel turnover, and an overall reduction of 3 percent in the crime rate.[110]

In addition to recruitment standards emphasizing good moral character, emotional stability, and above-average intelligence and advanced education, minimum standards concerning the physical health, strength, stature, and agility of the potential police officer are also important. After all, as the National Advisory Commission appropriately underscores, "Cops still have to slug it out in back alleys, chase fleet-footed burglars, and physically disarm dangerous persons."[111] These requirements can be unduly restrictive, however, and many otherwise exceptional applicants are summarily rejected because of their height, weight, or vision. For this reason, the National Advisory Commission has recommended the establishment of flexible standards that would allow physical requirements to be assessed on an individual basis. It has proposed the establishment of "minimum standards that incorporate compensating factors such as education, language skills, or experience in excess of that required if such factors can overcome minor deficiencies in physical requirements such as age, height, or weight."[112]

These improved recruitment standards will obviously enhance both the professionalism and the effectiveness of police departments. But, a problem arises: The exceptional men who meet these rigid qualifications are not likely to be attracted to police work, at least not at the present time. To begin with, police functions are not divided among personnel on a rational basis. In the words of the President's Commission:

> At present, a patrolman is equally responsible for the most complex and the most menial of police tasks. The wide range of skills required in performing all of these tasks seems possible of attainment for only limited numbers of personnel. This being so, these tasks should be divided according to the skills required to perform them. For example, instead of having all patrol officers respond to all demands placed upon a department, the most competent officers should devote their time to the police work that requires the greatest degree of ability, education and judgment.[113]

To accomplish this more rational division of police functions, the President's Commission recommended the establishment of three classes of officers:

the police agent, the police officer, and the community service officer (CSO). Tasks would be assigned to these officers on the basis of the skills, the intelligence, and the education necessary to perform them well. Thus, police agents would receive those tasks that require the highest degree of judgment, intelligence, education, initiative, and understanding of community and human behavior. The President's Commission anticipated that they would be assigned such complicated, sensitive, and demanding tasks as serving as uniformed patrol officers in high-crime and high-tension areas, investigating major crimes in a plainclothes capacity, making difficult arrests, enforcing gambling, vice, and narcotic statutes, and maintaining contact with citizens in the community to ascertain potential signs of strife. In contrast, police officers would perform less demanding tasks such as performing routine patrol, rendering emergency services, enforcing traffic regulations and investigating traffic accidents, and investigating those crimes that can be solved by immediate follow-up investigations or that are most likely to have suspects close to the crime scene. Finally, the President's Commission perceived community service officers as relieving police agents and police officers of lesser police duties, increasing the opportunity for minority-group members to serve in law enforcement, enabling police to hire persons who can provide a greater understanding of minority-group problems, tapping new reservoirs of manpower by helping talented young men who have not yet been able to complete their education to qualify for police work, and, thereby, improving police service in areas with high crime rates.

This recommendation is significant in two respects. First, it offers an alternative perspective for approaching the problem of how properly to divide police tasks among officers. Rather than dividing them functionally between law enforcement and community service as Garmire suggests, it divides them among officers on the basis of the task's complexity and significance. Critical and sensitive tasks—be they of a law enforcement or community service nature—are to be performed by the most competent personnel, those having the highest degree of judgment, intelligence, education, initiative, and understanding. Likewise, the mundane and the menial tasks of policing—again, be they related to law enforcement or community service—are to be performed by those with lesser skills, intelligence, and education. This alternative to a functional division of police tasks has much to commend it. Thus, it would be likely to attract and retain high-caliber personnel by providing them with tasks, status, and compensation commensurate with their abilities. Moreover, it would be likely to avoid many of the interface problems that a functional separation of police departments into law enforcement and community service agencies would stimulate.

This recommendation for a more rational division of police functions is significant in a second respect as well. As you will have observed, most of the tasks assigned to those with the highest degree of ability, education, and judgment—that is, to the police agents—tend to be of a law enforcement nature, and most of the tasks assigned to those of lesser skills, education, and intelligence—

that is, to the community service officer—tend to be of a community service nature. The President's Commission obviously considers law enforcement and order maintenance to be the most important police role and wants it to be entrusted to the most competent police personnel. It is at this juncture that the functional division of police roles merges with the division based on complexity and significance, with compliance analysis providing the bridge. Coercive power, as essential to the successful operation of law enforcement and order maintenance as it ultimately is to that of the criminal justice system as a whole, must be exercised by the best men.

Even if this division of police tasks were to be implemented, it would not be sufficient by itself to attract recruits of high caliber to police work. To begin with, salaries are presently so low in many departments that they are interpreted by the police as palpable evidence of the contempt in which they are held by the public and its elected representatives. For police departments to recruit successfully the high-quality personnel they need, salaries must be competitive. Police departments must meet or exceed the salaries offered by other employers seeking individuals with similar qualifications. This simply has not been the case. In 1972, for the first time in the nation's history, the median income for the average family of four exceeded $10,000. However, as of January 1, 1975, despite 3 years of rampant inflation, the median annual base salary for entering patrolmen was only $9,464 and the median annual base salary for patrolmen receiving maximum compensation was $11,377.[114] If police departments are serious about improving the quality of their personnel and the success of their police-community relations programs, they simply must provide salaries that keep pace.

Once qualified men have been attracted to police work, they must be retained. Here, too, changes are necessary. Thus, police departments must establish procedures that assure that only the best-qualified personnel are promoted or advanced to positions of greater authority and responsibility in higher pay grades and ranks. Likewise, they must provide for the recruitment of personnel through the means of lateral entry.[115] Unlike the private sector and most public agencies (including the military) where lateral entry is common, police departments recruit only at the lowest levels. Officers are expected to work their way up the bureaucratic hierarchy. As a consequence, however, the entire organizational hierarchy is composed of persons who are, or at one time were, patrolmen. Police administrators simply "fish ladder" their way up through the ranks without ever being prepared in a systematic way for the difficult and demanding roles they are required to play in the complex enterprise that is the hallmark of contemporary police work.[116] Thus, lateral entry is essential if truly professional police leadership is to be achieved and if high-quality police recruits are to be retained.

Finally, other police personnel practices that discourage career-oriented persons from entering or staying in law enforcement must also be altered. Early retirement benefits are a case in point. Although they have the effect of making way for younger officers, the prospect of retirement at age 40 or 45 also tends to discourage police officers from developing skills and qualifications required for higher managerial positions. The police officer's aim is often to get out (in order to start a second career) rather than to get ahead.[117]

Even when all of these obstacles to the successful employment of improved recruitment standards are overcome, one more remains and is all but insurmountable. It is contained in the language of *Griggs* v. *Duke Power Company*.[118] In this 1971 decision, the U.S. Supreme Court unanimously held that Title VII of the Civil Rights Act of 1964 removed all "artificial, arbitrary, and unnecessary barriers to employment where the barriers operate invidiously to discriminate on the basis of racial or other impermissible classifications."[119] Speaking for the Court, Chief Justice Burger noted that only testing and measuring procedures that are "demonstrably a reasonable measure of job performance" are permissible.[120] Employers may adopt job requirements without any "intention to discriminate against Negro employees," the Court admitted. Nonetheless, "good intent or absence of discriminatory intent does not redeem employment procedures or testing mechanisms that operate as 'built-in headwinds' for minority groups and are unrelated to measuring job capability."[121]

Because most police departments' recruitment standards have been adopted "without meaningful study of their relationship to job-performance ability" and cannot be shown to be essential to the "successful performance" of police work, many police departments are now simply abandoning standards altogether. Thus, for example, many departments have dropped all minimum height requirements. They are unable to establish that a certain stature is essential either to protect the police officer from assault or to assure successful policing,[122] and, of course, this requirement has served to screen many applicants, especially women, Orientals, and Chicanos, from possible service. Weight requirements have met with much the same fate. Moreover, in their haste to rid themselves of all recruitment standards that cannot be empirically validated as "reasonable measures of job performance," many departments have even abandoned requirements pertaining to moral character. Thus, for example, some departments are now accepting applicants who have been arrested and convicted of criminal offenses.[123] They feel obliged to do so, because over 50 percent of all male ghetto youths have had some brush with the law, and the requirement of an unblemished criminal record tends, as a consequence, to have a racially discriminatory effect.

Thus, recruitment standards in many departments have been largely abandoned, both because of their inadvertent promotion of racial discrimination and because of police inability to establish a "demonstrated relationship" between them and successful police performance.[124] However, a serious problem now arises: With the abandonment of most if not all recruitment standards, police departments find it increasingly difficult to justify either their acceptance or rejection of particular applicants and find themselves ever less able to resist the pressure of those who would have them engage in reverse discrimination in their recruitment practices so as to help eliminate "root and branch" the effects of pervasive and historic discrimination suffered by America's minority citizens.[125] Although the Supreme Court stressed in *Griggs* that "discriminatory preference for any group, minority or majority, is precisely and only what Congress has proscribed,"[126] a number of lower federal courts have nonetheless interpreted the Fourteenth Amendment as occasionally authorizing ameliorative racial preference. As the First Circuit argued in *Associated General Contractors v. Altshuler*, "Our society cannot be completely color blind in the short term if we are to have a color-blind society in the long term. After centuries of viewing through colored lenses, eyes do not quickly adjust when the lenses are removed. Discrimination has a way of perpetuating itself, albeit unintentionally, because the resulting inequalities make new opportunities less accessible."[127] Thus, particular courts have argued that the Constitution must be "color conscious to prevent discrimination [from] being perpetuated and to undo the effects of past discrimination,"[128] and have authorized preference among applicants on the basis of race as part of a specific remedy for past discriminations. Certain members of the legal community go even further and argue that the Fourteenth Amendment not only authorizes, but requires, such preference.[129] But, whatever the ultimate formulation, the effect of this practice on police departments will be increasingly devastating. Thus, efforts to increase police professionalization will be dealt a severe blow; professional norms are, after all, unabashedly nonegalitarian.[130] With professional standards rendered ineffectual and dismissed as irrelevant, the limits they presently impose on the exercise of police discretion will be lifted. The police will become increasingly irresponsible (in the sense that there are no criteria, no norms, no standards to which they are accountable), and police-community relations, tenuous at best, will be rendered all the more problematic. Obviously, these untoward consequences on police professionalism cannot be tolerated, and every effort must be made by police departments to establish and validate recruitment standards that bring to them men of the highest caliber.

Improved preservice and in-service training No recruit, regardless of his individual qualifications, is prepared to perform police work on native ability alone. Thus, another recommendation for improved police professionalism is directed toward improved preservice and in-service training. Presently, however, most police departments are providing neither as much nor as extensive training as they should. Granted, they are providing more training than that described by a metropolitan police chief to the Wickersham Commission (U.S. National Commission on Law Observance and Enforcement) in 1931:

> I say to him that he is a policeman, and I hope he will be a credit to the force. I tell him he doesn't need anybody to tell him how to enforce the law, that all he needs to do is go out on the street and keep his eyes open. I say: "You know the Ten Commandments, don't you? Well, if you know

the Ten Commandments, and you go out on your beat, and you see somebody violating one of those Ten Commandments, you can be pretty sure he is violating some law."[131]

Nonetheless, a recent study by the International Association of Chiefs of Police revealed that the average police officer receives less than 200 hours of formal training.[132] In striking contrast, physicians receive more than 11,000 hours, lawyers more than 9,000 hours, teachers more than 7,000, embalmers more than 5,000 hours, and barbers more than 4,000 hours.[133] With the possible exception of the physician, none of these other professions has anywhere near the power of life or death over individual citizens that the police do, and yet, the length of their training is on average only one-twentieth of that required for a barber.

Police training must be upgraded. The National Advisory Commission recommends that every police recruit should successfully complete at least 400 hours of basic police preservice training. In addition to such traditional police subjects as patrol, traffic training, criminal law, evidence, and investigation, it recommends that this training should also include (1) instruction in law, psychology, and sociology, specifically as they relate to interpersonal communication, the police role, and the community the police officer will serve; (2) assigned activities away from the training academy to enable the officer to gain specific insight into the community, the criminal justice system, and local government; and (3) where necessary, remedial training for individuals who are deficient in their training performance but who demonstrate potential for satisfactory performance.[134]

As with any profession, effective performance can be maintained only with continual training. Thus, the National Advisory Commission also recommends that every police officer, up to and including the rank of captain, should receive at least 40 hours of in-service training a year.[135] Because this is designed to maintain, update, and improve the officer's necessary knowledge and skills, the subject matter of these in-service programs will often vary with the specific needs of individual departments and officers. However, common subject areas include the law and recent Supreme Court decisions in the realm of criminal procedure, newly developed field practices (especially control of civil disorders), weapons use, evidence collection, interpersonal communication, and advances in "technological enforcement."[136]

The benefits to be derived from this recent emphasis on training are threefold: increased police effectiveness, fewer interface problems, and improved police-community relations. With the newly acquired knowledge and technical skills that the training provides, the ability of the police to perform their tasks effectively and expeditiously is enhanced. Because such training instills greater appreciation for, and insight into, the criminal justice system, the likelihood of police involvement in interface problems is minimized. After all, the more the police come to realize and accept the "differences in philosophy, purpose, and practice" that exist among the components of the criminal justice system, the more inclined they will be to cooperate with courts and corrections to achieve the basic overall goal for which they are all striving, namely, the reduction and ultimately the prevention of crime.[137] This is especially true as the police come to appreciate more fully the unique responsibility of courts in the realm of criminal procedure.[138] With the greater technological sophistication that this training supplies, the opportunity for the police to use the awe that this technology stimulates in the public mind to promote improved police-community relations is heightened. And finally, as the officer gains, by means of this training, greater appreciation for the community he will serve, the overall professional attitude of the police officer is further assured. This professional attitude—a pride and confidence that former Kansas City, Missouri, Police Chief Bernard C. Brannon has described as a combination of respect for the public and respect for one's abilities as an officer—promotes even more secure police-community relations.[139]

Departmental Professionalization

Regionalization of police forces Like individual professionalization, departmental professionalization also seeks to enhance public respect for the police and to contribute to the overall effectiveness of law enforcement. It does so by stressing the importance of changes in the organizational structure of police departments and by striving to develop more sophisticated criteria for evaluating delivery of police services.

The most widely recommended proposal for police organizational change is the consolidation of all police service on a metropolitan-wide or regional basis. As former New Haven Police Chief James F. Ahern argues:

> One of the most important ways in which a department can increase its efficiency and the quality of its service is to cooperate with other departments and to move toward regionalization. This is the only way in which small- and medium-sized departments will be able to gain the resources for proper support services like training, and for effective elimination of complex crime problems. . . . Regionalization is perhaps the ultimate step in the attempts of a professional police department to meet the responsibilities of the law enforcement profession as it applies to them.[140]

Miami Police Chief Bernard L. Garmire agrees: "The consolidation of police agencies, accompanied by a rationalization of police structure and function, could be the first step down the long road toward the reform of the police system and the resolution of its problems."[141] So does the prestigious Committee for Economic Development;[142] it places the blame for much "wasted energies and lost motion" squarely on the extreme "fragmentation of police forces" that exists in the United States.[143] The extent of this problem is highlighted in Figure 3.1. It displays the conditions of overlap and fragmentation of police government that exist in the Detroit metropolitan area.

THE POLICE

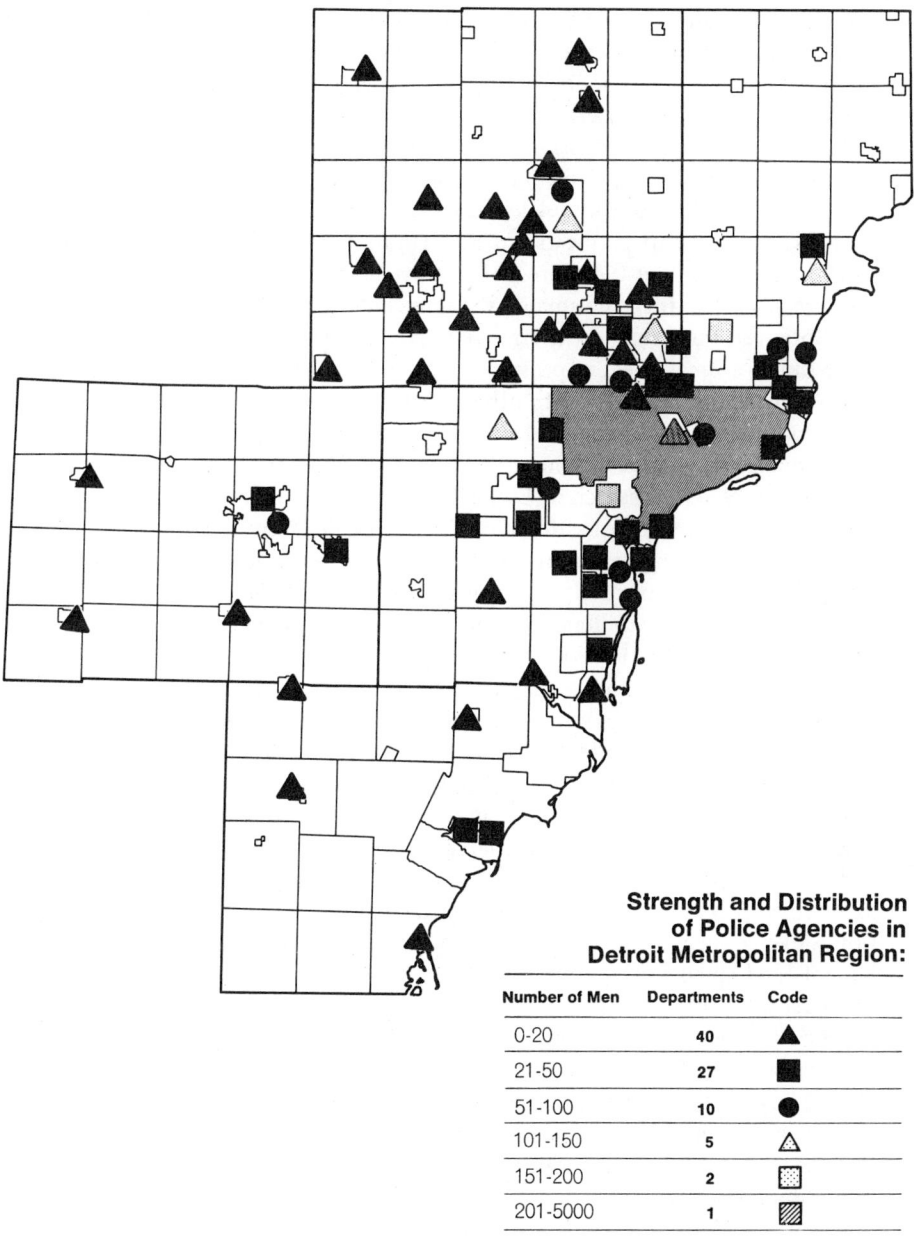

Figure 3.1 Fragmentation of urban police. [Source: President's Commission on Law Enforcement and Administration of Justice, *Task Force Report: The Police* (Washington, D.C.: Government Printing Office, 1967), p. 69.]

Recently, however, the ardor for consolidation has cooled somewhat. As Robert L. Bish and Vincent Ostrom have pointed out, two relationships are implicit in the thinking of those who favor police consolidation: (1) An increase in the size of police departments through consolidation will be associated with improved output of police service, increased efficiency, increased responsibility, and increased citizen satisfaction with police performance. (2) A reduction in the number of police departments in a metropolitan area will also be associated with increased police output, efficiency, and responsibility and increased citizen satisfaction.[144] A critical question arises: Do these relationships, in fact, hold true? If they do, then the more police consolidation the better. However, if the reverse is true, then the smaller the units and the more duplication the better. Moreover, there may be intermediate possibilities. "An increase in size for some functions may yield improvements to some degree and yield net disadvantages beyond that magnitude. In other circumstances a decrease in size might yield improvements to some magnitude but yield net disadvantages if reduced to a still smaller size."[145] These intermediate possibilities have only recently come under scrutiny. The research of Elinor Ostrom, Roger B. Parks, and Gordon P. Whitaker explores these questions. In "Do We Really Want to Consolidate Urban Police Forces? A Reappraisal of Some Old Assertions," they suggest that neither total consolidation nor total decentralization is likely to lead to more efficient police service in metropolitan areas. Rather, they conclude the "conscious use of overlapping jurisdictions of varying sizes may be necessary to combine the advantages of both small and large scale."[146] In brief, they argue that a two-tier approach must be employed to solve the problems of delivery of police services,[147] with a consolidated upper tier performing such metropolitan-wide functions as training and crime lab analysis and a lower tier of smaller local units providing patrol and service functions and dealing with community and neighborhood problems within the large consolidated unit.

The proper mixture of organizational arrangements is, of course, yet to be ascertained. However, even when this obstacle to departmental professionalization is overcome and the proper mixture of large-scale metropolitan-wide components and small-scale locally controlled components that can provide for the most efficient delivery of police services is achieved, problems will remain, for the findings of Ostrom and her associates also challenge the appropriateness and importance of efficiency as a criterion for evaluating delivery of police services. They contend instead that effectiveness, as measured at least in part by citizen satisfaction, and not mere efficiency, as measured on a cost-per-unit basis, is the appropriate criterion for evaluating service delivery by professional police departments.[148]

Emphasis on professional "effectiveness" criteria over bureaucratic "efficiency" criteria As Ostrom and her associates note, departmental professionalization requires more than changes in the organizational structures of police departments;

it also requires a more sophisticated set of criteria for evaluating both the quantity and quality of delivery of police services. Thus, it is not enough that departments be efficient; they must also be effective. They must be as concerned with crime prevention as with crime apprehension; they must be as interested in the quality of professional police service as measured by citizen satisfaction as they are with high productivity as measured by lower crime rates or high clearance rates.

Police efficiency is extremely important. Police departments are continuously striving to make more efficient use of their personnel. Those who advocate consolidation of all police services on a metropolitan-wide basis typically do so to promote this goal.[149] The President's Commission on Law Enforcement and Administration of Justice was also motivated by this same concern when it spelled out the various steps that police departments should take to obtain maximum utilization of their field personnel.[150]

In addition to seeking ways by which to increase police efficiency, departments have also been concerned with developing techniques by which to measure this efficiency. Standard productivity measures include the crime rate and the clearance rate. Although readily available, these indicators are so general that they tell little about the efficiency of a particular department. Consequently, other measures have been devised that allow for a more comparative evaluation of police efficiency. One such measure is arrest per police department employee or per $1,000 expenditure. It is the most readily available single measure of apprehension productivity.[151] Another is clearance per police employee or per $1,000 expenditure, which is closely related to arrest per employee or per dollar. Although arrests provide a better count of the total number of criminals involved, clearances provide a better measure of the number of recorded crimes that have been solved. Finally, another commonly employed traditional productivity measure is population served per employee or per dollar expenditure.

Unfortunately, none of these efficiency measures tells anything about the quality of police service. They indicate quantity, not quality; and by so doing, actually serve to undermine high-quality police service. This can be seen by focusing on just one of these measures: arrest per employee or per dollar. Because this measure in no way indicates the "quality of arrest," it actually biases the resulting productivity measurement in favor of those police departments with a large number of poor-quality arrests.[152] Thus, although it is important to have efficiency measures that reveal the quantity of service delivered on some cost-per-unit basis, it is also imperative to develop effectiveness measures that assess the quality of service on the basis of professional competence and public satisfaction.

If programs designed to improve police-community relations are ever to be successful, the concern for professional effectiveness and for the development of qualitative measures must also come to dominate the thinking in police departments. High rates of criminal apprehension are not enough; they must be accompanied by high rates of crime prevention, and this, of course, requires citizen satisfaction. As George Barbour and Stanley Wolfson declare: "The percent of population expressing satisfaction with police services is a basic objective of a police force and of concern to the community. Public acceptance and cooperation enable the police to be more effective in deterring crime and in apprehending criminals."[153] Police effectiveness, however, is hard to measure. As the National Advisory Commision on Criminal Justice Standards and Goals points out:

> Perhaps the major problem related to measuring police effectiveness lies in identifying the relationship between police activity and crime prevention or deterrence. It is difficult, if not impossible, to estimate the amount of crime that does not occur because of police prevention. It is obvious, however, that the relative success of a police agency in preventing the occurrence of crime or in deterring criminal behavior will make its criminal control function more effective.[154]

Difficult though the task may be, there are a number of measures that can be employed to ascertain police effectiveness. They include, but are by no means limited to, the following: crime rates based on victimization survey data, which give improved estimates of criminal activity; clearance rates based on victimization survey data; percent of arrests that survive initial review by courts of limited jurisdiction, which measures to a considerable extent the quality of arrests; average response time for calls of service; percent of population expressing a feeling of security, which indicates the extent to which police are successful in making citizens less fearful of crime; and percent of population expressing satisfaction with police services. At present, these effectiveness measures are not being developed and employed as they might be, in large part because they require additional data collection. Nonetheless, as Barbour and Wolfson stress, until an attempt is made "to measure the effectiveness, efficiency, and productivity of police services, no clear picture of effective resource allocation can be gained."[155]

Even when adequate qualitative measures are devised, police effectiveness will still be difficult to achieve for two reasons. To begin with, the present rewards systems of most police departments do not recognize efforts in this direction, and there are few incentives for individual officers to direct their attention and talents to this end. Moreover, as noted above, many of the methods and measures that police departments employ to encourage efficiency serve to undermine effectiveness. Thus, foot patrols have been abandoned by most departments because they are highly expensive, geographically restrictive, and wasteful of manpower—in short, because they are inefficient, even though they provide an intimate, personal police-citizen contact and a police presence that contributes to citizen satisfaction, assists in deterring crime, brings existing but otherwise unreported crime to the attention of the police, and helps in the apprehension of criminals. Both of these reasons, however, are subsumed in what is perhaps the principal obstacle to the successful incorporation of effectiveness criteria in the delivery of police services: the inevitable incompatibility of professional criteria and bureaucratic criteria. Professional criteria tend to be normative and are concerned with isolating and legitimating particular ends or objectives; bureaucratic criteria, in contrast, tend to be calculative and instrumental and are designed to promote the most rational means to whatever end or objective others decide upon. In short, professional criteria provide the ends, bureaucratic criteria the means. In practice, however, bureaucracy inexorably prevails, and professional ends are rendered subordinate to bureaucratic means. Max Weber explains why: "The decisive reason for the advance of bureaucratic organization has always been its purely technical superiority over any other form of organization. The fully developed bureaucratic mechanism compares with other organization exactly as does the machine with the non-mechanical modes of production."[156] Bureaucracy has "precision, speed, unambiguity, knowledge of the files, continuity, discretion, unity, strict subordination, reduction of friction and material and personal costs" and has raised these attributes "to the optimum point."[157] It is, however, frightfully devoid of an awareness of, or a concern for, ultimate ends or objectives. Every end is treated as equal and is viewed as a means for a more remote end in a process that repeats itself *ad infinitum.* In this instrumental process, the bureaucrat is reduced to a mere "cog in an ever-moving mechanism which prescribes to him an essentially fixed route of march."[158] His only interest is "in seeing that the mechanism continues its functions," not in seeing that the ends for which the mechanism ostensibly functions are achieved.[159] Thus, the ineluctable consequence of this bureaucratization is the establishment of what Weber calls a "cryptoplutocracy" of technically superior, efficiency-oriented instrumental bureaucrats who prevail over ends-oriented, effectiveness-directed professionals.[160] Police departments have been no more successful in escaping this inevitable bureaucratic domination than have any other organizations.

The Problematic Nature of Police-Community Relations

Even if these monumental problems to police professionalization were eventually to be overcome, improved police-community relations would still remain problematic. This is so for two principal reasons: (1) the inevitable antipathy that exists between professionalism and democracy; and (2) the inescapable fact that the essential police role is fundamentally coercive.

Looking first at the antipathy between professionalism and democracy, it should be noted that professionalized departments are often held in no higher esteem by the public than are traditional departments.[161] When citizens of cities with professionalized departments have been asked to evaluate the fairness, honesty, and abusiveness of their police force, their responses differ little from citizens of cities with traditional departments: About the same percentage believe that being black makes a difference in the treatment one receives by the police, about the same percentage see the police as using unnecessary force; and about the same percentage have "little respect" or "great respect" for the police.[162] This fact is in large part the inevitable consequence of police professionalization. It tends to make police officers "increasingly separated from those they serve."[163] James Q. Wilson considers this separation to be the

> result both of what the professional doctrine requires (substituting patrol cars for officers walking beats, increasing the size of police districts, rotating men among assignments and discouraging police involvement in political affairs) and of what the ethos of professionalism assumes (that the impersonal rules of law enforcement are correct and appropriate regardless of what a hostile or indifferent citizenry may think).... A professional force, in principle at least, devalues citizen opinion as manifested in personal relations; professionalism, in this sense, means impersonalization. Relations with the community are no longer handled by the officers' informal contacts—some legitimate, some illegitimate—with neighborhoods and individuals but are given over to a specialized and bureaucratic agency within the police organization.[164]

This professional impersonalization obviously diminishes the prospects for improved police-community relations. How much any professional police department can (or, for that matter, should) reduce this impersonalization remains a question, for just as there is an inherent incompatibility between professionalism and bureaucracy, so, too, there is an unavoidable antipathy between professionalism and democracy. Professionalism stresses responsibility and constraints; democracy, in contrast, stresses rights and freedoms. So long as some members of the public exercise these freedoms in an irresponsible manner and have to be coercively restrained by professional police from affecting the rights and freedoms of others, antipathy will exist between the police and these irresponsible members of the public. If these individuals constitute a majority or a large and significant minority of the public, good police-community relations will be all but impossible.

This is, however, exactly the state of affairs in which many police departments find themselves. They must enforce the law and maintain order so that those fit for self-rule can enjoy their rights and exercise their freedoms without fear. And, to do so, they must rely on coercion to discipline and restrain those who have no self-discipline or self-restraint. The police view this use of coercion as absolutely indispensable, and this fact constitutes the second major obstacle to improved police-community relations—an obstacle that the use of compliance analysis has helped to explore. As long as the police are called upon to protect the law-abiding public through the enforcement of laws and the maintenance of order, they will consider the use of coercive power—the very foundation of the entire criminal justice system—to be absolutely imperative. Efforts to improve police-community relations will be, in their estimation, of less importance.

Consequently, they will resist efforts to employ normative and remunerative powers to promote good police-community relations through expanding the definition of police role to include social service and police advocacy. They will regard the simultaneous presence of these three kinds of power as serving only to neutralize the effective employment of coercion. The likely consequence of all of this will be to exacerbate, not improve, police-community relations. After all, as a police department is rendered increasingly powerless and ineffective and as it becomes unable to perform even essential law enforcement and order maintenance functions, it loses its ability to command much respect in the community. As it becomes increasingly ineffective, it also becomes increasingly dependent upon the discretionary actions of its individual officers, who find this the only way to circumvent organizational ineffectiveness. This, however, adds to a further deterioration in police-community relations. Even if a department is able to avoid these more immediate pitfalls, it will be likely, nonetheless, to find itself subjected to charges of mendacity. Thus, to the extent that the public perceives police officers to be simultaneously employing normative and remunerative power along with coercion in the performance of their duties, it is likely to feel betrayed and confused and to regard the police as not only coercive but also hypocritical.

As this chapter has explored at some length, the prospects for improved police-community relations are not good. The essentially coercive nature of the police prevents them from being so, at least as long as there are men who violate the law and disturb the peace. Those who would seek to ameliorate police-community relations by concealing this bitter pill with a sugar coating of normative and remunerative power will find that their efforts not only have failed but have proved to be counterproductive as well. Unpleasant as it might be, there are times when bitter medicine must be taken. For those who would expand the nature of the police role to establish the limits of police discretion and to improve police-community relations, perhaps that time has arrived.

Notes

1. Alan Edward Bent, *The Politics of Law Enforcement* (Lexington, Mass.: Heath, 1974), pp. 2-5.
2. They employ approximately 508,000 men and women in some 40,000 separate police agencies and expend annually over $4,491,000,000. Michael J. Hindelang et al., *Sourcebook of Criminal Justice Statistics, 1973,* Law Enforcement Assistance Administration, U.S. Department of Justice (Washington, D.C.: Government Printing Office, 1973), pp. 30-31, 36-37.
3. Michael Lipsky, "Street-Level Bureaucracy and the Analysis of Urban Reform," *Urban Affairs Quarterly* 4, no. 4 (June 1971): 392.

4. President's Commission on Law Enforcement and Administration of Justice, *The Challenge of Crime in a Free Society* (Washington, D.C.: Government Printing Office, 1967), p. 91.
5. *Report of the National Advisory Commission on Civil Disorders* (New York: Bantam Books, 1968), p. 299.
6. Ibid.
7. See Tim C. Ryles and William H. Wilken, "Citizen Evaluations of the Police: Their Political Implications" (Paper delivered at the National Convention of the American Society for Public Administration, New York, N.Y., 1972).
8. Lipsky, "Street-Level Bureaucracy," p. 392.
9. Joseph R. Gusfield, "Moral Passage: The Symbolic Process of Public Designations of Deviants," in *Law and The Behavioral Sciences,* ed. L. Friedman and S. McCauley (Indianapolis: Bobbs-Merrill, 1969), p. 308. However, just as the police, to the extent that they symbolize the entire criminal justice system, are likely to be blamed for failures elsewhere in the system, so, too, the police, to the extent that they symbolize the authority of the entire society, are likely to become virtual "lightning rods" for public dissatisfaction with that society. In *Minorities and the Police: Confrontation in America* (New York: The Free Press, 1969), David H. Bayley and Harold Mendelsohn write: "Those who would ameliorate the relations between the police and minorities must also realize that it may not be within the power of the police to do much more than palliate the situation, no matter how heroic their efforts to change. In order to produce better police-community relations, changes in police behavior and practice must be one part of a program touching all those aspects of human interaction which create minority status. For the police will continue to function as a lightning rod for minority discontent so long as they must enforce laws created by a community with which minority people only imperfectly identify" (p. 142).
10. See Jesse Rubin, "Police Identity and the Police Role," in *The Police and the Community,* ed. Robert F. Steadman (Baltimore: The Johns Hopkins University Press, 1972), pp. 23-25.
11. Ramsey Clark, *Crime in America: Observations on its Nature, Causes, Prevention and Control* (New York: Simon and Schuster, 1971), p. 139.
12. David C. Perry and Paula A. Sornoff, "Politics at the Street Level: The Select Case of Police Administration and the Community" (Paper delivered at the Annual Meeting of the American Political Science Association, Washington, D.C., 1972), p. 13.
13. See James Q. Wilson, *Varieties of Police Behavior: The Management of Law and Order in Eight Communities* (Cambridge, Mass.: Harvard University Press, 1968), p. 7.
14. Ibid. Emphasis in the original.

15. Bent, *The Politics of Law Enforcement*, p. 4.
16. Albert J. Reiss, Jr., *The Police and the Public* (New Haven, Conn.: Yale University Press, 1971), pp. 179-180. See also Elmer H. Johnson, "Police: An Analysis of Role Conflict," *Police,* January-February 1970, pp. 50-51.
17. This comment is not meant to suggest that the complete and total rule of law is either possible or desirable. See Kenneth Culp Davis's critique of "the extravagant version of the rule of law," in Davis, *Discretionary Justice: A Preliminary Inquiry* (Baton Rouge: Louisiana State University Press, 1969), pp. 28-33, 36-39.
18. National Advisory Commission on Criminal Justice Standards and Goals, *Report on Police* (Washington, D.C.: Government Printing Office, 1973), p. 21. See also William C. Louthan, "Paradigms of Police Community: A New Critique of Legal Order," *Public Administration Review* 34, no. 3 (May-June 1975): 296-299.
19. See Alan E. Bent and Ralph A. Rossum, *Police, Criminal Justice, and the Community* (New York: Harper & Row, 1976), p. 260.
20. Bernard L. Garmire, "The Police Role in an Urban Society," in *The Police and the Community,* ed. Steadman, p. 2.
21. Ibid., pp. 2-3.
22. Arthur Niederhoffer, *Behind the Shield: The Police in Urban Society* (Garden City, N.Y.: Doubleday, 1967), p. 1.
23. Richard H. Ward, "The Police Role: A Case of Diversity," *Journal of Criminology, Criminal Law and Police Science,* December 1970, pp. 581-582.
24. Amitai Etzioni, *A Comparative Analysis of Complex Organizations: On Power, Involvement, and Their Correlates* (New York: The Free Press, 1961), p. 7.
25. See Leonard Ruchelman, "Police Policy," *Policy Studies Journal* 3, no. 1 (Autumn 1974): 48-53. "Until we come up with a clearer understanding of what we expect our police to do, effective standards of police performance will continue to hang under a cloud of ambiguity" (p. 49).
26. Jerome H. Skolnick, *Justice Without Trial: Law Enforcement in Democratic Society* (New York: Wiley, 1966), p. 9.
27. As Skolnick observes, "Law is not merely an instrument of order, but may frequently be its adversary." *Justice Without Trial,* p. 7. For a discussion others of the distinction between law enforcement and order maintenance, see Michael Banton, *The Policeman in the Community* (New York: Basic Books, 1964), pp. 6-7 and Wilson, *Varieties of Police Behavior,* pp. 16-17.
28. For others who treat these two functions as one, see Ivan Gabor and Christopher Low, "The Police Role in the Community," *Criminology,* 10, no. 4 (February 1973): 385-389; Garmire, "The Police Role in an Urban Society," pp. 2-7; and National Advisory Commission on Criminal Justice Standards and Goals, *Report on Police,* p. 12.

29. Garmire, "The Police Role in an Urban Society," p. 4. See also Garmire's catalog of the essential tasks in law enforcement and order maintenance in "Understanding Others: The Police and the Citizen," in *Police and Community Relations: A Sourcebook,* ed. A.F. Brandstatter and Louis A. Radelet (Beverly Hills, Calif.: Glencoe Press, 1968), p. 233.
30. Jesse Rubin, "Police Identity and the Police Role," p. 32.
31. William A. Westley, "Violence and the Police," *American Journal of Sociology* 59 (1953).
32. See Bent and Rossum, *Police, Criminal Justice, and the Community,* pp. 6-8, and Wilson, *Varieties of Police Behavior,* pp. 17-18.
33. Order maintenance functions may be more mundane than crime fighting activities, but they are often no less dangerous. Domestic quarrels are especially dangerous; 22 percent of all police fatalities occur during investigations of altercations between husband and wife or parent and child. See Suzanne K. Steinmetz, "The Family Is Cradle of Violence," *Social Science and Modern Society* 10, no. 6 (September-October 1973): 51.
34. Ray J. Blackmore, "The Law Enforcement Image: A Partnership with the Community," in *Police Yearbook* (Washington, D.C.: International Association of Chiefs of Police, 1964), pp. 227-230. Thus, A.C. Germann in "Community Policing: An Assessment," *Journal of Criminology, Criminal Law and Police Science,* March 1969, pp. 89-96, suggests that police officers should be renamed "human affairs officers," "public welfare officers," "public service officers," or "human relations officers." See also Bruce J. Terris, "The Role of the Police," *The Annals of the American Academy of Political and Social Science* 374 (November 1967): 58-69.
35. "Patrol officers should encourage negotiation . . . rather than rely exclusively on the coercive power of the police." Robert Wasserman, Michael Paul Gardner, and Alana S. Cohen, *Improving Police-Community Relations: A Prescriptive Package,* Law Enforcement Assistance Administration, U.S. Department of Justice (Washington, D.C.: Government Printing Office, 1973), p. 29. This view is in keeping with David J. Bordua's assessment that American society is shifting "away from coercion as a means of social control." Bordua, "Comments on Police-Community Relations," in *Police-Community Relations,* ed. Paul F. Cromwell, Jr., and George Keefer (St. Paul: West, 1973), p. 53. See also Police Chief James C. Parsons, "Police-Community Relations: A Candid Analysis of the Problem" (unpublished paper, Birmingham, Ala., 1972), who contends that police must "encourage more supportive services to offset problems created by [the] coercive role inherent in police work."
36. See Johnson, "Police: An Analysis of Role Conflict," pp. 49-50.
37. See Garmire, "The Police Role in an Urban Society," pp. 4-5.
38. See Donald F. Norris, *Police-Community Relations* (Lexington, Mass.: Heath, 1973), pp. 2, 122.

39. *The Challenge of Crime in a Free Society,* p. 98. We shall have more to say on this important consideration later.
40. Bordua, "Comments on Police-Community Relations," pp. 75-79. See note 68 below.
41. *The Challenge of Crime in a Free Society,* p. 98.
42. Wasserman et al., *Improving Police-Community Relations,* p. 55.
43. Ibid.
44. Bordua, "Comments on Police-Community Relations," p. 78. See also Bent and Rossum, *Police, Criminal Justice, and the Community,* pp. 309-311, 324-325.
45. James Q. Wilson, "The Police in the Ghetto," in *The Police and the Community,* ed. Steadman, p. 81.
46. *Report on Police,* p. 12. Also, "The fundamental purpose of the police throughout America is crime prevention through law enforcement" (p. 13).
47. *The Challenge of Crime in a Free Society,* pp. 97-98. The following discussion relies heavily on this source.
48. Thus, as Jesse Rubin observes in "Police Identity and the Police Role": "There are no built-in rewards for good performance as a peacekeeper. Pats on the back, compliments about doing a good job, and other verbal and nonverbal rewards from the peer, supervisory, or command levels rarely follow the successful completion of a peacekeeping or community-service activity" (p. 26).
49. See Ruchelman, "Police Policy," pp. 50-51.
50. Reiss, *The Police and the Public,* p. 46. Emphasis in the original.
51. Ibid., pp. 48-62. Reiss concludes that "citizens who behave antagonistically toward the police are more likely to be treated in a hostile, authoritarian, or belittling manner by the police than citizens who behave with civility or who extend deference" (p. 52).
52. Garmire, "The Police Role in an Urban Society," pp. 4-5.
53. For discussions of role conflict, see James S. Campbell, Joseph R. Sahid, and David P. Stang, *Law and Order Reconsidered,* a Staff Report to the National Commission on the Causes and Prevention of Violence (Washington, D.C.: Government Printing Office, 1969), pp. 290-292; Garmire, "The Police Role in an Urban Society," p. 3; Rubin, "Police Identity and the Police Role," pp. 20-24; and Johnson, "Police," pp. 47-52.
54. Campbell et al., *Law and Order Reconsidered,* p. 290.
55. See Bent and Rossum, *Police, Criminal Justice, and the Community,* pp. 81-82. See also Rubin, "Police Identity and the Police Role," pp. 26-29.
56. Joseph Wambaugh, *The New Centurions* (New York: Dell, 1970), p. 161. Emphasis in the original. For a further discussion of this "isolation syndrome," see Banton, *The Policeman in the Community:* "Couple this experience of the public with the policeman's feeling that in his social life he is a pariah, scorned by citizens who are more respectable but no more

honest, and it need surprise no one that the patrolman's loyalties to his department and his colleagues are often stronger than those to the wider society" (p. 170).
57. The efforts of some to impose external control on the police through such means as citizen review boards have contributed greatly to this conviction. See Campbell et al., *Law and Order Reconsidered,* pp. 293-295.
58. Bent and Rossum, *Police, Criminal Justice, and the Community,* p. 277. See also Hervey A. Juris and Peter Feuille, *The Impact of Police Unions: Summary Report,* U.S. Department of Justice, Law Enforcement Assistance Administration (Washington, D.C.: Government Printing Office, 1973), pp. 9-13.
59. Louis A. Radelet, *The Police in the Community* (Beverly Hills, Calif.: Glencoe Press, 1973), p. 492; and James Q. Wilson, *Thinking about Crime* (New York: Basic Books, 1975), p. 105. Niederhoffer found that 72 percent of those New York police officers he questioned believe that newspapers "seem to enjoy giving an unfavorable slant to news concerning the police" *(Behind the Shield,* p. 234).
60. See James Q. Wilson, "The Police and Their Problems: A Theory," *Public Policy,* no. 12 (1963), pp. 189-216. "The awareness that he is viewed with hostility and judged in terms of inconsistent standards can, unless other factors intervene, lead a policeman to believe that he has chosen an occupation that sets him apart from others. Even during off-duty hours, he is rarely allowed to forget he is a policeman—even if by nothing more than the joking remarks of his friends."
61. For further discussions of "the pariah feelings" that police officers experience, see James Q. Wilson, "The Police and Their Problems"; Banton, *The Policeman in the Community,* p. 170; and William Westley, "Violence and the Police," *American Journal of Sociology* 59 (July 1953): 34-41.
62. See Paul K. Hatt and C. North, "Prestige Ratings of Occupations," in *Man, Work, and Society,* ed. Sigmund Nosow and William H. Form (New York: Basic Books, 1962), pp. 277-283.
63. See Robert W. Hodge, Paul N. Siegel, and Peter H. Rossi, "Occupational Prestige in the United States, 1925-1963," *American Journal of Sociology* 70 (1964): 291.
64. It should be observed, however, that not all police officers enjoy such low occupational prestige. When the positions of police captain and lieutenant are included in the list of occupations separate from that of patrolman, they end up near the top of the status scale, not very far behind the level of the professions. See Niederhoffer, *Behind the Shield,* pp. 23-24. However, see Bent, *The Politics of Law Enforcement,* p. 100, where the total civilian sample in Memphis, Tennessee, ranked patrolmen higher than detectives in terms of occupational prestige.
65. Richard N. Harris, *The Police Academy, The Inside View* (New York: Wiley, 1973), p. 3.

66. Harlan Hahn, "The Public and the Police: A Theoretical Perspective," in *Police in Urban Society,* ed. Harlan Hahn (Beverly Hills, Calif.: Sage Publications, 1971), p. 26.
67. See *Report on Police,* pp. 469-473; *Task Force Report: The Police,* pp. 28-35.
68. The ombudsman is an institution that originated in Scandinavia. Whether one person or an office, the ombudsman is empowered to gain redress against administrative abuse. See Stanley V. Anderson, ed., *Ombudsmen for American Government?* (Englewood Cliffs, N.J.: Prentice-Hall, 1968). Within that volume, see especially William B. Gwyn, "Transfering the Ombudsmen," pp. 37-69, and Stanley V. Anderson, "Proposals and Politics," pp. 136-155.
69. Wilson, "The Police in the Ghetto," p. 53.
70. Michael J. Hindelang et al., *Sourcebook of Criminal Justice Statistics,* Law Enforcement Assistance Administration, U.S. Department of Justice (Washington, D.C.: Government Printing Office, 1973), p. 132.
71. American Institute of Public Opinion, Study No. 749.
72. Lewis Harris & Associates, Study No. 2,043.
73. American Institute of Public Opinion, Study No. 861. Emphasis in the original.
74. American Institute of Public Opinion, Study No. 841. This was reflected in a 1973 Gallup Poll that revealed that 73 percent of the people believe that the courts do not deal harshly enough with criminals. See Hazel Erskine, "The Polls: Causes of Crime," *Public Opinion Quarterly* 38, no. 2 (Summer 1974): 294.
75. Wilson, "The Police in the Ghetto," p. 61.
76. Ibid.
77. Jack L. Kuykendall, "Police and Minority Groups: Toward a Theory of Negative Contacts," *Police* 15, no. 1 (September-October 1970): 53-54.
78. See Gary L. McDowell and Rosemary Hogan, "Perceptions of the Criminal Justice System: The Memphis Study," Institute of Governmental Studies and Research, Memphis State University, *Public Affairs Forum* 4, no. 3 (January 1975), who found that black high school age respondents view the police and the administration of police services with much less favor than do white high school age respondents. See also John Moland, Jr., "Application of the Likert Scaling Technique to Black and White Perceptions of Police Behavior" (Paper delivered at the Annual Meeting of the American Political Science Association, New Orleans, 1973), who found that white respondents and older respondents perceive police behavior as less abusive than blacks and younger respondents.
79. See Reiss, *The Police and the Public,* pp. 102-111.
80. See Terris, "The Role of the Police," p. 61.

81. Skolnick, *Justice Without Trial*, p. 45.
82. Clayton A. Hartjen, "Police Citizen Encounters: Social Order in Interpersonal Interaction," *Criminology* 10, no. 1 (May 1972): 72-77.
83. Garmire, "The Police Role in an Urban Society," p. 6.
84. Ibid., p. 8.
85. Bent and Rossum, *Police, Criminal Justice, and the Community*, p. 368.
86. Wilson, "The Police in the Ghetto," p. 69. See also James Baldwin, *Nobody Knows My Name* (New York: Dell, 1962): "The only way to police a ghetto is to be oppressive" (p. 61).
87. See, for example, Niederhoffer, *Behind the Shield*, pp. 109-161; and Algernon D. Black, *The People and the Police* (New York: McGraw-Hill, 1968), pp. 6-7.
88. Robert W. Balch, "The Police Personality: Fact or Fiction?" *Journal of Criminology, Criminal Law, and Police Science*, March 1972, pp. 106-119.
89. See Bayley and Mendelsohn, *Minorities and the Police*, pp. 14-30.
90. Balch, "The Police Personality," pp. 114-115, and Bent and Rossum, *Police, Criminal Justice, and the Community*, pp. 73-85.
91. Bent, *The Politics of Law Enforcement*, p. 99.
92. Ibid., p. 16.
93. See New Haven Police Chief James F. Ahern, *Police in Trouble, Our Frightening Crisis in Law Enforcement* (New York: Hawthorn Books, 1972): "Some [police officers] said they believe police work to be honorable, reliable and steady. A few admitted the attraction of a secure pension at the end of twenty-five years of service. But none admitted that they wanted exciting jobs. None admitted that they wanted action and were willing to take certain risks to get it. None admitted that they were eager to put themselves against people who had committed criminal offenses and had challenged society to deal with them if they could. But this is why most of them become cops" (pp. 4-5).
94. For a discussion of preconventional, conventional, and postconventional morality, see Edward C. Banfield, *The Unheavenly City* (Boston, Little, Brown, 1970), p. 161. See also Banfield, *The Unheavenly City Revisited* (Boston: Little, Brown, 1974), p. 182.
95. Balch, "The Police Personality," pp. 109-110.
96. Bent, *The Politics of Law Enforcement*, p. 105.
97. Bayley and Mendelsohn, *Minorities and the Police*, pp. 144-147.
98. Balch, "The Police Personality," p. 117.
99. President's Commission on Law Enforcement and Administration of Justice, *Task Force Report: The Police* (Washington, D.C.: Government Printing Office, 1967), p. 125.
100. See Charles B. Saunders, Jr., *Upgrading the American Police: Education and Training for Better Law Enforcement* (Washington, D.C.: The Brookings Institution, 1970), pp. 40-48.

101. Ibid., p. 41.
102. Ibid., p. 42.
103. *Task Force Report: The Police*, p. 129.
104. Saunders, *Upgrading the American Police*, p. 42. See also Melany E. Baehr, David R. Saunders, Ernest C. Froemal, and John E. Furcon, "The Prediction of Performance for Black and for White Patrolmen," *Professional Psychology* 2, no. 1 (Winter 1971): 46-57.
105. *Task Force Report: The Police*, p. 126.
106. *Report on Police*, p. 369. See also Larry T. Hoover, *Police Educational Characteristics and Curricula*, U.S. Department of Justice (Washington, D.C.: Government Printing Office, 1975).
107. Saunders, *Upgrading the American Police*, p. 89.
108. Bernard Cohen and Jan M. Chaihen, *Police Background Characteristics and Performance: Summary* (New York: Rand Institute, 1972).
109. Melany E. Baehr et al. *Psychological Assessment of Patrolman Qualifications in Relation to Field Performance* (Washington, D.C.: Government Printing Office, 1968).
110. See David Patrick Geary, "College Educated Cops—Three Years Later," *Police Chief,* August 1970. Increased educational requirements also tend to minimize interface problems, at least between the police and the judiciary. Thus, Ferinez Phelps has found that police officers' perceptions of the role of the trial judge improve with greater education. Likewise, he has found that the more education an officer has, the less likely he is to believe that the police are hindered by the exclusionary rule. See Phelps, "The Policeman's Perception of the Role of the Trial Judge" (Paper delivered at the Annual Meeting of the Southwestern Political Science Association, San Antonio, Texas, 1975).
111. *Report on Police*, p. 335.
112. Ibid, p. 334. See also *Task Force Report: The Police*, p. 130.
113. *Task Force Report: The Police*, p. 122. The division of police functions between the complex and the menial is not to be confused with the division of police functions between law enforcement and community service that is discussed above. The two proposals are somewhat related, however, as the subsequent discussion will establish.
114. The mean annual base salary for entering patrolmen was $9,523 and the mean annual base salary for patrolmen receiving maximum compensation was $11,438. Carol A. Pigeon, *Personnel, Compensation, and Expenditures in Police, Fire, and Refuse Collection and Disposal Departments,* Urban Data Services Reports, vol. 7, no. 4 (Washington, D.C.: International City Management Association, April 1975), p. 3. These figures were up by $700 to $900 over 1974 figures. See David Lewin, *Expenditure, Compensation, and Employment Data in Police, Fire, and Refuse Collection and Disposal Departments,* Urban Data Services Reports, vol. 6, no. 9

(Washington, D.C.: International City Management Association, September, 1974), p. 4. See also *Report on Police,* p. 357.
115. See Committee for Economic Development, *Reducing Crime and Assuring Justice* (New York: Committee for Economic Development, 1972), pp. 32-33.
116. Samuel G. Chapman, "Developing Personnel Leadership," *Police Chief* 33 (March 1966): 24.
117. See Ford Foundation, *Law and Justice* (New York: Ford Foundation, 1974), p. 13.
118. 401 U.S. 424 (1971). However, see also *Washington* v. *Davis,* 426 U.S. 229 (1976), in which Justice Stewart held for a seven member majority that a law is not unconstitutional solely because it has a racially disproportionate impact.
119. 401 U.S. at 431. Mr. Justice Brennan did not participate in this unanimous decision.
120. Ibid., p. 436.
121. Ibid., p. 432.
122. See, for example, Cheryl G. Swanson and Charles D. Hale, "A Question of Height Revisited: Assaults on Police," *Journal of Police Science and Administration* 3, no. 2 (June 1975), pp. 183-188, wherein the authors review statistics that show taller officers are, in fact, assaulted more frequently than are shorter officers.
123. Many states have statutes that prohibit individuals convicted of felonies from being employed by the state or any of its political subdivisions. See, for example, *Tennessee Code Annotated,* 40-2714: "Every person convicted of a felony and sentenced to the penitentiary, except for manslaughter, is also disqualified for holding any office under the State." The Tennessee Supreme Court held that this language pertained to police officers in *State ex rel Harvey* v. *Knoxville,* 166 Tenn. 550, 64 S.W. (2d) 7 (1933). Nonetheless, successful police applicants may previously have been charged and convicted of misdemeanors. Moreover, because many misdemeanor convictions have been plea-bargained down from felony offenses, this still represents a substantial erosion to standards of moral character.
124. *Griggs* v. *Duke Power Company,* 401 U.S. at 431.
125. *Green* v. *County School Board of New Kent County,* 391 U.S. 430, 437-438 (1968).
126. 401 U.S. at 430-431.
127. 490 F. 2d 9 (1st Cir. 1973).
128. *United States* v. *Jefferson County Board of Education,* 372 F. 2d 836, 876 (5th Cir., 1966). See also *Norwalk CORE* v. *Norwalk Redevelopment Agency,* 395 F. 2d 920, 931, 932 (2d Cir. 1968).
129. See, for example, Brief for the Board of Governors of Rutgers, the State University of New Jersey, and the Student Bar Association of Rutgers

THE POLICE

School of Law at Newark as Amicae Curiae at 12, *DeFunis* v. *Odegaard,* 416 U.S. 312 (1974). See also Ralph A. Rossum, "Ameliorative Racial Preference and the Fourteenth Amendment: Some Constitutional Problems," *Journal of Politics* 38, no. 2 (May 1976): 346-366.
130. See Etzioni, *A Comparative Analysis of Complex Organizations,* pp. 201-232.
131. Quoted in Saunders, *Upgrading the American Police,* p. 117.
132. There are, of course, exceptions to this general finding. Thus, both Chicago and Los Angeles provide 1,040 hours of training; Richmond, Virginia, provides a 16-week live-in preservice training program, as does the Michigan State Police; Dayton, Ohio, provides 960 hours of training; and Dade County, Florida, provides 949 hours. *Report on Police,* p. 393.
133. Ibid., p. 380.
134. Ibid., p. 392.
135. Ibid., p. 404.
136. See, for example, Thomas F. Coon, "Law Enforcement Technology Welcomes the 'Chopper Copper,'" *Police* 13 (May-June 1969): 6-8: "Law enforcement does not want to be left at the post and its hopes for professionalization revolve a good deal around expertise in the areas of technological enforcement." See also Kent W. Colton, *Computers and the Police: Police Departments and the New Information Technology,* Urban Data Service Reports, vol. 6, no. 11 (Washington, D.C.: International City Management Association, November 1974).
137. Robert H. Scott, "Problems in Communication and Cooperation in the Administration of Criminal Justice," in *Police and Community Relations: A Sourcebook,* ed. Brandstatter and Radelet, p. 430.
138. See Phelps, "The Policeman's Perception of the Role of the Trial Judge," p. 33.
139. Bernard C. Brannon, "Professional Development of Law Enforcement Personnel," in *Police and Community Relations: A Sourcebook,* ed. Brandstatter and Radelet, pp. 311-315.
140. Ahern, *Police in Trouble,* p. 225.
141. Garmire, "The Police Role in an Urban Society," p. 9.
142. Committee for Economic Development, *Reducing Crime and Assuring Justice,* p. 30.
143. The President's Commission on Law Enforcement and Administration of Justice also agrees: "A fundamental problem confronting law enforcement today is that of fragmented crime repression efforts resulting from the large number of uncoordinated local government and law enforcement agencies. . . . Formal cooperation or consolidation is an essential ingredient in improving the quality of law enforcement." *Task Force Report: The Police,* p. 68.
144. Robert L. Bish and Vincent Ostrom, *Understanding Urban Government:*

Metropolitan Reform Reconsidered (Washington, D.C.: American Enterprise Institute for Public Policy Research, 1973), p. 10.
145. Ibid.
146. Elinor Ostrom, Roger B. Parks, and Gordon P. Whitaker, "Do We Really Want to Consolidate Urban Police Forces? A Reappraisal of Some Old Assertions," *Public Administration Review* 33, no. 5 (September-October 1973): 430.
147. For a discussion of the two-tier approach, see Joseph F. Zimmerman, "Metropolitan Reform in the U.S.: An Overview," *Public Administration Review* 30, no. 5 (September-October 1970): 531-543.
148. For a further discussion of these themes, see Alan E. Bent and Ralph A. Rossum, eds., *Urban Administration: Management, Politics, and Change* (New York: Dunellen, 1976), chap. 6.
149. "Police departments in metropolitan areas should consider consolidation for greater efficiency." Earl F. Morris, "The Police and the Community: A Lawyer's View," *F.B.I. Law Enforcement Bulletin,* May 1968, p. 4. See also Ahern, *Police in Trouble,* pp. 225-226.
150. *Task Force Report: The Police,* pp. 52-56.
151. See George P. Barbour, Jr., and Stanley M. Wolfson, "Productivity Measurement in Police Crime Control," *Public Management,* April 1973, pp. 16-19. See also George P. Barbour, Jr., "Measuring Local Governmental Productivity," *The Municipal Yearbook–1973* (Washington, D.C.: International City Management Association, 1973), pp. 39-44.
152. As Barbour and Wolfson observe: "If policemen, individually or by departments, are rated by the number of arrests per employee, this may lead to excessive pressure to make arrests, even in instances where justice and order are better served by avoiding arrest (as in family crisis intervention)." "Productivity Measurement in Police Crime Control," p. 18.
153. Ibid., p. 19.
154. *Report on Police,* pp. 151-152.
155. Barbour and Wolfson, "Productivity Measurement in Police Crime Control," p. 19.
156. Max Weber, "Bureaucracy," in *Max Weber, Essays in Sociology,* trans. and ed. H.H. Gerth and C. Wright Mills (New York: Oxford University Press, 1958), p. 214.
157. Ibid.
158. Ibid., p. 228.
159. Ibid., pp. 228-229.
160. Ibid., p. 230. See also Reiss, *The Police and the Public:* "All bureaucracies, then, pose problems for the exercise of professional discretion. These problems are exacerbated for the police, who, in a command bureaucracy, are expected to obey the rules and follow the orders of superiors and, at the same time, to exercise their professional discretion. In other words, a

typical line policeman is expected both to adhere to commands and be held responsible for all discretion exercised in the line of duty" (p. 124).
161. See Ostrom et al., "Do We Really Want to Consolidate Urban Police Forces?" p. 430. Ostrum and her colleagues conclude that high degrees of specialization and professionalization are not required for effective police services as perceived by the public.
162. See Wilson, "The Police in the Ghetto," pp. 69-70.
163. Gabor and Low, "The Police Role in the Community," p. 397. Police departments are not the only public agencies to experience increasing separation from the community they serve as they become more professional. See, for example, the effects of professionalization on welfare agencies as presented in Frances Fox Piven and Richard A. Cloward, *Regulating the Poor: The Functions of Public Welfare* (New York: Pantheon Books, 1971), p. 176; and Gilbert Steiner, *Welfare Options and Welfare Politics* (Washington, D.C.: The Brookings Institution, 1969), p. 14.
164. James Q. Wilson, "Police Morale, Reform, and Citizen Respect: The Chicago Case," in *The Police: Six Sociological Essays,* ed. David J. Bordua (New York: Wiley, 1967), pp. 159-160. See also Elinor Ostrom, "The Design of Institutional Arrangements and the Responsiveness of the Police," in *People vs. Government: The Responsiveness of American Institutions,* ed. Leroy N. Rieselbach (Bloomington: Indiana University Press, 1975), pp. 276-284.

Bibliography

Ahern, James E. *Police in Trouble: A Frightening Crisis in Law Enforcement.* New York: Hawthorn, 1972.

Balch, Robert W. "The Police Personality: Fact or Fiction?" *Journal of Criminology, Criminal Law, and Police Science,* March 1972, pp. 106-119.

Banton, Michael. *The Police in the Community.* New York: Basic Books, 1964.

Barbour, George P., Jr., and Wolfson, Stanley M. "Productivity Measurement in Police Crime Control." *Public Management,* April 1973.

Bayley, David H., and Mendelsohn, Harold. *Minorities and the Police: Confrontation in America.* New York: The Free Press, 1969.

Bent, Alan Edward. *The Politics of Law Enforcement: Conflict and Power in Urban Communities.* Lexington, Mass.: Heath, 1974.

Bent, Alan Edward, and Rossum, Ralph A., eds. *Urban Administration: Management, Politics, and Change.* New York: Dunellen, 1976.

Bish, Robert L., and Ostrom, Vincent. *Understanding Urban Government: Metropolitan Reform Reconsidered.* Washington, D.C.: American Enterprise Institute for Public Policy Research, 1973.

Black, Algernon D. *The People and the Police.* New York: McGraw-Hill, 1968.

Brandstatter, A. F., and Radelet, Louis A., eds. *Police and Community Relations: A Sourcebook.* Beverly Hills, Calif.: Glencoe Press, 1968.

Cohen, Bernard, and Chaiken, Jan M. *Police Background Characteristics and Performance: Summary.* New York: Rand Institute, 1972.

Cromwell, Paul F., Jr., and Keefer, George, eds. *Police-Community Relations.* St. Paul: West, 1973.

Davis, Kenneth Culp. *Police Discretion.* St. Paul: West, 1975.

Hahn, Harlan, ed. *Police in Urban Society.* Beverly Hills, Calif. Sage Publications, 1971.

Kuykendall, Jack L. "Police and Minority Groups: Toward a Theory of Negative Contacts." *Police* 15, no. 1 (September-October 1970).

Lipsky, Michael. "Street-Level Bureaucracy and the Analysis of Urban Reform." *Urban Affairs Quarterly* 6, no. 4 (June 1971).

National Advisory Commission on Criminal Justice Standards and Goals. *Report on Police.* Washington, D.C.: Government Printing Office, 1973.

Niederhoffer, Arthur. *Behind the Shield: The Police in Urban Society.* Garden City, N.Y.: Doubleday, 1969.

Ostrom, Elinor, Parks, Robert B., and Whitaker, Gordon P. "Do We Really Want to Consolidate Urban Police Forces? A Reappraisal of Some Old Assertions." *Public Administration Review* 33, no. 5 (September-October 1973): 423-432.

Perry, David C. *Police in the Metropolis.* Columbus, Ohio: Merrill, 1975.

President's Commission on Law Enforcement and Administration of Justice. *Task Force Report: The Police.* Washington, D.C.: Government Printing Office, 1967.

Reiss, Albert J., Jr. *The Police and the Public.* New Haven, Conn.: Yale University Press, 1971.

Rossum, Ralph A. "Ameliorative Racial Preference and the Fourteenth Amendment: Some Constitutional Problems." *The Journal of Politics* 38, no. 2 (May 1976): 346-366.

Ruchelman, Leonard. "Police Policy." *Policy Studies Journal* 3, no. 1 (Autumn 1974): 48-53.

Saunders, Charles B., Jr. *Upgrading the American Police: Education and Training for Better Law Enforcement.* Washington D.C.: The Brookings Institution, 1970.

Skolnick, Jerome H. *Justice Without Trial: Law Enforcement in Democratic Society.* New York: Wiley, 1966.

Steadman, Robert F., ed. *The Police and the Community.* Baltimore: Johns Hopkins University Press, 1972.

Westley, William. *Violence and the Police: A Sociological Study of Law, Custom, and Morality.* Cambridge, Mass.: M.I.T. Press, 1970.

Wilson, James Q. "Police Morale, Reform, and Citizen Respect: The Chicago Case." In *The Police: Six Sociological Essays,* ed. by David J. Bordua.

New York: Wiley, 1967.
——. "The Police and Their Problems: A Theory." *Public Policy,* no. 12 (1963), pp. 189-216.
——. *Thinking About Crime.* New York: Basic Books, 1975.
——. *Varieties of Police Behavior: The Management of Law and Order in Eight Communities.* Cambridge, Mass.: Harvard University Press, 1968.

THE SUPREME COURT, THE CONSTITUTION, AND CRIMINAL PROCEDURE

The courts constitute that component of the criminal justice system charged with a twofold responsibility: They are both participants in the criminal process and supervisors of its practice. As participants, they are instrumental in determining the guilt or innocence of those accused of crime and imposing appropriate sanctions. As supervisors, they act as guardians of the requirements of the Constitution and statutory law. Thus, when the practices of the criminal justice system, and especially the police, come into conflict with other values in the society, the courts in their supervisory role must determine which takes precedence over the other. In recent years, the courts, and especially the U.S. Supreme Court, have generally determined that those values reflected in the Constitution must take precedence over the efficient administration of criminal justice.

Compliance analysis has already been helpful in explaining why these dual roles have led to extensive interface problems;[1] in addition, however, it is also of great utility in evaluating in what manner and how satisfactorily the courts have discharged their twofold responsibility. Thus, of the three components of the criminal justice system, the courts, especially in their supervisory capacity, depend completely upon the exercise of normative power. As *Federalist* No. 78 observes, they have neither the power of the sword (coercion) nor the power of the purse (remuneration) but only that of judgment.[2] How well the courts exercise this normative power of judgment will in large part determine how successful they will be in checking the dominance of coercive and remunerative power (that is, police and corrections) and ensuring that those values reflected in the Constitution and statutory law continue to take precedence over the efficient administration of justice. Consequently, the next two chapters will explore the courts' exercise of judgment in the realm of criminal procedure. This chapter will critically examine how adequately the U.S. Supreme Court has given meaning and substance to those values found in the Constitution, especially the Bill of Rights. Chapter 5 will then go on to assess to what extent the Supreme Court has been able to translate these normative requirements into reality not only in the lower courts themselves as they participate in the criminal process and supervise its practices but also in the other components of the criminal justice system as well.

The Constitution and Criminal Procedure

The protection of criminal procedural rights receives a special emphasis in the U.S. Constitution. Thus, in the original document itself, there are seven provisions specifically addressed to this matter. Article I, Section 9, restricts the suspension of the privilege of the writ of habeas corpus "unless when in cases of rebellion or invasion the public safety may require it" and prohibits the passage of bills of attainder and ex post facto laws. Article II, Section 2, provides the president with the power to grant reprieves and pardons. Article III, Section 2, provides for trial by jury for "all crimes except in cases of impeachment" and further directs that the trial "shall be held in the state where the said crimes shall have been committed." Article III, Section 3, narrowly and precisely defines what shall constitute treason against the United States, and Article IV, Section 2, provides for extradition of criminal defendants.

The Bill of Rights places an even greater stress on criminal procedure. Of the twenty-three separate rights enumerated in the first eight amendments, thirteen are concerned with the treatment of criminal defendants. Thus, the Fourth Amendment guarantees the right of the people to be secure "in their persons, houses, papers, and effects," against unreasonable searches and seizures and prohibits the issuance of warrants without probable cause. The Fifth Amendment requires prosecution by indictment of a grand jury for commission of all "infamous crimes" (except in certain military cases) and prohibits placing a person "twice in jeopardy of life or limb" for the same offense or compelling him to be "a witness against himself." The Sixth Amendment lists several rights that apply "in all criminal prosecutions": the right to a speedy and public trial by an impartial jury of the state and district in which the crime has been committed; notice of the "nature and cause of the accusation"; confrontation of hostile witnesses; compulsory process for obtaining favorable witnesses; and assistance of counsel. The Eighth Amendment adds prohibitions against the imposition of excessive bails and fines and the infliction of cruel and unusual punishments. Finally, in addition to these specific guarantees, the Fifth Amendment adds the general prohibition against deprivation of life, liberty, or property without due process of law.

These provisions, however, are not self-defining, and, as a consequence, two major questions have arisen: (1) Are these Constitutional protections available to defendants in state as well as federal proceedings? (2) What, in fact, is the meaning or substance of some of these provisions? What, for example, makes a search or seizure "unreasonable"? What constitutes "probable cause"? What does it mean to be put "twice in jeopardy of life or limb," and what constitutes the "same" offense? What is a "speedy" trial? Does right to counsel mean right to court-appointed counsel for indigents? And, what is a "cruel and unusual punishment"? Amost all of these constitutional provisions are like so many empty vessels into which the courts, and especially the U.S. Supreme Court, have had to pour meaning. The remainder of this chapter will examine the meaning that the courts have poured into these provisions. More specifically, it will detail the current meaning or interpretation which the Supreme Court has given to each of the major constitutional protections in the realm of criminal procedure, and it will critically analyze the adequacy, validity, and reasonableness of these interpretations. After all, as Justice Felix Frankfurter observed, "the ultimate touchstone of constitutionality is the Constitution itself, and not what [the justices] have said about it,"[3] and interpretations of criminal procedural protections that depart from, or are inconsistent with, the overall intention of the Constitution itself are appropriately the objects of critical scrutiny.

The Fourteenth Amendment and the Bill of Rights

The first question that must be taken up when examining the Supreme Court's interpretation of these constitutional provisions pertaining to criminal procedure is the equal applicability of these provisions (whatever meaning the Court may subsequently give them) to state as well as federal proceedings. Obviously, those provisions spelled out in the original Constitution were intended to apply only to the federal government; but what about the subsequent provisions of the Bill of Rights? Are these protections of criminal procedure to apply to the states —where, after all, most criminal proceedings take place?[4] The initial answer to this question was provided by Chief Justice John Marshall in an 1833 decision in *Barron* v. *Baltimore*.[5] He declared that the first ten amendments to the U.S. Constitution were enacted as limitations solely upon the national government. Marshall's reasoning was on firm ground. After all, the opening sentence of the First Amendment begins with the phrase "Congress shall make no law," and nowhere in the subsequent provisions of the Bill of Rights are there to be found any limitations upon state action. And, as Marshall observed:

> Had the framers of these amendments intended them to be limitations on the powers of the state governments, they would have imitated the framers of the original Constitution, and have expressed that intention. Had Congress engaged in the extraordinary occupation of improving the constitutions of the several states by affording the people additional protection from the exercise of power by their own governments in matters which concerned themselves alone, they would have declared this purpose in plain and intelligible language.[6]

However, with the adoption of the Fourteenth Amendment in 1868, Marshall's ruling in *Barron* had to be reconsidered. Among the various provisions of that Amendment is the following: "No state shall . . . deprive any person of life, liberty, or property, without due process of law." The bearing of these words on state criminal procedure is unequivocal: States cannot deprive defendants, either charged with, or convicted of, crime, of life, liberty, or property without due process. However, the words themselves are ambiguous. What, after all, constitutes due process? Does it impose on the states the same restrictions the Bill of Rights imposes on the national government? Or, alternatively, does it impose either more lenient or more severe restrictions? From the onset, the Supreme Court has had to grapple with the relationship between the limitations imposed on the states by the Fourteenth Amendment's Due Process Clause and the limitations imposed upon the federal government by the first eight amendments. Three separate and distinct views of the appropriate relationship between these amendments have been advanced: the "fundamental rights" interpretation, total incorporation, and selective incorporation.

The "Fundamental Rights" Interpretation

The "fundamental rights" interpretation finds no necessary relationship between the Fourteenth Amendment and the guarantees of the Bill of Rights. Rather, it understands the Fourteenth Amendment as protecting "traditional notions" of due process, described variously by Justice Brown in *Holden* v. *Hardy* as those "certain immutable principles of justice which inhere in the very idea of free government which no member of the Union may disregard"[7] and by Justice Cardozo in *Palko* v. *Connecticut* as those principles "implicit in the concept of ordered liberty."[8] Applied to criminal procedure, the "fundamental rights" interpretation requires that a state grant the defendant "that fundamental fairness essential to the very concept of justice."[9] Although the Bill of Rights is regarded as a likely indicator of "fundamental fairness," it is not necessarily conclusive. As Justice Harlan observed in *Griswold* v. *Connecticut:* "The Due Process Clause of the Fourteenth Amendment stands in my opinion on its own bottom."[10]

Just as the "fundamental rights" interpretation of due process does not "impose upon the States all the requirements of the Bill of Rights," neither does it "restrict the reach of the Fourteenth Amendment" only to those rights enumerated in the first eight amendments.[11] Its concern is with fundamental fairness, not mere compliance with the Bill of Rights. Consequently, a state procedure may violate due process even though its operation is not contrary to any specific guarantee in the first eight amendments. For example, Justice Harlan, following this interpretation in his concurrence in *Estes* v. *Texas,* was able to declare unconstitutional the use of television in the courtroom even though he believed that practice was not contrary to the Sixth Amendment right to a "public trial by an impartial jury." The crucial question for him was whether this practice might prove to be so potentially prejudicial that it infringed upon the defendant's "fundamental right to a fair trial assured by the Due Process Clause of the Fourteenth Amendment."[12]

Critics of the "fundamental rights" interpretation contend that it fosters "subjective considerations of 'natural justice'" and, thereby, helps to promote an ad hoc, personal application of the Fourteenth Amendment.[13] Justice Black was chief among these critics. He dismissed it as nothing more than "natural law due process philosophy."[14] Based on this "mysterious and uncertain natural law concept,"[15] the "fundamental fairness" test was to him so imprecise a standard that it gave "unconfined power . . . to judges in our Constitution that is a written one in order to limit governmental power."[16] As he wrote in *Duncan* v. *Louisiana,* the "fundamental rights" interpretation "depends entirely on the particular judge's idea of ethics and morals instead of requiring him to depend on the boundaries fixed by the written words of the Constitution."[17] Supporters of this interpretation reply, however, that its application is not subjective but rests on a consensus of society that can be determined quite independently of the justice's personal views.[18] Various "objective" factors are available to the Court as it determines whether a particular procedural right has been traditionally recognized as an essential ingredient of fairness. Justice Curtis gave expression to two of these in *Murray's Lessee* v. *Hoboken Land and Improvement Company:* the significance attached to the right by the framers of the Constitution and the importance of the right as recognized by "those settled usages and modes of proceedings existing in the common and statute law of England, before the immigration of our ancestors, and which are shown not to have been unsuited to their civil and political conditions by having been acted on by them after the settlement of this country."[19] Two other objective factors also exist: the subsequent treatment of the right in state courts and legislatures and the significance attached to the right in other countries with similar jurisprudential traditions. Supporters of this interpretation note that although these factors do not provide "a mathematical calculus" for application of the Fourteenth Amendment, they go as far as is possible.[20] After all, as Justice Frankfurter observed:

> "Due Process," unlike some legal rules, is not a technical conception with a fixed content unrelated to time, place, and circumstances. Expressing as it does in its ultimate analysis respect enforced by law for that feeling of just treatment which has been evolved through centuries of Anglo-American constitutional history and civilization, "due process" cannot be imprisoned within the treacherous limits of any formula. Representing a profound attitude of fairness between man and man, and more particularly between the individual and the government, due process is compounded

of history, reason, the past course of decisions, and stout confidence in the strength of the democratic faith which we profess. Due process is not a mechanical instrument. It is not a yardstick. It is a process.[21]

The proponents of the "fundamental rights" interpretation appreciate that due process is neither "a technical conception" nor "a mechanical instrument." Moreover, they refuse to imprison due process "within the treacherous limits of any formula." Rather, they insist that a judgment be made on a case-by-case basis as to what due process requires. This interpretation, they continue, should prevail if for no other reason than this: that it is the only interpretation of the Fourteenth Amendment that, in fact, requires judges to engage in judgment—the activity that uniquely defines the behavior of a judge—rather than to adopt such simplistic surrogates for judgment as total or selective incorporation.

Total Incorporation

The second view of the relationship between the Fourteenth Amendment and the Bill of Rights is the "total incorporation" interpretation. Proponents of this view argue that the Fourteenth Amendment was intended simply and exclusively "to extend to all the people of the nation the complete protection of the Bill of Rights."[22] Not only do they believe that the legislative history and language of the amendment support total incorporation,[23] they also make the pragmatic argument that it avoids much of the subjectivity inherent in a "fundamental rights" approach by restricting the judges to the specific language of the Bill of Rights. As Justice Black observed:

> To pass upon the constitutionality of statutes by looking to the particular standards enumerated in the Bill of Rights and other parts of the Constitution is one thing; to invalidate statutes because of application of "natural law" deemed to be above and undefined by the Constitution is another. "In the one instance, courts proceed within clearly marked constitutional boundaries to seek to execute policies written into the Constitution; in the other, they roam at will in the limitless area of their own beliefs as to reasonableness and actually select policies, a responsibility which the Constitution entrusts to the legislative representatives of the people."[24]

Critics of total incorporation challenge these contentions. They argue that neither the legislative history nor the language of the amendment supports this view. Thus, for example, they point out that the Due Process Clause of the Fourteenth Amendment merely restates a single provision of the Fifth Amendment of the Bill of Rights. Reflecting on this fact in *Hurtado* v. *California,* an 1884 decision that concluded that the Fourteenth Amendment's Due Process

Clause did not require indictment by grand jury in state prosecutions, Justice Mathews observed:

> According to a recognized canon of interpretation, especially applicable to formal and solemn instruments of constitutional law, we are forbidden to assume, without clear reason to the contrary, that any part of . . . [the Fifth] Amendment is superfluous. The natural and obvious inference is, that in the sense of the Constitution, "due process of law" was not meant or intended to include . . . the institution and procedure of a grand jury in any case. The conclusion is equally irresistible, that when the same phrase was employed in the Fourteenth Amendment to restrain the action of the States, it was used in the same sense and with no greater extent; and that if in the adoption of that amendment it had been part of its purpose to perpetuate the institution of the grand jury in all the States, it would have embodied, as to the Fifth Amendment, express declaration to that effect.[25]

Critics of total incorporation also reject the notion that it avoids much of the subjectivity inherent in the "fundamental rights" approach. They criticize Justice Black—this interpretation's leading exponent—for merely shifting the focus of judicial inquiry from the flexible concept of fundamental fairness to equally flexible terms in the specific amendments. Thus, for example, they observe that such terms as "probable cause," "speedy and public trial," and "cruel and unusual punishments" are hardly self-defining and must be interpreted in light of the same contemporary notions of fairness that are considered in applying a "fundamental rights" standard.[26] As Justice Harlan chided Justice Black in *Griswold:* "'Specific' provisions of the Constitution, no less than 'due process' lend themselves readily to 'personal' interpretations by judges whose constitutional outlook is simply to keep the Constitution in supposed 'tune with the times.'"[27] To illustrate his point, Justice Harlan turned to *Wesberry* v. *Sanders,*[28] where Justice Black himself had interpreted the words "by the People" as found in Article I, Section 2, "to command 'one person, one vote,' an interpretation that was made in the face of irrefutable and still unanswered history to the contrary."[29] Finally, the critics of total incorporation argue that it imposes an undue burden on the states and deprives them of any opportunity to act as social and legal laboratories—experimenting with reforms designed to enhance the protections and freedom of the people.

Selective Incorporation

The "selective incorporation" interpretation is the third view of the appropriate relationship between the Fourteenth Amendment and the Bill of Rights. It combines aspects of both the "fundamental rights" and "total incorporation" interpretations. It accepts the basic premise of the "fundamental rights" interpretation that the Fourteenth Amendment encompasses all rights, substantive and procedural, that are "of the very essence of a scheme of ordered liberty."[30] It recognizes that not all rights enumerated in the Bill of Rights are fundamental and, moreover, that other rights may, in fact, be fundamental even though they are not specifically guaranteed in the Bill of Rights.[31] However, in determining whether an enumerated right is fundamental, this interpretation, like total incorporation, focuses on the total right guaranteed by the individual amendment and not merely on the element of that right before the Court or the application of that right in a particular case. In other words, once the Supreme Court has decided that a particular guarantee within the first eight amendments is fundamental, it incorporates that guarantee into the Fourteenth Amendment "whole and intact" and enforces it against the states in every case according to the same standards that it applies to the federal government.[32]

Proponents of selective incorporation contend that it represents an improvement over both other interpretations. Thus, they claim, a fundamental right should not be denied merely because the "totality of circumstances" in a particular case does not disclose "a denial of fundamental fairness." After all, they point out, judicial evaluation of the factual circumstances surrounding any particular case is often extremely subjective and discretionary. Moreover, they continue, selective incorporation avoids the rigidity and extremism of total incorporation. Thus, for example, they are not obliged to explain why the Seventh Amendment's right of trial by jury in all suits at common law in excess of $20.00 should not be incorporated. Critics respond, however, by charging that selective incorporation is an unacceptable compromise between the "fundamental rights" and "total incorporation" doctrines that is inconsistent with the logic and historical support of either. Proponents of total incorporation charge that it imports the same element of "natural law due process philosophy" as the "fundamental rights" doctrine. Proponents of fundamental rights, on the other hand, contend that selective incorporation fails to appreciate the special burdens it imposes on the administration of criminal justice at the state level. They fear that the imposition of a single standard regulating both state and federal practice will result in either the placing of an unrealistic "constitutional strait-jacket" on the states or a relaxing of standards as applied to both state and federal officials in order to meet the special problems of the states.[33]

Despite the shortcomings, however, selective incorporation has replaced the "fundamental rights" interpretation as the dominant view. Although Justice William Brennan advanced this doctrine for the first time in his 1961 dissent in *Cohen* v. *Hurley,* by 1963 it had the basic support of at least four justices. In addition, it was accepted by Justice Black, who, although he remained committed to total incorporation, accepted selective incorporation as a lesser evil than the "mysterious and uncertain law concepts" of the "fundamental rights" interpretation.[34] With this majority support, it has been instrumental in making the following Bill of Rights guarantees applicable to the states: protection against unreasonable searches and seizures and the right to have excluded from criminal trials any evidence obtained in violation thereof, *Mapp* v. *Ohio*;[35] the prohibition against compulsory self-incrimination, *Malloy* v. *Hogan*;[36] the guarantee against double jeopardy, *Benton* v. *Maryland*;[37] the right to assistance of counsel, *Gideon* v. *Wainwright*[38] and *Argersinger* v. *Hamlin*;[39] the right to a speedy trial, *Klopfer* v. *North Carolina*;[40] the right to a jury trial in nonpetty criminal cases, *Duncan* v. *Louisiana*;[41] the right to confront opposing witnesses, *Pointer* v. *Texas*;[42] the right to compulsory process for obtaining favorable witnesses, *Washington* v. *Texas*;[43] and the protection against "cruel and unusual punishments," *Robinson* v. *California*.[44] When the earlier cases of *In re Oliver*,[45] which incorporated the right to a "public" trial, and *Cole* v. *Arkansas*,[46] which required states to provide defendants with notice of the nature and cause of the accusation against them, are added to this list, the only remaining Bill of Rights guarantees directly related to criminal procedure that have not been held by the Supreme Court to apply to the states are the Eighth Amendment prohibition against excessive bail and the Fifth Amendment requirement of prosecution by grand jury indictment. Remarkably, the opportunity has never presented itself for the Supreme Court to rule on the prohibition against excessive bail, but it is generally assumed that this guarantee will be incorporated if the issue is squarely presented.[47] The Fifth Amendment requirement of grand jury indictment, on the other hand, was specifically held by the Court not to be guaranteed by the Fourteenth Amendment in the 1884 decision of *Hurtado* v. *California,* and that decision cotinues to be followed as valid precedent[48] (see Table 4.1).

On the basis of the "fundamental rights" interpretation and, more recently, through selective incorporation, the Supreme Court has come to hold that virtually all of the protections enumerated in the Bill of Rights are equally applicable in state as well as federal criminal prosecutions. But, what substantively is the meaning of these protections? What, for example, constitutes an unreasonable search and seizure, compulsory self-incrimination, or cruel and unusual punishment? The discussion that follows examines the substantive content that the Supreme Court has poured into the "vague contours" of these Bill of Rights protections—protections now equally applicable in both federal and state proceedings.

The Law of Search and Seizure

The Fourth Amendment to the Constitution provides that "the right of a people to be secure in their persons, houses, papers, and effects, against unreasonable searches and seizures shall not be violated and no Warrants shall issue but upon probable cause supported by Oath or Affirmation, and particularly describing the place to be searched, and the persons or things to be seized." One point

THE SUPREME COURT

Table 4.1 Application of Criminal Procedural Rights to the States

Rights	Case and Year
Fourth Amendment	
Unreasonable search and seizure	*Mapp* v. *Ohio* (1961)
Fifth Amendment	
Grand jury clause	Not incorporated
Double jeopardy clause	*Benton* v. *Maryland* (1969)
Self-incrimination clause	*Malloy* v. *Hogan* (1964)
Sixth Amendment	
Speedy trial clause	*Klopfer* v. *North Carolina* (1967)
Public trial clause	*In re Oliver* (1948)
Jury trial clause	*Duncan* v. *Louisiana* (1968)
Notice clause	*Cole* v. *Arkansas* (1948)
Confrontation clause	*Pointer* v. *Texas* (1965)
Compulsory process clause	*Washington* v. *Texas* (1967)
Right-to-counsel clause	*Gideon* v. *Wainwright* (1963)
	Argersinger v. *Hamlin* (1972)
Eighth Amendment	
Excessive fines and bails clause	Not incorporated
Cruel and unusual punishments clause	*Robinson* v. *California* (1962)

must be immediately stressed: The Constitution does not prohibit all searches, but only those that are unreasonable. This raises a serious question, however; what makes a search unreasonable? As with so many other provisions of the Constitution, the Supreme Court has had to pour substance and meaning into these Fourth Amendment words.

The general rule that the Supreme Court has adopted in response to this question is that searches are reasonable if they are based on a warrant obtained from a magistrate. The judicial officer will issue the warrant only if the law enforcement officials can demonstrate through introduction of evidence that probable cause exists that some evidence of criminal activity will be uncovered by the search. This is accomplished by the presentation to the magistrate of an affidavit that sets forth the facts that would lead a reasonably discreet and prudent man to believe that the offense charged has in fact been committed. An affidavit may also rest on hearsay—that is, it may rely on the observation of an informant rather than an officer—in which case probable cause can be established if the informant has previously given correct information and if there is corroboration from other sources.[49]

Failure to obtain a warrant, however, does not automatically render the search or seizure unreasonable. The Supreme Court has provided for three exceptions to the warrant requirement: (1) searches where the evidence seized is in "plain view" of the police; (2) searches of vehicles that can be quickly moved out of the jurisdiction in which the warrant must be sought; and (3) searches incident to a lawful arrest.

The "plain view" doctrine is a fundamental part of search and arrest procedures.[50] As the Supreme Court held in *Harris* v. *United States,* "It has long been settled that objects falling in the plain view of an officer who has a right to be in the position to have that view are subject to seizure and may be introduced in evidence."[51] The "plain view" doctrine has been applied in cases in which officers standing on public property have peered into car windows or the windows of dwellings.[52] It has also been employed to justify observations made by officers while on a defendant's property in the pursuit of legitimate business.[53] The "plain view" doctrine is considered by some to be potentially inconsistent with the Supreme Court's decision in *Katz* v. *United States,* in which Justice Stewart held that "the Fourth Amendment protects people, not places. What a person knowingly exposes to the public, even in his own home or office, is not a subject of Fourth Amendment protection . . . but what he seeks to preserve as private, even in an area accessible to the public, may be constitutionally protected."[54] However, any possible inconsistency between the "plain view" doctrine and *Katz* is eliminated when it is recalled that the defendant should have reasonably anticipated that such observations could be made by others in the normal pursuit of their daily activities.[55]

The right to search a vehicle on probable cause without a warrant is the second major exception to the warrant requirement of the Fourth Amendment. The Supreme Court first recognized this right during the prohibition era in *Carroll* v. *United States,* the justification being that a vehicle can be quickly moved out of the locality or jurisdiction in which the warrant must be sought.[56] The Court did not, however, regard the Fourth Amendment as totally inapplicable to moving vehicles, as it might have done by stressing their obvious differences from fixed structures. Rather, it held that where the securing of a warrant is reasonably practical, it must be used.

For many years, the *Carroll* rule was seldom utilized, for most vehicle searches were justified as incident to the arrest of the driver and, hence, as falling under the third major exemption to the warrant requirement. The need to define its precise reach was not all that great.[57] However, with the Supreme Court's recent decision in *Chimel* v. *California,*[58] this need became imperative. *Chimel* limited the permissible scope of a search incident to a lawful arrest to the arrestee's person and areas within his immediate control. Once the *Chimel* rule had become effective, could *Carroll* still be relied upon to justify a warrantless search of a car after the arrest of the driver? The Court was confronted with this question in *Chambers* v. *Maroney.*[59] In response to the contention that *Carroll* was not applicable on the facts in question because the automobile in which the defendant was arrested could simply have been held until a search warrant was obtained, Justice White declared for the Court majority:

Arguably, because of the preference for a magistrate's judgment, only the immobilization of the car should be permitted until a search warrant is obtained; arguably, only the "lesser" intrusion is permissible until the magistrate authorized the "greater." But which is the "greater" and which the "lesser" intrusion is itself a debatable question and the answer may depend on a variety of circumstances. For constitutional purposes, we see no difference between on the one hand seizing and holding a car before presenting the probable cause issue to a magistrate and on the other hand, carrying out an immediate search without a warrant. Given probable cause to search, either course is reasonable under the Fourth Amendment.[60]

The Court's continued commitment to *Carroll* is further highlighted by its 1974 decision in *Cardwell* v. *Lewis*.[61] In this case, Justice Blackmun held that the police did not violate the Fourth Amendment when, without a warrant, they seized from a public parking lot the automobile of an Ohio murder defendant and examined it the next day for tire and exterior paint matchings. He stressed that a person "has a lesser expectation of privacy in a motor vehicle because its purpose is transportation and it seldom serves as one's residence or as the repository of personal effects."[62]

Finally, the third major exception to the rule that warrants must be secured pertains to searches incident to a lawful arrest. The major justification for these searches involves the need for an officer to search a defendant to remove weapons—thus protecting the officer's safety—and evidence—thus preventing the defendant from destroying it. However, this justification does not permit an officer to search just anybody and then use evidence thereby obtained to justify the original arrest. Generally speaking, an officer cannot use the fruits of a search as justification for the arrest; the grounds for arrest must exist if the search incident to the arrest is to be valid.

This third major exception to the warrant requirement has, however, been modified somewhat by recent Supreme Court decisions. Thus, in *Terry* v. *Ohio*, decided near the end of its 1967 term, the Court, over the lone dissent of Justice Douglas, upheld laws permitting police officers to "stop and frisk" suspicious persons without having to meet the "probable cause" standard of the Fourth Amendment.[63] Chief Justice Warren stressed that the Court was not retreating from the warrant requirement of the Fourth Amendment but was simply applying a more practical standard, one that exempts from the probable cause requirement a limited search for weapons only if the search is otherwise reasonable. He declared:

> When an officer is justified in believing that the individual whose suspicious behavior he is investigating at close range is armed and presently dangerous to the officer or to others, it would appear completely unreasonable to deny the officer the power to take necessary measures to

determine whether the person is in fact carrying a weapon and to neutralize the threat of physical harm . . . there must be a narrowly drawn authority to permit a reasonable search for weapons for the protection of the police officer, where he has reason to believe that he is dealing with an armed and dangerous individual, regardless of whether he has probable cause to arrest the individual for a crime. The officer need not be absolutely certain that the individual is armed; the issue is whether a reasonably prudent man in the circumstances would be warranted in the belief that his safety or that of others was in danger.[64]

The 1973 decisions of *United States* v. *Robinson*[65] and *Gustafson* v. *Florida*[66] have further modified the general rule that a warrantless search will be valid only if it is incident to a lawful arrest. Both of these cases involved arrests for motor vehicle violations, and in both, subsequent searches of the offenders uncovered possession of narcotics. The evidence so obtained was admitted at subsequent trials where convictions resulted. In affirming both convictions, Justice Rehnquist for the majority in *Robinson* and for a plurality in *Gustafson* expanded the permissible limits of the "stop and frisk" doctrine of *Terry* and held that a search incident to a valid arrest under the circumstances of these cases was not limited to frisking the outer garments for weapons. He did not consider it unreasonable to conduct such a search, even though the arresting officer did not suspect that the offender was armed or that it was possible for him to destroy evidence of the crime for which the arrest was made. As Rehnquist declared in *Robinson*:

The authority to search the person incident to a lawful custodial arrest, while based upon the need to disarm and to discover evidence, does not depend on what a court may later decide was the probability in a particular arrest situation that weapons or evidence would in fact be found upon the person of the suspect. As custodial arrest of a suspect based on probable cause is a reasonable intrusion under the Fourth Amendment, that intrusion being lawful, a search incident to the arrest requires no additional justification. It is the fact of the lawful arrest which establishes the authority to search, and we hold that in the case of a lawful custodial arrest a full search of the person is not only an exception to the warrant requirement of the Fourth Amendment, but is also a "reasonable" search under that amendment.[67]

Finally, in *United States* v. *Edwards*,[68] the Supreme Court further authorized warrantless searches incident to a valid arrest. In this five-to-four decision, Justice White for the majority upheld the warrantless seizure of clothing worn by a jailed suspect whose arrest had taken place some 10 hours before, thereby further modifying the notion that the police must take advantage of every opportunity to secure a search warrant.

It was late at night; no substitute clothing was then available for Edwards to wear, and it would certainly have been unreasonable for the police to have stripped respondent of his clothing and left him exposed in his cell throughout the night. . . . When the substitutes were purchased the next morning, the clothing he had been wearing at the time of arrest was taken from him and subjected to laboratory analysis. This was no more than taking from respondent the effects in his immediate possession that constituted evidence of crime. This was and is a normal incident of custodial arrest, and reasonable delay in effectuating it does not change the fact that Edwards was no more imposed upon than he could have been at the time and place of the arrest or immediately upon arrival at the place of detention. The police did no more . . . than they were entitled to do incident to the usual custodial arrest and incarceration.[69]

Although these cases have somewhat loosened restrictions on warrantless searches incident to a valid arrest, another recent case, *Chimel* v. *California*,[70] has narrowed considerably the permissible scope of these searches. Before *Chimel*, the Court had allowed the police rather wide latitude in searching premises under the control of validly arrested defendants. Thus, in *Harris* v. *United States*,[71] the Court validated an extensive search of a four-room apartment supported only by an arrest warrant, and in *United States* v. *Rabinowitz*,[72] it approved as incident to an arrest a 1½-hour search of an office, including desks, safes, and file cabinets. However, in *Chimel*, the Court substantially tightened the requirements of the Fourth Amendment and reversed the trend of *Harris* and *Rabinowitz*. Officers arrested Chimel in his house, and over his objections and without a search warrant, proceeded to search his entire three-bedroom house, including attic, garage, and small workshop. Items obtained from this search were subsequently admitted in evidence against him during his trial for burglary, and he was convicted. The Supreme Court, in a seven-to-two decision, declared that such a widespread search was unreasonable and overturned his conviction.[73] Justice Stewart held for the Court that:

It is entirely reasonable for the arresting officer to search for and seize any evidence on the arrestee's person in order to prevent its concealment or destruction. And the area into which an arrestee might reach in order to grab a weapon or evidentiary items must, of course, be governed by a like rule. A gun on a table or in a drawer in front of one who is arrested can be as dangerous to the arresting officer as one concealed in the clothing of the person arrested. There is ample justification, therefore, for a search of the arrestee's person and the area "within his immediate control"—construing that phrase to mean the area within which he might gain possession of a weapon or destructible evidence.

There is no comparable justification, however, for routinely searching any room other than that in which an arrest occurs—or, for that matter, for searching through all the desk drawers or other closed or concealed areas in that room itself. Such searches, in the absence of well-organized exceptions, may be made only under the authority of a search warrant. The "adherence to judicial processes" mandated by the Fourth Amendment requires no less.[74]

Once the Court has resolved the question of what constitutes a reasonable search, another question quickly emerges: What remedy should be available to a defendant whose Fourth Amendment rights have been violated—that is, one who has been the subject of an unreasonable search or seizure? The Supreme Court dealt with this question for the first time in its 1914 decision in *Weeks* v. *United States*.[75] In *Weeks,* it declared that the appropriate remedy was exclusion of the illegally obtained evidence. The Court did not hold that the Fourth Amendment of its own force barred from criminal prosecution the use of illegally seized or "tainted" items; it did not consider the Fourth Amendment to constitute a rule of evidence. However, it went on to state that unless such an exclusionary rule were adopted, the Fourth Amendment would present no effective deterrent to improper searches and seizures. Thus, the Court held in *Weeks* that as a federal rule of evidence, which in its supervisory function it could impose on the entire federal judiciary, illegally obtained evidence could not be used in federal prosecutions.

The *Weeks* decision, however, dealt only with federal prosecutions, and because the Fourth Amendment was not yet incorporated through the Fourteenth Amendment to apply to the states, most states continued to follow the old common-law rule that relevant evidence however obtained was admissible. It was not until *Wolf* v. *Colorado*[76] in 1949 that the Supreme Court had occasion to rule on these state practices. In that decision, the Court concluded in an opinion written by Justice Frankfurter that "the security of one's privacy against arbitrary intrusion by the police—which is at the core of the Fourth Amendment—is basic to a free society. It is therefore implicit in 'the concept of ordered liberty' and as such enforceable against the States through the Due Process Clause."[77] However, while *Wolf* held that the Fourth Amendment guarantee against unreasonable searches and seizures was enforceable against the states through the Fourteenth Amendment, it did not consider the exclusionary rule announced in *Weeks* to be an "essential ingredient" of that guarantee.[78] The Court denied that the exclusionary rule had any constitutional status and asserted instead that it was merely a pragmatic remedy developed under the Court's powers to supervise the federal judicial system. It was not until *Mapp* v. *Ohio*[79] that the Supreme Court finally abandoned the *Wolf* doctrine and imposed the exclusionary rule on state proceedings as well.[80] Justice Clark concluded for the five-man majority that the exclusionary rule provided "the only effective available way . . . to compel respect for the constitutional guarantee."[81] It was no less than "an essential part of both the Fourth and Fourteenth Amendments."[82] Clark acknowledged that there was some truth to Justice Cardozo's argument that the exclusionary rule permits "the criminal . . . to go free because the constable has blundered." However, he believed "another consideration, the imperative of judicial integrity," to have priority. "The criminal goes free, if he must, but it is the law that sets him free. Nothing can destroy a government more quickly than its failure to observe its own laws, or worse, its disregard of the charter of its own existence."[83]

Since *Mapp*, however, the exclusionary rule has come under increasingly heavy attack. Justice Clark's moving language to the contrary, the operation of the exclusionary rule has been seen by many, including Chief Justice (then Court of Appeals Judge) Warren E. Burger, as bringing "to the public gaze a spectacle repugnant to all decent people—the frustration of justice."[84] As Monrad Paulsen observes, the exclusionary rule "destroys respect for law because it provides the spectacle of the courts letting the guilty go free."[85] These consequences are considered all the more indefensible in light of the rule's limited effectiveness. After all, the primary justification offered on behalf of the exclusionary rule is that exclusion of evidence obtained by illegal means will deter law enforcement officials from illegal behavior. Yet, as Chief Justice Burger has noted, "A fair conclusion is that the record does not support a claim that police conduct has been substantially affected by the suppression of the prosecution's evidence."[86] In his estimation, the notion that the exclusionary rule effectively deters the future action of particular police officers or the police more generally is no "more than wishful thinking on the part of the courts."[87]

Chief Justice Burger's suspicions appear to be fully confirmed, as there are at least five limitations on the deterrent effectiveness of the exclusionary rule.[88] First, in terms of its immediate remedial effect, the exclusionary rule benefits only the defendant incriminated by illegally obtained evidence. It provides no remedy, however, for the violation of Fourth Amendment rights suffered by the victim of an unreasonable search that turns up nothing incriminating. In short, it provides nothing for the innocent but freedom for the guilty.

Second, the exclusionary rule constitutes a deterrent only if the police are interested in obtaining a conviction. However, as Jerome Skolnick has pointed out, a variety of goals and motivations other than obtaining convictions may prompt arrest and search and seizure.[89] Thus, the police may be interested in developing informants and information on other offenders. They may also wish to impose punitive sanctions, as is common in gambling and liquor law violations. The upper echelons of police departments may be more concerned with crime prevention than with crime solving; consequently, an officer may search a suspect without probable cause on the basis of a furtive movement to gain the approval of his superiors, even though the evidence obtained is inadmissible. Because a large proportion of police behavior is traceable to these motivations for arrest and search and seizure, it is not likely to be responsive to any deterrent effect of the exclusionary rule.

A third limitation on the deterrent effectiveness of the exclusionary rule is that it fosters what may be referred to as "police perjury." Because of the exclusionary rule, Skolnick concludes that police officers often feel compelled to "reconstruct a set of complex happenings in such a way that, subsequent to the arrest, probable cause may be found according to Appellate Court standards. In this way, as one District Attorney expressed it, 'The policeman fabricates probable cause.'"[90] Skolnick's observations are supported by the research of a group of law students at Columbia University Law School who analyzed the evidentiary grounds for arrest and subsequent disposition of misdemeanor narcotics cases in New York City for 6-month periods before and after the *Mapp* decision. In the period after the *Mapp* decision, they observed a substantial increase in the percent of cases in which the police alleged that the evidence was obtained not from a search of the suspect's person, but rather because the suspect had, when the officer approached him, attempted to dispose of the evidence by dropping or throwing it to the ground (see Table 4.2). Because this was at the very time when the Court had extended to these suspects the protection against such searches of their persons without probable cause, the law students were forced to conclude that the police were induced to commit "police perjury" in an attempt to legalize their arrests and thereby avoid the effect of the exclusionary rule.[91] To the extent that the exclusionary rule encourages police officers to give such deliberately false testimony about the circumstances of arrests or searches and seizures, it not only fails to achieve its own objectives but also corrupts law enforcement personnel and degrades the entire criminal justice system.

Table 4.2 New York City Police Officers' Allegations Regarding Discovery of Evidence in Misdemeanor Narcotics Offenses, 1960-1962

How evidence found	Percent of arrests during 6-month period		Percent change
	Before Mapp	After Mapp	
Narcotics Bureau			
Hidden on person	35	3	−32
Dropped or thrown to ground	17	43	+26
Uniform			
Hidden on person	31	9	−22
Dropped or thrown to ground	14	21	+ 7
Plainclothes			
Hidden on person	24	4	−20
Dropped or thrown to ground	11	17	+ 6

Source: Dallin H. Oaks, "Studying the Exclusionary Rule in Search and Seizure," *University of Chicago Law Review* 37 (1970): 698.

A fourth reason for the limited deterrent effect of the exclusionary rule is that it does not proscribe, and often positively encourages, police imposition of extrajudicial punishments. Dallin Oaks reports that police on occasion feel compelled to control gambling through the use of harassing searches without probable cause because of the strict requirements of the laws of search and seizure and the light penalties imposed on gambling offenses.[92]

Finally, a fifth limitation on the deterrent effectiveness of the exclusionary rule is that it allows for the possibility that police may immunize criminals from prosecution by deliberately overstepping legal bounds in obtaining vital evidence. On the basis of his examination of the high proportion of gambling-raid cases in Chicago in which the defendants were released after they were granted motions to suppress, Professor Samuel Dash has concluded that these raids were made to "immunize the gamblers while at the same time satisfying the public that gamblers are being harassed by the police."[93]

Recently, awareness of these limitations has grown, and with it, so has the conviction that the exclusionary rule must be either modified substantially or abandoned altogether.[94] Professor John Kaplan proposes the former and advocates two "practical modifications" to accomplish this objective.[95] He first proposes that the exclusionary rule be modified so that it does "not apply in the most serious cases—treason, espionage, murder, armed robbery, and kidnapping by organized groups."[96] Kaplan sees definite advantages in not applying the exclusionary rule to the most serious crimes. Perhaps the most important of these is that "freed of the concern that the Fourth Amendment doctrine they announce would later result in the release of people guilty of the most serious crimes, judges would be able to interpret more fully and more honestly the commands of the Fourth Amendment in all the remaining cases. Such a result would not be surprising. Increases in the range of the exclusionary rule sanction tend to cause the contraction of the substantive rights protected."[97]

Kaplan's second proposal is of greater significance. Noting that departmental sanctions and rewards are far more important to a police officer than the threat of exclusion of any evidence he might illegally seize, Kaplan argues that the focus of the exclusionary rule should be changed so that its application is directed against the police department rather than against the misbehavior of the individual police officer. Thus, his second proposed modification would "hold the exclusionary rule inapplicable to cases where the police department in question has taken seriously its responsibility to adhere to the Fourth Amendment."[98]

While Professor Kaplan would attempt to provide for a substantial modification of the exclusionary rule, Chief Justice Burger would go even further, as he did in his dissent in *Bivens* v. *Six Unknown Named Agents*[99] when he proposed to eliminate the exclusionary rule altogether and to develop in its place a "meaningful and effective remedy against unlawful conduct by government officials."[100] Burger conceded that private damage actions against individual police officers are inadequate in this respect; consequently, he urged Congress to develop an administrative or quasi-judicial remedy against the government itself to afford compensation and restitution for persons whose Fourth Amendment rights have been violated. According to Burger, such a statutory scheme would have two advantages: it would eliminate the "universal capital punishment we inflict on all evidence when police error is shown in its acquisition";[101] and it would provide "some remedy to completely innocent persons who are sometimes the victims of illegal police conduct."[102] Thus, Burger used his *Bivens* dissent to propose to Congress that it enact a statute that would (1) waive sovereign immunity as to the illegal acts of law enforcement officials committed in the performance of assigned tasks; (2) create a cause of action for damages sustained by any persons aggrieved by conduct of governmental agents in violation of the Fourth Amendment or statutes regulating official conduct; (3) create a quasi-judicial tribunal, perhaps patterned after the U.S. Court of Claims, to adjudicate all claims under the statute; (4) substitute this remedy for the exclusionary rule; and (5) direct that no evidence, otherwise admissible, shall be excluded from any criminal proceeding because of violation of the Fourth Amendment.[103]

Chief Justice Burger's recommendation that the exclusionary rule be abandoned in favor of a more "meaningful alternative" has not received a favorable congressional response, but it does appear to have struck a responsive chord in Justices Blackmun, Stewart, White, Rehnquist, and Powell. Thus, in *United States* v. *Calandra*,[104] these six members of the Court joined together in refusing to apply the exclusionary rule to grand jury proceedings.[105] Justice Powell contended for this majority that the "historic role and function of the grand jury" in ensuring effective law enforcement would be compromised by its introduction. "It is evident that this extension of the exclusionary rule would seriously impede the grand jury. Because the grand jury does not finally adjudicate guilt or innocence, it has traditionally been allowed to pursue its investigative and accusatorial functions unimpeded by the evidentiary and procedural restrictions applicable to a criminal trial. Permitting witnesses to invoke the exclusionary rule before a grand jury would precipitate adjudication of issues hitherto reserved for the trial on the merits and would delay and disrupt grand jury proceedings."[106]

The Privilege Against Self-Incrimination and Coerced Confessions

The Fifth Amendment provides that no person "shall be compelled in any criminal case to be a witness against himself." As with other provisions of the Bill of Rights, this privilege was originally restricted to federal prosecutions. In both *Twining* v. *New Jersey* [107] and *Adamson* v. *California*,[108] the Supreme Court rejected the argument that the exception to compulsory self-incrimination was a "fundamental right" and hence necessary to a system of "ordered liberty."

However, in the 1964 case of *Malloy* v. *Hogan*,[109] it overruled these longstanding precedents and extended this protection through the Fourteenth Amendment to the states as well. As Justice Brennan stated for the Court: "The Fourteenth Amendment secures against state invasion the same privilege that the Fifth Amendment guarantees against federal infringement—the right of a person to remain silent unless he chooses to speak in the unfettered exercise of his own will, and to suffer no penalty—for such silence."

The justification for this protection was perhaps best stated by Chief Justice Earl Warren in his opinion for the Court in *Miranda* v. *Arizona:* "The constitutional foundation underlying the privilege is the respect a government—state or federal—must accord to the dignity and integrity of its citizens. To maintain a 'fair state-individual balance,' to require the government 'to shoulder the entire load' . . . to respect the inviolability of the human personality, our accusatory system of criminal justice demands that the government seeking to punish an individual produce the evidence against him by its own independent labors, rather than by the cruel, simple expedient of compelling it from his own mouth."[110] However, a question now arises: What does the protection really involve? In the context of a criminal trial, the Supreme Court's answer to this question has been rather straightforward. A criminal defendant cannot be forced to take the witness stand.[111] Neither opposing counsel nor the judge in the case can call attention to the failure of the defendant to take the witness stand in his own defense; and by federal statute, a judge must instruct the jury that the defendant's failure to testify creates no presumption against him.[112]

When the focus changes, however, and brings within its purview police interrogation of suspects, this question becomes much more difficult for the Supreme Court to answer. What constitutes being "compelled"? That is, what constitutes coercion in violation of the privilege? The answers the Court has given to this question not only highlight the extent to which these words in the Fifth Amendment are empty vessels into which the Court has from time to time poured different meanings but also reveal a cause of considerable interface problems between the Court and the police.

Although the Court did not rule until *Malloy* v. *Hogan* in 1964 that the protection against self-incrimination applied to the states, since *Brown* v. *Mississippi* in 1936 it has placed limitations upon police interrogation techniques and upon the admissibility of confessions thereby obtained.[113] In that case, the Court overturned the conviction of three defendants whom police had physically tortured in order to extort confessions. Chief Justice Hughes made abundantly clear the Court's belief that the use of such confessions violated the Due Process Clause of the Fourteenth Amendment: "The freedom of the state in establishing its policy is the freedom of constitutional government and is limited by the requirement of due process of law. Because a state may dispense with a jury trial, it does not follow that it may substitute a trial by ordeal. The rack and torture chamber may not be substituted for the witness stand."[114]

Brown was extended in 1940 in *Chambers* v. *Florida*,[115] in which the Court again overturned a state conviction, not because the defendant had been subjected to blatant physical methods of coercion, but because he had been arrested on suspicion without a warrant, denied contact with friends or attorneys, and questioned for long periods of time by different squads of police officers. *Brown* and *Chambers* were followed by a long line of cases in which the Court dealt with the admissibility of confessions on an ad hoc basis. It employed the "totality of circumstances" rule: In the evaluation of the Court, did the circumstances surrounding the obtaining of a particular confession—for example, the nature of the charge, the age, maturity, and educational achievements of the defendant, the degree of pressure put upon him, the length of interrogation, and so on—constitute coercion and thereby render the confession inadmissible? The "totality of circumstances" rule was plagued with one major problem, however; it provided neither the police nor the prosecution with much guidance on what practices did or did not pass constitutional muster. As a consequence, the Court found itself continually confronted with a barrage of "coerced confessions" cases dealing with such police practices as attempts to gain the sympathy of the defendant through a childhood friend on the police force;[116] threats to bring a defendant's wife into custody for questioning;[117] threats to place the defendant's children in the custody of welfare officials;[118] and the interrogation of a wounded defendant under the influence of a so-called truth serum.[119]

In an effort to free itself from this perpetual litigation, the Supreme Court finally sought to establish some general guidelines on the meaning of self-incrimination and coerced confessions. *Escobedo* v. *Illinois* provided it with such an opportunity.[120] In *Escobedo,* the defendant made damaging admissions while being interrogated, despite the fact that he had asked for, but had been denied, an opportunity to consult with his attorney. In overturning his conviction, Justice Goldberg laid down the following rule:

> Where, as here, the investigation is no longer a general inquiry into an unsolved crime but has begun to focus on a particular suspect, the suspect has been taken into police custody, the police carry out a process of interrogation that lends itself to eliciting incriminating statements, the suspect has requested and been denied an opportunity to consult with his lawyer, and the police have not effectively warned him of his absolute constitutional right to remain silent, the accused has been denied 'the Assistance of Counsel' in violation of the Sixth Amendment to the Constitution as 'made obligatory upon the States by the Fourteenth Amendment' . . . and . . . no statement elicited by the police during the interrogation may be used against him at a criminal trial.[121]

Escobedo, however, was only a faltering step toward the establishment of general guidelines for police interrogation. As Justice Goldberg's opinion indicates, it was still couched in the "particularized language of the totality-of-circumstances rule."[122] It was not until 2 years later in the celebrated case of *Miranda* v. *Arizona* that the Court finally broke completely with past cases, rejected the ad hoc "totality of circumstances" rule, announced specific procedures that the police would have to follow during interrogation, and declared that any statements elicited in violation of these procedures would be inadmissible.[123] In the language of Chief Justice Warren:

> The prosecution may not use statements, whether exculpatory or inculpatory, stemming from custodial interrogation of the defendant unless it demonstrates the use of procedural safeguards effective to secure the privilege against self-incrimination. By custodial interrogation, we mean questioning initiated by law enforcement officers after a person has been taken into custody or otherwise deprived of his freedom of action in any significant way. As for the procedural safeguards to be employed, unless other fully effective means are devised to inform accused persons of their right of silence and to assure a continuous opportunity to exercise it, the following measures are required. Prior to any questioning, the person must be warned that he has a right to remain silent, that any statement he does make may be used as evidence against him and that he has a right to the presence of an attorney, either retained or appointed. The defendant may waive effectuation of these rights, provided the waiver is made voluntarily, knowingly, and intelligently. If, however, he indicates in any manner and at any stage of the process that he wishes to consult with an attorney before speaking there can be no questioning. Likewise if the individual is alone and indicates in any manner that he does not wish to be interrogated, the police may not question him. The mere fact that he may have answered some questions or volunteered some statements on his own does not deprive him of the right to refrain from answering any further inquiries until he has consulted with an attorney and thereafter consents to be questioned.[124]

Miranda was approved only over the bitter denunciations of Justices Harlan, White, Stewart, and Clark. Justice Harlan branded it a "dangerous experimentation" at a time of a "high crime rate that is a matter of growing concern" and a "new doctrine" without substantial precedent, reflecting a "balance in favor of the accused."[125] He saw the Court's opinion as unable to "serve due process interests in preventing blatant coercion" for "those who use third-degree tactics and deny them in court are equally able and destined to lie as skillfully about warnings and waivers." Thus, he concluded, "the rules work for reliability in confessions almost only in the Pickwickian sense that they can prevent some from being given at all."[126] Most importantly, however, Justice Harlan saw this desire to escape from the "totality of circumstances" rule and to establish in its place a general set of guidelines to govern police interrogation of defendants as a fundamental departure from the "judicial" function. The approach abandoned by the majority in *Miranda* was "'judicial' in its treatment of one case at a time, flexible in its ability to respond to the endless mutations of fact presented, and ever more familiar to the lower courts."[127] This now disgraced approach lacked "strict certainty," but Harlan insisted, "this is often so with Constitutional principles, and disagreement is usually confined to that borderland of close cases where it matters least."[128] Moreover, a considerable question was raised whether the *Miranda* decision came any closer to providing this "strict certainty." This obviously was the intention of the Court majority when it laid down the general policy guidelines that it did; however, as Justice White in his dissent stressed, these efforts were destined to fail. *Miranda* raised other questions that would have to be resolved on a case-by-case basis:

> Today's decision leaves open such questions as whether the accused was in custody, whether his statements were spontaneous or the product of interrogation, whether the accused has effectively waived his rights, and whether non-testimonial evidence introduced at trial is the fruit of statements made during a prohibited interrogation, all of which are certain to prove productive of uncertainty during investigation and litigation during prosecution. For all these reasons, if further restrictions on police interrogation are desirable at this time, a more flexible approach makes much more sense than the Court's constitutional straightjacket which forecloses more discriminating treatment by legislative or rule-making pronouncements.[129]

Justice White's call for a "more flexible approach" to self-incrimination has not been ignored by the more recent Burger Court. Reluctant to confine police interrogations to the "constitutional straitjacket" of *Miranda,* the Court has shown an increasing willingness to modify its general policy guidelines announced in that case and to return to a case-by-case adjudication of the issues involved. Thus, in *Harris* v. *New York,* a six-member majority joined in Chief Justice Burger's opinion holding that statements made to police by a defendant who has not been advised of his *Miranda* rights, while they cannot be introduced at a trial court for the prosecution's case in chief, nonetheless can be employed to impeach the credibility of the defendant should he testify on his own behalf and, in so doing, contradict his earlier statements.[130] The Chief Justice refused to construe the privilege against self-incrimination to include the right to commit perjury. "Every criminal defendant is privileged to testify in his own defense, or to refuse to do so. But . . . the shield provided by *Miranda* cannot be perverted into a license to use perjury by way of a defense free from the risk of confrontation with prior inconsistent utterances. We hold, therefore, that petitioner's credibility was appropriately impeached by the use of his earlier conflicting statements."[131] This trend was continued in *Michigan* v. *Tucker*[132] in 1974 and *Oregon* v. *Hass*[133] in 1975. *Tucker* held that failure to advise the defendant of his right to court-appointed counsel when the other *Miranda* rights were given was not by itself so serious an error as to require suppression of damaging testimony by a third party whose identity was revealed by the defendant during police interrogation. Justice William Rehnquist spoke for an eight-member majority when he observed: "Just as the law does not require that a defendant receive a perfect trial, only a fair one, it cannot realistically require that policemen investigating serious crimes make no errors whatsoever. The pressures of law enforcement and the vagaries of human nature would make such an expectation unrealistic. Before we penalize police error, therefore, we must consider whether the sanction serves a valid and useful purpose."[134] *Oregon* v. *Hass* went beyond *Harris* in limiting *Miranda.* In an opinion written by Justice Blackmun, the Court held that when a suspect in police custody has been given and accepts the full warnings prescribed by *Miranda* and later states that he would like to telephone a lawyer but is told he cannot do so until reaching the station, and he then provides inculpatory information, such information is admissible in evidence at the suspect's trial solely for impeachment purposes after he has taken the stand and testified to the contrary knowing that such information has been ruled inadmissible for the prosecution's case in chief.[135]

The Right to Counsel

The Sixth Amendment declares that "in all criminal prosecutions, the accused shall enjoy the right . . . to have Assistance of Counsel for his defense." As with so many other provisions of the Bill of Rights, these words raise questions that the Supreme Court has had to resolve. To begin with, what does the right to have assistance of counsel involve? Does it require, for example, appointment of counsel for indigents—and, if so, in what cases? When that question is resolved, another arises. The Sixth Amendment guarantees the right to assistance of counsel "in all criminal prosecutions"; however, it makes no mention of detention, interrogation, preliminary hearings, or other pretrial or posttrial stages that an accused must face. Does the Sixth Amendment ensure the right to assistance of counsel at each of these stages? The Court's answers to these questions will be taken up, as they illustrate to what extent the Court has had to pour normative meanings into these empty constitutional provisions.

The original meaning of the Sixth Amendment right to assistance of counsel was most restrictive. It guaranteed the accused the right to employ and bring to trial a lawyer of his own choosing. However, it made no provision for the indigent defendant who might want and even badly need assistance of counsel but who was unable to afford an attorney. As Professor M. Glenn Abernathy observes, the provision was "permissive only. It imposed no duty on the government to provide free counsel."[136] This interpretation extended well into the twentieth century and was still in force as late as 1931, when the Wickersham Commission, appointed by President Hoover to investigate law observance and enforcement, stated in its *Report on Prosecution:* "The right guaranteed is one of employing counsel, not one of having counsel provided by the government."[137]

In 1932, however, the Court began to expand this interpretation. In *Powell* v. *Alabama*,[138] it held that in capital felony cases, right to counsel is secured by the Due Process Clause of the Fourteenth Amendment. Mr. Justice Sutherland observed that even "the intelligent and educated layman has small and sometimes no skill in the science of law"; as a consequence, he lacks "both the skill and knowledge adequately to prepare his defense, even though he have a perfect one." Without the "guiding hand of counsel at every step in the proceedings against him," a defendant, "though he be not guilty, . . . faces the danger of conviction because he does not know how to establish his innocence." Consequently, Justice Sutherland concluded for the Court majority that "the right to have counsel appointed, when necessary, is a logical corollary from the constitutional right to be heard by counsel."[139] Six years later, in *Johnson* v. *Zerbst*,[140] the Court further extended this interpretation and held that right to counsel extends to appointment of counsel for indigent defendants in all federal criminal proceedings—capital or non-capital.[141] "The Sixth Amendment withholds from federal courts, in all criminal proceedings, the power and authority to deprive an accused of his life or liberty unless he has or waives the assistance of counsel."[142] Justice Black justified this new interpretation by quoting from *Powell:* "The right to be heard would be, in many cases, of little avail if it did not comprehend the right to be heard by counsel."[143]

Although the Court held that the Sixth Amendment required appointment of counsel for indigent criminal defendants in federal prosecutions, it was reluctant to interpret the Due Process Clause of the Fourteenth Amendment in such a way as to impose the same requirement on the states. When presented with the opportunity to do so in *Betts* v. *Brady*,[144] Mr. Justice Roberts examined the "constitutional and statutory provisions subsisting in the colonies and the States prior to the inclusion of the Bill of Rights in the National Constitution" and reviewed "the constitutional, legislative and judicial history of the States to the present date" and concluded for a six-member majority that "this material demonstrates that, in the great majority of the States, it has been the considered judgment of the people, their representatives and their courts that appointment of counsel is not a fundamental right essential to a fair trial. On the contrary, the matter has generally been deemed one of legislative policy. In the light of this evidence, we are unable to say that the concept of due process incorporated in the Fourteenth Amendment obligates the States, whatever may be their own views, to furnish counsel in every such case."[145] Justice Black dissented and was joined by Justices Douglas and Murphy; he insisted that right to court-appointed counsel for indigent defendants was an inherent part of "common and fundamental ideas of fairness and right." Moreover, he stressed, "whether a man is innocent cannot be determined from a trial in which, as here, denial of counsel has made it impossible to conclude, with any satisfactory degree of certainty, that the defendant's case was adequately presented."[146]

Justice Black's dissent was eventually vindicated some 20 years later in

Gideon v. *Wainwright.*[147] In that celebrated case, the Court overruled *Betts* and unanimously concluded that the right to court-appointed counsel is fundamental and essential to a fair trial of an indigent defendant in state as well as federal felony prosecutions. Justice Black declared for the Court that precedent, reason and reflection all "require us to recognize that in our adversary system of criminal justice, any person hailed into court, who is too poor to hire a lawyer, cannot be assured a fair trial unless counsel is provided for him."[148] Observing that the government hires lawyers to prosecute and defendants with money hire lawyers to defend, he concluded that "lawyers in criminal courts are necessities, not luxuries."[149]

As a result of *Gideon,* the right to assistance of counsel was extended to all indigent defendants in both federal and state felony prosecutions. *Gideon* did not, however, extend this right to "all criminal prosecutions." Misdemeanor offenses were still excluded from coverage, and it was not until 1972 in *Argersinger* v. *Hamlin*[150] that right to counsel was guaranteed in these cases as well. In that decision, the Court noted that the volume of misdemeanor cases was far greater than the number of felony prosecutions; as a consequence, there was in many trial courts "an obsession for speedy dispositions, regardless of the fairness of the result."[151] Prejudice had crept into this "assembly-line justice." Justice Douglas cited favorably an American Civil Liberties Union report that concluded that misdemeanants represented by counsel were five times more likely to emerge from municipal courts with all charges dismissed than were defendants who faced similar charges without counsel. Consequently, he held for a unanimous Court that "absent a knowing and intelligent waiver, no person may be imprisoned for any offense, whether classified as petty, misdemeanor, or felony, unless he was represented by counsel at his trial."[152] Because Argersinger had been convicted of carrying a concealed weapon and had been sentenced to 90 days in jail, the Court left unconsidered the question of whether counsel is also required even in cases where there is no prospect of imprisonment. However, Justice Powell in his concurrence did take up this question and concluded that the requirements of the Sixth Amendment apply whether or not the loss of liberty is involved. "The Fifth and Fourteenth Amendments guarantee that property, as well as life and liberty, may not be taken from a person without affording him due process of law. The majority opinion suggests no constitutional basis for distinguishing between deprivations of liberty and property. In fact, the majority suggests no reason at all for drawing this distinction. The logic it advances for extending the right to counsel to all cases in which the penalty of imprisonment is imposed applies equally well to cases in which other penalties may be imposed. Nor does the majority deny that some 'non-jail' penalties are more serious than brief jail sentences."[153]

The Court's decisions from *Powell* to *Argersinger* holding that no defendant can be convicted and imprisoned unless he has been accorded the right to assistance of counsel have recently raised a serious question: Does a defendant in a criminal trial have a constitutional right to proceed without counsel when he voluntarily and intelligently elects to do so? Stated another way, can a state constitutionally hail a person into its criminal courts and there force a lawyer upon him, even when he insists that he wants to conduct his own defense? The Court was confronted with this question for the first time in the 1975 case of *Faretta v. California*.[154] In this case, Justice Stewart concluded for a six-member majority that a state cannot. Justice Stewart acknowledged that this was not "an easy question"; furthermore, he conceded that "the basic thesis" of the Court's previous right-to-counsel opinions "is that the help of a lawyer is essential to assure the defendant a fair trial."[155] However, despite his admission that "a strong argument can surely be made that the whole thrust of those decisions must inevitably lead to the conclusion that a State may constitutionally impose a lawyer upon even an unwilling defendant," he nevertheless insisted that "the right to self-representation—to make one's own defense personally—is . . . necessarily implied by the structure of the [Sixth] Amendment. The right to defend is given directly to the accused; for it is he who suffers the consequences if the defense fails."[156] He stressed that the language of the provision provides for "assistance" of counsel, and, he observed, "an assistant, however expert, is still an assistant." Developing this argument further, he concluded that to thrust counsel upon an unwilling defendant violates the logic of the Sixth Amendment. "In such a case, counsel is not an assistant, but a master; and the right to make a defense is stripped of the personal character upon which the Amendment insists."[157]

Chief Justice Burger dissented, as did Justices Blackmun and Rehnquist. Their arguments go a long way toward explaining the genuinely conciliatory nature of Justice Stewart's majority opinion. To begin with, Chief Justice Burger stressed that in all but "an extraordinarily small number of cases," the defendant will lose whatever defense he may have if he undertakes to conduct the trial himself. Such an easy conviction, obtained as a result of the defendant's ill-advised decision to waive counsel "would, moreover serve to undermine the integrity of and public confidence in the system of criminal justice."[158] Justice Blackmun took this argument even further. "The Court seems to suggest that so long as the accused is willing to pay the consequences of his folly, there is no reason for not allowing a defendant the right to self-representation. . . . That view ignores the established principle that the interest of the State in a criminal prosecution 'is not that it shall win a case, but that justice shall be done.'"[159] Justice Blackmun refused to subordinate the danger of "unjust" convictions and the "interest of the State in seeing that justice is done in a real and objective sense" to "the individual defendant's right of free choice."[160]

In addition to these more theoretical objections to the right of self-representation, both Chief Justice Burger and Justice Blackmun feared the "potential effect" that this would have on "an already malfunctioning criminal justice system." Chief Justice Burger predicted "added congestion in the courts" and a decline in the "quality of justice."[161] Moreover, he expected that many convictions would be reversed by the appellate courts: "Unless, as may be the case, most people accused of crime have more wit than to insist upon the dubious benefit that the Court confers today, we can expect that many expensive and good-faith prosecutions will be nullified on appeal for reasons that trial courts are now deprived of the power to prevent."[162] Justice Blackmun expressed concern over the "host" of procedural questions this right would raise.

> Must every defendant be advised of his right to proceed *pro se?* If so, when must that notice be given? Since the right to assistance of counsel and the right to self-representation are mutually exclusive, how is the waiver of each right to be measured? If a defendant has elected to exercise his right to proceed *pro se,* does he still have a constitutional right to assistance of standby counsel? How soon in the criminal proceeding must a defendant decide between proceeding by counsel or *pro se?* Must he be allowed to switch in midtrial? May a violation of the right to self-representation ever be harmless error? Must the trial court treat the *pro se* defendant differently than it would professional counsel?[163]

Justice Blackmun concluded that these many "procedural problems spawned by an absolute right to self-representation will far outweigh whatever tactical advantage the defendant may feel he has gained by electing to represent himself."[164]

The question of who has right to assistance of counsel has now been examined; the right extends to all defendants—be they affluent or indigent, be their offenses serious or petty—unless they knowingly and intelligently waive it. However, a second question then arises: When in the "criminal prosecution" does the right to counsel accrue and for how long does it continue? The seminal answer to this question was provided in 1932 in *Powell* v. *Alabama* when Justice Sutherland declared that the defendant "requires the guiding hand of counsel at every step in the proceedings against him."[165] Through the years, the Court has held that this constitutional principle is not limited simply to the presence of counsel at trial. As it declared in *United States* v. *Wade,* "it is central to that principle that in addition to counsel's presence at trial, the accused is guaranteed that he need not stand alone against the state at any stage of the prosecution, formal or informal, in court or out, where counsel's absence might derogate from the accused's right to a fair trial."[166] On the basis of that principle, the Court has ruled that the accused has the right to counsel at such "critical stages" as in-custody police interrogation following arrest, *Escobedo* v. *Illinois*[167] and *Miranda* v. *Arizona;*[168] the police lineup held for eye-witness identification, *United States* v. *Wade*[169] and *Gilbert* v. *California;*[170] the preliminary hearing, *Coleman* v. *Alabama;*[171] the arraignment, *Hamilton* v. *Alabama;*[172] at his appeal, *Douglas* v. *California;*[173] and even at a posttrial proceeding for the revocation of probation and parole, *Mempa* v. *Rhay.*[174] In short, the meaning that the Court has poured into the broad language of the Sixth Amendment provision of right to assistance of counsel provides that in all federal and state criminal proceedings and in the absence of a knowing and intelligent waiver, a defendant is entitled to representation by counsel at every step where substantial rights may be affected.[175]

The Protection Against Double Jeopardy

In archaic language, the Fifth Amendment forbids the government to put any person twice "in jeopardy of life or limb" for the same offense.[176] The underlying justification for this provision, as Justice Black has noted, "is that the State with all its resources and power should not be allowed to make any repeated attempts to convict an individual for an alleged offense, thereby subjecting him to embarrassment, expense and ordeal and compelling him to live in a continuing state of anxiety and insecurity, as well as enhancing the possibility that even though innocent he may be found guilty."[177] The amount of protection afforded by this provision is dependent, however, upon the answers given to such questions as what constitutes "jeopardy" in a legal proceeding and what constitutes "sameness" in an offense. These questions have become of equal importance and concern to both federal and state governments since the Supreme Court found in *Benton* v. *Maryland* in 1969 "that the double jeopardy prohibition of the Fifth Amendment represents a fundamental ideal in our constitutional heritage and that it should apply to the States through the Fourteenth Amendment."[178]

On the first question, an accused has, of course, been placed in jeopardy when he has been tried by a court of competent jurisdiction and either acquitted or convicted. The government cannot appeal such a verdict or institute a second prosecution for the same offense. However, it is not necessary to have reached the verdict stage to bring the jeopardy rule into operation. Otherwise, when it began to appear that a jury might not convict, a prosecutor or judge would be inclined to secure a mistrial in order to leave the way open for a second trial. As a result, the following rule has emerged: If it is a bench trial, jeopardy commonly attaches when the first witness is sworn or when the court has begun to hear evidence; if the case is tried by a jury, jeopardy begins when the jury is impaneled and sworn.[179] Only under exceptional circumstances can a trial be halted after this stage and the accused subjected later to a second trial. Such would be the case where a juror is disqualified or the jury fails to reach a verdict.

As with other Bill of Rights guarantees, the accused may waive his constitutional immunity against double jeopardy. He does this when he moves for a new trial, or appeals from a verdict of guilty. If his conviction is overturned on appeal, the defendant may be tried a second time for the same offense, and he assumes the risk of receiving a heavier penalty than in the first trial. As the Supreme Court ruled in *North Carolina* v. *Pearce*,[180] neither the Double Jeopardy nor the Equal Protection Clauses automatically prohibit, on retrial of a defendant whose original conviction was set aside, the imposition of a more severe sentence than that imposed following the original conviction. The defendant is protected, however, by the Due Process Clause, which prohibits the imposition of a more severe sentence for the purpose of discouraging the exercise of the statutory right to appeal. To curb such improper motivation, the Court in *Pearce* also ruled that "whenever a judge imposes a more severe sentence upon a defendant after a new trial, the reasons for his doing so must affirmatively appear."[181]

The question of what constitutes the "same offense" is much more complicated. It has been complicated by three factors. First, the criminal law has developed in such a fashion that a single criminal act may in fact be chargeable as two or more offenses. For example, a burglary may actually be broken down into the separate charges of conspiracy to commit burglary, possession of burglar's tools with intent to commit burglary, and burglary. Second, a criminal may commit several crimes on a single occasion, as for example by robbing five different customers in a tavern. In so doing, he has committed five separate crimes and may be so charged. However, problems arise when he is tried seriatim on these charges rather than at one trial. Third, in the American federal system, a single criminal act may constitute both a federal crime and a state crime. The Court has had to confront each of these complicating factors.

In response to the first of these factors, the Court has concluded that the test of constitutionality of trying a defendant on closely related charges is usually determined by whether additional facts must be proved in the additional charges. If additional facts must be proved, then there is no double jeopardy. However, if the same facts would support a conviction on the additional charges, then double jeopardy occurs. For example, there is no constitutional bar against trying an accused for conspiracy to commit a crime (for example, conspiracy to commit bank robbery) and for the substantive crime itself (the actual bank robbery). If, however, the additional charge is an included offense, the situation is quite different. Conspiracy to commit bank robbery and bank robbery are capable of different treatment. They may even be tried at different trials, because either crime may take place without the other. However, because murder includes the lesser crime of manslaughter, if a trial is held on either charge, a later trial on the other is precluded.

The Court has also had to face the double jeopardy problem raised by the prosecution of different offenses at consecutive trials, even though the crimes have arisen out of the same event. This problem was at the heart of *Hoag* v. *New Jersey*.[182] In that case, a man alleged to have robbed five tavern patrons was tried for the robbery of three of them. He was acquitted when four of the state's witnesses unexpectedly failed to identify the defendant. The state then tried Hoag for the robbery of a fourth patron, the only witness at the first trial to identify the defendant. This time he was convicted. The Supreme Court upheld Hoag's conviction on the ground that, while a single trial would have been "preferable practice," the Fourteenth Amendment did not make multiple trials unconstitutional, and the circumstances surrounding Hoag's conviction did not result in "fundamental unfairness." Once the Court in *Benton* extended the Fifth Amendment's double jeopardy protections to the states, *Hoag* had to be reconsidered. After all, the question no longer was, did the *Hoag* doctrine meet the requirements of due process, but did it meet the Fifth Amendment's guarantee against double jeopardy? This reconsideration came in *Ashe* v. *Swenson*.[183] In that 1970 decision, the Court overruled *Hoag* and espoused the view that the double jeopardy provision of the Fifth Amendment embraces the doctrine of "collateral estoppel," a test defined by Justice Stewart as meaning that "when an issue of fact has been determined by a valid and final judgment, that issue cannot be litigated between the same parties in any future lawsuit."[184] In this instance, Ashe was charged with robbing one of six players at a poker game but was acquitted for lack of positive identification. At a second trial for the robbery of another player, he was convicted and sentenced to 35 years in prison. The Court declared that because the jury had determined in the first prosecution that Ashe had not been one of the robbers, a second prosecution was barred, because it would require a redetermination of the same fact.

The third complicating factor in determining what constitutes double jeopardy for "the same offense" arises when a defendant is tried in both federal and state courts for a single act that is a crime against both jurisdictions.[185] In the 1959 decision of *Bartkus* v. *Illinois*,[186] the Supreme Court in a five-to-four decision reaffirmed *United States* v. *Lanza*[187] and held that it is not double jeopardy for each government to prosecute and punish.[188] In that particular case, a man who was tried and acquitted by a federal court for robbery of an Illinois bank was subsequently indicted for the same crime by an Illinois grand jury, convicted, and sentenced to life imprisonment. Justice Frankfurter upheld this dual prosecution, observing that "were the federal prosecution of a comparatively minor offense to prevent state prosecution of so grave an infraction of state law, the result would be a shocking and untoward deprivation of the historic right and obligation of the State to maintain peace and order within its confines."[189] Any other interpretation by the Court would, as Frankfurter pointed out, "be in derogation of our federal system" because it would "displace the reserved power of States over state offenses by reason of prosecution of minor federal offenses by federal authorities beyond the control of the States."[190]

The Supreme Court has been considerably less receptive, however, to efforts to extend the same logic to dual prosecutions under both state law and municipal ordinances. In *Waller* v. *Florida*,[191] it rejected the notion that "the relationship between a municipality and a state is analogous to the relationship between a State and the Federal Government." Instead, it declared that "the apt analogy of the relationship between the municipal and state governments is to be found in the relationship between the government of a Territory and the

Government of the United States . . . [where] a prosecution in a court of the United States is a bar to a subsequent prosecution in a territorial court, since both are arms of the same sovereign."[192] In so doing, it vacated the judgment of a second trial in a state court for grand larceny, because the defendant had already been convicted in city court of the included offenses of destruction of city property and disorderly breach of the peace.[193]

The Right to a Fair Trial

The Sixth Amendment provides that "in all criminal prosecutions, the accused shall enjoy the right to a speedy and public trial, by an impartial jury of the State and district wherein the crime shall have been committed." Among its other provisions, it also grants the accused the right "to be confronted with witnesses against him [and] to have compulsory process for obtaining witnesses in his favor." Once again, the bare language of the amendment raises a number of questions: What is a speedy trial? What is an impartial jury? And, what is the right to confrontation? The answers the Court has given to each of these questions must be given some consideration.

The Right to a Speedy Trial

The Sixth Amendment assures the accused of the right to a speedy trial.[194] But, what is a speedy trial? As Justice Powell acknowledged in *Barker* v. *Wingo,* "the right to a speedy trial is a more vague concept than other procedural rights. It is, for example, impossible to determine with precision when the right has been denied. We cannot definitely say how long is too long in a system where justice is supposed to be swift but deliberate."[195] The Court has been reluctant to hold "that the Constitution requires a criminal defendant to be offered a trial within a specified time period." To do so would require the Court "to engage in legislative or rule-making activity." Instead, it has identified four factors that have to be "balanced" against each other on an ad hoc basis: the length of the delay, the reason for the delay, the defendant's assertion of his right to a speedy trial, and the prejudice such a delay works on the defendant. If, on balance, it appears that the defendant has been denied a speedy trial, the Court has held that there is only one "possible remedy"—dismissal of the indictment.[196]

The Right to an Impartial Jury

Once the question of a speedy trial has been resolved, another question arises: What is an impartial jury?[197] In answering this question, the Court has had to consider three crucial issues: the composition of the jury, prejudicial pretrial and trial publicity, and the question of jury size and the requirement of unanimity.

The Composition of the Jury

The composition of the jury has been the subject of considerable litigation. Most of it has centered on the question of racial discrimination. Thus, for example, in its 1880 ruling in *Strauder* v. *West Virginia*,[198] the Supreme Court employed the Equal Protection Clause of the Fourteenth Amendment to declare formal exclusion of blacks from juries to be unconstitutional. It expanded this holding in *Norris* v. *Alabama*,[199] when it held that failure by a state to place the names of blacks on jury lists also violated the Constitution. Aware of the difficulties involved in proving discrimination, it held in *Eubanks* v. *Louisiana*[200] that a prima facie case of discrimination could be established by showing that only a small percentage of blacks have been called to jury duty despite a much larger percentage of blacks in the total population. Finally, the Court held in *Swain* v. *Alabama*[201] that, although a prosecutor's use of peremptory challenges to strike all prospective black jurors in a particular case did not constitute denial of due process, a different result might be reached if it could be shown that he regularly followed that practice. However, the Court has never held that each black defendant is entitled to a jury made up entirely or in part of blacks. As it stressed in *Atkins* v. *Texas*,[202] "fairness in selection has never been held to require proportional representation of races upon the jury."

Until 1975, claims of sexual discrimination in jury selection had not fared as well as claims of racial discrimination. *Hoyt* v. *Florida* was representative of this fact.[203] In that case, the Court held that a state could reasonably exclude all women from jury duty unless they volunteered. It accepted as reasonable the state's argument that the woman's role in the home was so significant that the state could reasonably relieve her of jury duty unless she determined herself that such services were consistent with her other responsibilities. However, in *Taylor* v. *Louisiana*,[204] the Court reversed *Hoyt*[205] and, in an eight-to-one decision, declared that this sort of exclusion of women from jury service deprived a defendant of the Sixth Amendment right to a jury drawn from a fair cross section of the community. Justice White spoke for the majority when he observed that "the unmistakeable import" of the Court's decisions over the past 35 years is that the presence of a fair cross section of the community on the jury venire "is essential to the Sixth Amendment's guarantee of an impartial jury trial."[206]

Prejudicial Pretrial and Trial Publicity

Directly related to the question of the demographic composition of the jury is the second major issue involved in the right to an impartial jury: protection of the defendant and the jury from prejudicial pretrial and trial publicity.

This issue presents the Court with an especially vexing dilemma: What should it do when the constitutionally protected right to a fair trial clashes with the constitutionally protected right of a free press? In Great Britain, this issue has not aroused nearly the controversy that it has in the United States. The right of every person to a free and impartial trial simply takes precedence over the right of a free press. Thus, the general rule in Great Britain is that, upon pain of contempt of court, nothing that might conceivably affect the attitude of a potential juror may be published unless and until it is formally disclosed at trial.[207] Large fines are meted out to newspapers that violate this general rule, and stiff jail sentences are imposed on their editors.[208] In the United States, however, the way in which the Constitution's First Amendment guarantees of free speech and free press have been interpreted has precluded this solution to the problem. As a consequence, on a number of occasions the Supreme Court has had to reverse the criminal convictions of defendants because of adverse pretrial or trial publicity. This practice was begun in 1961 in *Irvin* v. *Dowd,* when, for the first time, the Court reversed the conviction of a criminal defendant on the grounds of prejudicial pretrial publicity.[209] Justice Clark stressed that when a defendant's life is at stake, "it is not requiring too much that the petitioner be tried in an atmosphere undisturbed by so huge a wave of public passion [that 90 percent of the prospective jurors examined entertained some opinion as to guilt] and by a jury other than one in which two-thirds of the members admit, before hearing any testimony, to possessing a belief in his guilt." It was expanded in *Rideau* v. *Louisiana,* in which the Court reversed a defendant's conviction in the absence of a particularized showing of juror prejudice. Justice Stewart declared for a seven-member majority that due process had been denied the defendant who had been refused a request for a change of venue despite the fact that the entire community had been "exposed repeatedly and in depth" to the "spectacle" of the defendant confessing to a crime in a police interview broadcast on local television.[210] Finally, in *Estes* v. *Texas*[211] and *Sheppard* v. *Maxwell,*[212] the principles of *Irvin* and *Rideau* were extended to publicity during the trial as well. In those decisions, the Court declared that the presence at trial of a large, ill-controlled news media contingent can deny a defendant the "judicial serenity and calm" that are essential for a fair trial—even in the absence of proof that the jury was in fact prejudiced by the publicity.

In an effort to avoid the effects of this prejudicial publicity, the Court in *Sheppard* admonished judges, lawyers, and journalists to adopt guidelines for disclosure and reporting of information in criminal proceedings. As a consequence, most states have now adopted voluntary bar-media codes, in which both the legal community and the news media agree not to disclose or report such information as the prior criminal record of the accused, the existence or content of any confession, the refusal of the accused to make a statement, the results of fingerprints, polygraph examinations, or ballistics tests, the identity or credibility of prospective witnesses, the possibility of a plea of guilty to the charge, or any opinion on the guilt or innocence of the accused.[213]

Jury Size and the Requirement of Unanimity

With these decisions regulating the jury's composition and ensuring its impartiality, the Court has felt free to allow states to depart from the traditional requirements that juries must consist of twelve members and that they must render their verdicts unanimously. Thus, in *Williams* v. *Florida*,[214] the Court upheld the conviction of a defendant by a jury composed of only six members. Justice White justified this decision, noting that "the purpose of the jury trial ... is to prevent oppression by the Government."

> Given this purpose, the essential feature of a jury trial obviously lies in the interposition between the accused and his accuser of the commonsense judgment of a group of laymen, and in the community participation and shared responsibility that results from that group's determination of guilt or innocence. The performance of this role is not a function of the particular number of the body that makes up the jury ... [and] we find little reason to think that these goals are in any meaningful sense less likely to be achieved when the jury numbers six, than when it numbers twelve.[215]

Likewise, in *Johnson* v. *Louisiana*,[216] it departed from the requirement of unanimity. The Court rejected appellant's due process and equal protection claims and sustained provisions of both the Louisiana Constitution and its Code of Criminal Procedure, which provided that in noncapital cases, a vote of nine of the twelve jurors is sufficient either to convict or acquit.

The Right to Confrontation

The final question raised by the Sixth Amendment guarantee of a fair trial is the right of confrontation. This provision was made applicable to the states under the Fourteenth Amendment in *Pointer* v. *Texas*.[217] In its effort to give meaning to this right, the Court has held in *Barber* v. *Page*[218] that a state may not introduce into evidence the testimony of a witness at a preliminary hearing unless it has made a "good-faith effort to obtain his presence at trial" and in *Bruton* v. *United States*[219] has barred the admission in a joint trial of a confession of one co-defendant that implicates the other.[220] The right to confrontation is not absolute, however; as the Court declared in *Illinois* v. *Allen*,[221] an obstreperous defendant "can lose his right to be present at trial if, after he has been warned by the judge that he will be removed if he continues his disruptive behavior, he nevertheless insists on conducting himself in a manner so disorderly, disruptive, and disrespectful of the court that his trial cannot be carried on with him in the courtroom."[222] Justice Black declared that there are at least three constitutionally permissible ways of handling such a contumacious defendant: He can be held in criminal contempt; he can be ordered from the courtroom until he "is willing to conduct himself consistently with the decorum and respect inherent in the concept of courts and judicial proceedings"; or, as a "last resort," he can be ordered bound and gagged.

The Protection Against Cruel and Unusual Punishments

The Eighth Amendment protects against the infliction of "cruel and unusual punishments." Again, as with other provisions of the Bill of Rights, these words are like so many empty vessels into which the Court has had to pour meaning. The amendment's particular phraseology derives from the English Bill of Rights of 1689 and was originally understood to prevent such ancient practices as branding, drawing and quartering, burning alive, and crucifixion. The death penalty as such was not held to violate its provisions so long as it did not involve unnecessary cruelty. As the Court observed in *Wilkerson* v. *Utah,* in which it upheld execution by a firing squad, "difficulty would attend the effort to define with exactness the extent of this constitutional provision which provides that cruel and unusual punishments shall not be inflicted, but it is safe to affirm that punishments of torture, . . . and all others of the same line of unnecessary cruelty, are forbidden by that Amendment to the Constitution."[223] The amendment was understood to be a limitation not only on the manner of punishment but also on the severity of the punishment in relation to the crime itself. Thus, in *Weems* v. *United States,* the Court condemned a Philippine statute prescribing a fine and imprisonment of from 12 to 20 years for entering a known false statement in a public record, on the ground that the gross disparity between this punishment and that imposed for other more serious offenses made it cruel and unusual and, hence, repugnant to the Bill of Rights.[224]

However, as Chief Justice Warren noted in *Trop* v. *Dulles,* the scope of the Eighth Amendment "is not static. The Amendment must draw its meaning from the evolving standards of decency that mark the progress of a maturing society."[225] Put simply, whatever the amendment was originally intended to mean is of less importance to the Court than what "evolving standards of decency" require. Just what the Court holds these standards to be is now of as much interest to the states as to federal government, because *Robinson* v. *California* made this particular provision applicable to the states as well through the Fourteenth Amendment.[226]

Robinson invalidated a California statute that made it a misdemeanor subject to a mandatory jail sentence of not less than 90 days for a person to "be addicted to the use of narcotics." Justice Stewart spoke for a five-member majority when he observed that the statute did not prohibit the use, purchase, sale, or possession of narcotics but rather was directed toward making the "'status' of narcotics addiction a criminal offense for which the offender may be prosecuted 'at any time before he reforms.'" He concluded by holding that "a state law which imprisons a person thus afflicted as a criminal, even though he has never touched any narcotic drug within the State or been guilty of any irregular behavior there, inflicts a cruel and unusual punishment in violation of the Fourteenth Amendment. To be sure, imprisonment for 90 days is not, in the abstract, a punishment which is either cruel or unusual, but the question cannot be considered in the abstract. Even one day in prison would be a cruel and unusual punishment for the 'crime' of having a common cold."[227]

Robinson was significant for three principal reasons. Not only did it incorporate the constitutional guarantee against imposition of cruel and unusual punishments into the Fourteenth Amendment, but it also set as an absolute minimum condition of validity that all criminal statutes assign liability on the basis of the behavior and not the status or condition of the alleged offender and recognized in the Eighth Amendment a general constitutional command that the punishment fit the crime.[228]

The potential sweep of these propositions is awesome, and the Court thus far has only begun to scratch the surface. Thus, in *Powell* v. *Texas* in 1968, the Court came within one vote of holding that jailing a chronic alcoholic for public drunkenness constitutes cruel and unusual punishment.[229] Justice Thurgood Marshall in his plurality opinion feared the danger of undermining the common-law doctrine of criminal responsibility with an extension of the *Robinson* holding to cases like *Powell.* If the Court were to hold that a chronic alcoholic could not be convicted for public drunkenness because of a claim that he suffers from a compulsion to drink over which he has no control, then, Marshall stressed, it would be difficult to see how a person could be convicted for murder if a claim were also made in that case that the person "while exhibiting normal behavior in all other respects, suffers from a compulsion to kill."[230] Consequently, Marshall sought to distinguish *Robinson* and *Powell,* noting that in *Robinson* the Court condemned the state action because it inflicted punishment for the mere status of addiction, whereas in *Powell,* the state had properly "imposed upon the appellant a criminal sanction for public behavior which may create substantial health and safety hazards both for the appellant and for members of the general public, and which offends the moral and esthetic sensibilities of a large segment of the population."[231]

Perhaps the most dramatic issue to date arising out of *Robinson* and its incorporation of the protection against cruel and unusual punishments has been the question of capital punishment. In 1972 in *Furman* v. *Georgia,* a badly split Court rendered inoperable every state death penalty statute then in existence.[232] In a brief *per curiam* order, the five members of the majority were able to agree that "the imposition and the carrying out of the death penalty in these cases constitute cruel and unusual punishment in violation of the Eighth and Fourteenth

Amendments." However, they could agree on little more, as attested by the fact that each member of the majority wrote a separate opinion. Thus, Justices Marshall and Brennan both argued that the imposition of the death penalty is per se unconstitutional: Justice Marshall found it to be not only "abhorrent to currently existing moral values" but also excessive and unnecessary;[233] Justice Brennan, on the other hand, contended that it was "offensive to human dignity," because "death is an unusually severe and degrading punishment."[234] Justice Douglas's objections were less far reaching; thus, although he did not consider capital punishment to be per se unconstitutional, he did find imposition of the death penalty as presented in *Furman* and its companion cases to be incompatible with the notion of equal protection that he found implicit in the Eighth Amendment. In these cases, "the discretion of judges and juries in imposing the death penalty enables the penalty to be selectively applied, feeding prejudices against the accused if he is poor and despised, poor and lacking political clout, or if he is a member of a suspect or unpopular minority, and saving those who by social position may be in a more protected position."[235]

The objections of Justices Stewart and White were by far the narrowest and pertained to what they considered to be the uncontrolled discretion that judges and juries were free to exercise under the state death penalty statutes then in force. Thus, Justice Stewart found the sentences imposed on the defendants in *Furman* and its companion cases to be "cruel and unusual in the same way that being struck by lightening is cruel and unusual." He saw "the petitioners . . . [as] among a capriciously selected and random handful" of all those convicted of the crimes of rape and murder, and this fact is what made their sentences unconstitutional. As Justice Stewart stressed, the Eighth Amendment "cannot tolerate the infliction of a sentence of death under legal systems that permit this unique penalty to be so wantonly and so freakishly imposed."[236] Neither Justices Stewart nor White saw capital punishment as per se unconstitutional; both, however, stressed that the Eighth Amendment does not tolerate, in the slightest, capriciousness in the imposition of this punishment.[237]

Although *Furman* foreclosed executions under state statutes then in existence, it did not declare that capital punishment was inevitably unconstitutional. Encouraged by the fact that only Justices Brennan and Marshall seemed to regard all death penalty statutes as per se unconstitutional, state legislatures were quick to adopt new capital punishment statutes that attempted to meet the objections of the other members of the *Furman* majority, especially Justices Stewart and White. Ultimately, new death penalty schemes providing for either controlled discretion or mandatory death sentences were adopted by at least thirty-five states. With the enactment of these new laws, the Court was forced once again to confront the question of the constitutionality of the death penalty. When it finally did in 1976, it held in a seven-to-two vote that the death penalty is a constitutionally permissible punishment, at least for carefully defined categories of murder. However, the same plurality that spoke for the Court on this basic issue went on to say that the Eighth Amendment requires the sentencing authority to be provided with carefully controlled discretion: A bifurcated trial was seen as the ideal procedure.[238] Mandatory death penalty statutes, on the other hand, were generally regarded as unconstitutional.[239]

Considering in five separate sets of opinions the constitutionality of five different state capital punishment statutes, the Court was unable to muster a majority for any one analysis of these statutes. However, seven justices, with Justices Brennan and Marshall dissenting, did agree that capital punishment does not inevitably violate the Eighth Amendment. The same seven voted to uphold the "controlled discretion" schemes of the states of Georgia, Texas, and Florida. On the other hand, the "mandatory" death penalty statutes of the states of North Carolina and Louisiana were struck down by five-to-four majorities.[240]

The key opinion in each of the five cases was jointly written by Justices Stewart, Powell, and Stevens. Taken together, their five plurality opinions make it clear that the Eighth Amendment not only permits controlled discretion on the part of the sentencing authority but in fact demands it. Their analysis is worth some attention.

Justices Stewart, Powell, and Stevens began by stressing that the Eighth Amendment, which has been interpreted in a flexible and dynamic manner in accord with evolving standards of decency, forbids the use of punishment that is "excessive" either because it involves the unnecessary and wanton infliction of pain or because it is grossly disproportionate to the severity of the crime.[241] They went on to point out, however, that these standards must be applied with an awareness of the judiciary's limited role in assessing the constitutionality of a punishment selected by a democratically elected legislature. "We may not require the legislature to select the least severe penalty possible so long as the penalty selected is not cruelly inhumane or disproportionate to the crime involved. And a heavy burden rests on those who would attack the judgments of the representatives of the people."[242] They stressed that both the weight of the legislative judgment in assessing contemporary standards and considerations of federalism would have to be taken into consideration, as would also the fact that the selection of punishments is peculiarly within the legislative sphere. The plurality went on to analyze both contemporary standards and the question of the death penalty's excessiveness as a sanction for deliberate murder and concluded that the penalty satisfied both standards. Thus, it concluded that the enactment of death penalty schemes by the legislatures of at least thirty-five states, the passage of death penalty legislation by Congress in 1974 for aircraft piracy that results in death, and the willingness of juries or courts in some 460 cases to impose the death penalty under these laws were significant and reliable indicators of the punishment's acceptability to contemporary society.[243]

Justices Stewart, Powell, and Stevens also found that the penological justification for capital punishment was sufficient to comport "with the basic concept of human dignity at the core of the Amendment." They were not persuaded that capital punishment did not serve the purposes of retribution and deterrence. Their willingness to accept retribution as a legitimate social purpose reflected the view expressed by Justice Stewart in *Furman:* It was based on the recognition that "in part, capital punishment is an expression of society's moral outrage at particularly offensive conduct. This function may be unappealing to many, but it is essential in an ordered society that asks its citizens to rely on legal processes rather than self-help to vindicate their wrongs."[244] On the hotly debated question of whether capital punishment is an effective deterrent, the plurality declared that "the results simply have been inconclusive. . . . The value of capital punishment as a deterrent of crime is a complex factual issue the resolution of which properly rests with the legislatures, which can evaluate the results of statistical studies in terms of their own local conditions and with a flexibility of approach that is not available to the courts."[245] Thus, a state legislature's judgment that capital punishment is necessary in some cases cannot be deemed "clearly wrong," the plurality concluded.[246] The death penalty is not a form of punishment that may never be imposed, regardless of the circumstances of the offense, regardless of the character of the offender, and regardless of the procedure followed in reaching the decision to impose it.[247]

However, while Justices Stewart, Powell, and Stevens acknowledged that the death penalty is not a form of punishment that may never be imposed, they were insistent that it be accompanied by adequate constitutional safeguards. Capital punishment, they held, is permissible only where there is controlled discretion on the part of the sentencing authority. The statutes of Georgia, Texas, and Florida controlled sufficiently the discretion of the sentencing authority by requiring it to weigh a number of statutory aggravating and mitigating circumstances in making the life-or-death decision and in providing for automatic appellate review of death sentences. This controlled discretion, however, was altogether absent in the "mandatory" capital punishment schemes of North Carolina and Louisiana. Put simply, the mandatory approach was "unduly harsh and unworkably rigid."[248] It conflicted with the evolving standards of decency that inform the Eighth Amendment's prohibition against cruel and unusual punishment. After all, the respect for human dignity underlying the Eighth Amendment requires consideration of aspects of the character of the individual offender and the circumstances of the particular offense as a constitutionally indispensable part of the process of imposing the ultimate punishment of death. Thus, the plurality joined with Justices Brennan and Marshall in invalidating the Louisiana and North Carolina statutes because they impermissibly treated all persons convicted of a designated offense "not as uniquely individual human beings, but as members of a faceless, undifferentiated mass to be subjected to the blind infliction of the death penalty."[249]

Four other justices (Chief Justice Burger and Justices White, Blackmun, and Rehnquist) concurred with the Stewart, Powell, and Stevens plurality in upholding the capital punishment statutes of Georgia, Florida, and Texas.

Justice White spoke for them, declaring that if the statutes in question were to operate as designed, the "wanton and freakish" imposition of the death penalty condemned in *Furman* would not occur.[250] However, they found no significant difference between these statutes and those of North Carolina and Louisiana, and, accordingly, they would have upheld the latter statutes as well. As Justice White stressed, a state may conclude that the commission of certain crimes adequately establishes the criminal's character and that the need for deterrence and the likelihood of its success support a mandatory scheme.[251]

Justices Brennan and Marshall, the only members of the *Furman* majority who would have declared capital punishment per se unconstitutional, held fast to that position. They continued to stress that the issue is essentially a moral one. As Justice Brennan insisted, the cruel and unusual punishment clause "embodies in unique degree moral principles restraining the punishments that our civilized society may impose on those persons who transgress its laws." Capital punishment, no less than "the rack, the screw, and the wheel, is no longer morally tolerable in our civilized society."[252] Reiterating one of the points he made in *Furman,* Justice Brennan declared that the fatal constitutional infirmity of the death penalty is its treatment of human beings "as objects to be toyed with and discarded."[253] Justice Marshall likewise expanded upon themes he had introduced in his *Furman* concurrence. In part, this was an attempt to meet directly the claim that subsequent developments had undercut his *Furman* conclusion about the unacceptability of capital punishment under current moral standards. Thus, he declared: "I would be less than candid if I did not acknowledge that these developments have a significant bearing on a realistic assessment of the moral acceptability of the death penalty to the American people. But if the constitutionality of the death penalty turns, as I have urged, on the opinion of an *informed* citizenry, then even the enactment of new death statutes cannot be viewed as conclusive."[254] Justice Marshall also used his dissent to express his alarm that the Court majority was willing to accept "the notion that retribution can serve as moral justification for the sanction of death."[255] "It is this notion that I find to be the most disturbing aspect of today's unfortunate decision," he declared. The taking of a wrongdoer's life because "he deserves it . . . surely must fall, for such a punishment has as its very basis the total denial of the wrongdoer's dignity and worth."[256]

Posttrial Procedures

The Supreme Court has also found it necessary to protect the constitutional rights of defendants in such posttrial procedures as sentencing, appeals, and postconviction remedies. Traditionally, the Court has not subjected sentencing to the same constitutional limitations it has imposed on the trial process. This has been justified in part on the historical separation of the trial and sentencing stages and in part on the grounds that fulfillment of the basic objectives of sentencing—especially the emphasis on fitting the punishment to the individual as well as to the crime—requires more flexible procedural standards than those applied in the determination of guilt.[257] However, recently the Court has restricted somewhat this flexibility as inconsistent with the demands of the Due Process and Equal Protection Clauses of the Fourteenth Amendment. *Williams* v. *Illinois*[258] and *Tate* v. *Short*[259] illustrate this point. In *Williams,* the Court declared that an indigent defendant may not be held in confinement beyond the maximum term specified by law because of his failure to satisfy the monetary provisions of his sentence. Such a practice, Chief Justice Burger held, constituted a denial of equal protection of the laws in that it imposed a far heavier burden on the indigent than on the solvent offender. Speaking for a unanimous Court, he stressed that "since only a convicted person with access to funds can avoid the increased imprisonment, the Illinois statute in operative effect exposes only indigents to the risk of imprisonment beyond the statutory maximum. By making the maximum confinement contingent upon one's ability to pay, the State has visited different consequences on two categories of persons since the result is to make incarceration in excess of the statutory maximum applicable only to those without the requisite resources to satisfy the money portion of the judgment."[260] Likewise, in *Tate,* the Court denied that a state can, consistent with the Equal Protection Clause, limit the punishment of an offender to payment of fines if he is able to pay, yet convert the fines into a prison term if he is indigent and without means to pay his fine.[261]

The constitutionally protected procedural rights of the defendant continue even when the sentencing stage is complete. Although the Supreme Court held in *McKane* v. *Durston*[262] that a state is not constitutionally obligated to provide for appellate review of criminal convictions, in *Griffin* v. *Illinois*[263] in 1956, it declared that if a state does establish appellate review, and all states have now done so, this review must be available to all, regardless of financial status. Most constitutional decisions relating to appellate review since *Griffin* have been concerned with the application and extension of the *Griffin* principle; for example, *Douglas* v. *California*[264] held that a state must provide indigent defendants with court-appointed counsel on appeal. The Court has not gone so far, however, as to require that a state provide an indigent appellee with every advantage that may be enjoyed by a more affluent appellee. Thus, in the 1974 case of *Ross* v. *Moffitt,*[265] a six-to-three Court held that a state is not required to provide counsel to indigent defendants for discretionary state appeals or for application for review by the U.S. Supreme Court. As Justice Rehnquist explained the Court's position:

> There are significant differences between the trial and appellate stages of a criminal proceeding. The purpose of the trial stage from the State's point of view is to convert a criminal defendant from a person presumed innocent to one found guilty beyond a reasonable doubt. . . . Under the

circumstances . . . "reason and reflection require us to recognize that in our adversary system of criminal justice, any person hailed into court who is too poor to hire a lawyer cannot be assured of a fair trial unless counsel is provided for him."

By contrast, it is ordinarily the defendant, rather than the State, who initiates the appellate process, seeking not to fend off the efforts of the State's prosecutor, but rather to overturn a finding of guilt made by a judge or jury below. The defendant needs an attorney on appeal, not as a shield to protect him against being "hailed into court" by the State and stripped of his presumption of innocence, but rather as a sword to upset the prior determination of guilt. This difference is significant for, while no one would agree that a State may simply dispense with the trial stage of proceedings without a criminal defendant's consent, it is clear that the State need not provide any appeal at all. . . . The fact that an appeal has been provided does not automatically mean that a State then acts unfairly by refusing to provide counsel to indigent defendants at every stage of the way.[266]

The constitutional limitations imposed on postconviction remedies are roughly akin to the limitations imposed on appellate review. Several Supreme Court opinions suggest that a state is not required to provide postconviction remedies; however, once again, if it does, the *Griffin* principle applies. Postconviction relief in federal courts is subject to the limitations of Article I, Section 9, as well as the requirements of the Due Process Clause of the Fifth Amendment. Article I, Section 9, provides that the privilege of the writ of habeas corpus shall not be suspended except in times of rebellion or invasion when the public safety may require it. In *Fay* v. *Noia*,[267] the Court extended significantly the availability of habeas relief for state prisoners "in custody in violation of the Constitution." *Fay* held that federal habeas corpus proceedings are a proper way to challenge a previously obtained unconstitutional state conviction. Before *Fay*, the Supreme Court had restricted habeas corpus in such a way that federal courts would never consider the merits of a constitutional claim if the petitioner had a fair opportunity to raise his arguments in the original proceeding. Even after *Brown* v. *Allen*,[268] which liberalized somewhat habeas corpus relief, the petitioner still had to have raised a "new" constitutional argument both at his original trial and on appeal in order to raise the argument again in a habeas corpus proceeding. However, in *Fay,* the Court held for the first time that in certain instances, a habeas corpus petitioner may collaterally attack his conviction despite the fact that the "new" issue on which he bases his attack had not even been suggested in the original proceedings. In so doing, it has opened the door for a large number of prisoners to relitigate their convictions each time a "new" constitutional rule is announced by the Court.[269]

Retroactive Application of Criminal Procedural Guarantees

One further question must be considered in this analysis of the Supreme Court, the Constitution, and criminal procedure. Once the Supreme Court has interpreted the provisions of the Bill of Rights in such a manner as to expand the procedural protections of criminal defendants and once it has incorporated these provisions through the Fourteenth Amendment to apply to the states, are these new interpretations and incorporations to be given retroactive effect—that is, are they to be made available to criminal defendants whose cases have already been litigated under different rules deemed constitutionally permissible at the time? Until 1965, this question was always answered in the affirmative. The reasons for this answer have been provided by Professor Herman Schwartz. "New constitutional doctrines are not new conceptions but rather reflections of principles of 'ordered liberty' fundamental to our legal system. Such principles are equally applicable to past and present trials, for an ethical society cannot seek to retain the fruits of past defaults."[270] According to Professor Schwartz, the Court's most recent decisions in criminal procedure have neither discovered nor created new rights; rather, thay have granted new federal remedies for old wrongs. These remedies have been granted only recently, not because the rights they protect are newly conceived or newly relevant, but because sensitivity for these rights has increased.[271] This commitment by the Court to unlimited retroactivity was abandoned, however, in *Linkletter* v. *Walker.*[272] In that particular case, Justice Clark concluded for a seven-member majority that "the Constitution neither prohibits nor requires retrospective effect."[273] Instead, he argued, "We must . . . weigh the merits and demerits in each case by looking to the prior history of the rule in question, its purpose, effect, and whether retrospective operation will further or retard its operation."[274] To assist the Court in weighing the various merits and demerits of applying particular decisions retroactively, Justice Clark announced three standards or criteria: (1) the purpose to be served by the new decision; (2) the extent of reliance by the law enforcement authorities on the old decision; and (3) the effect on the administration of justice of a retroactive application of the new decision.[275] When Justice Clark applied these standards to the case under consideration, which addressed the possible retroactive effect of *Mapp* v. *Ohio,* he concluded that "we are not able to say that the *Mapp* rule requires retrospective application."[276] To begin with, the states had justifiably relied on *Wolf* v. *Colorado,* which had exempted them from the strictures of the exclusionary rule: "Again and again this Court refused to reconsider *Wolf* and gave its implicit approval to hundreds of cases in their application of its rule."[277] Likewise, the retroactive application of *Mapp* "would tax the administration of justice to the utmost."[278] Over half of the states would be affected and would now be required to hold new hearings on the possible exclusion of evidence long since destroyed, misplaced, or deteriorated. Witnesses would perhaps be unavailable, or, if located, they might have trouble recalling details of the case. "To thus legitimate such an extraordinary procedural weapon that has no bearing on guilt would seriously disrupt the administration of justice."[279] Most importantly, however, Justice Clark stressed that *Mapp* had as its prime purpose the enforcement of the Fourth Amendment through application of the exclusionary rule. This, he continued, was the only effective deterrent to lawless police action. But, "we cannot say that this purpose would be advanced by making the rule retrospective. The misconduct of the police prior to *Mapp* has already occurred and will not be corrected by releasing the prisoners involved."[280] The purpose of *Mapp* did not reach to the fundamental fairness of the trial, to the very integrity of the fact-finding process. The fairness of the trial was not at issue. All that Linkletter could attack was the admissibility of evidence, the reliability and relevancy of which was not questioned. In overturning *Wolf*, the purpose had been to deter the lawless action of the police and to enforce the Fourth Amendment effectively. Justice Clark felt that that purpose would not be served by the "wholesale release of the guilty victims."[281]

Since *Linkletter,* the Court has remained faithfully wedded to the three criteria enunciated in this seminal decision.[282] To the extent that there is any alteration in the Court's thinking on retroactivity, it has occurred in the new and singular emphasis that the Court now places on the sole criterion of purpose. As Justice Stewart noted in the Court's opinion in *Desist* v. *United States,* "foremost . . . is the purpose to be served by the new constitutional rule."[283] The criteria of reliance and effect on the administration of justice are invoked only "when the purpose of the rule in question [does] not clearly favor either retroactivity or prospectivity."[284] With these criteria firmly established and with the number of retroactivity issues on the decline now that virtually all the provisions of the Bill of Rights have been incorporated through the Fourteenth Amendment to apply to the states, the controversy surrounding retroactivity has subsided, and the reasons for the Court's abandonment of unlimited retroactivity can now be dispassionately examined.

Perhaps the most important reason for the Court's efforts to limit the retroactive effect of its decisions is the essentially activistic character of the recent Court. Ineluctable retroactivity would seem to be an automatic check and "inherent restraint" on judicial innovations, because it would compel the Court to confront in a most direct manner the possible undesirable consequences of adopting a new rule. As Justice Black observed in *James* v. *United States:*

> In our judgment one of the great inherent restraints upon this Court's departure from the field of interpretation to enter that of lawmaking has been the fact that its judgments could not be limited to prospective application. This Court and in fact all departments of the government have always heretofore realized that prospective law-making is the function of

Congress rather than the Court's. We continue to think that this function should be exercised only by Congress under our Constitutional system.[285]

The activist Warrent Court, however, chafed at these restraints and established its criteria to limit the immediate ill-effects of its lawmaking, much to the consternation of Justice Black, who condemned this practice in his dissent in *Lee* v. *Florida:* "Waiting for Congress to rewrite its laws, however, is too slow for the Court in this day of rapid creation of new judicial rules."[286]

A second reason for the Court's departure from unlimited retroactivity is its desire to forestall hostile public reaction to its more controversial decisions. *Johnson* v. *New Jersey* is a case in point.[287] It limited the retroactive effect of *Escobedo* v. *Illinois* and *Miranda* v. *Arizona* only to those cases in which the trial had actually begun after the dates that *Escobedo* and *Miranda* had been decided. *Johnson* thus appears to be an intensely practical decision by the Court, which was attempting to minimize the hostility that *Escobedo* and *Miranda* had generated. Its *Linkletter* criteria were employed for the prospective result they could accomplish rather than for the method of analysis they could provide. These efforts by the Court to limit the retroactive effect of its more controversial decisions so as to minimize adverse public reaction to them has also prompted individual justices to employ similar strategies. Thus, a particular justice may seek to limit the retroactive operation of certain decisions not only because of public disapprobation but also because he is himself fundamentally at odds with the decision and wishes to limit its effect as much as possible. As Justice Harlan rather candidly confessed in *Desist:* "I did so [voted against unlimited retroactivity] because I though it important to limit the impact of constitutional decisions which seemed to me profoundly unsound in principle."[288]

Finally, a third reason (closely related to the second) for the Court's departure from unlimited retroactivity is the volatile and provocative problem of federalism. The need to sustain and, indeed, encourage viable and healthy federal-state relationships often intrudes into the Court's considerations of retroactivity. Each time the Supreme Court extends another Bill of Rights guarantee to the states, it imposes a quantum-level increase in both the quality and extent of the states' responsibility in the realm of criminal procedure. The shock that these quantum-level increases have caused the states has been profound; and the consequence has been hostility to federal court intervention, couched in the rhetoric of states' rights and state sovereignty. Thus, the Court, aware of the exacerbating influence that its incorporation of the Bill of Rights has had on already strained federal-state relations, has often sought to mitigate this tension by limiting the impact of its decisions through prospective application. Such Court awareness is apparent in *Linkletter* v. *Walker,* where Justice Clark unabashedly announced, "nor would it [retroactive application of *Mapp*] add harmony to the delicate state-federal relationship."[289]

Basic Themes

From this basic review of what the Supreme Court has done in the realm of criminal procedure, four basic themes emerge. The first is the complete dependence of the Court upon the exercise of normative power. It is required to pour meaning into the many ambiguous provisions of the Bill of Rights, and it can accomplish this only through the normative power of judgment. On the quality of this judgment, the whole society depends. As Chief Justice Earl Warren declared in *Coppedge* v. *United States,* "no general respect for, nor adherence to, the law as a whole can well be expected without judicial recognition of the paramount need for prompt, eminently fair and sober criminal law procedures. The methods we employ in the enforcement of our criminal law have aptly been called the measures by which the quality of our civilization may be judged."[290]

A second theme closely related to the first is the emphasis the Court has placed on achieving equality in the administration of criminal justice. The Court has recognized the unequal impact that criminal procedure has tended to have on the poor and racial minorities and has undertaken to eliminate the official aspects of this inequality.[291] The same emphasis on equality has also been apparent in the treatment of juveniles as well. Thus, as a result of the 1967 decision of *In re Gault,*[292] juvenile defendants are now guaranteed such rights as effective and specific notice of charges, representation by counsel and appointment of counsel if the defendant is indigent, confrontation and cross examination of witnesses, and protection of the privilege against self-incrimination.

A third basic theme is the Court's growing insistence upon uniform constitutional standards applicable in both the state and federal systems. The Court has all but repudiated the traditional view that states are to serve as laboratories, experimenting with novel social and legal schemes and thereby sparing the whole nation of the need to suffer the consequences of failure. Although this requirement ensures a certain uniformity of criminal procedure throughout the land, it does stifle creativity and check innovation.

Finally, a fourth basic theme that emerges from this review of the Court's decisions in criminal procedure is its movement toward broadly stated rulings. In such decisions as *Miranda* and *Wade,* it has gone far beyond the proscription of particular unconstitutional practices and has prescribed affirmative standards of conduct that it regards as essential to safeguard against such unconstitutional practices. Thus, in *Miranda,* to avoid the potential violation of a defendant's privilege against self-incrimination during pretrial police interrogations, it required that the defendant be advised of his rights and given the right to consult with counsel before and during any interrogation. In *Wade,* it similarly required that the state make available to the defendant assistance of counsel in order to protect him from the unconstitutional manipulation of lineup identification procedures.

The use of such prescriptive rulings has certain obvious advantages. To begin

THE SUPREME COURT

with, it reduces uncertainty and provides the police, prosecutors, and personnel of lower courts with specific instruction as to which procedures do or do not pass constitutional muster. By so doing, the Court is spared the need to pass individual judgment on each and every criminal prosecution and is able to devote its time and attention to the further development and refinement of fundamental constitutional protections. However, the movement toward broadly stated rulings is not an unmixed blessing. Thus, it represents a substantial departure from the "judicial" function. Instead of judging the merits of a particular "case or controversy" as charged by Article III of the Constitution, the Court has become increasingly engaged in general lawmaking. The consequences of this shift are rather far-reaching. Thus, lawmaking typically emphasizes general society-wide policies and the general administration of these policies. It is not concerned with the fates of particular individuals or the alleviation of specific instances of injustice. Traditionally, these concerns have been left to the judiciary, which has rejected the idea of general lawmaking and has understood its function to be the dispensation of justice and equity on the individual, case-by-case level. As the Court abandons this traditional role, however, there appears to be no other institution ready to step in and take its place.

Whatever the advantages or disadvantages of the Court's more prescriptive decisions, they have not always had the full effect that the Supreme Court has anticipated.[293] As Theodore L. Becker and Malcolm M. Feeley have observed, there is often a "rather wide gap between what the Court says *ought* to be done and what in fact *is* actually done."[294] The extent of this discrepancy between the "ought" of doctrine and the "is" of behavior and the reasons that account for it must be closely assessed, because they reveal the true limits of the Court's capacity effectively to employ normative power. With the aid of compliance analysis, these questions will be explored in Chapter 5.

Notes

1. See the discussion in Chapter 2, pp. 50-54, 57-58.
2. Alexander Hamilton, James Madison, and John Jay, *The Federalist,* ed. Jacob E. Cooke (New York: World, 1961), p. 523.
3. *Graves* v. *New York ex rel. O'Keefe,* 306 U.S. 466, 492 (1939). Mr. Justice Frankfurter concurring.
4. "The state is mainly responsible for the maintenance of law and order; most crimes are defined by state legislatures; and enforcement is in the hands of state police and judicial agencies." David Fellman, "The Supreme Court's Changing View of Criminal Defendants' Rights," in *Crime in Urban Society,* ed. Barbara N. McLennan (New York: Dunellen, 1970), pp. 96-97. The states' major responsibility in the realm of criminal justice is also reflected in a comparison of state and federal prison populations. Thus, for

example, in 1970 there were 176,384 adult felony offenders in state correctional instututions, but only 19,623 such persons in federal penal institutions. See Federal Bureau of Prisons, *National Prisoners Statistics: Prisoners in State and Federal Institutions for Adult Felons, 1968, 1969, 1970.* U.S. Department of Justice (Washington D.C.: Government Printing Office, 1971), p. 6.

5. 7 Peters 243 (1833).
6. Ibid., p. 250.
7. *Holden* v. *Hardy,* 169 U.S. 366, 389 (1898). Quoted by Justice Moody in *Twining* v. *New Jersey,* 211 U.S. 78, 102 (1908).
8. *Palko* v. *Connecticut,* 302 U.S. 319 (1937). Henry J. Abraham refers to these "fundamental rights" protected by the Fourteenth Amendment as belonging to the "Honor Roll of Superior Rights." *Freedom and the Court: Civil Rights and Liberties in the United States,* 2nd ed. (New York: Oxford University Press, 1972), p. 58.
9. *Lisemba* v. *California,* 314 U.S. 219, 236 (1941). Mr. Justice Roberts employed this language in his majority opinion for the Court.
10. 381 U.S. 479, 500 (1965). Mr. Justice Harlan concurring in the judgment of the Court.
11. Ibid.
12. *Estes* v. *Texas,* 381 U.S. 532, 587 (1965). On much the same grounds, Justice Harlan concurred in the judgment of the Court in striking down Connecticut's birth control law. "In my view, the proper constitutional inquiry in this case is whether this Connecticut statute infringes upon the Due Process Clause of the Fourteenth Amendment because the enactment violates basic values 'implicit in a concept of ordered liberty'. . . . I believe it does." 381 U.S. at 500.
13. *Griswold* v. *Connecticut,* 381 U.S. 479, 522 (1965). Justice Black dissenting.
14. Ibid., pp. 515, 516, 524. See also his dissent in *Adamson* v. *California,* 332 U.S. 46, 91-92 (1947).
15. *Griswold* v. *Connecticut,* 381 U.S. at 522.
16. *Duncan* v. *Louisiana,* 391 U.S. 145, 168 (1967).
17. Ibid., p. 169. Justice Black made much the same point in *Griswold,* when he argued that the "fundamental rights" interpretation permits "judges to determine what is or is not constitutional on the basis of their own appraisal of what laws are unwise or unnecessary." 381 U.S. 479, 511-512.
18. Jerold H. Israel and Wayne R. LaFave, *Criminal Procedure: Constitutional Limitations,* 2nd ed. (St. Paul: West, 1975), p. 9.
19. 18 Howard 272, 276 (1856).
20. Israel and LaFave, *Criminal Procedure,* p. 9.
21. *Joint Anti-Fascist Refugee Committee* v. *McGrath,* 341 U.S. 123, 162-163 (1951). Mr. Justice Frankfurter concurring.

THE SUPREME COURT 165

22. *Adamson v. California,* 332 U.S. 46, 89 (1947). Mr. Justice Black dissenting. See Howard Ball, *The Vision and the Dream of Justice Hugo L. Black* (University, Ala.: University of Alabama Press, 1975), pp. 78-135, and Wallace Mendelson, *Justices Black and Frankfurter: Conflict in the Court* (Chicago: University of Chicago Press, 1966), pp. 64-73.
23. See Justice Black's famous dissent in *Adamson,* in which he argued that the history of the Fourteenth Amendment "conclusively demonstrates that the language of the first section of the Fourteenth Amendment, taken as a whole, was thought by those responsible for its submission to the people, and by those who opposed its submission, sufficiently explicit to guarantee that thereafter no state could deprive its citizens of the privileges and protections of the Bill of Rights." 332 U.S. at 74-75. For a historical examination that disagrees with Justice Black's conclusion, see Charles Fairman, "Does the Fourteenth Amendment Incorporate the Bill of Rights? The Original Understanding," *Stanford Law Review* 2 (December 1949): 5-139. See also Charles Fairman and Stanley Morrison, eds., *The Fourteenth Amendment and the Bill of Rights: The Incorporation Theory* (New York: DaCapo Press, 1970).
24. *Adamson v. California,* 332 U.S. at 91-92. In this passage, Mr. Justice Black quotes from his concurrence in *Federal Power Commission v. Natural Gas Pipeline Company,* 315 U.S. 575, 601, n. 4 (1942).
25. 110 U.S. 516, 534-535 (1884).
26. For example, see Chief Justice Warren's comments on the Eighth Amendment's protection against "cruel and unusual punishments" in *Trop v. Dulles,* 356 U.S. 86 (1958): "This Amendment is not static. The Amendment must draw its meaning from the evolving standards of decency that mark the progress of a maturing society."
27. 381 U.S. at 501.
28. 376 U.S. 1 (1964).
29. 381 U.S. at 501.
30. *Cohen v. Hurley,* 366 U.S. 117 (1961). Mr. Justice Brennan dissenting.
31. Justice Douglas's establishment of the right of "privacy" in *Griswold v. Connecticut,* 381 U.S. 479 (1965), is a case in point.
32. Israel and LaFave, *Criminal Procedure,* p. 13.
33. *Baldwin v. New York,* 399 U.S. 66 (1970). Mr. Justice Harlan dissenting. See also Ralph A. Rossum, "New Rights and Old Wrongs: The Supreme Court and the Problem of Retroactivity," *Emory Law Journal* 23 (Spring 1974): 414-416.
34. *Griswold v. Connecticut,* 381 U.S. 479, 522.
35. 367 U.S. 643 (1961).
36. 378 U.S. 1 (1964).
37. 395 U.S. 784 (1969).
38. 372 U.S. 335 (1963).

39. 407 U.S. 25 (1972).
40. 386 U.S. 213 (1967).
41. 391 U.S. 145 (1968).
42. 380 U.S. 400 (1965).
43. 388 U.S. 14 (1967).
44. 370 U.S. 660 (1962).
45. 333 U.S. 257 (1948).
46. 333 U.S. 196 (1948).
47. See Henry J. Abraham, *Freedom and the Court,* p. 81; see also Israel and LaFave, *Criminal Procedure,* pp. 20-21.
49. 110 U.S. 516 (1884).
49. U.S. Department of Justice, *Handbook on the Law of Search and Seizure* (Washington, D.C.: Government Printing Office, 1971), pp. 2-5.
50. Ibid., p. 21
51. 390 U.S. 234 (1968)
52. *Nunez v. United States,* 370 F. 2d 538 (5th Cir., 1967), and *P. v. Wright,* 242 N.E. 2nd 180 (Ill. 1968).
53. *Ellison v. United States,* 206 F. 2d 476 (D.C. Cir., 1953).
54. 389 U.S. 347 (1967).
55. Israel and LaFave, *Criminal Procedure,* p. 93. *Katz* may, however, require a reassessment of "the use of bifocals, field glasses, or the telescope" to focus "upon what one supposes to be private indiscretions." *On Lee v. United States,* 343 U.S. 747 (1952). The use of these artificial means of making observations appears to conflict with the *Katz* rationale and may have to be reconsidered in the light of the reasonableness of the defendant's privacy considerations. See, for example, the decision of the United States District Court for Hawaii, 19 CrL 2281 (1976), which held that plain view means "unaided plain view" and proscribed any governmental use of binoculars and telescopes. *U.S. v. Kim.*
56. 267 U.S. 132 (1925).
57. Although, see *Brinegar v. United States,* 338 U.S. 160 (1949), *Preston v. United States,* 376 U.S. 364 (1964), and *Cooper v. California,* 386 U.S. 58 (1967).
58. 395 U.S. 752 (1969).
59. 399 U.S. 42 (1970).
60. 399 U.S. at 51-52.
61. 417 U.S. 583 (1974).
62. *Cardwell* was, however, a five-to-four decision, with Justice Powell concurring in the judgment of the Court for reasons quite apart from the Fourth Amendment argument of Justice Blackmun.
63. 392 U.S. 1 (1968).
64. 392 U.S. at 24, 27.
65. 414 U.S. 218 (1973).

THE SUPREME COURT

66. 414 U.S. 260 (1973).
67. 414 U.S. at 235.
68. 415 U.S. 800 (1974).
69. 415 U.S. at 805. Justices Douglas, Brennan, and Marshall joined with Justice Stewart in his dissent.
70. 395 U.S. 752 (1969).
71. 331 U.S. 145 (1947).
72. 339 U.S. 56 (1950).
73. Justices White and Black dissented.
74. 395 U.S. at 763.
75. 232 U.S. 383 (1914).
76. 338 U.S. 25 (1949).
77. 338 U.S. at 27-28.
78. Ibid., p. 29.
79. 367 U.S. 643 (1961).
80. See also *Ker* v. *California,* 374 U.S. 23 (1963), where the Court asserted that "the standard of reasonableness is the same under the Fourth and Fourteenth Amendments." See also *Aguilar* v. *Texas,* 378 U.S. 108 (1964), in which the Court held that requirements for obtaining a search warrant are the same in both federal and state jurisdictions.
81. 367 U.S. at 656.
82. Ibid., p. 657.
83. Ibid., p. 659.
84. Warren E. Burger, "Who Will Watch the Watchmen?" *American University Law Review* 14 (1964): 22.
85. Monrad Paulsen, "The Exclusionary Rule and Misconduct by the Police," *Journal of Criminal Law, Criminology, and Police Science* 52 (1961): 256.
86. Burger, "Who Will Watch the Watchmen?" pp. 11-12.
87. Ibid., p. 12.
88. The following discussion relies heavily on Dallin H. Oaks, "Studying the Exclusionary Rule in Search and Seizure," *University of Chicago Law Review* 37 (1970): 665-753.
89. Jerome Skolnick, *Justice Without Trial: Law Enforcement in Democratic Society* (New York: Wiley, 1966). See also John Kaplan, "The Limits of the Exclusionary Rule," *Stanford Law Review* 26, no. 5 (May 1974): 1050-1051.
90. Skolnick, *Justice Without Trial,* p. 215.
91. Comment, "Effect of *Mapp* v. *Ohio* on Police Search and Seizure Practices in Narcotics Cases," *Columbia Journal of Law and Social Problems* 4 (1968): 87.
92. Oaks, "Studying the Exclusionary Rule in Search and Seizure," pp. 750-751.
93. Samuel Dash, "Cracks in the Foundation of Criminal Justice," *Illinois Law Review,* 46 (1951): 391-392.

94. However, see Bradley C. Canon, "Is the Exclusionary Rule in Failing Health? Some New Data and a Plea Against a Precipitous Conclusion," *Kentucky Law Journal* 62, no. 3 (1974): 681-730, who argues that more recent empirical evidence casts "considerable doubt on earlier conclusions that the rule is ineffective in deterring illegal police searches" (p. 725).
95. Kaplan, "The Limits of the Exclusionary Rule," pp. 1046-1052. See also *United States v. Lee,* 19 CrL 2193 (1976), in which the Fourth Circuit Court of Appeals held that a federal district court judge can properly consider illegally seized evidence when sentencing a convicted offender.
96. Ibid., p. 1046. Kaplan would, nonetheless, still preserve the standard of *Rochin v. California,* 342 U.S. 165 (1952), that evidence is to be suppressed if the violation of civil liberties is of such a nature that it "shocks the conscience."
97. Ibid., p. 1047.
98. Ibid., p. 1050. See also Anthony Amsterdam, "Perspectives on the Fourth Amendment," *Minnesota Law Review* 58 (1974): 436-438.
99. 403 U.S. 388 (1971). See also his concurrence in *Stone v. Powell,* 428 U.S. 465 (1976), in which Chief Justice Burger again declared that the time has come to modify the exclusionary rule's reach, "even if it is retained for a small and limited category of cases."
100. 403 U.S. at 421.
101. Ibid., p. 419.
102. Ibid., p. 422.
103. Ibid., pp. 422-423.
104. 414 U.S. 338 (1974). In this same connection, see also *Stone v. Powell,* 428 U.S. 465 (1976), in which Justice Powell held for a six-member majority that a state prisoner who has had an opportunity at the state level to fully and fairly litigate his claim that evidence admitted at his trial was the product of an illegal search or seizure is not entitled to federal habeas corpus consideration of his Fourth Amendment claims. Justice Powell's regard for the exclusionary rule is perhaps best captured in the following: "The disparity in particular cases between the error committed by the police officer and the windfall afforded a guilty defendant by application of the [exclusionary] rule is contrary to the idea of proportionality that is essential to the concept of justice." For a general discussion of the modifications in criminal procedure from the Warren Court to the Burger Court, see Stephen L. Wasby, *Continuity and Change: From the Warren Court to the Burger Court* (Pacific Palisades, Calif.: Goodyear, 1976), pp. 167-205. See also William R. Thomas, *The Burger Court and Civil Liberties* (Brunswick, Ohio: King's Court Communications, 1976), pp. 40-74.
105. See also *United States v. Weir,* 15 CrL 2164 (1974), in which the Ninth Circuit Court of Appeals expanded *Calandra* and declared that grand jury use of coerced confessions is not barred.

THE SUPREME COURT 169

106. 414 U.S. at 349. Justice Brennan, with whom Justices Douglas and Marshall joined, dissented. He charged that the Court majority had disregarded the central purpose of the exclusionary rule, which is to assure the people that the government does not profit from its own lawless behavior. 414 U.S. at 360. Justice Powell responded, however, by noting that "the incentive to disregard the requirement of the Fourth Amendment solely to obtain an indictment from a grand jury is substantially negated by the inadmissibility of the illegally seized evidence in a subsequent criminal prosecution of the search victim. For the most part, a prosecuter would be unlikely to request an indictment where a conviction could not be obtained." 414 U.S. at 351.
107. 211 U.S. 78 (1908).
108. 331 U.S. 46 (1947).
109. 378 U.S. 1 (1964).
110. 384 U.S. 436, 360 (1966). See also Justice Felix Frankfurter's opinion for the Court in *Rodgers* v. *Richmond,* 365 U.S. 534 (1961).
111. See, however, *Andreson* v. *Maryland,* 96 S. Ct. 2737 (1976), in which the Court held, in a seven-to-two decision, that use in court of incriminating records seized validly under the Fourth Amendment does not raise any Fifth Amendment problems. After all, the party in question was not compelled to say or do anything that might incriminate him.
112. However, if the defendant does take the stand, he lays himself open to cross examination that may bring out evidence damaging to his case. See C. Herman Pritchett, *The American Constitution,* 2nd ed. (New York: McGraw-Hill, 1968), p. 617. See also *Griffin* v. *California,* 380 U.S. 609 (1965).
113. 297 U.S. 278 (1936).
114. Ibid., pp. 285-286. Chief Justice Hughes continued: "It would be difficult to conceive of methods more revolting to the sense of justice than those taken to procure the confessions of these petitioners, and the use of the confessions thus obtained as the basis for conviction and sentence was a clear denial of due process." 297 U.S. at 286.
115. 309 U.S. 227 (1940).
116. *Spano* v. *New York,* 360 U.S. 315 (1959).
117. *Rodgers* v. *Richmond,* 365 U.S. 534 (1961).
118. *Lynumn* v. *Illinois,* 372 U.S. 528 (1963).
119. *Townsend* v. *Sain,* 372 U.S. 293 (1963). In each of these cases, the confessions involved were considered by the court to be 'coerced," and the convictions of the defendants were overturned.
120. 378 U.S. 478 (1964).
121. Ibid., pp. 490-494.
122. Jonathan D. Casper, *The Politics of Civil Liberties* (New York: Harper & Row, 1972), p. 261.

123. 384 U.S. 436 (1966).
124. Ibid., pp. 444-445.
125. Henry J. Abraham, *Freedom and the Court: Civil Rights and Liberties in the United States,* 2nd ed. (New York: Oxford University Press, 1972), p. 125.
126. 384 U.S. at 516.
127. Ibid., p. 508.
128. Ibid., p. 509.
129. Ibid., p. 545.
130. 401 U.S. 222 (1971).
131. Ibid., pp. 225-226. See also *United States* v. *Mandujano,* 96 S. Ct. 1768 (1976), in which a unanimous Court agreed that the Fifth Amendment privilege against self-incrimination does not entitle a grand jury witness to answer falsely questions put to him or prevent introduction of false answers at his subsequent perjury trial.
132. 417 U.S. 433 (1974).
133. 420 U.S. 714 (1975). In only one recent case has the Burger Court really departed from this general trend. See *Doyle* v. *Ohio,* 96 S. Ct. 2240 (1976), in which the Court raised to constitutional status its ruling in *United States* v. *Hale,* 421 U.S. 171 (1975), that forbids the impeachment use of an accused's silence after he has been given his *Miranda* rights.
134. 417 U.S. at 489. Mr. Justice Douglas was the lone dissenter in this decision.
135. Justices Brennan and Marshall dissented, observing in part that *Hass* removed whatever incentive police may have had to follow the *Miranda* requirement that if a suspect wants to consult with his attorney, no interrogation can take place until he is present. 420 U.S. at 725. Justice Blackmun responded by declaring that the Court's ruling would not undermine deterrence; "there is sufficient deterrence when the evidence in question is made unavailable to the prosecution in its case in chief." 420 U.S. at 722.
136. M. Glenn Abernathy, *Civil Liberties Under the Constitution,* 2nd ed. (New York: Dodd, Mead, 1972), p. 181.
137. U.S. National Commission on Law Observance and Enforcement, *Report on Prosecution* (Washington, D.C.: Government Printing Office, 1931), p. 30.
138. 287 U.S. 45 (1932).
139. Ibid., p. 69.
140. 304 U.S. 458 (1938).
141. The Federal Crimes Act of 1790 had already provided that counsel must be provided in all capital cases at the request of the defendant. *Johnson,* however, went further and declared that appointment of counsel was not only statutorily but also constitutionally required and extended to noncapital cases as well.

142. 304 U.S. at 463.
143. 287 U.S. at 463.
144. 316 U.S. 455 (1942).
145. Ibid., p. 471.
146. Ibid., p. 476.
147. 372 U.S. 335 (1963).
148. Ibid., p. 344.
149. Ibid. See also Anthony Lewis, *Gideon's Trumpet* (New York: Random House, 1964).
150. 407 U.S. 25 (1972).
151. Ibid., p. 34.
152. Ibid., p. 37. In his concurrence, Mr. Justice Powell expressed some apprehensions about the effect this decision would have on "hundreds of communities in the United States with no or very few lawyers, with meager financial resources, but with the need to have some sort of local court system to deal with minor offenses." He feared that "to require that counsel be furnished virtually every indigent charged with an imprisonable offense would be a practicable impossibility for many small town courts. The community could simply not enforce its own laws." 407 U.S. at 61. Justice Douglas, however, remained largely unconcerned with the plight of these communities and simply reiterated that: "We do not sit as an ombudsman to direct state courts how to manage their affairs but only to make clear the federal constitutional requirement." 407 U.S. at 38.
153. 407 U.S. at 51-52.
154. 422 U.S. 806 (1975).
155. Ibid., pp. 807, 811.
156. Ibid., pp. 819-820.
157. Ibid., p. 820.
158. Ibid., p. 839.
159. Ibid., p. 849. Justice Blackmun's quotation comes from *Berger* v. *United States*, 295 U.S. 78, 88 (1935).
160. 422 U.S. at 849.
161. Ibid., p. 837
162. Ibid., p. 846.
163. Ibid., p. 852. See, for example, *United States* v. *Swinton,* 18 CrL 2035 (1975), wherein one such question arose. The United States District Court for Southern New York ruled in that particular case that the defendant who was already represented by an attorney had no right to participate in her trial as co-counsel.
164. 422 U.S. at 852.
165. 287 U.S. at 69.
166. 388 U.S. 218, 226 (1967).

167. 378 U.S. 478 (1964).
168. 384 U.S. 436 (1966).
169. 388 U.S. 218 (1967).
170. Ibid., p. 263.
171. 399 U.S. 1 (1970).
172. 368 U.S. 52 (1961).
173. 372 U.S. 353 (1963). See however, *Ross* v. *Moffitt,* 417 U.S. 600 (1974), in which the Court in a six-to-three vote limited the requirement of appointment of counsel for indigent defendants to their first appeal as of right and refused to extend this requirement to discretionary state appeals or to applications for review by the U.S. Supreme Court.
174. 389 U.S. 128 (1967).
175. There remains, of course, one glaring exception to this general statement, as Justice Harlan so effectively noted in his dissent in *Miranda:* "Certainly the purchase of narcotics by an undercover agent from a prospective defendant may . . . be 'critical,' yet provision of counsel and advice on that score have never been thought compelled by the Constitution in such cases." 384 U.S. at 514.
176. The language very much suggests that a person can be put once "in jeopardy of life or limb" and supports thereby the constitutionality not only of the death penalty but also of dismemberment.
177. *Green* v. *United States,* 335 U.S. 184 (1957). However, this protection is aimed primarily against governmental appeals to verdicts of acquittal. As Justice Thurgood Marshall observed in *United States* v. *Wilson,* 421 U.S. 309 (1975), "The development of the Double Jeopardy Clause from its common-law origins . . . suggests that it was directed at the threat of multiple prosecutions, not at government appeals, at least where those appeals would not require a new trial."
178. 395 U.S. 784 (1969).
179. Abernathy, *Civil Liberties Under the Constitution,* p. 205.
180. 395 U.S. 711 (1969).
181. 395 U.S. at 726. See also *Blackledge* v. *Perry,* 417 U.S. 21 (1974), in which Justice Stewart held for a seven-member majority that the Due Process Clause of the Fourteenth Amendment prevents the state from bringing felony charges against a misdemeanant who has exercised his right to a trial *de nova.*
182. 356 U.S. 464 (1958).
183. 397 U.S. 436 (1970).
184. Ibid., p. 443.
185. See Jay A. Sigler, *Double Jeopardy: The Development of a Legal and Social Policy* (Ithaca, N.Y.: Cornell University Press, 1969), pp. 38-76.
186. 359 U.S. 121 (1959).
187. 260 U.S. 377 (1922).

188. See also the companion case of *Abbate* v. *United States,* 359 U.S. 187 (1959).
189. 359 U.S. at 137.
190. Ibid.
191. 397 U.S. 387 (1970).
192. Ibid., p. 393.
193. See *Breed* v. *Jones,* 421 U.S. 519 (1975), in which the Supreme Court employed the same logic it did in *Waller* and unanimously concluded that the Double Jeopardy Clause was violated when a youthful defendant, who was found by a California juvenile proceeding to have committed the crime with which he was charged, was subsequently tried as an adult, after a determination that he was not amenable to juvenile court care and treatment. Chief Justice Burger observed that the juvenile adjudicatory hearing to which the defendant was initially subjected, no less than his subsequent criminal trial, "engenders elements of 'anxiety and insecurity' in the juvenile, and imposes a 'heavy personal strain.'"
194. See *United States* v. *Marion,* 404 U.S. 307 (1971), in which Justice White spoke for a unanimous Court in holding that the right to a speedy trial enters into play only after a defendant has been indicted. No constitutional violation occurs so long as the indictments are handed down within the period of the applicable statute of limitations.
195. 407 U.S. 514 (1972).
196. This drastic remedy was reaffirmed by the Court in *Strunk* v. *United States,* 412 U.S. 434, 440 (1973).
197. It should be noted at the outset that the Court has never held that all defendants are entitled to a jury trial; rather, it has reserved this right only for those charged with serious crimes, thereby differentiating between serious and petty offenses. The standard that the Court has employed to distinguish between these two classes of crimes is the length of sentence the law authorizes a judge to impose for a violation. Currently, the standard appears to be 6 months' imprisonment. If the law authorizes penalties of more than 6 months, the defendant is entitled to a jury trial; if less, he is not. See *Duncan* v. *Louisiana,* 391 U.S. 145 (1968).
198. 100 U.S. 313 (1880).
199. 294 U.S. 587 (1935).
200 356 U.S. 584 (1958).
201. 380 U.S. 202 (1965).
202. 325 U.S. 398 (1945). See *Ristaino* v. *Ross,* 96 S. Ct. 1017 (1976), in which Justice Powell, in a six-to-two decision, reversed a grant of habeas corpus relief for a black Massachusetts murder defendant whose request that prospective jurors be asked the following specific question about racial bias was refused by the trial judge: "Are there any of you who believe that a white person is more likely to be telling the truth than a black person?"

203. 368 U.S. 57 (1961).
204. 419 U.S. 522 (1974).
205. Technically, the Court did not overrule *Hoyt* but rather distinguished it. *Hoyt* was upheld against equal protection and due process claims and did not involve a defendant's Sixth Amendment right to a jury chosen from a fair cross-section of the community.
206. 419 U.S. at 528. The language of *Taylor* would seem to call into question the authority of *Fay* v. *New York,* 332 U.S. 261 (1947), in which the Court upheld New York's use of "blue-ribbon juries"—juries used for especially important or complex cases and comprised of the more affluent, highly educated members of the community.
207. Alfred Friendly and Ronald Goldfarb, *Crime and Publicity* (New York: The Twentieth-Century Fund, 1967), p. 141.
208. For a further discussion of the extent to which Great Britain places a higher priority on a fair trial than a free press, see Abraham, *Freedom and the Court,* pp. 152-154.
209. 366 U.S. 717 (1961).
210. 373 U.S. 73 (1963).
211. 381 U.S. 532 (1965).
212. 384 U.S. 333 (1966).
213. See *The Rights of a Fair Trial and Free Press* (Chicago: American Bar Association, 1969), pp. 22-28, for a comparative assessment of the voluntary bar-media codes of Oklahoma, Oregon, and Massachusetts. For a critique of these bar-media codes, especially mandatory codes, see the lecture of Clifton Daniel of the *New York Times* in the American Enterprise Institute's rational debate series, Paul C. Reardon and Clifton Daniel, *Fair Trial and Free Press* (Washington, D.C.: American Enterprise Institute for Public Policy Research, 1968), p. 37. Mr. Daniel believes that those who wish to impose these codes are, in a sense, "using a sledgehammer to kill a gnat," the gnat being "a tiny fraction of criminal cases . . . [that] is ever reported in the press. And in only a fraction of this fraction is there any question of doing violence to the rights of the defendant." This heavy-handedness, he fears, "may wreck freedom of the press as well; it may shatter the very keystone of our democracy."
214. 399 U.S. 78 (1970).
215. Ibid., p. 100.
216. 406 U.S. 356 (1972). See also the companion case of *Apodaca* v. *Oregon,* 406 U.S. 404 (1972).
217. 380 U.S. 400 (1965). The collateral right to compulsory process was also held by the Court to be applicable in state criminal prosecutions in *Washington* v. *Texas,* 388 U.S. 14 (1967).
218. 390 U.S. 719 (1968).
219. 391 U.S. 123 (1968).

THE SUPREME COURT 175

220. In so doing, it overruled *Delli Paoli* v. *United States,* 352 U.S. 232 (1957).
221. 397 U.S. 337 (1970).
222. Ibid., p. 343.
223. 99 U.S. 130 (1879).
224. 217 U.S. 349, 371, 389 (1910). See *Downey* v. *Perini,* 17 CrL 2324 (1975), in which the Sixth Circuit Court of Appeals held that a first-time marijuana offender's 10-year sentence imposed by an Ohio court was so disproportionate to the crime as to violate the cruel and unusual punishment provision of the Eighth Amendment.
225. 356 U.S. 86 (1958).
226. 370 U.S. 660 (1962).
227. Ibid., p. 667.
228. Harold W. Chase and Craig R. Ducat, *Constitutional Interpretation: Cases, Essays, and Materials* (St. Paul: West, 1974), p. 927.
229. 392 U.S. 514 (1968).
230. Ibid., p. 534.
231. Ibid., p. 532.
232. 408 U.S. 238 (1972).
233. Ibid., p. 369.
234. Ibid., p. 305.
235. Ibid., p. 255.
236. Ibid., p. 310. Whereas Justice Stewart objected to the "wanton" and "freakish" manner in which the death penalty was imposed, Justice White focused on the "infrequency" of its imposition. "As the statutes before us are now administered, the penalty is so infrequently imposed that the threat of execution is too attenuated to be of substantial service to criminal justice." Ibid., p. 313.
237. Chief Justice Burger and Justices Powell, Rehnquist, and Blackmun dissented. Justice Powell, in the most comprehensive of the dissents, concluded that the majority opinions would have a "shattering effect" on "the root principles of *stare decisis,* federalism, judicial restraint and—most importantly—separation of powers." Ibid., p. 376.
238. A bifurcated trial consists of two stages: a trial stage, which establishes the guilt or innocence of the defendant; and a penalty stage, which determines the sentence that will be imposed.
239. See *Gregg* v. *Georgia,* 428 U.S. 153 (1976); *Jurek* v. *Texas,* 428 U.S. 262 (1976); *Proffitt* v. *Florida,* 428 U.S. 242 (1976); *Woodson* v. *North Carolina,* 428 U.S. 280 (1976); and *Roberts* v. *Louisiana,* 428 U.S. 325 (1976).
240. Justices Brennan and Marshall, the only members of the *Furman* majority who would have declared capital punishment per se unconstitutional, stood by that position and joined the plurality of Justices Stewart, Powell, and Stevens in invalidating these laws.
241. *Gregg* v. *Georgia,* 428 U.S. at 173.

242. Ibid., p. 175.
243. Ibid., pp. 179-182.
244. Ibid., 183. "Indeed," Justice Stewart continued, "the decision that capital punishment may be the appropriate sanction in extreme cases is an expression of the community's belief that certain crimes are themselves so grievous an affront to humanity that the only adequate response may be the penalty of death." Ibid., 184.
245. Ibid., pp. 184-186.
246. Ibid., p. 186.
247. Ibid., p. 187.
248. *Woodson v. North Carolina,* 428 U.S. at 293.
249. Ibid., p. 304.
250. *Gregg v. Georgia,* 428 U.S. at 221.
251. *Roberts v. Louisiana,* 428 U.S. at 358. Mr. Justice White dissenting.
252. 428 U.S. at 229. Mr. Justice Brennan dissenting in *Gregg, Jurek,* and *Proffitt.*
253. Ibid., p. 230.
254. Ibid., p. 232. Mr. Justice Marshall dissenting in *Gregg, Jurek* and *Proffitt.* Emphasis in the original.
255. Ibid., p. 237.
256. Ibid., p. 241.
257. Israel and LaFave, *Criminal Procedure,* p. 70.
258. 399 U.S. 235 (1970).
259. 401 U.S. 395 (1971).
260. 399 U.S. at 242. In *Williams,* Chief Justice Burger declared that "we are not unaware that today's holding may place a further burden on States in administering criminal justice." However, he emphasized that "the constitutional imperatives of the Equal Protection Clause must have priority over the comfortable convenience of the status quo." 399 U.S. at 245. For a full discussion of the effect that *Williams* and *Tate* have had on municipal courts, see Ralph A. Rossum, "Problems in Municipal Court Administration and the Stress of Supreme Court Decisions: A Memphis Case Study," *American Journal of Criminal Law* 3, no. 1 (Summer 1974): 53-84.
261. Although *Williams* and *Tate* have restricted somewhat the flexibility judges have in sentencing, Federal District Judge Marvin E. Frankel continues to be extremely critical of "the almost wholly unchecked and sweeping powers we give to judges in the fashioning of sentences," which he finds "terrifying and intolerable for a society that professes devotion to the rule of law." Marvin E. Frankel, *Criminal Sentences: Law Without Order* (New York: Hill & Wang, 1973), p. 5. He proposes additional means to check this "unbounded discretion" such as greater appellate review of sentences and either sentencing councils, which utilize other judges to advise and

assist collectively the sentencing judge on sentencing decisions, or mixed sentencing tribunals, which employ panels of three, including a judge, a psychiatrist or a psychologist, and a sociologist or educator, to impose sentences. *Criminal Sentences,* pp. 69-85.
262. 153 U.S. 684 (1894).
263. 351 U.S. 12 (1956).
264. 372 U.S. 352 (1963).
265. 417 U.S. 500 (1974).
266. 417 U.S. 610-611 (1974).
267. 372 U.S. 391 (1963).
268. 344 U.S. 433 (1953).
269. However, see *Stone* v. *Powell,* 428 U.S. 465 (1976), in which the Supreme Court closed the door somewhat by withdrawing federal habeas corpus jurisdiction for state prisoners who had the opportunity to litigate their Fourth Amendment and exclusionary rule claims fairly and fully at the state level. As Justice Powell declared for the six-member majority: "There is no reason to believe, however, that the overall educative effect of the exclusionary rule would be appreciably diminished if search and seizure claims could not be raised in federal habeas corpus review of state convictions. Nor is there reason to assume that any specific disincentive already created by the risk of exclusion of evidence at trial or the reversal of convictions on direct review would be enhanced if there were the further risk that a conviction obtained in state court and affirmed on direct review might be overturned in collateral proceedings often occurring years after the incarceration of the defendant." See also *Francis* v. *Henderson,* 425 U.S. 536 (1976), in which the Court held that failure of a state prisoner to make a timely challenge to the allegedly unconstitutional composition of the grand jury that indicted him deprives him of the opportunity to obtain federal habeas relief on that issue.
270. Herman Schwartz, "Retroactivity, Reliability, and Due Process: A Reply to Professor Mishkin," *University of Chicago Law Review* 33 (1966): 753.
271. Ralph A. Rossum, "New Rights and Old Wrongs: The Supreme Court and the Problem of Retroactivity," *Emory Law Journal* 23, no. 2 (Spring 1974): 387.
272. 381 U.S. 618 (1965).
273. Ibid., p. 629.
274. Ibid.
275. Ibid., p. 636.
276. Ibid., p. 640.
277. Ibid., p. 637.
278. Ibid.
279. Ibid., pp. 637-638.
280. Ibid., p. 637.

281. Ibid.
282. For example, it has relied on these criteria in such cases as *Stovall* v. *Denno*, 388 U.S. 293 (1967), which denied retroactivity to *United States* v. *Wade*, 388 U.S. 218 (1967); *DeStefano* v. *Woods*, 392 U.S. 631 (1968), which denied retroactive effect to *Duncan* v. *Louisiana*, 392 U.S. 145 (1968); *Desist* v. *United States*, 394 U.S. 244 (1969), which denied retroactive operation to *Katz* v. *United States*, 389 U.S. 347 (1968); *Williams* v. *United States*, 401 U.S. 646 (1971), which denied retroactive application to *Chimel* v. *California*, 395 U.S. 752 (1969); *Adams* v. *Illinois*, 405 U.S. 278 (1972), which denied retroactivity to *Coleman* v. *Alabama*, 399 U.S. 1 (1970); and *Michigan* v. *Payne*, 412 U.S. 47 (1973), which limited the retroactive effect of *North Carolina* v. *Pearce*, 395 U.S. 711 (1969).
283. 394 U.S. at 249.
284. Ibid., p. 250.
285. 366 U.S. 213, 225 (1961).
286. 392 U.S. 378, 388 (1968). Mr. Justice Black dissenting.
287. 384 U.S. 719 (1966).
288. *Desist* v. *United States*, 394 U.S. 244, 258 (1969). Mr. Justice Harlan dissenting. See also his dissent in *Mackey* v. *United States*, 401 U.S. 667, 676 (1971). Mr. Justice Harlan is not the only justice to have acted in this manner. See Mr. Justice Black's concurrence in *Desist* v. *United States*, 394 U.S. 244 (1969), for a less candid but no less illuminating admission by Mr. Justice Black. See also Rossum, "New Rights and Old Wrongs," pp. 411-413.
289. 381 U.S. at 637.
290 369 U.S. 438 (1962).
291. See Israel and LaFave, *Criminal Procedure*, p. 80. This effort, however, has not been altogether successful, as the next chapter will establish.
292. 387 U.S. 1 (1967).
293. In fact, the Supreme Court has lately been abandoning such efforts at judicial policy making. See, for example, *Harris* v. *New York*, 420 U.S. 714 (1975); *Michigan* v. *Tucker*, 417 U.S. 433 (1974); *Oregon* v. *Hass*, 16 CrL 3120 (1975); and *United States* v. *Calandra*, 414 U.S. 338 (1974).
294. Theodore L. Becker and Malcolm M. Feeley, eds., *The Impact of Supreme Court Decisions*, 2nd ed. (New York: Oxford University Press, 1973), p. 3. Emphasis in the original.

Bibliography

Abernathy, M. Glenn. *Civil Liberties Under the Constitution.* 2nd ed. New York: Dodd, Mead, 1972.

Abraham, Henry J. *Freedom and the Court: Civil Rights and Liberties in the United States.* 2nd ed. New York: Oxford University Press, 1972.

Ball, Howard. *The Vision and the Dream of Justice Hugo L. Black.* University, Ala.: University of Alabama Press, 1975.

Becker, Theodore L., and Feeley, Malcolm M., eds. *The Impact of Supreme Court Decisions.* 2nd ed. New York: Oxford University Press, 1973.

Bent, Alan Edward, and Rossum, Ralph A. *Police, Criminal Justice, and the Community.* New York: Harper & Row, 1976.

Black, Charles L., Jr. *Capital Punishment: The Inevitability of Caprice and Mistake.* New York: Norton, 1974.

Burger, Warren E. "Who Will Watch the Watchmen?" *American University Law Review* 14 (1964).

Casper, Jonathan D. *The Politics of Civil Liberties.* New York: Harper & Row, 1972.

Chase, Harold W., and Ducat, Craig R. *Constitutional Interpretation: Cases, Essays, and Materials.* St. Paul: West, 1974.

Fairman, Charles, "Does the Fourteenth Amendment Incorporate the Bill of Rights? The Original Understanding." *Stanford Law Review* 2 (December 1949): 5-139.

Fairman, Charles, and Morrison, Stanley, eds. *The Fourteenth Amendment and the Bill of Rights: The Incorporation Theory.* New York: Da Capo Press, 1970.

Fellman, David. "The Supreme Court's Changing View of Criminal Defendants' Rights." In *Crime in Urban Society,* edited by Barbara L. McLennan. New York: Dunellen, 1970.

Frankel, Marvin E. *Criminal Sentences: Law Without Order.* New York: Hill & Wang, 1973.

Friendly, Alfred, and Goldfarb, Ronald. *Crime and Publicity.* New York: The Twentieth-Century Fund, 1967.

Goldberg, Steven. "On Capital Punishment." *Ethics* 85, no. 1 (October 1974): 67-74.

Israel, Jerold H., and LaFave, Wayne R. *Criminal Procedure: Constitutional Limitations.* 2nd ed. St. Paul: West, 1975.

Kaplan, John. *Criminal Justice: Introductory Cases and Materials.* Mineola, N.Y.: Foundation Press, 1973.

———, "The Limits of the Exclusionary Rule." *Stanford Law Review* 26 (May 1974): 1027-1055.

Lewis, Anthony. *Gideon's Trumpet.* New York: Random House, 1964.

Mendelson, Wallace. *Justices Black and Frankfurter: Conflict in the Court.* Chicago: University of Chicago Press, 1966.

Oaks, Dallin H. "Studying the Exclusionary Rule in Search and Seizure." *University of Chicago Law Review* 37 (1970): 665-753.

Pritchett, C. Herman. *The American Constitution.* 2nd ed. New York: McGraw-Hill, 1968.

Reardon, Paul C., and Daniel, Clifton. *Fair Trial and Free Press.* Washington, D.C.: American Enterprise Institute for Public Policy Research, 1968.

Rights of a Fair Trial and Free Press. Chicago: American Bar Association, 1969.

Rossum, Ralph A. "New Rights and Old Wrongs: The Supreme Court and the Problem of Retroactivity." *Emory Law Journal* 23, no. 2 (Spring 1974): 381-420.

Schlesinger, Steven R. *Exclusionary Injustice.* New York: Marcel Dekker, Inc., 1977.

Sigler, Jay A. *Double Jeopardy: The Development of a Legal and Social Policy.* Ithaca, N.Y.: Cornell University Press, 1969.

Skolnick, Jerome. *Justice Without Trial: Law Enforcement in Democratic Society.* New York: Wiley, 1966.

Wasby, Stephen L. *Continuity and Change: From the Warren Court to the Burger Court.* Pacific Palisades, Calif.: Goodyear, 1976.

5

THE LOWER COURTS AND THE ADMINISTRATION OF "JUSTICE"

Chapter 4 explored at length what the U.S. Supreme Court has done in the realm of criminal procedure. It stressed the Court's reliance upon judgment—upon the exercise of normative power—to give substance and meaning to the many ambiguous provisions of Amendments Four through Eight. However, at the very end, it also suggested that this normative power of judgment is extremely limited. The normative compliance structure of the Supreme Court has not been sufficient to ensure that the mandates of its decisions in criminal procedure are followed. As Howard James has trenchantly observed, there is "a wide gap between what we say is true about justice in the United States and what is really true."[1] This chapter will examine the extent of this discrepancy "between the 'ought' of doctrine and the 'is' of behavior"[2] as well as the factors that contribute to it. It will also assess the various proposals that have been advanced to minimize this discrepancy and, on the basis of that analysis, suggest that the prospects for substantial judicial reform are not bright.

The Limited Normative Power of the Supreme Court

The study of the impact of Supreme Court decisions has recently become an important and fruitful field of research in public law. These empirical investigations of the Court's ability to implement the constitutional principles it enunciates have revealed the very limited power of the Court's normative compliance structures.[3] Decisions in the realm of criminal procedural protections have received special scrutiny.[4] Studies of this sort have typically sought to establish to what extent Court decisions—especially *Mapp* v. *Ohio*[5] and *Miranda* v. *Arizona*[6] —have succeeded in modifying either police behavior or courtroom procedure. These studies have generally concluded that there is a rather substantial discrepancy between what the Court says ought to be done and what in fact is actually done.[7] Thus, Professor Michael Ban, in his study of the impact of *Mapp* v. *Ohio*, points out that the effectiveness of the exclusionary rule was wholly dependent upon a number of Supreme Court assumptions:

> The first and seemingly the safest of the Court's assumptions was that defense lawyers would move to suppress illegally obtained evidence and that they would do it with some skill. The Court also assumed that prosecuting attorneys would aid, or at least not actively impede, the judicial process. Next, the Court was assuming that lower court judges would grant valid motions to suppress and would, it was hoped, help to make the rules clear to police. And finally, the Court, by assuming that the actors in the local system of criminal justice would play their assigned roles, was assuming that in fact an adversary system of justice was operative at the lower court level, that the lower courts would be responsive to the Supreme Court.[8]

As Ban's research suggests, however, "such assumptions were unwarranted." The findings of a Columbia University research team are somewhat at odds with Ban's, but this conflict can hardly provide comfort for the Court. Analyzing the evidentiary grounds for arrest and subsequent disposition of misdemeanor narcotics cases in New York City before and after *Mapp,* this team concluded that the effect of *Mapp* has been to encourage "police perjury" designed to legalize arrests and thereby avoid the effect of the exclusionary rule.[9] Studies of the effectiveness of *Miranda*—with its insistence on an accused's rights to silence and counsel during interrogation after arrest or detention—reinforce these assessments of the Court's limited power to secure compliance with its rulings. Neal Milner, for instance, argues that the "effectiveness of Supreme Court-imposed restraints on police behavior . . . is mitigated by the milieu in which the police officer operates, by the characteristics of the police decision-making process, and by the relationship police have with their reference groups."[10] Jonathan D. Casper reflects the general picture that can be drawn from studies of this sort:

> The Court spoke in its *Miranda* opinion of redressing the balance between law enforcement officials and the suspect, of permitting him to make intelligent choices about how to proceed without coercion and with the advice of competent counsel should he so desire it. The studies on the impact of *Miranda* suggest that this goal has not been reached. The decision was no doubt a movement toward this goal, but the dynamics of the legal system —the gap between the "ought" of doctrine and the "is" of behavior—again demonstrate that the protection of civil liberties depends upon much more than the words of the Court.[11]

The picture that Casper presents of the limited normative power of the Supreme Court is made all the more dramatic when it is viewed in light of the fact that plea bargaining presently takes place in over 90 percent of all criminal prosecutions in the United States. In plea bargaining, the defendant surrenders

THE LOWER COURTS

an "entire array of constitutional rights designed to protect . . . [him] against unjustified conviction, including the right to remain silent, the right to confront witnesses against him, the right to trial by jury, and the right to be proven guilty by proof beyond a reasonable doubt."[12] In other words, the defendant waives virtually all those Bill of Rights guarantees that the Supreme Court is attempting to protect and, in the process, renders the Court's power almost totally ineffectual.[13]

Two Models of the Criminal Process

What accounts for this discrepancy between the rulings of the Supreme Court and the behavior of the rest of the criminal justice system? What explains the limited effectiveness of the Court's normative compliance structure? Part of the answer is provided by the late Alexander Bickel:

> The judicial process is too principle-prone and principle-bound—it has to be, there is no other justification or explanation for the role it plays. It is also too remote from conditions, and deals, case by case, with too narrow a slice of reality. It is not accessible to all the varied interests that are in play in any decision of great consequence. It is, very properly, independent. It is passive. It has difficulty controlling the stages by which it approaches a problem. It rushes forward too fast, or it lags; its pace hardly ever seems just right. For all these reasons, it is, in a vast, complex, changeable society, a most unsuitable instrument for the formation of policy.[14]

The substantial discrepancy that exists between the Court's judgments in the criminal procedural realm and the actual practices of the criminal justice system cannot, however, be fully explained simply by reference to the unsuitability of the Court as an "instrument for the formation of policy." Bickel's comments, significant as they are, must be considered in conjunction with those of Herbert L. Packer. Packer, in one of the most influential contributions to the understanding of the administration of criminal justice, suggests that the answer to these questions is also to be found in the fact that there are in the United States two distinct views—two alternative ways of looking at the goals and procedures—of the criminal process: the crime control model and the due process model.[15]

The Crime Control Model

According to Packer, "The crime control model is based on the proposition that the repression of criminal conduct is by far the most important function to be performed by the criminal process."[16] If the laws go unenforced, a general disregard for legal controls tends to develop, and law-abiding citizens become the victims of unjustifiable invasions of their interests. Their security of person and property is drastically reduced, and, as a result, so is their liberty to function as members of society. Thus, the crime control model regards the criminal process as the positive guarantor of social freedom. In order to achieve this lofty objective, it focuses primary attention on the efficiency with which the criminal justice system operates to screen suspects, ascertain guilt, and secure appropriate dispositions of persons convicted of crime.

This emphasis on efficiency encourages informality, uniformity, and, above all, a "presumption of guilt." The importance of informality to achieve efficiency is obvious enough. "The process must not be cluttered up with ceremonious rituals that do not advance the progress of the case."[17] Because the facts of a case can be more quickly established through informal interrogation at a police station than through the formal process of examination and cross-examination in a court, the crime control model favors extrajudicial processes over judicial processes, informal operations over formal ones. For informality to be effective, it must also be accompanied by uniformity; "Routine, stereotyped procedures are essential if large numbers are being handled."[18] Thus, the crime control model is an administrative, bureaucratic model. As Packer observes:

> The image that comes to mind is an assembly-line conveyor belt down which moves an endless stream of cases, never stopping, carrying the cases to workers who stand at fixed stations and who perform on each case as it comes by the same small but essential operation that brings it one step closer to a finished product, or, to exchange the metaphor for the reality, a closed file. The criminal process, in this model, is seen as a screening process in which each successive stage—pre-arrest investigation, arrest, post-arrest investigation, preparation for trial, trial or entry of plea, conviction, disposition—involves a series of routinized operations whose success is gauged primarily by their tendency to pass the case along to a successful conclusion.[19]

For this "assembly-line" justice to operate efficiently, however, an early determination must be made of probable innocence or guilt. It is necessary that the probably innocent be immediately screened out, thereby allowing the probably guilty to be passed quickly through the remaining stages of the process. "The key to the operation of the model regarding those who are not screened out" is what Packer calls "a presumption of guilt."[20] It is this presumption of guilt that makes it possible for the crime control model to deal effectively with a large volume of cases. It considers the screening processes of the police and prosecutors to be reliable indicators of probable guilt. "Once a man has been arrested without being found to be probably innocent, or, to put it differently, once a determination has been made that there is enough evidence of guilt to permit holding him for further action, then all subsequent activity directed toward him is based on the view that he is probably guilty."[21]

The Due Process Model

If the crime control model can be likened to an assembly line, the due process model can be likened to an obstacle course. As Packer describes it, "each of its successive stages is designed to present formidable impediments to carrying the accused any further along in the process."[22] The due process model places a premium on reliability rather than on efficiency. In a sense, it "resembles a factory that has to devote a substantial part of its input to quality control. This necessarily cuts down on quantitative output."[23]

The priority that the due process model places on reliability is related to its understanding of legal guilt. According to the due process model, an accused is not guilty of a crime merely because he has, in fact, committed the offense for which he is charged. The doctrine of legal guilt requires more than mere factual guilt. Rather, an accused is guilty if and only if the state can prove, under various procedural restraints dealing with admissibility of evidence, the burden of proof, and the requirement that guilt be proved beyond a reasonable doubt, that he did in fact commit the crime. As Packer acknowledges, "None of these requirements has anything to do with the factual question of whether the person did or did not engage in the conduct that is charged as the offense against him; yet favorable answers to any of them will mean that he is legally innocent."[24]

Much as the crime control model's preoccupation with efficiency and productivity is based on the presumption of guilt, so, too, the due process model's concern for reliability and legal guilt is grounded on the presumption of innocence. According to the due process model, even if a murderer were to kill his victim in plain view of a large number of people and were then to declare to the police upon their arrival, "I did it and I'm glad," the criminal justice system must presume the suspect to be innocent, for the presumption of innocence is not a "prediction of outcome" but "a direction to officials about how they are to proceed."[25] It directs them to ignore the presumption of guilt in their treatment of the suspect and to close their eyes to what will frequently seem to be factual probabilities. It encourages them to prefer reliability as measured through the determination of legal guilt in an adversary proceeding to efficiency and the adequacy of factual guilt.

These two models are, as Packer describes them, "polarities"; they represent competing schemes of values. They are not intended to constitute "a program for action" but rather are introduced as "an aid to analysis" that is useful in providing an answer to the question of why "the Court's prescriptions about how the process ought to operate does not automatically become part of the pattern of official behavior in the criminal process."[26] With them, an answer to this question can be given: Although the due process model is preached by the U.S. Supreme Court, the crime control model is in fact practiced by the lower courts. It is practiced because of its remunerative value and utility to each element in the criminal justice system. The next section will explore in detail the extent to which this is the case.

The Performance of the Lower Courts

The extent to which the crime control model is practiced by lower courts is dramatically apparent when it is recalled that plea bargaining occurs in over 90 percent of all criminal prosecutions in the United States.[27] In plea bargaining, or "copping a plea," as it is often called in the vernacular, the defendant agrees to plead guilty in exchange for a lesser sentence. It is efficient in that it spares the criminal justice system of the need for a trial. Yet, it is clearly in conflict with the due process model, for the defendant who enters such a plea not only admits guilt but also surrenders his rights to an entire array of procedural protections all designed by the Supreme Court to shield him from unjustified conviction. There are a variety of reasons why lower courts prefer plea bargaining under the crime control model to an adversary proceeding under the due process model. For the most part, they can be grouped under two general rubrics: the problem of system overload and the bureaucratization of the lower courts.

The Problem of System Overload

According to Uniform Crime Reports statistics, it is estimated that the police in 1974 made a total of 9,055,800 arrests.[28] This figure was up from 3,242,574 recorded arrests in 1960 and 4,257,707 in 1968.[29] Police and law enforcement agencies have recently become much more effective in the apprehension of criminal suspects. They have generally enjoyed the lion's share of Law Enforcement Assistance Administration (LEAA) grants from the federal government, receiving approximately 70 percent of all such funding, whereas courts and correctional agencies have had to be content with the remainder.[30] Because of this increased funding and because of soaring crime rates, the police have been able to bring ever-increasing numbers of criminal defendants into the criminal justice system. This, however, has contributed greatly to system overload. The other components of the criminal justice system—the courts and corrections—have simply not been able to keep pace with this dramatic increase in the number of cases. Given these conditions, plea bargaining under the crime control model has become a practical necessity.

The lower courts in the United States are simply unable to adhere to the "obstacle course" provisions of the due process model when they are required to pass judgment on the validity of over 9 million arrests a year. If they were to attempt to do so, the entire criminal justice system would grind to a halt. As the President's Commission of Law Enforcement and Administration of Justice was quick to point out, "If a substantial percentage of . . . [criminal cases] were not dropped or carried to negotiated conclusions administratively, justice would be not merely slowed down; it would be stopped."[31] Chief Justice Warren Burger's remarks to the American Bar Association in 1970 support this assessment.

THE LOWER COURTS

Aware that the lower courts in the United States have been based "on the premise that approximately 90 percent of all defendants will plead guilty, leaving only 10 percent, more or less, to be tried," Chief Justice Burger declared that "the consequence of what might seem on its face a small percentage change" in the rate of plea bargaining "can be tremendous. A reduction from 90 percent to 80 percent in guilty pleas requires the assignment of twice the judicial manpower and facilities—judges, court reporters, bailiffs, clerks, jurors, and court rooms. A reduction to 70 percent trebles this demand."[32] Carrying Chief Justice Burger's logic through to a complete elimination of plea bargaining under the crime control model, it is apparent that a ten-fold increase in manpower, facilities, and financial support for the lower courts would be required—an eventuality that most observers of the criminal justice system consider unlikely at best.[33] Thus, the huge volume of criminal cases necessarily compels the lower courts to adopt remunerative-calculative compliance structures and to tolerate and, in fact, encourage plea bargaining—the entire criminal justice system would simply overload and, hence, cease to function were the trial courts to attempt to provide a full adversary proceeding for every criminal defendant. Given these realities, the normative power of the Supreme Court is simply inadequate to obtain the compliance of these lower courts concerning its understanding of due process. Moreover, the future holds no bright prospects in store. In fact, the long-range consequences of the Speedy Trial Act of 1974, which requires that all federal criminal defendants be brought to trial within 100 days and which will doubtless emerge at some future date as a constitutionally mandated requirement for state court prosecutions as well, will certainly contribute all the more to the lower courts' embrace of the crime control model. Only by so doing can system overload be avoided and the overall objectives of the criminal justice system be efficiently realized.

The Bureaucratization of the Lower Courts

The specter of the consequences of system overload is not the only reason for the lower courts' embrace of plea bargaining and the crime control model. Another also exists and must be carefully examined. Plea bargaining as it is presently practiced remunerates every major participant in the criminal justice system, including the defendant, the police, the prosecutor, the judge, and the defense attorney. Because of the benefits that it provides for every participant, the traditional combative adversary proceeding that one associates with the criminal justice system has been replaced by what Abraham Blumberg calls an "administrative, ministerial, rational-bureaucratic one."[34] No longer are the defendant and defense attorney locked in a contest for truth with the prosecutor and police before an impartial and detached judge. Rather, all are "integrated into a bureaucratic matrix"[35] based fundamentally on a remunerative compliance structure. The participants in the criminal justice system comply with the dictates of the crime control model, not because it is morally compelling, but because they are remunerated or benefited for doing so. The normative power of the Supreme Court has, at this juncture, little real influence; all it can do is to remind the participants of how far the criminal justice system has departed from the due process model. This, however, only fosters further bureaucratization, as the participants bind together all the more closely in their "web of complicity."[36] These points merit elaboration.

Plea Bargaining in the "Bureaucratic Matrix"

Plea bargaining, as it is presently practiced, tends to benefit every participant in the criminal justice system. However, the clearly guilty defendant probably benefits the most. By waiving his right to require the prosecution to prove guilt at trial, he can be remunerated in at least four different ways. First, he can agree to plead guilty in return for a lesser or different charge. There are a number of advantages for doing so. Thus, the offense to which he pleads guilty may have a lower maximum penalty, thereby assuring that his sentence will not be longer than a given period of time. On the other hand, the offense may have a lower minimum sentence, thereby enabling him to be eligible for parole earlier. This advantage is especially attractive in California, where there is considerable incentive for a defendant to plead guilty to a lesser charge where punishment will be confinement for a particular period of time in a county jail rather than to go to trial, in which case conviction will, in all probability, subject him to the indeterminate sentences of the state prison system. Reduction or change in charge may also have advantages for the defendant quite independent of sentencing. Thus, a defendant may be willing to plead guilty to a charge such as disorderly conduct or assault in order to avoid being labeled as a child molester or a homosexual.

Second, he can agree to plead guilty to a single charge in a multiple-charge indictment in return for the dropping of all other charges. The plea bargaining involving former Vice-President Spiro T. Agnew is illustrative of this; Agnew agreed to resign as vice-president and to enter a plea of *nolo contendere* to a single count of income tax evasion in return for a government agreement to quash all other charges that may have been pending.

A third way in which a defendant can be remunerated for his willingness to plead guilty is for the prosecution to agree to recommend a sentence to the judge for the original charge. Although this recommendation is not binding on the judge, he is likely to follow it. Thus, the defendant trades his trial rights for the prosecution's promise to attempt to influence the sentence by means of a recommendation. Finally, a fourth way in which a defendant can be remunerated for his plea of guilty involves judge shopping. In many jurisdictions, there are wide sentencing disparities among judges. A defendant may agree to plead guilty in exchange for assurances from the prosecution that he will be brought before a particular judge for sentencing.[37]

These benefits that the defendant derives from plea bargaining can be neutralized, to a certain extent, by "overcharging" on the part of the prosecutor. Overcharging occurs when the prosecutor charges a defendant with a variety of counts, not with the intention of obtaining a conviction for each count but in an effort to induce the defendant to plead guilty to a few of the charges in exchange for a dismissal of the rest. Overcharging can be either horizontal or vertical. Horizontal overcharging may include charging the defendant with either a separate offense for every criminal transaction in which he is alleged to have participated (for example, charging an embezzler who has falsified evidence in his employer's books over a long period of time with hundreds of counts) or with several offenses arising out of a single act (for example, charging a defendant accused of burglary with three separate counts: burglary third degree, possession of burglar's tools, and breaking and entering.) Vertical overcharging, on the other hand, typically occurs when a prosecutor charges robbery when he should charge larceny of the person or auto theft when he should charge joy riding—a less serious offense that does not involve an intention to deprive the owner permanently of his property.

However, although this tendency of the prosecutor to overcharge has reduced somewhat the benefits to be derived from plea bargaining, most defendants still prefer it to an actual trial, where, if convicted, far harsher sentences are likely. In an attempt to examine the administration of criminal justice from the perspective of the defendant, Jonathan D. Casper conducted interviews with seventy-one different defendants charged with felonies in the state of Connecticut. He queried them on many issues, including their attitudes toward the plea bargain. The following exchange between Casper and a convicted offender is perhaps typical of most defendants' attitudes:

> "You think you did about as good as you could [through plea bargaining]?"
>
> "I think I made out like a bandit. I mean I had forty years hanging, the maximum. They could have gave me a ten-to-twenty on just one of them, because twenty years is the maximum on burglary. They could have gave me ten-to-twenty; they could have gave me anything. They gave me a twenty, nineteen, on the way down. Or they could have gave me a one-to-two or a two-to-five, but whatever he offers you, you better take it, because if you don't, you're going to get more than he offered; so take what you get. . . . Yeah, I mean from forty years down to one year you know—good."[38]

The defendant who pleads guilty is likely to receive a less severe sentence than the defendant who is convicted after trial. There are a number of reasons for this. To begin with, the sentencing judge may consider a plea of guilty as evidence of repentance. He may regard the defendant who pleads guilty as less culpable than the one who denies guilt in that the confession itself demonstrates a readiness on the part of the defendant to accept responsibility for his criminal acts. Judges commonly feel that such a confession of wrongdoing is indicative of a penitent attitude and thus constitutes an important first step toward rehabilitation of the accused. A second reason for imposing a less severe sentence on a defendant who pleads guilty than on one who is convicted after trial is the notion that the latter may well have committed perjury in his defense. (This inference can be drawn, of course, only when the defendant has taken the witness stand.) It presumes the commission of perjury from the fact of conviction. Because the defendant is also a perjurer, an increased sentence is justified. It is justified either as an additional sentence imposed by the judge because the defendant has committed the second crime of perjury or as an appropriate sentence for the defendant, who, through his perjurious conduct, has increased the difficulty of his ultimate reformation. After all, perjury is a culpable act that bears upon the character of the accused. A third reason for granting a defendant who pleads guilty some discount in punishment is the aid his plea provides to the efficient administration of criminal justice. This reason is, of course, altogether pragmatic, but it is important, nonetheless. By entering a plea of guilty, the defendant thereby permits the state to assign its limited judicial manpower and resources elsewhere. Finally, a fourth reason for imposing shorter sentences on those who plead guilty is that the brutal circumstances that often accompany a criminal activity are not emphasized by the prosecution or vividly recounted at trial. In a "cop-out" ceremony, the defendant is more sanitized, more antiseptic; he appears to be less of a threat to society.

The prospect that the defendant is likely to face a more severe sentence if he is unable to prove his innocence at trial is quite an incentive to engage in plea bargaining, especially if he has been unable to post bond. Thus, if the defendant has already spent a number of months in jail because he has been unable to post bond, he may be induced to plead guilty even though he knows himself to be innocent. If the sentence is short and if he is given credit for the time he has already served awaiting trial, he may be released immediately or in a short period of time. However, if he protests his innocence and demands a full adversary proceeding, he may have to spend an additional 2-to-3 months in jail awaiting a formal trial at which, if convicted, he may receive a far more severe prison sentence —in which case pretrial jail time may not count. For the defendant caught in this dilemma, the pressures to plead guilty are tremendous: If he pleads guilty, he goes free; if he pleads not guilty, he remains in jail and faces far greater risks.

Plea bargaining would not be so widely practiced if it benefited only the defendant. It has, however, proven to be advantageous to virtually all the participants in the criminal justice system, including the police, the prosecution, the judge, and even the defense attorney. The police, although they often complain about plea bargaining and point to it as one of the chief causes of interface problems between law enforcement personnel and the judiciary, have many reasons for supporting it. To begin with, they save time otherwise spent waiting around and testifying in trials. More importantly, plea bargaining proves to be useful in clearing cases—that is, "solving" crimes—and thereby improves the department's clearance rate. As previously noted, the clearance rate is one of the most commonly used indicators in evaluating police performance employed by superiors, political figures, and the public at large. On many occasions, a defendant charged with a particular offense will, after negotiation with the police, admit to a number of other crimes with an agreement that he will be charged with, plead guilty to, and be leniently punished for, only his most recent arrest. As a result of this negotiation, the police are able to clear several other cases on the basis of admissions by the defendant. Finally, another incentive police have for supporting plea bargaining is that it suppresses legal issues. A plea of guilty deprives the defendant of the opportunity to raise questions concerning the possible admissibility of the evidence against him or the activities of the police in their treatment of him.[39] Because 90 percent of all cases end in plea bargaining, the police know that strict adherence to procedural rules relating to searches and seizures and to interrogations is not as paramount a concern as it would be if every defendant were likely to use every procedural imperfection as a weapon in his defense at trial. Thus, the plea bargain buries much police conduct not conforming to legal doctrine.

The prosecutors also gain from plea bargaining. As with the police, guilty pleas avoid time-consuming trials and, thus, promote the "conservation of scarce resources."[40] Such pleas also suppress legal issues in potentially damaging challenges to the state's case and dispose of the need for complainants and witnesses to cooperate in the prosecution. Finally, the use of guilty pleas, even at the cost of conviction on lesser charges, takes all the risk out of the prosecution and assures the prosecutor a high conviction record, or "batting average," so useful at election time.

Judges also benefit from plea bargaining. Like the prosecutors, they too seek to avoid "the time-consuming, expensive, unpredictable snares and pitfalls of an adversary trial."[41] They see the plea bargain as essential if they are to keep their court dockets current; a full adversary proceeding for every criminal defendant would, after all, result in a huge backlog of cases and mounting delay. Moreover, as Abraham Blumberg has pointed out, a plea of guilty by the defendant enables certain judges to engage in a social-psychological fantasy: "The accused becomes an already repentant individual who has 'learned his lesson' and deserves lenient treatment."[42]

Even the defense attorney, whether a public defender, court assigned, or privately retained, is likely to favor plea bargaining.[43] The defense attorney who bargains for his client is often pursuing more than the best possible deal for his client.[44] He may also be pursuing personal goals and acting as a representative of the organizational matrix that the criminal court comprises.[45] Many attorneys who practice criminal law in trial courts can maximize their incomes only through a rapid turnover of a relatively large number of cases in which they represent clients paying small fees. Because plea bargaining is an efficient and quick method for turning over a large number of cases, it has considerable appeal.[46] Moreover, as Blumberg stresses, no other participant in the criminal justice system is more strategically located or ideally suited to promote plea bargaining than is the defense attorney. Both prosecutors and judges recognize this fact, and, because they, too, gain from plea bargaining, they frequently cooperate with the defense attorney in ways designed to assist him in persuading the defendant to plead guilty. Thus, the prosecution may deceptively engage in horizontal or vertical overcharging as part of a sham staged to benefit the defense attorney. These additional charges will in all probability be dismissed during plea negotiation; however, they help to establish the defense attorney's credibility and, hence, help to justify his fee. He can tell the defendant that there were initially five felony charges against him but that he has been able to whittle the prosecution down to one. At that juncture, the defense attorney is in a strong position to tell his client: "I've gotten you quite a deal, please don't blow it." Judges can also provide similar assistance. Thus, they have been known to recess the case of a defendant who is in jail awaiting plea or sentence if it is requested by his attorney. This may be done for an ostensibly legitimate reason, but the real purpose may be to permit the attorney to press for collection of his fee, which is likely to go uncollected if it is not obtained prior to the conclusion of the case.[47]

The defense attorney is bound to the court and encouraged to induce his client to plead guilty by other factors as well. Thus, if he is a court regular, he is likely to have developed interpersonal relationships and dependencies in his dealings with the prosecutors and judges and, as a consequence, may accede to the wishes of the prosecutor in one case in order to gain a favor that can be collected in another. Moreover, because his contact with the client is typically brief, whereas his contact with the prosecutors and judges is continuous, the pressures to become what Blumberg calls a "double agent" are all the more intense.[48] The operational reality of the crime control model and its presumption that someone brought this far into the criminal justice system is guilty spares the defense attorney of much of the anxiety that one would normally expect to attach to such actions. Because his client is probably guilty, he is acting in his client's interest by encouraging him to plead guilty in return for some consideration.

As is apparent, plea bargaining tends to serve the best interests of all the participants of the criminal justice system. The police, prosecutors, judges, and defense attorneys all benefit by it; so, too, does the guilty defendant who obtains in return for his acquiescence and cooperation a more favorable disposition. There are only two losers: the clearly innocent defendant and society as a whole. The innocent defendant finds himself enmeshed in the calculative crime control model with its presumption of guilt and its emphasis on efficiency over reliability. Once enmeshed in this remunerative compliance structure, there is, as Blumberg has emphasized, "little chance of escaping conviction."[49]

The loss to society as a whole is perhaps less visible but no less serious. To begin with, reliance on plea bargaining and the crime control model transfers considerable sanctioning authority from the courts to the police, who "make the major decisions about sanctions by deciding whether to pull someone into the machinery of justice."[50] This critically affects that distribution of authority and power that was intended to exist among the components of the criminal justice system.[51] Society suffers from the plea bargain in other respects as well, however. Thus, because of plea bargaining, most defendants (especially professional criminals) are not dealt with as severely as might be appropriate. This leniency reduces the deterrent effectiveness the law may have. Plea bargaining further endangers the security and well-being of society in yet another respect: It makes the correctional task of rehabilitation more difficult. Thus, in some defendants, plea bargaining reinforces the belief that they can manipulate the criminal justice system, and, as a consequence, it minimizes their motivation to participate in correctional programs.[52] In other defendants, plea bargaining simply promotes cynicism, which is also destructive of the rehabilitative enterprise. As the New York State Special Commission on Attica noted, "What makes inmates most cynical about their preprison experience is the plea-bargaining system. . . . Even though an inmate may receive the benefit of a shorter sentence, the plea-bargaining system is characterized by deception and hypocrisy which divorce the inmate from the reality of his crime."[53] The consequences of this cynicism on correctional programs is devastating. As the Attica Commission continued, "The large segment of prison population who believe they have been 'victimized' by the courts or Bar 'are not likely to accept the efforts of another institution of society, the correctional system, in redirecting their attitudes.'" After all, "No program of rehabilitation can be effective on a 'prisoner who is convinced in his own mind that he is in prison because he is the victim of a mindless, undirected, and corrupt system of justice.'" The cynicism described by the Attica Commission is not an isolated phenomenon occurring in but a few prisoners. The New York State Joint Legislative Committee on Crime found that almost 90 percent of the inmates they surveyed had been solicited to enter a plea bargain. Most were bitter, believing that they had not received effective legal representation or that the judge had not kept the state's promise of a lenient sentence, which had induced them to enter guilty pleas.[54] These findings are consistent with those of Burton M. Atkins and Emily W. Boyle.[55] In a survey of the attitudes of 200 selected inmates at two South Carolina prisons, they found that 79.3 percent of the respondents indicated that "they were not pleased with their attorney's performance."[56] Furthermore, 73.9 percent of the sample declared that they would rather have a different type of attorney in any future encounters with the criminal justice system—i.e., they were dissatisfied regardless of whether they had court-appointed, privately retained, or public defender representation.

Finally, plea bargaining complicates the correctional task of rehabilitation in still another respect. Plea bargaining tends to limit the sentencing alternatives of the court, and, to the extent that it does, it encourages sentences inconsistent with correctional goals, generates further interface conflict between courts and corrections, and ultimately contributes to the greater inefficiency of the entire criminal justice system.

The Politics of the Lower Courts

As the costs to society as a whole imposed by plea bargaining become more pronounced, public awareness of, and hostility to, plea bargaining also mounts. The results of a 1974 public opinion survey in Memphis, Tennessee, are revealing. A total of 557 respondents were interviewed to determine their awareness of, and attitudes toward, plea bargaining.[57] Although the sample was randomly selected,[58] it closely resembled the demographic characteristics of the city as a whole (see Table 5.1). The respondents were read the following statement: "Plea bargaining is the practice of permitting a criminal defendant to plead guilty to a lesser charge than the one for which he was originally charged, thereby enabling the state to avoid the expense and uncertainty of a trial." They were then asked whether or not they were aware that plea bargaining in fact took place in the American criminal justice system. An overwhelming 86.9 percent of the sample population admitted that they were (see Table 5.2). They were then asked if they approved of such a practice. Altogether, 76.3 percent declared that they did not. White female respondents registered the strongest opposition, with 91.8 percent of the sample declaring that they were opposed to plea bargaining. In contrast, only 44.7 percent of black male respondents expressed similar opposition (see Table 5.3).

Very little empirical research has been conducted on the question of public awareness of, and attitudes toward, plea bargaining. Nonetheless, the results recorded here are completely in keeping with the collateral findings of the Gallup organization and the National Opinion Research Center. They report that

Table 5.1 Demographic Characteristics of Plea Bargaining Sample

Race and sex	Number polled	Percent of sample	Percent of city population[a]
White males	166	29.8	28.9
White females	914	34.8	31.9
Black males	85	15.3	18.0
Black females	112	20.1	20.8
Totals	557	100.0	99.6

[a] U.S. Bureau of the Census, *Census of Population, 1970*, vol. 1, *Characteristics of the Population*, Part 44, Tennessee (Washington, D.C.: Government Printing Office, 1973), pp. 63-64.

Table 5.2 Awareness of Plea Bargaining by Race and Sex

Race and sex	Aware of plea bargaining	
	Number	Percent
White males	155	96.9
White females	164	84.5
Black males	76	89.4
Black females	89	79.5
Totals	484	86.9

nationwide, approximately 75 percent of the population believes that the courts do not deal "harshly enough with criminals."[59] Because, as this analysis has shown, plea bargaining is the major factor contributing to this judicial leniency, public opposition to plea bargaining is only one step or, more precisely, one question away.

Despite this massive public opposition to plea bargaining, the lower courts have been generally opposed to its wholesale elimination. This aversion can be attributed in large part to the politics of complicity that operates in the lower courts. This politics of complicity arises out of the fact that lower courts are simply compelled by the volume of cases with which they are confronted to operate on the basis of the remunerative-calculative compliance structure of the crime control model. Given these imperatives, departures from the normative requirements of due process are inevitable. As Abraham Blumberg writes: "Heavy work volume, impossible case loads, and unrealistic work schedules exert

Table 5.3 Attitude toward Plea Bargaining by Race and Sex

Race and sex	Favor		Oppose		No opinion		Total
	Number	Percent	Number	Percent	Number	Percent	
White males	19	11.4	144	86.8	3	1.8	100.0
White females	6	3.1	178	91.8	10	5.2	100.1[a]
Black males	38	44.7	38	44.7	9	10.6	100.0
Black females	31	27.7	65	50.0	16	14.3	100.0
Totals	94	16.9	425	76.3	38	6.8	

[a]Due to rounding, does not add to 100 percent.

inordinate pressures for innovation—the search for short cuts, the use of forbidden procedures and devices, and the like—in order that production norms may be met."[60] These departures do more, however, than ensure that production norms are met. They also entangle all who are a party to these departures in a web of complicity and, thereby, make them amenable to control from within. If a party to these departures should eventually find his continued participation in them intolerable and should suggest the need for a renewed dedication and commitment to the due process model, his past indiscretions and violations of that same due process model, even though he may have been encouraged by his colleagues to engage in them, are available to be invoked against him. Thus, the politics of complicity discourages individual effort by various members of the lower courts to eliminate plea bargaining and to substitute in its place the full adversary proceedings of the normative due process model. Everyone is tainted; as a consequence, no one is worthy to lead the crusade.

Problems of Judicial Administration

Although the problem of system overload and the increased bureaucratization of the judiciary constitute perhaps the major causes for the lower courts' embrace of plea bargaining and the crime control model and their departure from the requirements of the due process model as spelled out by the Supreme Court, other considerations are also present. One such consideration is the rather dismal state of present-day judicial administration. As former Senator Joseph D. Tydings, Jr., has observed: "Our courts are administered today in essentially the same way that they were two centuries ago."[61]

Chief Justice Warren Burger made much the same point in his 1968 address to the American Bar Association, generally known as the First State of the Judiciary message. In it, he made reference to a famous speech delivered 62 years earlier by Dean Roscoe Pound to that same association. In 1906, Pound warned that the work of twentieth-century courts could not be conducted through the use of nineteenth-century methods and machinery. Chief Justice Burger, in commenting on how little Dean Pound's admonition had been heeded, declared:

> We are still trying to operate the courts with fundamentally the same basic methods, procedures, and machinery he [Pound] said were not good enough in 1906. In the supermarket age, we are like a merchant trying to operate a cracker barrel corner grocery store with the methods and equipment of 1900.[62]

Many factors, typically related to the uniqueness of the courts and to the constraints and conflicts that their unusual role creates, help frustrate the attainment of better and more orderly judicial administration. Ernest C. Friesen, Jr.,

THE LOWER COURTS

former administrative director of the U.S. courts, has explored six of these.[63] First, courts are almost totally dependent upon political processes for their resources. Although the governmental system has come to place increased responsibility on the courts for solving complex social problems, it has not given them the requisite resources for their effective resolution. Second, traditional adversary theory requires judges to assume passive roles, thereby placing principal responsibility for the administration of justice upon the performance, quality, availability, and attitudes of the American lawyer.[64] Third, lawyers tend to be highly individualistic. "Their legal training and practice emphasize legal rather than administrative skills and individual effort rather than teamwork."[65] This professional independence, exhibited by attorneys and judges alike, thwarts strong administration. Fourth, the jury system is a special constraint upon court management. Jurors, after all, are not employees of the court; their incentives for performance are substantially different from those of employees generally. Thus, courts often face massive problems in getting an impartial jury and in keeping it for a protracted trial. Fifth, methods of selection and tenure of judges affect the performance of the judicial establishment. Efforts at reform, such as the Missouri Plan, often have made the judges less effective in court management and more dependent upon the good will of the lawyer.[66] Sixth, and finally, the statutory division of jurisdiction among courts (limited jurisdiction versus general jurisdiction) prohibits flexible administration. As Friesen notes:

> Though there are clearly areas of the law and of justice which require more or less skill on the part of judges, the distribution of labor along traditional lines has not taken this into account. The critical legal problems of today are probably in the area of the relations of a tenant to his landlord, consumer credit, or juvenile behavior. The jurisdiction over these matters has traditionally been allocated to courts with lower-paid and lower-status judges.[67]

These factors have all limited the effectiveness of judicial administration. They have contributed to the archaic management and record-keeping systems of most lower courts. As Leonard Downie, Jr., writes:

> To step inside the local courthouse, in this age of space travel, transoceanic television, and computers, is to travel backward in time—if not to the Dark Ages, then certainly to an era generations ago. Modern improvements in management techniques, record keeping, and communications are all but unheard of inside courthouse walls. Instead, U.S. courts continue to follow slavishly many of the same procedures as did courts in early-world America and the shires of England before that.[68]

Thus, at a time when computerized data processing could print out a daily calendar for the judges in each division of court; could provide additional information on case loads so that the judges' time could be properly scheduled; could determine how many cases each attorney has and when each case is scheduled for its next court hearing; could be used for legal research—yielding data, for example, on how many defendants have been arrested for a particular offense during a certain period and what happened to them in court; and could be of benefit to court administrators, enabling them to determine accurately how well each division is coping with its business, whether methods need to be changed, or whether more judges or support personnel are required, most courts continue to waste considerable time and effort by keeping most records and preparing most dockets in long hand.[69]

As a consequence of these "cracker barrel corner grocery store" methods, congestion and delay in the lower courts are rife. Downie has described this unfortunate situation as follows:

> Cases pile up because the methods for moving them to trial are archaic, feeble and slow. Cases are postponed when ready for trial because judges will not work full, properly scheduled days and lawyers, greedy for too many cases at one time, miss court appearances or come unprepared. Cases are lost in the system because judges and clerks with no management skills are trying to run a large, complicated business.[70]

The typical response to these problems in most lower courts has been "not to modernize an out-moded system but rather to short-circuit it."[71] Thus, plea bargaining and crime control are stressed. However, this response serves only to convert "courthouses into counting houses"[72]—or, to state the matter in terms of compliance analysis, it serves to supplant normative compliance structures with remunerative ones.

The Impact of Positivist Jurisprudence

Finally, another major factor contributing to the lower courts' emphasis on plea bargaining and the crime control model is the impact of the positivist critique of declaratory theory. Simply put, declaratory theory holds that the function of a judge is only to declare the law. Sir William Blackstone provided the classic formulation and intellectual justification for declaratory theory in his *Commentaries on the Laws of England*. His argument may be succinctly stated: Because "it is an established rule to abide by former precedents," it is the duty of a judge not to "pronounce new law, but to maintain and expound the old one."[73] Consequently, in deciding a case, the judge is bound to find the law as it existed when the controversy arose and to declare it as being the controlling principle in the case. As Blackstone said, it is not "in the breast of any subsequent judge to alter or vary from [precedent], according to his private judgment, but according to the known laws and customs of the land."[74] Blackstone did acknowledge that

THE LOWER COURTS

this rule does "admit of exceptions, where the former determination is most evidently contrary to reason."[75] However, even in such cases,

> subsequent judges do not pretend to make a new law, but to vindicate the old one from misrepresentation. For if it be found that the former decision is manifestly absurd or unjust, it is declared, not that such a sentence was *bad law*, but that it was *not law;* that it is not the established custom of the realm, as has been erroneously determined.[76]

This view of Blackstone—that it is not the duty of a judge to expound new law but to discover and declare the old law—has been harshly criticized by the positivist school of jurisprudence.[77] For example, Jeremy Bentham scornfully observed that if we ask "who is it that the common law has been made by, we learn, to our unexpressible surprise that it has been made by nobody."[78] And certainly it has not been made by the judges, for

> they know their duty better, their bounden duty, their only right is, not to *make* law, but to *declare* it. Declare what? Declare that to have been made, which to their own perfect knowledge never was made? Give their fictions, their own interest—begotten falsehoods, for realities . . .?[79]

Bentham asserted that "the truth is—that, on each occasion, the rule to which a judge gives the force of law, is one which, on this very occasion he makes out of his own head: and this—not till the act for which the man is thus dealt with has been done."[80]

John Austin was subsequently to join Bentham in these criticisms. He argued that what hindered Blackstone from seeing this reality "was the childlike fiction employed by our judges, that judiciary or common law is not made by them, but is a miraculous something made by nobody, existing, I suppose, from eternity, and merely *declared* from time to time by the judges."[81] Consequently, for Austin, all that remained from Blackstone was "absurd . . . conceits."[82] He likewise expanded upon Bentham's view of the nature of the law, arguing that law is constantly evolving and that the law today is frankly recognized to be different from the law yesterday. He maintained that judges do more than discover law: They make it interstitially by filling in with judicial interpretation the vague, indefinite, or generic statutory or common-law terms that alone are but, as Justice Tom Clark has described them, the "empty crevices of the law."[83] Austin received sound backing for this positivist understanding of judicial decision making from Justice Benjamin Cardozo in his classic study, *The Nature of the Judicial Process*.[84] In it, a pensive Cardozo observed:

> I have grown to see that the [judicial] process in its highest reaches is not discovery, but creation; and that the doubts and misgivings, the hopes and fears, are part of the travail of the mind, the pangs of death

and the pangs of birth, in which principles that have served their day expire, and new principles are born.[85]

He rejected the view that law was predicated on the existence of a universal and immutable set of principles embedded in human nature. He stressed rather that there is no "solid land of fixed and settled rules, [no] paradise of a justice that would declare itself by tokens plainer and more commanding than its pale and glimmering reflections in . . . [the judge's] own vacilitating mind and conscience."[86] As a consequence, he admitted that there are many cases in which plausible and fairly persuasive reasons can be found for one conclusion as well as for another. And, at this juncture "here come into play that balancing of judgment, that testing and sorting of considerations of analogy and logic and utility and fairness: . . . Here it is that the judge assumes the function of a *lawgiver.*"[87]

This positivist jurisprudence received perhaps its classic formulation in the writings of Oliver Wendell Holmes. Holmes heaped scorn on Blackstonian declaratory theory that, he declared, believed law to be "a brooding omnipresence in the sky." "The life of the law," he insisted, "has not been logic: it has been experience. The felt necessities of the time, the prevalent moral and political theories, intuitions of public policies, avowed or unconscious, even the prejudices which judges share with their fellow-men, have had a good deal more to do than the syllogism in determining the rules by which men should be governed."[88] He insisted that "the very considerations which judges most rarely mention, and always with an apology, are the secret root from which the law draws all the juices of life. I mean, of course, considerations of what is expedient for the community concerned."[89] This positivist critique of declaratory theory has won the massive support of both the academic and legal communities, so much so that most judges now govern their actions as Justice Cardozo advised, "not by metaphysical conceptions of the nature of judge-made law, nor by the fetich of some implacable tenet, such as that of the division of governmental powers, but by considerations of convenience, of utility, and of the deepest sentiments of justice."[90] This jurisprudential view, however, has prompted the sort of performance of the lower courts described earlier in this chapter. If the law is not based on a set of immutable universal principles everywhere applicable but is rather reflective of the prejudices and the "felt necessities of the time," how are "the deepest sentiments of justice" to be distinguished from "considerations of convenience . . . [and] utility"? And if so, how is any one value to be favored over another? How is due process to be preferred to crime control—a full adversary proceeding to plea bargaining? How is a court system based upon normative power to be preferred to one based on remuneration? Because plea bargaining under the remunerative crime control model is, in most courts, a "felt necessity," are not its claims to advancing considerations of convenience and utility, and hence, of justice, surely as compelling as those of a full adversary proceeding under the normative due process model.

The Prospects for Judicial Reform

Given all of the inducements for the lower courts to engage in the calculative crime control model, how realistic are the prospects for any thoroughgoing judicial reform and for a return to the normative due process model? The recent National Advisory Commission on Criminal Justice Standards and Goals stressed the need for such reform when it proposed as one of its standards that plea bargaining be entirely abolished. It declared:

> Negotiations between prosecutors and defendants—either personally or through their attorneys—concerning concessions to be made in return for guilty pleas should be prohibited. In the event that the prosecution makes a recommendation as to sentence, it should not be affected by the willingness of the defendant to plead guilty to some or all of the offenses with which he is charged. A plea of guilty should not be considered by the court in determining the sentence to be imposed.[91]

How realistic is this proposed standard? The next section focuses attention on this pressing question.

Recommendations of the National Advisory Commission on Criminal Justice Standards and Goals

To meet this standard, the commission stressed the need for reducing the huge volume of cases that has made plea bargaining necessary through possible decriminalization of "victimless" crimes, increased use of screening and pretrial diversion, and expanded funding for the criminal justice system sufficient to provide the manpower and facilities necessary to handle this volume. Each of these recommendations is, however, open to criticism.

Decriminalization of "Victimless" Crimes

Removal of criminal sanctions from such "victimless" crimes as marijuana use, prostitution, pornography, drunkenness, and gambling would certainly help to reduce the heavy volume of cases the lower courts are required to hear.[92] Despite these advantages, however, a serious question arises concerning how well, in the long run, the normative power of the courts and the due process model is served through decriminalization of "victimless" crimes. After all, the call for decriminalization is but a further acknowledgment of the limited normative power of the law generally. Moreover, decriminalization of "victimless" crimes is an extremely controversial proposal and is unlikely to gain the support of the public.

Increased Use of Screening and Pretrial Diversion

Extensive use of screening and diversion of cases would also contribute to a decline in the incidence of plea bargaining in the lower courts. As described in Chapter 2, screening involves a discretionary decision to stop, prior to trial or plea, all formal proceedings against a person who has become involved in the criminal justice system; pretrial diversion, on the other hand, involves a decision to encourage a suspect to participate in a noncriminal rehabilitative program by suspending or dismissing formal proceedings. The City of Philadelphia has employed these methods with impressive results. Although, as mentioned earlier, over 90 percent of the cases in most major American cities involve plea bargaining, only 32 percent of the cases in Philadelphia are concluded by guilty pleas.[93] However, screening and especially pretrial diversion are mixed blessings. Although they are proposed as methods by which to reduce the heavy volume of cases that the lower courts must hear and that leads those courts to embrace the crime control model and plea bargaining, they are themselves based on crime control principles. Thus, for example, pretrial diversion involves the disposition of criminal charges without a conviction. The disposition, however, does not imply a finding of not guilty; rather, it often assumes guilt. This, of course, is clearly contrary to the tenets of the due process model, but this is only the beginning. "Program restrictions regarding which offenders are eligible for diversion may violate the equal protection clause of the Fourteenth Amendment of the United States Constitution. The defendant's right to a speedy trial must be waived in order to have sentence withheld. As with pre-sentence investigations, the issue of self-incrimination emerges when the defendant, still presumed to be innocent, may be required to discuss the details of his alleged offense with his diversion counselor."[94]

Increased Financial Support

Finally, increased financial support for the criminal justice system in general and for the courts in particular would also be required for a complete elimination of plea bargaining. This expanded funding, however, is not all that likely to be forthcoming. The public has, for the most part, exactly the kind of criminal justice system it is willing to support.[95] It would rather pay higher insurance premiums to protect against the consequences of crime than higher taxes to combat its root causes. Nonetheless, the National Advisory Commission was adamant: "Basic to the Commission's position on plea negotiations is its conclusion that lack of resources should not affect the outcome of the processing of a criminal defendant and that it is not unrealistic to expect that the criminal justice system can and will be provided with adequate resources."[96]

Bail Reform

Even if criminal sanctions were removed from "victimless" crimes, if screening and pretrial diversion were more extensively employed, and if additional financial support were provided for the lower courts, total elimination of plea bargaining would still by no means be assured. These measures would have to be supplemented with a comprehensive program of bail reform and with a genuine commitment to administrative modernization.

Bail may be defined as a sum of money posted by a defendant or his representative to secure his release from jail until the disposition of his case. The bail process typically operates as follows: An arrested person is brought by the police before a committing magistrate or judge who fixes an amount of money as security for his appearance at trial.[97] In some courts, bail schedules set an amount for each offense, and if the defendant can post that amount, the judge seldom considers the case individually. In either case, if the defendant can post the required amount or can pay a bail bondsman to post it for him, he is released until trial. If he cannot, he remains in jail.

Under normal bail procedures where a bail bond is obtained from a private bail bondsman, the accused pays 10 percent of the bond to the bondsman, who then becomes financially responsible to the state for the defendant's appearance at trial. If the defendant fails to appear, the bail bondsman forfeits the entire amount of the bond. On the other hand, if the defendant does appear, he does not recoup the 10 percent that he has paid to the bondsman—after all, the bondsman is in business for a profit. Because of the loss of the 10 percent premium, many defendants are unable to afford bail if it is set at more than $500. For example, in New York City, 25 percent of all defendants fail to make bail at $500, 45 percent fail at $1,500, and 63 percent fail at $2,500.[98] Although the percentage of defendants who fail to make bail varies widely from place to place, in some jurisdictions it is as high as 90 percent.[99]

The results of these bail procedures, which leave a substantial portion of defendants in jail because they cannot post bond, have been twofold: They have encouraged plea bargaining and have promoted the crime control model. Thus, in many instances, these procedures may induce even an innocent defendant to plead guilty because he has already spent a number of months in jail, having been unable to post bond. If the sentence is short and if the defendant is given credit for the time he has already served in jail awaiting trial, he may be subject to immediate or imminent release. In contrast, if he protests his innocence, he may have to spend an additional 2 to 3 months in jail awaiting a formal trial at which, if convicted, he may receive a far more severe sentence in prison—in which case, as has been noted before, pretrial jail time may not count. Thus, for a defendant in this situation, the pressures to plead guilty are tremendous.

Present bail arrangements not only encourage plea bargaining, they also promote the crime control model and its presumption of guilt. Professor Caleb Foote conducted pioneer studies on the varying dispositions between bailed and nonbailed defendants in Philadelphia and New York. In Philadelphia, he traced the disposition of 529 serious criminal cases where the defendants were free on bail. Of that number 275 were convicted; and of these, only 61, or 22 percent, were sentenced to prison. In contrast, of 417 similar cases where the defendants were held in jail before trial, 340 were convicted, and 200, or 59 percent, of them were sentenced to prison.[100] In New York, he found much the same pattern. Of a sample of 2,000 defendants, the grand jury dismissed about 24 percent of those defendants free on bail but only 10 percent of those in jail. Jailed defendants pleaded guilty about 90 percent of the time, whereas those awaiting trial on bail did so only about 70 percent of the time. At trial, defendants awaiting trial in jail were acquitted about 20 percent of the time; in contrast, those who were free on bail were acquitted 31 percent of the time. Finally, suspended sentences were received by only 13 percent of jailed defendants who were tried and convicted; however, 54 percent of bailed defendants who were tried and convicted received suspended sentences.[101]

This discrepancy between bailed and jailed defendants is explained in large part by the fact that the pretrial period is a crucial stage in the administration of criminal justice. An incarcerated defendant is severely limited in what he can do to assist in the preparation of his defense.[102] He may be detained at an inconvenient location or have insufficient time available for working with the attorney, investigators, or witnesses. He may be unable to make amends with the complaining witness in an effort to have the charges dropped. He cannot help locate witnesses or evidence. He earns no money that could be used to help his case.[103] Moreover, he has no opportunity to establish himself as a dependable and stable member of the community and, hence, as one worthy of a suspended sentence, as does the defendant who is free on bail. More recent data gathered in conjunction with the Manhattan Bail Project serve to underscore just how crucial this stage is. They reveal that only one-third of all bailed defendants but a full 60 percent of all incarcerated defendants were subsequently convicted at trial.[104] Table 5.4 compares the disposition by charge for defendants who were free pending trial and for those who were in jail at the time of adjudication. They also reveal that of those convicted defendants who were at liberty before trial, 38 percent charged with felonies and 67 percent charged with misdemeanors received suspended sentences, whereas of those convicted defendants who were detained before trial, only 6 percent charged with felonies and 15 percent charged with misdemeanors had their sentences suspended (see Table 5.5).

In addition to these human costs, present bail procedures also impose a staggering financial burden on the units of government that must feed and clothe those detained for want of bail. Thus, for example, New York City annually spends well over $18 million and Los Angeles approximately $14 million

Table 5.4 Case Disposition, by Jail Status and Charge

Charge	At liberty before trial						Detained before trial					
	Convicted		Not convicted			Total cases	Convicted		Not convicted			Total cases
	Number	Percent	Number	Percent			Number	Percent	Number	Percent		
Assault	29	23	97	77		126	76	59	52	41		128
Grand larceny	41	43	55	57		96	112	72	44	28		156
Robbery	18	51	17	49		35	58	58	42	42		100
Dangerous weapons	10	43	13	57		23	12	57	9	43		21
Narcotics	17	52	16	48		33	16	38	26	62		42
Sex crimes	5	10	44	90		49	4	14	24	86		28
Others	14	30	33	70		47	18	78	5	22		23
Totals	134	33	275	67		409	296	60	202	40		498

Source: Charles E. Ares, Anne Rankin, and Herbert Sturz, "The Manhattan Bail Project: An Interim Report on the Use of Pre-Trial Parole," New York University Law Review 38 (1963): 84.

Table 5.5 Sentence, by Jail Status and Charge

Charge on which guilt determined	At liberty before trial					Detained before trial					
	Suspended sentence		Prison		Total cases	Suspended sentence		Prison		Total cases
	Number	Percent	Number	Percent		Number	Percent	Number	Percent	
Felonies										
Assaults	11	42	15	58	26	4	6	69	94	73
Dangerous weapons	3	30	7	70	10	1	9	10	91	11
Larceny	17	42	23	48	40	8	7	99	93	107
Narcotics	7	41	10	59	17	0	0	16	100	16
Robbery	4	22	14	78	18	2	3	57	97	59
Others	6	43	8	56	14	2	12	15	88	17
Subtotal	48	38	77	62	125	17	6	266	94	283
Misdemeanors[a]										
Assault	91	68	43	32	134	21	13	138	87	159
Dangerous weapons	32	49	33	51	65	11	25	32	75	43
Larceny	140	72	55	28	195	50	14	307	86	357
Subtotal	263	67	131	33	394	82	15	477	85	559
Total	311	60	208	40	519	99	12	743	88	842

[a] Although all charges entered the court as felonies, many were reduced and defendants pleaded guilty to misdemeanors.

Source: Charles E. Ares, Anne Rankin, and Herbert Sturz, "The Manhattan Bail Project: An Interim Report on the Use of Pre-Trial Parole," *New York University Law Review* 38 (1963): 67, 85.

on pretrial confinement.[105] These resources could well be used elsewhere in the criminal justice system—providing, for example, additional courtrooms, judges, prosecutors, and court staff sufficient to reduce the heavy volume of cases that has made plea bargaining necessary in the first place.

Programs of bail reform have been initiated in various jurisdictions to eliminate these enormous human and economic costs. They have generally been of three basic types. In a few jurisdictions, programs of citation in lieu of arrest have been instituted. Under these programs, such as the Oakland (California) Police Citation Program, police officers are authorized to issue citations in lieu of arrests for misdemeanor crimes where basic criteria are met. The defendant is instructed where to appear for booking and charging, thereby sparing the need for him to be taken into physical custody.[106] In many more cities and counties, ROR (Release on Recognizance) programs have been established, which allow selected defendants to be released simply on a promise to appear at trial. These programs are a means of eliminating the necessity for money bail and, hence, of avoiding the possible equal protection problems that it raises—after all, since the Supreme Court in *Tate* v. *Short*[107] invalidated postconviction imprisonment based on the inability to pay a fine, serious questions are raised concerning the constitutionality of money bail. Under these programs, arrested persons are interviewed at the police station by a staff member of a pretrial release program, who obtains and verifies information regarding the accused. This information typically includes residence, family ties, employment, and prior record. The staff member then submits copies of his report to the court, the district attorney, the public defender, and the ROR program agency. A point system that places values on ties to the community is applied to each accused, and from that system, a recommendation is made to the court as to whether the accused qualifies for ROR. This recommendation can then be either accepted or rejected by the judge at arraignment. [Table 5.6 lists the criteria employed by pretrial release in Memphis and Shelby County (Tennessee) to determine eligibility for ROR.]

ROR programs have proven to be quite successful. In Memphis, only 7 percent of ROR defendants fail to appear at trial, as opposed to 19 percent of defendants released under money bail.[108] Likewise, in Philadelphia, only 7.4 percent of defendants released on their own recognizance fail to appear at the designated time.[109] These high appearance rates can be attributed to the fact that pretrial release programs both carefully screen and closely supervise ROR defendants. Again, in Memphis, only one-third of all defendants interviewed are subsequently released on their own recognizance. Moreover, once a defendant is released, he is regularly contacted by telephone and letter during his pretrial period; in addition, he may be subject to special release conditions or provided with employment and rehabilitative services.[110]

Finally, in Illinois, Connecticut, and Philadelphia, bail bondsmen have been replaced with 10 percent cash-bond programs. Under traditional bail procedures, where a bail bond is obtained from a private bail bondsman, the accused is

Table 5.6 Pretrial Release Criteria for Memphis and Shelby County (Tennessee)

Point System

To be recommended, a defendant needs:
1. A Memphis address where he can be reached AND
2. A total of six points from the following:

Int.	Ver.	
		RESIDENCE (in Memphis area; NOT on and off)
4	4	Present residence 15 years OR buying home (has paid 3 or more years on mortgage).
3	3	Present residence 2 years OR present and prior 3 years.
2	2	Present residence 6 months OR present and prior 1 year.
1	1	Present resident 4 months OR present and prior 6 months.
		TIME IN MEMPHIS AREA
2	2	15 years or more.
1	1	5 years or more.
		FAMILY TIES (in Memphis area)
3	3	Lives with family.
2	2	Lives with nonfamily friend AND has contact with other members of his family.
1	1	Lives with nonfamily friend OR has contact with other members of his family.
		EMPLOYMENT OR SUBSTITUTES
5	5	Present job over 5 years where employer will take back.
4	4	Present job over 1 year where employer will take back.
3	3	Woman with children for whom she is responsible.
3	3	Present job over 6 months where employer will take back.
3	3	Receiving public assistance 3 or more years.
3	3	Student in GOOD standing with the school.
2	2	Worked less than 6 months at his job but employer can give satisfactory recommendation.

THE LOWER COURTS

2	2	Laid off his job for reasons other than personal or ability to carry out job.
2	2	Receiving public assistance at least one year.
1	1	(a) Present job 4 months or less OR present and prior job 6 months. OR (b) current job less than a month where employer will take back. OR (c) unemployed 3 months or less than 9 months or more single prior job from which not fired for disciplinary reasons. (d) Receiving unemployment compensation, welfare, etc. (e) Full-time student. (f) In poor health. (g) Pending workmen's compensation case.
−1	−1	Prior negligent no show. OR runaway from juvenile detention center.
−2	−2	Definite knowledge of drug addiction or alcoholism. (Rebuttable if on program.)

PRIOR RECORD

Note: Use chart below for single offenses and for combination of offenses.

Code: One adult felony = 7 units if 5 years ago and no previous record within the 5-year period.
One adult felony = 10 units if within a 5-year period from present charge.
One adult misdemeanor = 2 units if within a 5-year period from the date of present charge.
One adult misdemeanor = 1 unit if 5 years ago and no previous record within the 5-year period.

−1 −1
−2 −2
−3 −3
−4 −4
−5 −5
etc.

0	1	2	3	4	5	6	7	8	9	10	11	12	13	14	15	16	17	18	19	20	21	etc.
					−1						−2					−3					−4	

required to pay 10 percent to the bondsman, who then becomes financially responsible to the state for the appearance of the accused at trial. If the accused fails to appear, the bail bondsman forfeits the entire amount of the bond. If the accused appears, he does not recoup the 10 percent he has paid to the bondsman. Under this arrangement, the bail bondsman and not the individual has the financial interest in the appearance of the accused. Under the 10 percent cash-bond program, however, the court is allowed to accept the personal bond of the accused and a deposit of 10 percent of the bond in cash. When the accused appears at trial, 90 percent of the deposit is returned, the remainder, or 1 percent of the original bond, going toward the cost of operating the program. This gives the financial incentive to the accused rather than to the professional bail bondsman. This incentive has been sufficient in Philadelphia to reduce the rate of those who fail to appear at trial to 6.6 percent.[111]

These programs involving citation in lieu of arrest, release on recognizance, and a 10 percent cash bond are much needed if plea bargaining and the calculative crime control model are ever to be supplanted by a full adversary proceeding for every defendant under the due process model. However, these programs are rare exceptions. As of late 1973, there were throughout the nation only 106 bail reform programs either in operation or under consideration and only four of these were statewide.[112]

Administrative Modernization and Reform

Along with a comprehensive program of bail reform, extensive administrative modernization and reform is also essential to close the gap between what the Supreme Court says ought to occur in the lower courts and what in fact actually takes place. Various reforms have been suggested. Thus, for example, Abraham S. Blumberg advocates the creation of an ombudsman's office in the lower courts to oversee and review guilty pleas. This person, or group of persons, "would be wholly independent of the closed community of the criminal court and would scrupulously supervise each guilty plea to determine whether minimum standards had been met. . . ."[113] These standards would be used to ascertain whether the defendant fully appreciated the severity of the charges against him, understood the right to trial by jury, and actually desired to plead guilty. Moreover, the ombudsman's office would also press the prosecution to summarize in detail any evidence other than a confession that it had obtained against the defendant; investigate the precise circumstances of the defendant's arrest and all police practices and activities that preceded and followed the arrest; examine each negotiated plea to ascertain whether any secret arrangements had been made under the threat or the promise of some benefit that would or would not accrue to the defendant should he agree or fail to comply; evaluate the health, age, education, race, and other factors such as intelligence that might affect the defendant's ability to resist manipulation; and assess the effects of any period of confinement prior to pleading, including its duration, and the living conditions during such detention. Blumberg admits that these inquiries and assessments are presently the responsibility of judges, police, prosecutors, defense lawyers, and probation personnel but, he declares, "they cannot be relied upon . . . in many routine cases." After all, "all the various participants are so elaborately entangled with one another in occupational and organizational terms that their objectivity and evaluations are compromised by other goals they seek."[114] Thus, he seeks to establish the ombudsman as an "independent body, not enmeshed in the orgainzational framework of our court systems." A serious question arises, however. How is the independence of the ombudsman to be preserved? How is this office to be kept from becoming yet another participant in the "bureaucratic" matrix of the lower courts? The politics of the lower courts, which Blumberg elsewhere so ably describes, would seem to render the efficacy of this proposed reform altogether nugatory.

Perhaps the most realistic proposed reform is that of judicial unification. Presently there is in every state a statutory division of jurisdiction between courts of limited jurisdiction and general jurisdiction. This division presently constitutes a "virtually unsurmountable" barrier to "flexible administration."[115] There are, of course, areas of the law and of justice that require more or less skill on the part of judges, and divisions based on this rational criterion are unquestionable valid. However, as Ernest Friesen notes, the "distribution of labor" as it exists in the courts today "has not taken this into account."[116] As a consequence, the National Advisory Commission on Criminal Justice Standards and Goals proposed in its *Report on Courts* that "state courts should be organized into a unified judicial system financed by the State and administered through a state-wide court administrator or administrative judge under the supervision of the Chief Justice of the State Supreme Court."[117] It detailed its recommendations:

> All trial courts should be unified into a single trial court with a general criminal as well as civil jurisdiction. Criminal jurisdiction now in courts of limited jurisdiction should be placed in these unified trial courts of general jurisdiction, with the exception of certain traffic violations. The State Supreme Court should promulgate rules for the conduct of minor as well as major criminal prosecutions.
>
> All judicial functions in the trial courts should be performed by full-time judges. All judges should possess law degrees and be members of the bar.
>
> A transcription or other record of the pre-trial court proceedings and the trial should be kept in all criminal cases.
>
> The appeal procedure should be the same for all cases.
>
> Pre-trial release services, probation services, and other rehabilitative services should be available in all prosecutions within the jurisdiction of the unified trial court.[118]

Judicial unification would go a long way toward assisting the lower courts in meeting the heavy but often uneven case load that they are compelled to bear. It could help judges, prosecutors, defense attorneys, and defendants to resist the temptation to embrace the crime control model and engage in negotiated justice. However, judicial unification is not without its opponents. Resistance to it has typically come from three quarters. First, it has come from rural areas, where home town pride serves as a strong impediment to abolition of local courts and the move toward judicial consolidation.[119] Second, it has come from members of the legal community, where many lawyers have assiduously mastered the complex procedural labyrinth of most state judicial systems and are reluctant to see this advantage that they presently enjoy vanish. Third, it has come from judges themselves, who fear that a redistribution of jurisdiction will somehow reduce the importance of the courts on which they sit.[120] The question of unification subjects judges to cross pressures. On the one hand, they stand to benefit considerably from improved judicial administration. On the other hand, they are acutely aware of the status system in the judiciary. Most have become judges because of the status it affords them. Any reduction in their perceived status from unification may well reduce the number of lawyers willing to leave higher-paying jobs to accept this heavy responsibility.[121] Thus, the prospects for judicial unification are not all that encouraging.

Although the National Advisory Commission's call for judicial unification has received a very mixed response, its call for the establishment of local court administrators in all trial courts with five or more judges has received a far warmer reception.[122] These court administrators are to be responsible for the management of the nonjudicial business of the court. They are to prepare and submit the court's budgets; recruit, hire, train, evaluate, and monitor its personnel; manage its space, equipment, and facilities; disseminate information concerning it; procure its supplies and services; disperse its funds; engage in management of its jurors; study and improve its case flow, time standards, and calendaring; and develop further mechanization and computerization of its operations.[123] In a word, these court administrators are to make the courts more efficient, thereby reducing the need for plea bargaining and the crime control model.

Ironically, however, although the goal of judicial administration is to make the courts more efficient so that the normative due process model can be allowed to operate, it promotes this goal only by having the courts adopt the remunerative-calculative compliance structure of commercial enterprises in the business world. Even Chief Justice Burger has metaphorically cast the modern twentieth-century "supermarket" as the model for courts to emulate.[124] Compliance analysis helps to reveal this irony and, as a consequence, urges a cautious approach to judicial administration. After all, justice for individual defendants, no less than justice for society as a whole, may not be subject to mass production and mass merchandizing. It may require individualized attention on a case-by-case basis and may, to that extent, require courts that continue to employ normative power.

An End to Plea Bargaining?

By now it is apparent that massive obstacles stand in the way of realizing the National Advisory Commission's proposal that plea bargaining be eliminated altogether. As Blumberg realistically concedes, "the system of justice by negotiation without trial is likely to continue to be the major feature of criminal justice for the foreseeable future."[125] Various decisions by the U.S. Supreme Court reflect this same realism. Thus, in *Boykin* v. *Alabama*[126] and *McCarthy* v. *United States*,[127] the Court held that as a matter of constitutional law, a plea of guilty is valid so long as the trial court record affirmatively shows that the plea was intelligent and voluntary. Then, in *Brady* v. *United States*[128] in 1970, despite the plea bargain's obvious tie to the crime control model, the Court held that a plea is not involuntary when it is made in response to an assurance of a more lenient disposition. For all practical purposes, *Brady* effectively validated plea bargaining. Since then, the Supreme Court has been content with trying to improve the system of negotiated justice—by attempting to minimize the discrepancy in plea bargaining between the due process model and the crime control model as opposed to attempting to eliminate it altogether. Thus, for example, in *Santo Bello* v. *New York*[129] it held that if a defendant, relying upon a prosecutor's promise, enters a guilty plea, due process of law requires that the prosecutor's promise be kept or that the defendant be given some relief—for example, an opportunity to withdraw his guilty plea. The Court's most comprehensive effort to date to restore due process protections to plea bargaining came on August 1, 1975, when a set of amendments that it had proposed to the Federal Rules of Criminal Procedure became effective.[130] These amendments presently apply only to the federal courts; however, it is likely that as litigation continues, the Court will come to require these same procedures in state judicial systems as well. These amendments set forth the following requirements: They forbid the trial court from participating in the plea negotiations between the prosecutor and the defense attorney. Once a plea agreement has been reached that contemplates entry of a plea of guilty in the expectation that a specific sentence will be imposed or that other charges before the court will be dismissed, the trial court is required to disclose the agreement in open court at the time the plea is offered. At that juncture, the trial court is at liberty to accept or reject the agreement or to defer its decision until it has had an opportunity to consider the presentence report. If the trial court accepts the plea agreement, it informs the defendant of this fact and disposes of the case as provided for in the plea agreement. However, if the trial court rejects the plea agreement, it must then inform the parties of that fact, advise the defendant personally in open court that it is not bound by the plea agreement, offer the defendant the opportunity to withdraw his plea, and advise the defendant that if he persists in his plea of guilty, the disposition of the case may be less favorable to the defendant than that contemplated by the plea agreement. To aid in the orderly administration of justice, the trial court is to be notified of the existence of a plea agreement at the arraignment. Notwithstanding the acceptance of the guilty plea, the trial court is still to satisfy itself that there is a factual basis for the plea. Finally, throughout the entire proceeding at which the defendant enters his plea, a verbatim record is to be made that includes the court's advice to the defendant, the inquiry into the voluntariness of the defendant's plea, and the inquiry into the accuracy of the guilty plea.

Thus, the Court has been content to use its limited normative power to reduce as much as it can the gap between the "ought" of doctrine and the "is" of behavior. It has been reluctant to attempt to close the gap altogether, for fear that its normative-moral compliance structure will completely crumble before the essentially remunerative-calculative compliance structure present in the lower courts and that its actions will, thereby, only serve to widen the gap further. As a consequence, the discrepancy between the due process model and the crime control model will, in all probability, remain. There is only so much that a superior employing normative power can hope to accomplish if its subordinates are calculatively involved.

Notes

1. Howard James, *Crisis in the Courts,* rev. ed. (New York: McKay, 1971), p. 55.
2. Jonathan D. Casper, *The Politics of Civil Liberties* (New York: Harper & Row, 1972), p. 266.
3. See Stephen L. Wasby, *The Impact of the United States Supreme Court: Some Perspectives* (Homewood, Ill.: Dorsey Press, 1970); Theodore L. Becker and Malcolm M. Feeley, eds., *The Impact of Supreme Court Decisions,* 2nd ed. (New York: Oxford University Press, 1973); and Walter F. Murphy and Joseph Tanenhaus, *The Study of Public Law* (New York: Random House, 1972). See also Kenneth M. Dolbeare and Phillip E. Hammond, *The School Prayer Decisions: From Court Policy to Local Practice* (Chicago: University of Chicago Press, 1971); Robert H. Birkby, "The Supreme Court and the Bible Belt," *Midwest Journal of Political Science* 10 (August 1966): 304-319; William K. Muir, Jr., *Prayer in the Public Schools: Law and Attitude Change* (Chicago: University of Chicago Press, 1967); Gordon Patric, "Impact of a Court Decision: Aftermath of the *McCollum* Case," *Journal of Public Law* 4 (Fall 1952): 455-464; Frank J. Sorouf, *"Zorach* v. *Clauson:* The Impact of Supreme Court Decision," *American Political Science Review* 53 (September 1959): 777-791; Richard M. Johnson, "Compliance and Supreme Court Decision-Making," *Wisconsin Law Review* 1967 (Winter 1967): 170-185; and H. Frank Way, Jr., "Survey Research on Judicial Decisions: The Prayer and Bible Reading Cases," *Western Political Quarterly* 21 (June 1968): 189-205.

4. See Michael Ban, "Local Courts vs. the Supreme Court: The Impact of *Mapp* v. *Ohio*" (Paper delivered at the Annual Meeting of the American Political Science Association, New Orleans, 1973); Dallin H. Oaks, "Studying the Exclusionary Rule in Search and Seizure," *University of Chicago Law Review* 37 (1970): 665-753; David Manwaring, "The Impact of *Mapp* v. *Ohio,*" in *The Supreme Court as Policy-Maker: Three Studies on the Impact of Judicial Decisions,* ed. David Everson (Carbondale, Ill.: Public Affairs Research Bureau, Southern Illinois University, 1968); Stuart S. Nagal, "Testing the Effects of Excluding Illegally Seized Evidence," *Wisconsin Law Review* 1965 (Spring 1965): p. 283-310; Michael J. Murphy, "The Problem of Compliance by Police Departments," *Texas Law Review* 44 (1966): 936-946; Neal Milner, "Supreme Court Effectiveness and the Police Organization," *Law and Contemporary Problems* 36, no. 4 (Autumn 1971): 467-487; Milner, "Comparative Analysis of Patterns of Compliance with Supreme Court Decisions: *Miranda* and the Police in Four Communities," *Law and Society Review* 5, no. 1 (August 1970): 119-134; Michael Wald, Richard Ayres, David W. Hess, Mark Schantz, and Charles H. Whitebread II, "Interrogations in New Haven: The Impact of *Miranda,*" *Yale Law Journal* 76 (July 1967): 1519-1648; Richard H. Seeburger and R. Stanton Wettick, Jr., "*Miranda* in Pittsburgh—A Statistical Study," *University of Pittsburgh Law Review* 29 (October 1967): 1-26; and Richard J. Medalie, Leonard Zeitz, and Paul Alexander, "Custodial Police Interrogation in our Nation's Capital: The Attempt to Implement *Miranda,*" *Michigan Law Review* 66 (May 1968): 1347-1422.
5. 367 U.S. 643 (1961).
6. 384 U.S. 436 (1966).
7. Becker and Feeley, *The Impact of Supreme Court Decisions,* p. 3. Emphasis in the original.
8. Ban, "Lower Courts vs. the Supreme Court," p. 1.
9. Comment, "Effect of *Mapp* v. *Ohio* on Police Search-and-Seizure Practices in Narcotics Cases," *Columbia Journal of Law and Social Problems* 4 (1968): 87. For a further analysis of this research, see Chapter 4 of this book.
10. Milner, "Supreme Court Effectiveness and the Police Organization," p. 467. See also Medalie et al., "Custodial Police Interrogation in Our Nation's Capital, pp. 1347-1422, and Michael Wald et al., "Interrogations in New Haven," pp. 1519-1648.
11. Casper, *The Politics of Civil Liberties,* pp. 265-266.
12. National Advisory Commission on Criminal Justice Standards and Goals, *Report on Courts* (Washington, D.C.: Government Printing Office, 1973), p. 42. See also Michael E. Tigar, "Waiver of Constitutional Rights: Disquiet in the Citadel," *Harvard Law Review* 84, no. 1 (November 1970): 8.
13. Although, see *Lefkowitz* v. *Newsome,* 420 U.S. 283 (1975), in which the

Court held in a five-to-four decision that defendants who enter guilty pleas still have available to them federal habeas corpus relief as a means of raising constitutional claims. Justice Stewart insisted that this relief must be made available lest plea bargaining become "a trap for the unwary."

14. Alexander M. Bickel, *The Supreme Court and the Idea of Progress* (New York: Harper & Row, 1970), p. 175.
15. Herbert L. Packer, *The Limits of the Criminal Sanction* (Stanford, Calif.: Stanford University Press, 1968), pp. 149-173.
16. Ibid., p. 158.
17. Ibid., p. 159. See also Jerome Skolnick, *Justice Without Trial* (New York: Wiley, 1966), p. 241.
18. Packer, *The Limits of the Criminal Sanction*, p. 159.
19. Ibid.
20. Ibid., p. 160.
21. Ibid.
22. Ibid., p. 163.
23. Ibid., p. 165.
24. Ibid., p. 166.
25. Ibid., p. 161.
26. Ibid., p. 150.
27. In certain American major cities, the figures run even higher. Thus, for example, 94.5 percent of all criminal prosecutions in Shelby County, Tennessee (Memphis) and 94 percent of all criminal prosecutions in San Francisco, California, are achieved through a negotiated plea. See the *Memphis Commercial Appeal,* January 27, 1975, p. 15, and Herbert Jacob, *Urban Justice: Law and Order in American Cities* (Englewood Cliffs, N.J.: Prentice Hall, 1973), p. 110.
28. *Crime in the United States–Uniform Crime Reports–1974,* U.S. Department of Justice (Washington, D.C.: Government Printing Office, 1975), p. 179.
29. *Crime in the United States–Uniform Crime Reports–1973,* U.S. Department of Justice (Washington, D.C.: Government Printing Office, 1974), pp. 124-125.
30. Michael J. Hindelang et al., *Sourcebook of Criminal Justice Statistics, 1973,* Law Enforcement Assistance Administration, U.S. Department of Justice (Washington, D.C.: Government Printing Office, 1973), p. 28. Courts generally have received less than 10 percent of all monies available through LEAA. They have been reluctant to seek such aid for two principal reasons. First, courts generally perceive LEAA as being unreceptive to the needs of courts and correctional agencies. Second, even if such grants were available, they often involve so much red tape, require so many progress reports, and impose so many administrative difficulties that most courts—possessed of no grantsmen and few administrative resources—would

not be able to fulfill these administrative demands. However unrealistic this assessment may be of LEAA's posture toward the courts, LEAA funds have profoundly influenced the administration of justice. Through its grants, law enforcement agencies throughout the nation have been modernized and upgraded. They are now more efficient in their apprehension of offenders and have placed, thereby, even greater strains on the already overworked courts. See Ralph A. Rossum, "Problems in Municipal Court Administration and the Stress of Supreme Court Decisions: A Memphis Case Study," *American Journal of Criminal Law* 3, no. 1 (Summer 1974): 72-73.
31. President's Commission on Law Enforcement and Administration of Justice, *The Challenge of Crime in a Free Society* (Washington, D.C.: Government Printing Office, 1967), p. 130.
32. Chief Justice Warren Burger, "Speech Delivered before the American Bar Association," August 10, 1970, *American Bar Association Journal* 56 (October 1970): 931.
33. However, see *Report on Courts:* "Basic to the Commission's position on plea negotiations is its conclusion that lack of resources should not affect the outcome of the processing of a criminal defendant and that it is not unrealistic to expect that the criminal justice system can and will be provided with adequate resources" (p. 46).
34. Abraham S. Blumberg, *Criminal Justice* (Chicago: Quadrangle Books, 1970), p. 169.
35. Ibid., p. 181.
36. Ibid., pp. 83-86.
37. The President's Commission on Law Enforcement and Administration of Justice, *Task Force Report: The Courts* (Washington, D.C.: Government Printing Office, 1967), pp. 9-11.
38. Jonathan D. Casper, *American Criminal Justice: The Defendant's Perspective* (Englewood Cliffs, N.J.: Prentice-Hall, 1972), p. 65.
39. Although, see *Lefkowitz* v. *Newsome,* 420 U.S. 283 (1975).
40. Michael A. Mulkey, "The Role of Prosecution and Defense in Plea Bargaining," *Policy Studies Journal* 3, no. 1 (Autumn 1974): 56.
41. Blumberg, *Criminal Justice,* p. 65.
42. Ibid.
43. See Burton M. Atkins and Emily Wilson Boyle, "Prisoners' Perceptions of Their Constitutional Rights: A Client's View of the World of Criminal Justice," *Emory Law Journal* 24, no. 1 (Winter 1975): 67-91. The authors interviewed 200 selected inmates at two South Carolina prisons and found, among other things, that 72.2 percent of all defendants represented by court-assigned counsel, 86.1 percent of all defendants represented by public defenders, and 50.8 percent of all defendants represented by privately retained counsel entered pleas of guilty.

44. See Lynn Mather, "Some Determinants of the Method of Case Disposition: Decision-Making by Public Defenders in Los Angeles," *Law and Society Review* 8, no. 2 (Winter 1973): 187-216.
45. Blumberg, *Criminal Justice,* pp. 95-115.
46. Mulkey, "The Role of Prosecution and Defense in Plea Bargaining," p. 56.
47. See Leonard Downie, Jr., *Justice Denied: The Case for Reform of the Courts* (Baltimore: Penguin Books, 1972), p. 37. See also James Eisenstein, *Politics and the Legal Process* (New York: Harper & Row, 1973), pp. 105-108.
48. Blumberg, *Criminal Justice,* p. 113.
49. Ibid., p. 31.
50. Jacob, *Urban Justice,* p. 117.
51. For a more complete discussion of the distribution of authority and power that was intended to exist within the criminal justice system, see Alan E. Bent and Ralph A. Rossum, *Police, Criminal Justice, and the Community* (New York: Harper & Row, 1976), pp. 58-62.
52. See Jonathan D. Casper's perceptive comments on this matter in *American Criminal Justice,* p. 81.
53. New York Special Commission on Attica, *Attica* (1972), pp. 30-31. Quoted in *Report on Courts,* p. 44.
54. *Report on Courts,* p. 44.
55. Burton M. Atkins and Emily W. Boyle, "Prisoners' Perceptions of Their Constitutional Rights: A Client's View of the World of Criminal Justice," *Emory Law Journal* 34, no. 1 (Winter 1975): 67-91.
56. Ibid., p. 89.
57. This particular sample size was chosen so that the limits of tolerance would be 5 percent and the degree of assurance 99 chances out of 100, or 99 percent. See Mildren Parten, *Surveys, Polls, and Samples* (New York: Harper & Brothers, 1950), p. 314.
58. The sample for this survey was drawn from *Polk's Memphis City Directory, 1973, Section III: The Directory of Householders* (Detroit: Polk, 1973), pp. 1-663.
59. See Hazel Erskine, "The Polls: Causes of Crime," *Public Opinion Quarterly* 38, no. 2 (Summer 1974): 294.
60. Blumberg, *Criminal Justice,* p. 83.
61. *Congressional Record,* 91st Cong., 1st. Sess., 1969, 115, pt. 20: 27493. Quoted in Peter Graham Fish, *The Politics of Federal Judicial Administration* (Princeton, N.J.: Princeton University Press, 1973), p. 431.
62. "Report on the Federal Judicial Branch," Remarks of Warren E. Burger to the American Bar Association, St. Louis, Mo., August 10, 1968.
63. Ernest C. Friesen, Jr., "Constraints and Conflicts in Court Administration," *Public Administration Review* 31, no. 2 (March/April 1971): 120-124.

64. See Jerome Frank, *Courts on Trial: Myth and Reality in American Justice* (Princeton, N.J.: Princeton University Press, 1950), pp. 80-85.
65. Fish, *The Politics of Federal Judicial Administration,* p. 429.
66. For comprehensive discussion of the Missouri Plan, see Richard A. Watson and Rondal G. Downing, *The Politics of the Bench and the Bar: Judicial Selection Under the Missouri Nonpartisan Court Plan* (New York: Wiley, 1969).
67. Friesen, "Constraints and Conflicts in Court Administration," p. 123.
68. Downie, *Justice Denied,* pp. 138-139.
69. Rossum, "Problems in Municipal Court Administration," pp. 71-72.
70. Downie, *Justice Denied,* p. 146.
71. Ibid.
72. Ibid., p. 148.
73. William Blackstone, *Commentaries on the Laws of England,* 1: 69.
74. Ibid.
75. Ibid.
76. Ibid., p. 70. Emphasis in the original.
77. William G. Hammond, one of Blackstone's editors, has noted that "no ... passage of Blackstone has been the object of more criticism and even ridicule than this." See the Hammond Edition of Blackstone's *Commentaries* (San Francisco: Bancroft-Whitney, 1890), 1: 213.
78. Jeremy Bentham, *Works,* 5: 546.
79. Ibid., p. 552. Emphasis in the original.
80. Ibid., p. 546.
81. John Austin, *Jurisprudence* (1885), 2: 632. Emphasis in the original.
82. John Austin, *Jurisprudence* (1885), 1: 36.
83. *Linkletter* v. *Walker,* 381 U.S. 618, 623-624 (1965).
84. Benjamin N. Cardozo, *The Nature of the Judicial Process* (New Haven, Conn.: Yale University Press, 1921).
85. Ibid., pp. 166-167.
86. Ibid., p. 166.
87. Ibid., pp. 165-166. Emphasis added.
88. Oliver Wendell Holmes, *The Common Law* (Boston: Little, Brown, 1881), p. 1.
89. Ibid., p. 35.
90. Cardozo, *The Nature of the Judicial Process,* pp. 148-149.
91. *Report on Courts,* p. 46.
92. See National Advisory Commission on Criminal Justice Standards and Goals, *A National Strategy to Reduce Crime* (Washington, D.C.: Government Printing Office, 1973), pp. 203-204. As Chapter 1 noted, over 43 percent of the arrests made in the United States each year are for such offenses.
93. *Report on Courts,* p. 47.

94. Bent and Rossum, *Police, Criminal Justice, and the Community*, p. 183.
95. See David L. Bazelon, "The Realities of *Gideon* and *Argersinger*," *Georgetown Law Journal* 64, no. 4 (March 1976): 811-838, who argues that "we are receiving as much, or as little, justice as we are paying for" (p. 835).
96. *Report on Courts*, p. 46. See David W. Neubauer and George F. Cole, "A Political Critique of the Court Recommendations of the National Advisory Commission on Criminal Justice Standards and Goals," *Emory Law Journal* 24, no. 4 (Fall 1975): 1009-1036.
97. The major purpose of bail is to secure the court appearance of the defendant; however, bail may also be used to protect society from dangerous defendants and to punish defendants who, through various legal processes, are likely to obtain dismissal of all charges, in spite of obvious factual guilt. Michael P. Kirby, *An Evaluation of Pre-Trial Release and Bail Bond in Memphis and Shelby County* (Memphis: Southwestern at Memphis, The Police Research Institute, 1975), chapt. 2, p. 1.
98. *Task Force Report: The Courts*, p. 37.
99. See Silverstein, "Bail in the State Courts—A Field Study and Report," *Minnesota Law Review* 50 (1966): 621, 626-627, 630-631.
100. Caleb Foote et al., "Compelling Appearance in Court: Administration of Bail in Philadelphia," *University of Pennsylvania Law Review* 102 (1954): 1031.
101. Caleb Foote et al., "A Study of Administration of Bail in New York City," *University of Pennsylvania Law Review* 106 (1958): 693.
102. James S. Campbell, Joseph R. Sahid, and David E. Stang, *Law and Order Reconsidered*, a staff report to the National Commission on the Causes and Prevention of Violence (Washington, D.C.: Government Printing Office, 1969), p. 435.
103. Ibid.
104. Charles E. Ares, Anne Rankin, and Herbert Sturz, "The Manhattan Bail Project: An Interim Report on the Use of Pre-Trial Parole," *New York University Law Review* 38 (1963): 67, 85.
105. These figures were derived by conservatively estimating the daily cost of feeding and clothing a pretrial detainee at $6.25 and by multiplying this figure by the average daily number of pretrial detainees in New York City and Los Angeles jails. See *Local Jails: A Report Presenting Data for Individual County and City Jails from the 1970 Jail Census*, U.S. Department of Justice, Law Enforcement Assistance Administration (Washington, D.C.: Government Printing Office, 1973), pp. 16, 99.
106. National Advisory Commission on Criminal Justice Standards and Goals, *Report on Corrections* (Washington, D.C.: Government Printing Office, 1973), p. 107.
107. 401 U.S. 395 (1971).

THE LOWER COURTS

108. Kirby, *An Evaluation of Pre-Trial Release and Bail Bond in Memphis and Shelby County,* chapt. 3, p. 36.
109. *Report on Corrections,* p. 109.
110. Kirby, *An Evaluation of Pre-Trial Release and Bail Bond in Memphis and Shelby County,* chapt. 3, pp. 30-33.
111. *Report on Corrections,* p. 110.
112. Ibid., p. 108
113. Blumberg, *Criminal Justice,* p. 182.
114. Ibid., p. 183.
115. Friesen, "Constraints and Conflicts in Court Administration," p. 123.
116. Ibid.
117. *Report on Courts,* p. 164.
118. Ibid.
119. Ibid., p. 162.
120. Friesen, "Constraints and Conflicts in Court Administration," p. 124.
121. See Jacob, *Urban Justice,* p. 93.
122. *Report on Courts,* pp. 171-186.
123. Ibid., p. 183.
124. It must be acknowledged, however, that Chief Justice Burger did not leave the matter at that. In his 1973 Report on the Federal Judicial Branch, he declared: "Justice is not a commodity—and whether people experience the injustice of delay or injustice in some other form, it is not as tolerable as denial of some other services we ask from government.

    "We must never ration justice according to some hypothetical supply. We are not running a meat market or a gas station where the customers can be turned away when the supply of gas or beef is exhausted. Paralleling society's basic obligation to preserve order, so that each human being can develop his God-given talents to the fullest, is society's obligation to resolve conflicts—civil and criminal—and to do so fairly and justly according to announced rules, and to do so without delay. It is to serve these high objectives that we must have efficiency." Report on the Federal Judicial Branch, Remarks of Warren E. Burger to the American Bar Association, Washington, D.C., August 6, 1973.
125. Blumberg, *Criminal Justice,* p. 182.
126. 395 U.S. 238 (1969).
127. 394 U.S. 459 (1969).
128. 397 U.S. 742 (1970).
129. 404 U.S. 257 (1971).
130. See P.L. 93-361 (1974).

Bibliography

Atkins, Burton M., and Boyle, Emily Wilson. "Prisoners' Perceptions of Their Constitutional Rights: A Client's View of the World of Criminal Justice." *Emory Law Journal* 24, no. 1 (Winter 1975): 67-91.

Becker, Theodore L., and Feeley, Malcolm M. *The Impact of Supreme Court Decisions.* 2nd ed. New York: Oxford University Press, 1973.

Bent, Alan Edward, and Rossum, Ralph A. *Police, Criminal Justice, and the Community.* New York: Harper & Row, 1976.

Bickel, Alexander M. *The Supreme Court and the Idea of Progress.* New York: Harper & Row, 1970.

Blumberg, Abraham S. *Criminal Justice.* Chicago: Quadrangle Press, 1970.

Cannon, Mark W. "Can the Federal Judiciary Be an Innovative System?" *Public Administration Review* 33, no. 1 (January-February 1973): 74-79.

———. "The Federal Judicial System: Highlights of Administrative Modernization." *Criminology* 12, no. 1 (May 1974): 10-24.

Cardozo, Benjamin N. *The Nature of the Judicial Process.* New Haven, Conn.: Yale University Press, 1921.

Casper, Jonathan D. *American Criminal Justice: The Defendant's Perspective.* Englewood Cliffs, N.J.: Prentice-Hall, 1972.

———. *The Politics of Civil Liberties.* New York: Harper & Row, 1972.

Cole, George F. *Criminal Justice: Law and Politics.* 2nd ed. North Scituate, Mass.: Duxbury Press, 1976.

Downie, Leonard. *Justice Denied: The Case for Reform of the Courts.* Baltimore: Penguin Books, 1972.

Eisenstein, James. *Politics and the Legal Process.* New York: Harper & Row, 1973.

Fish, Peter Graham. *The Politics of Federal Judicial Administration.* Princeton, N.J.: Princeton University Press, 1973.

Friesen, Ernest C. "Constraints and Conflicts in Court Administration." *Public Administration Review* 31, no. 2 (March-April 1971): 120-124.

Jacob, Herbert. *Urban Justice: Law and Order in American Cities.* Englewood Cliffs, N.J.: Prentice-Hall, 1973.

James, Howard. *Crisis in the Courts.* Rev. ed. New York: McKay, 1971.

Milner, Neal. "Supreme Court Effectiveness and the Police Organization." *Law and Contemporary Problems* 34, no. 4 (Autumn 1971): 467-487.

Mulkey, Michael A. "The Role of Prosecution and Defense in Plea Bargaining." *Policy Studies Journal* 3, no. 1 (Autumn 1974): 60-66.

National Advisory Commission on Criminal Justice Standards and Goals. *A National Strategy to Reduce Crime.* Washington, D.C.: Government Printing Office, 1973.

———. *Report on Courts.* Washington, D.C.: Government Printing Office, 1973.

Neubauer, David W., and Cole, George F. "A Political Critique of the Court Recommendations of the National Advisory Commission on Criminal Justice Standards and Goals." *Emory Law Journal* 24, no. 4 (Fall 1975): 1009-1036.

Packer, Herbert L. *The Limits of the Criminal Sanction.* Stanford, Calif.: Stanford University Press, 1968.

President's Commission on Law Enforcement and Administration of Justice. *The Challenge of Crime in a Free Society.* Washington, D.C.: Government Printing Office, 1967.

Robertson, John A., ed. *Rough Justice: Perspectives on Lower Criminal Courts.* Boston: Little, Brown, 1974.

Rossum, Ralph A. "Problems in Municipal Court Administration and the Stress of Supreme Court Decisions: A Memphis Case Study." *American Journal of Criminal Law* 3, no. 1 (Summer 1974): 53-84.

Tigar, Michael E. "Waiver of Constitutional Rights: Disquiet in the Citadel." *Harvard Law Review* 84, no. 1 (November 1970): 1-28.

Wald, Michael, Ayres, Richard, Hess, David W., Schantz, Mark, and Whitebread, Charles H., II. "Interrogations in New Haven: The Impact of *Miranda,*" *Yale Law Journal* 76 (July 1967): 1519-1648.

Wasby, Stephen L. *The Impact of the United States Supreme Court: Some Perspectives.* Homewood, Illinois: Dorsey Press, 1970.

CORRECTIONS

As James Q. Wilson concludes his important new book, *Thinking About Crime*, so this chapter must begin: "We have trifled with the wicked, made sport of the innocent, and encouraged the calculators. Justice suffers, and so do we all."[1] In no component of the criminal justice system does this statement ring so true as in corrections. It does not adequately coerce the wicked or safeguard and protect the innocent; rather, it remunerates the manipulative. As a consequence, very little "correction" occurs. As Chief Justice Warren E. Burger lamented in his 1972 address to the National Conference of Christians and Jews:

> Since I first became a United States judge seventeen years ago, I have been deeply concerned at the "recall" rate, which, in American industry, is the rate at which products found defective are returned to the manufacturer for further processing and repair. The "recall" rate for the American penal system varies over the years, but for the present purposes it is safe to use the figure of two-thirds. By that I mean, at any given time, two-thirds of the persons found in prisons have prior criminal records. There is very little evidence that we have improved the situation in the past thirty or forty years—indeed, it has become worse with the passage of time.[2]

With the aid of compliance analysis, this chapter will attempt to explore why this is the case.

The Purpose of Criminal Sanctions

Perhaps the most important problem faced by corrections arises from the fact that there is no agreement to the question "Why punish crimes?" Three very different justifications for criminal punishment are possible: retribution, deterrence, and rehabilitation. As noted previously in Chapter 2, these three justifications correspond rather closely to coercive, remunerative, and normative compliance relationships. Each of these justifications is in conflict with the others; yet correctional personnel in the United States often attempt to rely on all of them and, as a consequence, fail to achieve the objectives of any of them. Each of these justifications must be examined in greater detail.

Retribution

Retribution rests on the idea that it is right for a wicked man to be punished. A man should be responsible for his actions and ought to receive his just deserts.[3] This retributive view can emphasize either revenge or expiation. The desire for revenge is deeply ingrained in human experience. It goes back at least as far as the *lex talionis,* or the law of retaliation, expressed most notably in the Mosaic formulation: "An eye for an eye, a tooth for a tooth." Retribution as revenge desires to make the offender suffer, not because it is good for him to suffer and thereby purge his guilt and not because suffering might deter him from further crime but simply because it is felt that he deserves to suffer. Alternatively, retribution can also emphasize expiation—the view that only through suffering punishment can the criminal expiate his sin. This view of atonement through suffering, important in both religious and secular thought, seeks to encourage the individual offender to reconcile himself to the social order—to make himself one with it.

Retribution is a much criticized justification for criminal punishment. It has been branded by behavioral science as "obsolete." "The retributive approach is too subjective and too emotional to solve problems that have their roots in social conditions and the consequent impact on individual personality. Such an approach can only obstruct the job of evolving techniques for social control utilizing what we now know about the forces that control human behavior."[4] Perhaps more seriously, it has been dismissed as a regrettable throwback to man's earlier barbarism. However, as Professor Morris Cohen has observed, retribution is too deeply grounded in human nature and too fundamental to so many moral and religious codes for it to be so lightly dismissed.

> All the sweetness and grace which make life in its happy moments so delectable have their seamy sides which cannot be hidden to an all-seeing eye. The effort to make life more decent, therefore, always involves a struggle against opposing forces. And in this struggle men find hatred as well as love, tonic emotions. Indeed, we must hate evil if we really love the good. (Undiscriminating love extended to everything is nonsense.) We must hate evil intensely if we are to fight it successfully, and we cannot hate theft, violence and fraud except when we see them embodied. It is thus impossible not to be indignant against certain criminals or not to wish to punish them.[5]

Furthermore, in punishing these criminals, retribution treats them as human beings, creatures who are responsible for their actions and deserve the punishment they receive as their just deserts. As Professor C. S. Lewis has pointed out: "To be punished, however severely, because we have deserved it, because we 'ought to have known better,' is to be treated as a human person made in God's image."[6] It is this concept of desert—and this alone—that provides "the only connecting link between punishment and justice."[7]

Finally, retribution can be defended on still another ground; it is firmly rooted in the principle that those who disobey the law should not gain an unfair advantage over those who obey voluntarily. Jeffrey Murphy has succinctly stated this case for retribution in a fundamentally just society:

> In order to enjoy the benefits that a legal system makes possible, each man must be prepared to make an important sacrifice—namely, the sacrifice of obeying the law even when he does not desire to do so. Each man calls on others to do this, and it is only just or fair that he bear a comparable burden when his turn comes. Now if the system is to remain just, it is important to guarantee that those who disobey will not thereby gain an unfair advantage over those who obey voluntarily. Criminal punishment thus attempts to maintain the proper balance between benefit and obedience by ensuring that there is no profit in criminal wrongdoing.[8]

Deterrence

The second justification for criminal punishment is deterrence. It is based on the view that punishment, either actual or threatened, will inhibit those who are otherwise disposed to commit crimes. It operates on a utilitarian premise: Punishment is justified insofar as it can be shown that more good is likely to result from inflicting punishment than from withholding it. The good that is sought from such punishment is the prevention or the reduction of the greater evil, crime.

The efficacy of deterrence is challenged on a number of grounds. To begin with, critics of deterrence claim that it simply does not work. They point to the high rate of repeat offenses or recidivism that exists in the United States as proof of their argument. To reiterate the words of Chief Justice Burger: "Two-thirds of the persons found in prisons have prior criminal records." Obviously, the critics assert, previously imposed criminal sanctions have not deterred these persons from continuing to engage in criminal activity. Many critics of deterrence also point to the experience of Great Britain after it abandoned capital punishment as an argument that not even the death penalty deters. After all, they observe, the murder rate in Great Britain is not increasing at a greater rate than it had before the abolition of the death penalty.

Deterrence, the critics charge, does not work. It does not work because it places too much faith on rationality and free will. In its classic form, deterrence can work if, and only if, the potential offender, in deciding whether or not to commit a crime, concludes that the probability that he will be apprehended and subjected to criminal punishment and the costs that he will therefore be forced to bear outweigh the probability that he will succeed and the benefits that success would bring him. This concept of deterrence is derided by the critics on psychological grounds. Individuals, they contend, do not engage in such a rational cost-benefit calculus before committing a crime; rather, they act upon obscure impulses that they can neither comprehend nor control.

Finally, deterrence is attacked on still another ground. It rests on the prediction that a person who has once committed a certain kind of crime is likely to commit more crime of the same or related sort. Herbert L. Packer has spelled out this charge:

> To the extent that we lock up burglars because we fear they will commit further offenses, our prediction is not that they will if left unchecked violate the anti-trust laws, or cheat on their income taxes, or embezzle money from their employers; it is that they will commit further burglaries, or other crimes associated with burglary, such as homicide or bodily injury. The premise is that the person may have the tendency to commit further crimes like the one for which he is now being punished and that punishing him will restrain him from doing so.[9]

Of course, it is an empirical question whether this prediction is valid; however, to the extent that it is empirically validated, it provides a justification or a basis for preventive detention, a practice at odds with the due process model and its presumption of innocence and repugnant to many supporters of deterrence.

The defenders of deterrence respond to each of these arguments. Regarding the charge that deterrence does not work, they cite the obvious but frequently overlooked fact that there are no data on how much higher the recidivism rates would be if there were no criminal punishment at all. There have been a few "natural experiments" in the effectiveness of deterrence. One occurred in 1944, during World War II, when the German Army deported the entire Danish police force. The result was a tenfold increase in property crimes such as theft and burglary but no noticeable increase in murder and sex crimes. Another occurred in Montreal in 1968, when both police and firemen went on strike. Within a day, two men had been shot dead, six banks had been robbed, and more than 100 shops had been looted. There were twelve major fires. More than forty carloads of glass were needed to replace shattered store fronts. Altogether, property damage totaled over $3 million. These natural experiments lend credence to the effectiveness of deterrence.

Moreover, the proponents of deterrence also point to various empirical studies that establish the effectiveness of deterrence. Isaac Ehrlich, an economist at the University of Chicago, has conducted perhaps the most detailed statistical analysis of the effects of criminal sanctions.[10] For the census years 1940, 1950, and 1970, he calculated the effect that probability of imprisonment and length of incarceration have on the known rates of the seven major index crimes. Controlling for the effects of the such factors as family income and percentage of nonwhites in the state's population, he found that both increased certainty of incarceration and increased length of sentence reduced the rate of recorded crimes in the states.[11] His data further supported the view that deterrence is as effective in preventing "crimes against the person" as "crimes against property."[12]

Proponents of deterrence also reject the notion that criminals are radically different from ordinary people in that they are utterly indifferent to the costs and rewards of their activities and respond only to deep passions, fleeting impulses, or uncontrollable social forces. As Ehrlich observes, "Offenders, as a group, respond to opportunities (costs and gains) available to them in legitimate and criminal activities in much the same way as those engaged in strictly legitimate activities do as a group."[13] Of course, not all criminals are so sensitive to these costs and gains. Thus, as James Q. Wilson remarks, "Some husbands will murder their wives though they are almost certain to be caught, some boys will steal cars in order to prove that they are not afraid of the police, and some madmen will plant bombs that destroy themselves as well as their victims."[14] But, he continues, this is not very different from observing that not all consumers are wholly rational in the marketplace. Some men continue to buy big and powerful automobiles even though the price of gasoline and maintenance has skyrocketed and the resale value of big cars has dropped. Their behavior might be determined by such factors as the need to accommodate their large family, the necessity to prove their masculinity, or the desire to impress their neighbors. But, however interesting this speculation might be, "We would not for a moment doubt that, for most people most of the time, the cost of cars is an important factor in predicting their automotive purchases."[15]

The fact that not every potential offender is deterred by the prospect of criminal sanctions no more denies the deterrent effectiveness of the law than the fact that not every consumer is sensitive to costs and benefits in his purchasing decisions denies the fundamental rationality of the market. This, the proponents of deterrence insist, is an important consideration that must be borne in mind when dealing with deterrence theory. As Steven Goldberg argues regarding the deterrent effectiveness of capital punishment: "No one who supports capital punishment and who has thought the problem through would predicate his support on the ability of capital punishment to deter the murderer; by definition the murderer has not been deterred by anything. The question that is of determinative importance, and the question that the opponents of capital punishment rarely attempt to even consider on a theoretical level, is what is it that deters those who are deterred; that is, not the murderer but the rest of us"[16]

Thus, the proponents of deterrence claim that it can and does work—that would-be criminals are no more indifferent to the risks associated with a proposed course of action than are ordinary citizens. Moreover, to the extent that deterrence seems to be failing, they insist that the fault lies not with deterrence theory or with the rational cost-benefit analysis on which it is based, but with the minimal criminal sanctions that the legal system presently invokes.[17] Thus, for example, they point with consternation to the facts that the median time served in prison for homicide in Massachusetts is less than 2½ years and that in Los Angeles over 90 percent of all burglars with major prior records receive no state prison sentence at all.[18]

Moreover, they continue, this leniency and reluctance on the part of the legal system to impose substantial punishments can have very serious long-range consequences. Thus, while the critics of deterrence argue that the fact that the murder rate in Great Britain has not increased since abolition of the death penalty offers proof of the ineffectiveness of deterrence, various advocates of deterrence point out that "the present population of Britain was socialized in a time when the seriousness of murder was emphasized by the use of the death penalty, and this may be the crucial factor (just as American society's traditional invocation of the death penalty may have served the reinforcing function even for the populations of states that did not practice capital punishment)."[19] Steven Goldberg's cogent argument must be addressed here. He emphasizes that an individual is deterred by capital punishment "because he has perceived, from childhood on, that murder is the most serious of social offenses. He has accepted this assessment of the seriousness of murder and internalized it in part because his society has emphasized the importance of this value by punishing it with a penalty stronger than that it imposes for any other crime."[20] By abolition of the death penalty, this educative or socializing effect is removed, and perhaps with it, the power of deterrence. This is, of course, somewhat speculative and hypothetical. But, the believers in the deterrent effectiveness of capital punishment insist, the benefit of the doubt must be given to them at this juncture. After all, if they are incorrect in their assumptions that the death penalty does deter but are nevertheless successful in their efforts to convince society to invoke capital punishment, they are responsible "merely" for the deaths of convicted *guilty* individuals who, if deterrence is the sole rationale for their execution, should not have been executed. If, on the other hand, the opponents of capital punishment are mistaken in their assumption that capital punishment does not deter and are successful in their efforts to convince society to abolish capital punishment, they are responsible for the death of *innocent* people. Moreover, as Goldberg stresses, "The number of innocent people who would not have been murdered if the deterrent of capital punishment had been invoked will be far greater than the number of innocent people who could conceivably be executed as a result of a mistaken conviction of innocent individuals for crimes they did not commit . . . and considerably greater, in all probability, than the total number of individuals who will be executed in a society that invokes capital punishment."[21]

Finally, proponents of deterrence deny that its imposition of criminal sanctions is based on the prediction that a person who has committed a certain kind of crime is likely to commit more crime of the same or related sort. They introduce a necessary distinction between specific deterrence—that is, after-the-fact inhibition of the person being punished—and general deterrence—that is, inhibition in advance through threat or example. Specific deterrence may be based on such a prediction, but general deterrence is not. Thus, for example, general deterrence punishes the burglar, not because it believes that this will restrain him from engaging in burglary again, but rather to discourage or dissuade others by his example. This, in turn, raises a serious ethical problem. In 1970 in New York City, there were 74,000 reported robberies, but only 13,000 defendants were arrested, only 4,000 were convicted, and only 300 were sentenced to prison. These figures force one to confront the possibility that prisons may serve more as sampling devices to show social disfavor of criminal activity than as institutions designed to treat or even punish all offenders; they force one to consider the question of exemplary punishments. The same question is often present during riots as well. Judges who have been imposing lenient penalties on offenders participating in a riot may conclude that this leniency, together with media publicity concerning it, is in fact encouraging further rioting; at some juncture, they may begin to introduce more severe penalties to discourage others from participating in the riot and may, therefore, help bring the riot to an end. This practice, however, poses an ethical problem; should the severity of the sentence an individual receives be determined by the deterrent effect it is likely to have on others? Not everyone can resolve this issue so easily as did Justice Oliver Wendell Holmes:

> If I were having a philosophical talk with a man I was going to have hanged (or electrocuted) I should say, "I don't doubt that your act was inevitable for you but to make it more avoidable by others we propose to sacrifice you to the common good. You may regard yourself as a soldier dying for your country if you like. But the law must keep its promises."[22]

Rehabilitation

Of the three justifications for criminal punishment, rehabilitation is perhaps the most immediately appealing.[23] Rehabilitation justifies punishment as necessary for the reformation of the offender, that is, as necessary to change his personality so that he will conform to the dictates of the law. As such, it is offender-oriented rather than offense-oriented. It denies that there is a generally postulated equivalent between the offense and the punishment, as is the case in either retributive or deterrent theories of punishment. Rather, it seeks to punish—or perhaps a better word, treat—each offender as an individual whose special needs and problems must be fully known and attended to if he is to be dealt with effectively.

This emphasis of rehabilitation on individualizing the punishment or therapy of the offender and thereby fully restoring him to society is not without its problems, however. To begin with, it tends to conflict openly with another enlightened value much touted today, due process. Rehabilitation stresses the need for administrative discretion to "treat" and, it is hoped, to "cure" the "patient" on an individualized basis. Due process, on the other hand, calls for standardized procedures, not in order to change the offender, but to make it easier for him to challenge the exercise of administrative discretion.

The rehabilitative justification for criminal punishment has also been attacked on other grounds. Thus, the language of rehabilitation has often been debased and exploited to serve a public relations function. It is frequently employed, either wittingly or unwittingly, to disguise the true state of affairs that prevails in custodial institutions and at other points in the correctional process. Professor Francis A. Allen's reflections on this debasement of the rehabilitative idea are telling:

> Recently, I visited an institution devoted to the diagnosis and treatment of disturbed children. The institution was established with high hopes and, for once, with the enthusiastic support of the state legislature. Nevertheless, 50 minutes of an hour's lecture, delivered by a supervising psychiatrist before we toured the building, were devoted to custodial problems. This fixation on problems of custody was reflected in the institutional arrangements which included, under a properly euphemistic label, a cell for solitary confinement. Even more disturbing was the tendency of the staff to justify these custodial measures in therapeutic terms. Perhaps on occasion the requirements of institutional security and treatment coincide. But the inducements to self-deception in such situations are strong and all too frequently provided a formidable obstacle to a realistic analysis of the conditions that confront us. And realism in considering these problems is the one quality that we require above all others.[24]

Rehabilitation has also come under fire for it has, ironically, led to increased severity of penal measures. The experiences of the California Adult Authority are typical. California operates under an indeterminate sentencing system—a clear offspring of the rehabilitative idea. Under the system, the judge merely decides whether or not a defendant will go to prison. The decision of when he will be released is determined by the Adult Authority—the parole board—within the limits of the legislatively set maximum sentence. The theory behind the system is simple, sensible, and progressive. Because the correctional goal is rehabilitation, and because each prisoner is likely to proceed toward rehabilitation at a different pace, the length of sentence should not be determined by the judge before this process of rehabilitation has begun; rather, it should be determined by a board of experts who will be able to evaluate continuously, throughout the period of incarceration, the prisoner's progress toward rehabilitation. In this way, punishment will be individualized and efficient: each prisoner will serve as long as it takes, but no longer than it takes, for him to become fully rehabilitated.

In practice, however, this program has not fared too well. Among other things, under this indeterminate sentencing system, maximum sentences have gone up. The state legislature has sought to provide the Adult Authority with sufficient flexibility to deal with those few especially dangerous persons for whom rehabilitation may take an extra long time; it has therefore increased the maximum possible sentences for most crimes. However, along with this increase in maximum sentences, California has also experienced a general increase in the length of confinement. Thus, from 1959 to 1969, the median time served in California increased from 24 to 36 months, thereby making it the longest in the country. A variety of factors have contributed to this increased severity, but the frustration and mental anguish the prisoner suffers from never knowing how long he will be confined and from the absence of any clear-cut and consistent criteria operative in determining rehabilitation and release are surely among them.

Finally, rehabilitation has been subjected to criticism for still another reason: It has replaced justice with mercy. Rehabilitation rejects the notion that a man is to be punished because he deserves it. Instead, it argues that punishment is legitimate only if it is intended to mend the criminal. Because proponents of rehabilitation tend to take the position that all crime is more or less pathological, mending becomes healing and curing, and punishment itself becomes therapeutic.[25] In brief, punishment is justified if it is used to cure the psychologically ill patient. In doing so, however, rehabilitation removes the idea of desert from punishment and with desert, so too, justice.[26] After all, it is only as deserved or undeserved that a sentence can be just or unjust. As Professor C. S. Lewis brilliantly states it, "If crime is only a disease which needs cure, not sin which deserves punishment, it cannot be pardoned. How can you pardon a man for having a gum boil or a club foot? . . . [Rehabilitation] wants simply to abolish justice and substitute mercy for it."[27]

These criticisms of rehabilitation as a justification for criminal punishment could perhaps be overlooked if there were any proof that rehabilitation was in fact more effective than retribution or deterrence. But, curiously, there is almost no evidence to support this contention—a rather remarkable situation in a field where controlled experiments are so comparatively easy to conduct. In fact, there is no evidence to suggest that the most advanced known "California" techniques of rehabilitation—including clinical analysis, intensive counseling, group therapy, work and school release and halfway houses—are in any way more rehabilitative than the benighted and savage "Arkansas" penal farm practices, which have been condemned for their failure to rehabilitate.[28] This is not to deny that California's methods may be preferable to those of Arkansas for all sorts of good reasons, but proved ability to "cure" inmates is not one of them. This is not surprising. The state of psychiatric science is still quite primitive. This fact is perhaps nowhere more impressively presented than in Professor D. L. Rosenhan's article "On Being Sane in Insane Places."[29] Rosenhan, a professor of psychology and law at Stanford University, found that psychiatrists are, by and large, unable to distinguish between sanity and insanity. If they are unable to make such gross judgments, how are they to determine when a person is fully "rehabilitated"?

In his research, Rosenhan conducted an experiment to determine whether the sane can be distinguished from the insane. It involved eight sane people— three psychiatrists, a pediatrician, a psychologist, a graduate student in psychology, a painter, and a housewife—who, as pseudopatients, gained admission to twelve different psychiatric hospitals. The twelve hospitals were located in five different states on the east and west coasts. Some of the hospitals were old and shabby, others were quite new; some were research-oriented, others were not; some were privately supported, others were supported by federal or state funds.

The eight pseudopatients gained admission by calling for an appointment and, thereupon, during the admissions interview, complaining of hearing hollow or empty voices. Beyond alleging these symptoms and falsifying their names, vocations, and employment, the pseudopatients made no other alterations of their personal histories or behavior, none of which were pathological in any way. All were admitted, and all but one were diagnosed to be schizophrenic. Once inside, they acted perfectly normally. In fact, they went to work openly recording their observations about the ward, its patients, and the staff. Length of hospitalization ranged from 7 to 52 days, with an average of 19 days. Yet, during that entire time period, not a single pseudopatient was detected. The regular patients at the institutions were able to recognize normality far better than the staff. As Rosenhan reports: "It was quite common for the patients to detect the pseudopatients' sanity. During the first three hospitalizations, when accurate counts were kept, 35 of the total of 118 admissions on the admissions ward voiced their suspicions, sometimes vigorously. 'You're not crazy. You're a journalist, or a professor [referring to the continual note-taking], you're checking up on the hospital.'"[30] As if Rosenhan has not questioned one's confidence in psychiatry enough already, he goes on to detail that the staff of one of these psychiatric hospitals, specializing in research and teaching, was informed that sometime during the following 3 months one or more of the pseudopatients would attempt to gain admission. Each staff member was asked to rate each patient who sought admission according to the likelihood that the patient was a pseudopatient. Judgments were obtained on 193 patients who were admitted for psychiatric testing. Of that number, 41 were deemed to be the pseudopatients by at least one member of the staff; 23 were suspected by at least one psychiatrist; and 19 were suspected by one psychiatrist and one other staff member. In actuality, no pseudopatient sought admission during that period.[31]

Obviously, considerable debate and controversy surrounds rehabilitation, just as it does retribution and deterrence. No single justification for criminal punishment has clearly established itself as solely legitimate. As a consequence, the correctional system in the United States has attempted to blend elements of all three into one correctional package. However, as high rates of recidivism make painfully apparent, this endeavor has not been especially successful. Too much emphasis on rehabilitation undercuts deterrence; too much concern for retribution interferes with rehabilitation; and too much stress upon deterrence, especially general deterrence and its inhibition in advance by example, obscures retribution's concept of desert.[32] Returning for a moment to compliance analysis, each justification tends to neutralize the effectiveness of the others. The presence of these contradictory justifications not only renders the correctional system virtually powerless, but also deprives its personnel of any standard or goal against which they can measure the success of their correctional endeavors. These problems, summed up in the question "Why punish?" confront every aspect of the correctional system.

Correctional Programs

The National Advisory Commission on Criminal Justice Standards and Goals defines corrections as follows: It is "the community's official reactions to the convicted offender, whether adult or juvenile."[33] In the United States, correctional programs have taken two distinct forms: incarceration and community-based alternatives to confinement. Incarceration, of course, refers to the institutionalization of offenders in prisons, camps, and jails. Community-based alternatives to confinement include probation, parole, and pretrial diversion.

Incarceration

Incarceration as a means of corrections is a relatively modern practice. As David P. Stang observes, "Before the eighteenth century, prisons were used not to punish but to detain the accused until the debtor paid his debt, the rapist was castrated, the thief's hands were cut off, or the perjurer's tongue was torn out."[34] It was not until 1786 in Pennsylvania that incarceration was instituted as a humane alternative to hanging and torture.[35] From this inauspicious beginning at Philadelphia's Walnut Street Prison, incarceration has emerged as a gigantic twentieth-century enterprise. On December 31, 1973, there were 204,349 prisoners confined in some 600 state and federal correctional institutions.[36] However, incarceration as an enterprise is fundamentally failing. The magnitude of this failure is told in the statistics of repeat offenders in the FBI's *Uniform*

Table 6.1 Percent Repeaters by Type of Crime, 1970-1974

Crime	Percent arrested before
Auto theft	79
Robbery	79
Stolen property	73
Forgery	73
Weapons	72
Murder	68
Rape	65
Assault	65
Gambling	65
Burglary	64
Narcotics	59
Fraud	58
Larceny	55
Embezzlement	28
All others	68
Total	65

Source: Crime in the United States—Uniform Crime Reports—1974, U.S. Department of Justice (Washington, D.C.: Government Printing Office, 1975), p. 49.

Crime Reports. During the period 1970-1974, 65 percent of all offenders arrested had been arrested before.[37] Table 6.1 presents the percentage of persons arrested for each type of crime who were repeat offenders. It should be kept in mind that these percentage figures are conservative and underestimate the amount of crime committed by these offenders. After all, they are based on arrest figures, and only 20 percent of all serious crimes reported to the police during the period of 1970-1974 were cleared by arrest. Nonetheless, certain generalizations concerning recidivism or criminal repeating are possible. Thus, repeaters range from 79 percent for robbery and auto theft to 28 percent for embezzlement. Moreover, five of these seven major index crimes have at least a 65 percent average rate of recidivism, with 79 percent of those arrested for auto theft and robbery, 68 percent of those arrested for murder, and 65 percent of those arrested for rape and assault being repeat offenders. On the basis of sex and race, males and blacks have the highest incidence of criminal repeating, with 68 percent of those males arrested and 71 percent of those blacks arrested being recidivists (see Table 6.2).

What accounts for this massive failure? Chief Justice Warren E. Burger offers a useful beginning in his famous "No Man Is an Island" address to the American Bar Association. In it, he declared:

Table 6.2 Percent Repeaters by Sex and Race, 1970-1974

	Total	Race		
		White	Black	Other
Total	65.2	61.6	71.0	48.5
Male	67.9	64.0	74.5	51.6
Female	47.8	43.0	53.3	29.6

Source: *Crime in the United States—Uniform Crime Reports—1974,* U.S. Department of Justice (Washington, D.C.: Government Printing Office, 1975), p. 48.

> Do you know or can you conceive of an industrial enterprise with two hundred thousand employees, which turns out a critical product and would use 50- to 150-year-old plants, equipments, and techniques, no research, low pay and little or no training for its output or quality control? This question answers itself.
>
> Yet, with notable exceptions in a few of the states and the federal system, this is a description of the process we use to deal with these 200,000 prisoners. Is it any wonder that we find a grim and distressing "recall" of 65 percent of the human output of these prisons "back to the factory"? This is a true pollution of society and it manifests itself in the highest crime rate in our 200 years of existence, with most crimes being committed by "graduates" from these penal institutions.[38]

Chief Justice Burger's observations are pertinent and altogether accurate. In many instances, America's correctional facilities are old and outmoded. Thus, 56 of its 113 maximum security prisons (virtually 50 percent) were opened in the nineteenth century (see Table 6.3). Yet, they house approximately 75,000 of the 110,000 felons who are confined to maximum-security institutions. Likewise, correctional personnel are overworked, underpaid, and typically preoccupied with custodial functions. Thus, the Joint Commission on Correctional Manpower and Training found that only 20 percent of all personnel employed in correctional institutions are engaged in treatment or rehabilitative activities. Table 6.4 presents the ratio of this 20 percent charged with treatment and rehabilitation to the total number of offenders they are supposed to be treating. It dramatically underscores Chief Justice Burger's concern. The staggering case load this 20 percent is required to bear is more than enough to render any serious efforts at "long-range planning" or "quality control" altogether impossible.

Table 6.3 Date of Opening of State Maximum Security Prisons Still in Operation

Date of opening	Number of prisons
Prior to 1830	6
1831-1870	17
1871-1900	33
1901-1930	21
1931-1960	15
1961-date	21
Total	113

Source: American Correctional Association, *1971 Directory of Correctional Institutions and Agencies of America, Canada, and Great Britain* (College Park, Md.: American Correctional Association, 1971).

Not all the blame, however, can be laid simply on old facilities, overworked and underpaid personnel, inadequate planning, and lack of quality control. These factors are themselves symptomatic of a more serious and profound problem, namely, the indecision generally experienced by the criminal justice system over what exactly is the purpose or objective of incarceration. This is a question that compliance analysis can help us to explore. After all, until there is some clear-cut agreement concerning the purpose of incarceration—be it

Table 6.4 Ratio of Treatment Personnel to Inmates

Position	Number of inmates per staff member
Classification worker	365
Counselor	758
Psychiatrist	1,140
Psychologist	803
Physician, surgeon	986
Social worker	295
Teacher: academic	104
Teacher: vocational	181
Vocational rehabilitation counselor	2,172

Source: Joseph S. Campbell, Joseph R. Sahid, and David P. Stang, *Law and Order Reconsidered* (Washington, D.C.: Government Printing Office, 1969), p. 573.

retribution, deterrence, or rehabilitation—and until there is some evidence that the entire criminal justice system is making a good-faith effort to achieve this purpose, public willingness to provide correctional institutions with the financial and political resources necessary to construct new facilities, train and reward competent personnel, engage in research and planning, and provide for quality control will remain in doubt, and the failure that incarceration is experiencing will continue.

Presently, incarceration is defended as necessary for both deterrence and rehabilitation. As noted earlier, however, deterrence and rehabilitation are fundamentally at odds with one another. Thus, deterrence is based on a rational cost-benefit analysis and on a remunerative-calculative compliance structure. Rehabilitation, on the other hand, is based on the employment of normative power to work such a change in the character and behavior of the offender that his actions will come to conform to the dictates of the law. The simultaneous presence of these competing compliance structures ends up neutralizing the potency and effectiveness of each; and, as a consequence, incarceration is increasingly dismissed as a valid correctional alternative. The extent to which this is true can be perhaps best established through examples. Thus, Martin Levin analyzed the sentencing decisions handed down to white males with prior criminal records who were convicted of still other offenses in the Pittsburgh (Allegheny County) Common Pleas Court in 1966; he found that approximately 75 percent of those convicted of narcotics possession or indecent assault, 60 percent of those convicted of grand larceny or burglary, and 50 percent of those convicted of aggravated assault and aggravated forgery were placed on probation despite their prior records. Even 26 percent of those convicted of aggravated robbery received probation.[39] Dean V. Babst and John W. Mannering uncovered the same reluctance to incarcerate in Wisconsin, where, of those male adults who were placed on probation upon their convictions for felonies from 1954 to 1959, 63 percent had already been convicted of a previous felony and 41 percent had two or more felony convictions.[40] Finally, Peter Greenwood, in his more recent study of sentencing practices in Los Angeles, found the tendency to dismiss incarceration as a valid correctional alternative even more pronounced. Among his sample, only 6 percent of those with serious prison records who were subsequently convicted of burglary were sent to prison, and only 12 percent of those convicted of burglary who had been in prison before were sent back.[41]

The lessons to be learned from these examples are apparent enough. As James Q. Wilson notes, the low proportion of prison sentences for those convicted of serious crimes who have prior convictions suggests that judges do not believe that incarceration has a deterrent effect, and the fact that they were convicted after previous contact with the correctional system implies that, for them at least, there has been no rehabilitation. In short, the criminal justice system today seems to operate on neither the deterrence nor the rehabilitative theory of sentencing.[42]

If, as Wilson argues, neither deterrence nor rehabilitation provides judges with a justification for the sentences they impose, on what principle does the criminal justice system operate? By the process of elimination, one is left with retribution; however, all available evidence seems to deny this and to suggest that there is, in fact, no currently operative underlying principle. Thus, retribution is based on the principle that it is important to guarantee that those who disobey the law will not gain thereby an unfair advantage over those who choose voluntarily to obey. It strives to maintain the proper balance between benefit and obedience by ensuring that there is no profit in criminal wrongdoing.[43] The actions of the present criminal justice system, however, do not appear to be directed toward striking such a balance. Thus, between 1960 and 1974, the number of *Uniform Crime Reports* index crimes increased by 203.0 percent and the number of violent crimes rose by 238.0 percent, but there was an actual decline in the population of state and federal prisons from approximately 213,000 to 204,000.[44] In New York State, the chances of a perpetrator of a given crime going to prison fell during the 1960s by a factor of six, and in Los Angeles County, the percentage of convicted robbers with major prior records who were sent to prison in 1970 dropped to a mere 27 percent.[45]

Although retribution does not now appear to be the underlying principle on which the criminal justice system operates, compliance analysis suggests that perhaps it should be, especially if it is combined with specific deterrence. As James Q. Wilson observes, perhaps the correctional system should be content with simply isolating and punishing offenders.[46] To begin with, such a policy would be at least as effective as current efforts at general deterrence or rehabilitation. Sociologist Robert Martinson and his colleagues have conducted what is perhaps the most comprehensive study of the correctional effectiveness of rehabilitation. They reviewed, initially at the request of the New York State Governor's Special Committee on Criminal Offenders, the findings of 231 experimental studies conducted between 1945 and 1967 on the efficacy of correctional treatment. Their conclusions are clear. As Martinson writes: "It is possible to give a rather bald summary of our findings: With few and isolated exceptions, the rehabilitative efforts that have been reported so far have had no appreciable effect on recidivism."[47] Moreover, studies completed since 1967 "do not present any major grounds for altering that conclusion."

More importantly, however, the policy of simply incapacitating convicted criminals may provide rather substantial benefits. Because much or most serious crime is committed by recidivists, isolating them from the rest of society, even for relatively brief periods of time, may produce a major reduction in the crime rate.[48] Shlomo and Reuel Shinnar have estimated what the effect on the crime rate would be if such a policy were implemented. At present levels of police efficiency, they conclude that the rate of serious crime would be reduced to only one-third of what it is now if every person convicted of a serious offense were to be incarcerated for 3 years.[49] This reduction would result simply by virtue of incarceration, and, in fact, the overall drop in the crime rate may well be even greater if this policy of mandatory minimum sentences should have any general deterrent effect and if improved rehabilitative techniques should prove to be at all successful.[50]

The Shinnars' estimate that the crime rate would be only one-third of what it is today is based on a number of assumptions that can be challenged—for example, assumptions concerning how many crimes each offender commits per year. Nonetheless, even if they have overestimated this reduction by a factor of two, a sizable decrease in crime would still ensue. Moreover, such a policy would be wholly in keeping with retributive theory in that it would subject to the solemn condemnation of the community those who disobeyed the law in hopes of gaining an unfair advantage over those who obey voluntarily. Further, it would also help to sustain the fundamental values and standards of the community. The use of coercive compliance structures to promote normative considerations has already been touched upon in Chapter 3. No more need be said here than this: That just as the police may have to employ coercion to ensure compliance with the normative judgments of the courts, so, too, correctional institutions may have to employ coercion to protect what Paul Eidelberg calls "the community's moral standards and sensibilities." As he writes:

> The holistic and binding persuasions of a political community are partly dependent upon coercive and punitive sanctions. This dependency should be neither minimized nor misunderstood. Viewed candidly, the coercive and punitive sanctions of a political community, though seemingly negative and sometimes harsh, really reflect, and, by example sustain, the community's moral standards and sensibilities, hence those positive values which endow human activity with gradations of importance on the one hand, and with different intensities of feeling on the other.[51]

Finally, the policy of simply incarcerating convicted offenders may be all that a democratic government can realistically hope to do to lower the crime rate. Government has no way of systematically altering family backgrounds, deep-seated attitudes, friendship patterns, or media images, all of which affect an individual's propensity to engage in criminal activity. Moreover, even if it had, the costs would be staggering—not only in monetary terms, as these programs would have to be directed at the entire citizenry in order to ensure that they would reach the small criminal population, but also in terms of those fundamental human values that would be jeopardized if government possessed the capacity to direct and mold so completely the family life and mental state of its citizens.[52]

This retributive policy of simply incarcerating all persons convicted of serious crime is not likely to generate much support. To begin with, it raises questions concerning the increased financial burden that this great use of incarceration is likely to impose both in additional prison space and judicial resources. It also raises questions concerning the propriety and humanity of mandatory minimum sentences for all offenders, regardless of extenuating or mitigating circumstances. The effect that such a policy is likely to have on the courts and due process also has to be considered. After all, if every defendant who is arrested for a serious crime knows that he faces a mandatory minimum sentence, his willingness to engage in plea bargaining will be dampened, and system-overload problems are likely to intensify. However, perhaps the major objection that is likely to be raised to this proposed policy is that it is clearly in conflict with the controlling correctional philosophy of the day, which may be summarized as follows: "Incarcerate only when nothing less will do, and then incarcerate as briefly as possible."[53] Exemplary of this philosophy is the National Advisory Commission on Criminal Justice Standards and Goals; it considers community-based alternatives to incarceration to be "the most promising means of accomplishing the changes in offender behavior that the public expects—and in fact now demands—of corrections."[54] It is convinced that community-based corrections is so fundamental and basic to the future of corrections that it has joined with the National Council on Crime and Delinquency (NCCD) in suggesting that incarceration and not community-based corrections should be regarded as the exception: "Imprisonment must be viewed as an alternative to community treatment."[55]

Community-Based Corrections: An Alternative to Incarceration

As the name implies, community-based corrections includes all correctional activities that take place in the community.[56] The proponents of community-based corrections typically advance three principal reasons for supporting it. First of all, they regard it as humanitarian. Incarceration often places inmates in physical jeopardy,[57] narrows their access to personal satisfaction, and destroys their self-confidence. These consequences are, of course, brought on by the offenders' own criminal actions; however, this in no way alters their reality. Thus, proponents of community-based corrections argue, to the extent that these unfortunate consequences can be abated by the use of community treatment, humanitarian objectives are realized. Second, community-based corrections is also justified in terms of its putative rehabilitative capability.[58] Those who have been subjects of community corrections are believed less likely to recidivate. The President's Commission on Law Enforcement and Administration of Justice fully embraced this view in its general report. It gave particular emphasis to the Community Treatment Project (CTP) of the California Youth Authority. In this controlled experiment to determine the effectiveness of community-based corrections, convicted juvenile defendants were assigned on a random basis to either an experimental group or a control group. The experimental group was returned to the community and received intensive individual counseling, group counseling, group therapy, and family counseling. The control group, on the other hand, was assigned to California's regular institutional-treatment program. The results of this particular study overwhelmingly supported community treatment: only 28 percent of the experimental group had their paroles revoked compared with 52 percent of the control group.[59] Third, community-based corrections can be justified in economic terms: It costs from ten to thirteen times more to maintain an offender in prison than it does to supervise him in the community.[60] This savings by itself is not decisive; the object of corrections is not simply to save money. However, the proponents of community treatment continue, because community-based alternatives to incarceration also appear to decrease rates of recidivism, this financial consideration merely provides additional justification for community-based corrections.

Beyond these three reasons typically given in support of community treatment, compliance analysis suggests still a fourth: It generally subjects the offender to just one type of compliance structure. In prison, inmates are typically subjected to a curious mixture of conflicting retributive, deterrent, and rehabilitative theories of incarceration. The simultaneous presence of these conflicting theories and the conflicting coercive, remunerative, and normative powers on which they are based end up neutralizing the efficacy of each and, thereby, diminish the overall correctional power of incarceration. In community-based treatment programs, however, the offender is placed in a normative-moral compliance structure with rehabilitation as the goal. Normative power does not have to compete nearly so much with coercion or remuneration and, hence, can be more effective.[61] Thus, for many proponents of community-based corrections, the goal is to "minimize the penetration" of offenders into the correctional system.[62] The further an offender penetrates the system, the more likely he is to be subjected to the simultaneous presence of conflicting correctional theories and compliance structures and the less likely it is that any valid correctional objectives will be achieved.

Community treatment typically takes on one of three forms: probation, parole, and pretrial diversion. The problems and prospects of each will be explored.

Probation

Probation may be defined as a sentence that does not involve incarceration but that instead places the offender under supervision in the community subject to the authority of the sentencing court. It attempts to "minimize the penetration" of the offender into the correctional system and relies almost exclusively on the normative power of the courts to accomplish its rehabilitative objectives. Probation consists of two basic operations: the presentence investigation and supervision of probationers. Both are crucial to its success.

The presentence investigation is conducted to determine which offenders will receive the sentence of probation. It is performed by a probation officer to

CORRECTIONS   243

ascertain the offender's family and social background, educational and occupational experiences, and previous criminal record and to uncover his strengths and his weaknesses with a view toward developing a treatment program. The presentence investigation report is then submitted to the judge after the offender has been convicted but before he is sentenced in order to assist the judge in his sentencing decision.[63] More specifically, the presentence investigation report can be used in five different ways. First, it can aid the judge in determining the appropriate sentence. Second, if the offender is placed on probation, it can aid the probation officer in rehabilitative efforts during probation supervision. Third, if, on the other hand, the offender is incarcerated, it can assist the correctional institution in designing a classification and treatment program for him. Fourth, it can furnish the parole board with information pertinent to the offender's release on parole. Fifth, it can serve as a source of information for systematic research on corrections.[64]

Once the presentence investigation has been completed and the offender sentenced to probation, the second basic operation of probation begins: supervision. Supervision involves a combination of both treatment and enforcement functions.[65] It employs such community resources as family agencies, child care or welfare agencies, child guidance clinics, mental hygiene clinics, vocational guidance agencies, and social work agencies in an attempt to rehabilitate the probationer for a full, productive, and law-abiding life. At the same time, however, it engages in surveillance and information gathering in efforts to control the activities and behavior of the probationer.

Probation is widely used; in fact, approximately 75 percent of all offenders receive suspended sentences and are placed on probation.[66] However, despite its wide use and despite its enthusiastic embrace by the 1967 President's Commission on Law Enforcement and Administration of Justice and the 1973 National Advisory Commission on Criminal Justice Standards and Goals, there is virtually no evidence to suggest that it is any more effective in reducing rates of recidivism than is simple incarceration. Robert Martinson, in his exhaustive review of 231 research reports dealing with offender rehabilitation, has this to say of the effectiveness of community treatment: "In sum, even in the case of treatment programs administered outside penal institutions, we simply cannot say that this treatment in itself has an appreciable effect on offender behavior."[67] The only "encouraging set of findings" that he could find in these reports is that "even if we can't 'treat' offenders so as to make them do better, a great many of the programs designed to rehabilitate them at least did not make them do worse."[68]

Earlier studies that claimed to have established the rehabilitative effectiveness of community-based correctional programs have been discredited. The Community Treatment Project (CTP) of the California Youth Authority, which the 1967 President's Commission singled out for special mention as evidence that rehabilitation is possible, is a case in point. Upon closer scrutiny, it has been subsequently determined that the experimental group (that is, those who were assigned directly to probation officers in small groups and exposed to intensive and individually tailored therapy programs) in fact committed more offenses than the controls (2.81 per experimental boy, 1.61 per control).[69] However, this relatively large number of offenses was not reflected in their failure rate because the experimentals' probation officers were using a more lenient revocation policy. In contrast, the control group had fewer offenses but a higher failure rate because parole was being revoked for less serious offenses. In reviewing all of this, Robert Martinson was forced to conclude that what the findings of the Community Treatment Project reveal is "not so much a change in the behavior of the experimental youths as a change in the behavior of the experimental *probation officers,* who knew the 'special' status of their charges and who had evidently decided to revoke probation status at a lower than normal rate. The experimentals continued to commit offenses; what was different was that when they committed these offenses, they were permitted to remain on probation."[70]

A number of factors help to explain why probation is not succeeding as its proponents would wish or once thought. To begin with, there is the problem of an "unbalanced allocation of staff personnel to offenders."[71] As James S. Campbell and his colleagues emphasize in their report to the Commission on the Causes and Prevention of Violence:

> Approximately 1.3 million people are under correctional authority in the United States. Of these, only one-third are in institutions; the other two-thirds are supervised in the community on probation or parole. But the ratios of staff and costs are inverse to these proportions: only one-fifth of the money and one-seventh of the staff are engaged with the two-thirds of the offenders who are in the community.[72]

To many proponents of community-based corrections, this "unbalanced allocation" of resources has led to unmanageable case loads—the average case load in probation, for example, is 100.[73] As a consequence of these heavy case loads, probation officers are too overworked to provide either treatment for, or control over, the probationer. Thus, the argument continues, for probation in fact to be effective in rehabilitation, case loads must be reduced. In keeping with this notion, the President's Commission on Law Enforcement and Administration of Justice recommended that the average ratio of offenders to probation officers should be reduced to thirty-five to one.[74]

Systematic research, however, does not lend much support to the claim that more intense supervision will enhance the rehabilitative effectiveness of probation. California's Department of Corrections has led the field in experimentation with case-load size in probation and parole. Its Special Intensive Parole Unit (SIPU) represents its most ambitious undertaking. The SIPU conducted a 10-year experiment designed to test the effects of variations in case load size on recidivism. In three of the four "phases" of this experiment, the results were "negative." Phase One tested the effect of reducing the regular case load from ninety to fifteen and found no measurable effect on the incidence of recidivism. Phase Two slightly increased the size of the case loads from fifteen to thirty but extended the length of this intensive supervision from 3 months to 6 months before transfer to a regular case load. Again, no evidence of the superiority of the reduced case load was demonstrated. Phase Four kept the case loads at fifteen or thirty and attempted to match the personality characteristics of the parole officer and parolee in a manner thought favorable to parole outcome. Once again, no significant results appeared. Only in Phase Three were positive results reported; in this phase, case loads were held to thirty-five persons, but the length of this intense supervision was increased to 1 year before transfer to a regular case load. A 2-year follow-up revealed that parolees who were part of a reduced case load did slightly better than those on regular case loads.[75] However, even here the significance of these findings must be qualified. When Martinson and his colleagues reexamined the SIPU's data, they found that much of the reduction in recidivism among experimental parolees was to be found in the northern region of the SIPU experiment. In this northern region, there was a policy of returning both experimental and control parolees to prison at relatively high rates. Yet, it was also in this region that more intense supervision did seem to produce a real improvement in the behavior of offenders. Martinson attributes this improvement to the "realistic threat" of severe sanctions that was manifestly present in the northern region. Martinson's conclusions from this reevaluation of the SIPU data are wholly consistent with the overall argument of this chapter: "What this suggests is that when intensive supervision *does* produce an improvement in offenders' behavior, it does so not through the mechanism of 'treatment' or 'rehabilitation,' but instead through a mechanism that our studies have almost totally ignored—the mechanism of *deterrence.*"[76]

The claims of the proponents of community-based corrections to the contrary, it appears that the failure of probation to reduce appreciably the rates of recidivism cannot be laid altogether on an "unbalanced allocation" of staff and financial resources and heavy case loads. Other factors must also be identified. One such factor is the simultaneous reliance of probation on both normative and remunerative powers and the resulting neutralization of the potency of both. This is most immediately apparent in an examination of the presentence investigation. As mentioned above, the presentence investigation is undertaken in order to evaluate the offender's social relationships, occupational strengths and weaknesses, educational background, criminal background, and all other factors pertinent to the sentencing decision. This process, however, can place the defendant in an altogether untenable position. Thus, in many jurisdictions, defendants at their arraignment are asked at that time to authorize initiation of a presentence investigation for the purpose of obtaining information that would be useful in the event of a subsequent guilty plea or conviction. The federal probation system's approval form is typical:

> I, _____ , hereby consent to a pre-sentence investigation by the probation officers of the United States District Courts. This investigation is for the purpose of obtaining information useful to the court in the event I should hereafter plead guilty or be found guilty.
>
> By this consent I do not admit any guilt or waive any rights and I understand that any report prepared will not be shown to the court or anyone else until after conviction or plea of guilty.
>
> I have read, or had read to me, the foregoing consent. No promise has been made to me as to what final disposition will be made in my case.

There are two rather compelling reasons for the defendant to give his approval. First, it can expedite matters later. The preparation of a presentence investigation report often takes anywhere from 6 to 8 weeks. If the defendant is found guilty, and if he has refused to authorize this investigation at the initial stages of the criminal process, he cannot be sentenced until this report is complete. For the defendant who has been unable to post bond, this will mean that he is likely to spend an additional 6 to 8 weeks in jail, time that often does not count against the time he may later be required to serve as punishment. In other words, it is simply lost time. Thus, beginning the presentence investigation immediately can expedite matters at the later stages.

A second reason for authorizing the investigation is that if in the preparation of the report, the probation officer finds a good record and discovers that the defendant has not been involved in these criminal activities in the past, he may be inclined to recommend him for pretrial diversion, the third community-based alternative to confinement to be discussed later in this chapter. However, despite these advantages, this authorization of the presentence investigation at the arraignment stage places the defendant in quite a dilemma. It subjects him to opposing pressures and tendencies of both the normative due process model and the remunerative crime control model. The quandary in which the defendant finds himself because of these two models' conflicting understandings of the privilege against self-incrimination is illustrative. The more the defendant exercises his due process model rights—that is, the more he protests his innocence and makes the prosecution carry the burden of proof—the more likely he is to be regarded by his probation officer as lacking the remorse or repentance commonly thought vital in considering mitigation and probation. On the other hand, the more he goes along with the crime control model—that is, the more he waives his privilege against self-incrimination and tells all—the more likely he is not only to be convicted but also to have any appeal or motion for a new trial eviscerated.[77] These cross-pressures cannot help but minimize the normative and rehabilitative effect that the operation of probation is intended to provide.

Even without this neutralization of normative power, the presence of still another factor militates agains the rehabilitative effectiveness of probation. Many criminal offenders are simply not receptive to the operation of normative power. As Justice Frankfurter observed in *United States* v. *Rabinowitz*, the criminal justice system is filled with "not very nice people"[78] —people who are capable of responding only to coercive power. The attempt to utilize normative power to rehabilitate an offender who is alienatively involved simply creates incongruence in probation's compliance structures and, as a consequence, leads to rehabilitative ineffectiveness.[79]

The proponents of community-based corrections are often reluctant even to acknowledge the possibility that probation may be no more successful than incarceration in reducing recidivism. As Gordon Tullock notes, this possibility directly challenges the conventional wisdom "so common in the social sciences, that 'all good things go together.'"[80] On occasion, they have even tried to suppress evidence damaging to their position. Thus, even though Robert Martinson and his colleagues were hired by the state of New York to undertake a comprehensive study of rehabilitative programs with the thought that such information would be a necessary basis for any reform that might be initiated, he reports that "the state's planning agency ended by viewing the study as a document whose disturbing conclusions posed a serious threat to the programs which, in the meantime, they had determined to carry forward."[81] As a consequence, the state planning agency not only failed to publish the study but refused to give him permission to publish it on his own. As he continues, "The document itself would still not be available to me or to the public today had not an attorney subpoenaed it from the State for use as evidence in a case before the Bronx Supreme Court."[82]

Of course, most proponents of community-based corrections renounce such suppression. They stress instead that even though probation has not been shown to be more effective in reducing recidivism than incarceration, neither has it been shown to be less effective. Moreover, because probation is so much less expensive and because it does not subject offenders—especially first offenders—to the brutality and dangers of prison life, it should still be embraced. To this, however, it can be responded that the true costs of probation and other community-based correctional programs include not only the costs of administering these programs but also the costs of maintaining in the community an offender population that is thereby made larger. This population may not be committing offenses at any higher rate, but the offender population will be larger in absolute numbers. As a consequence, the total number of offenses committed is likely to rise, and the chances of victimization are likely to rise also.[83] When these total costs are assessed, the putative advantages of probation may all but disappear.

Parole

Parole has been defined by the U.S. attorney general's *Survey of Release Procedures* as the "release of an offender from a penal or correctional institution, after he has served a portion of his sentence, under the continued custody of of the state and under conditions that permit his reincarceration in the event of misbehavior."[84] Most offenders released from correctional institutions reenter the community on parole. Thus, in 1973, of the 105,044 persons released from state and federal prisons, 78,262, or 75 percent were released by parole.[85] In a number of respects, parole resembles probation. To begin with, both attempt to adjust the correctional response to the circumstances of the offense and the characteristics of the offender. Both respond to crime through the employment of treatment in the form of counseling, guidance, and assistance. Both gather and present information about the offender to a decision-making authority with power to release him to community supervision under specific conditions. Finally, both probation and parole permit the offender who violates these conditions to be placed in, or returned to, a correctional institution.

Because of these similarities, parole is subject to many of the same problems that probation experiences. These do not need to be reiterated here, except to stress that they are even greater in parole. Edwin H. Sutherland and Donald R. Cressey suggest why this is the case:

> Probationers are considered as undergoing treatment while under the threat of punishment, should they violate the conditions of their probation. But probation is granted by the courts as a substitute for punishment as well as for mere suspension of sentence. Parolees are considered as "in custody" and undergoing both punishment and treatment while under the threat of more severe punishment—return to the institutions from which they have been released. Without the threat of return to prison, release from prison before the maximum term was served would merely represent the workings of an indeterminate sentence, not parole. Since parole is expected both to punish and to treat, the conflicts between punishment and treatment which are found in prisons are often found in parole.[86]

Parole "is expected both to punish and to treat." To the blend of normative and remunerative powers employed in other community-based correctional programs, parole also adds the very immediate element of coercion. All three kinds of power are simultaneously present and, as a consequence, foster even greater ineffectiveness in efforts to reduce rates of recidivism. This is especially apparent in supervision of parolees once they are released into the community. Two very different understandings of parole supervision have arisen that place varying degrees of emphasis on punishment and treatment. The first understanding considers most parolees as unrehabilitated and likely to commit new crime if given the opportunity. It views supervision as surveillance rather than assistance and regards parole work as, essentially, police work. It believes that the parole officer must coerce the parolee into conformity with the law by means of punishment or the threat of punishment. In contrast, the second understanding contends that reformation of the parolee, in the form of self-resolution to "make good," is not always sufficient to prevent recidivism. Parole supervision in the form of assistance is needed to improve the welfare of the parolee by helping him in his individual adjustment, within the limits of his capacity. Parole work, in this view, becomes social work.

Both understandings tend to be present to some degree in every parole system. However, the presence of these widely divergent understandings within the same system is the source of many of parole's difficulties. After all, these opposing understandings of supervision impose on the parolee very different kinds and degrees of control and elicit in return very different kinds of responses. Thus, the first understanding of supervision operates on a coercive-alienative compliance structure. It is primarily punitive and coercive and generates intense negative feelings of alienation. On the other hand, the second understanding tends to rely on a normative-moral compliance structure. It employs symbolic rewards and deprivations in the hopes of thereby promoting a moral reformation of the parolee. If a parolee is simultaneously subjected to these two opposing understandings, his response will, in all probability, be one of frustration, anxiety, and suspicion. If he expects surveillance and punishment, he will probably view any interest by his parole officer in assistance and treatment with mistrust and apprehension. If, alternatively, he expects assistance and treatment, he will doubtless respond to punitive measures with feelings of betrayal, frustration, and confusion. The presence of these mutually exclusive compliance structures neutralizes their individual efficacy and contributes to the high rate of failure for parole. And parole is failing. Thus, of 7,582 male offenders paroled in California in 1965, 47 percent had been declared violators by 1966.[87] What is true for California is true for the rest of the nation as well. As the National Council on Crime and Delinquency reports, 37 percent of all prisoners paroled from state correctional institutions in 1968 were declared violators by 1970.[88] Moreover, these figures refer only to the period of parole supervision and do not include the career of the offender after he is released from parole. When the subsequent period is also considered, the failure rate jumps considerably. This is documented by a whole range of empirical studies that examine the subsequent careers of ex-prisoners beyond the period of parole. The most intensive studies of this type have been undertaken by Sheldon and Eleanor Glueck. Analyzing the careers of 500 young male offenders paroled from the Massachusetts reformatory over a period of 15 years, they found that 79 percent committed new crimes during the first 5-year period after parole, 68 percent during the second 5-year period, and 68 percent during the third 5-year period.[89] The failure of parole is incontestable.

Pretrial Diversion

Because of the high failure rates of both probation and parole, correctional measures that seek to minimize even further the penetration of an offender into the criminal justice system are gaining increased attention. These measures are based on three assumptions that may be articulated in the language of compliance analysis as follows: By minimizing the offender's penetration into the criminal process, he will be subjected to the influence of only one kind of power—normative power; this normative power will be effective for it will not be neutralized by the simultaneous presence of coercion and remuneration, as is the case in other forms of community-based corrections; because this normative power will be effective, it will so be able to employ and manipulate symbolic rewards and deprivations that the offender will be less likely to recidivate. One such measure is pretrial diversion, which refers to "halting or suspending before conviction formal criminal proceedings against a person on the condition or assumption that he will do something in return."[90]

The most common use of diversion has been for the treatment of habitual public drunks in large cities. Instead of the traditional and largely ineffective cycle of arrest, hearing, jail or fine, and release, under these programs the drunk who is found on the streets by the police is taken directly to a detoxification or "drying out" center where he is treated and released with referral to an appropriate long-term rehabilitative program. Other diversion programs include noncriminal treatment of drug users and other offenders who would not appear to need or benefit from the costly process of prosecution, incarceration or probation, and release.[91] In many areas, to be eligible for pretrial diversion, a defendant must be youthful, charged with a nonserious crime, and a first offender. Moreover, he will have to consent to enter a program of counseling and job training or other community correction for a specified period. If the program is successfully completed, the program staff requests that the court dismiss prosecution, thereby permitting the defendant to escape the stigma of a conviction record.

Proponents of pretrial diversion catalog a number of distinct advantages that they claim it enjoys over incarceration, probation, and parole.[92] First, unlike these other correctional alternatives, pretrial diversion can help to reduce the heavy volume of cases that the lower courts must process. In so doing, it can help to ease the pressure on the criminal justice system to resort to plea bargaining and the remunerative crime control model to handle this volume. The discrepancy between what the Supreme Court says ought to be done and what in fact is actually done can thereby be diminished. Second, by taking the offender out of the criminal process before conviction, diversion avoids the destructive "labeling process"[93] and the stigma of conviction that makes rehabilitation and reform all the more difficult. The desire on the part of the offender to avoid the stigma of a criminal conviction often provides him with all the incentive he needs to fulfill all the conditions of his diversion program. Third, pretrial diversion can avoid subjecting the offender to the brutality and depravity that are so often characteristic of time spent in prison or jail.[94] Fourth, and perhaps most importantly, diversion can help to provide restitution or compensation to the victim. One of the conditions for participation in a pretrial diversion program can be that the offender must provide restitution.

For the most part, the fate of the victim has been generally ignored by corrections. As the old adage notes, "The victim is the Cinderella of the criminal law." He has been left largely without redress for the harm that he suffers. Recently, however, a new sensitivity for the fate of the victim has arisen. This concern to compensate the victim is the result of a number of factors, including rapidly escalating crime rates and the increasing anxiety that accompanies the growing recognition that anyone can be victimized—anytime, anywhere, and irrespective of the precautions taken. Even correctional officials are lending their support to this movement, seeing restitution as highly valuable from a penological point of view. Restitution, after all, focuses the offender's attention on the harm he has caused. It forces him to come to grips with consequences of his antisocial behavior. A variety of restitution schemes have been proposed; however, with the exception of restitution as a condition of a pretrial diversion program, all of these schemes have serious defects.

One scheme would require restitution as a condition for probation: Only when the convicted offender has compensated the victim for the wrong he has done to him is he eligible for probation. The problem with this scheme, as with so many other restitution schemes, is that it is altogether dependent on the offender's ability to give redress; as a consequence, it clearly favors the affluent over the indigent.[95] Another scheme would be to give a portion of the fine collected to the victim. There is, after all, no logical or penological imperative for the state to retain the entire sum levied upon the offender. This scheme would serve a rehabilitative effect by bringing home to the offender the price charged for his transgression and by giving him an increased awareness of his responsibility to the individual whom he has harmed. As with restitution by probation, however, the most obvious drawback of this proposal is that it, too, favors the more affluent. To eliminate the economic advantage that more wealthy offenders enjoy under these schemes, other proposals would institute systems of day fines or attachment of prison earnings. Day-fine systems, however, are dependent upon the availability of suitable and remunerative work, which is often lacking in those rural areas where prisons are typically located. Likewise, attachment of prison earnings is realistic only when the offender is adequately compensated for his labor while incarcerated, something the present state of prison industries is simply unable to do. Still other schemes are also proposed, including both private and public insurance plans. Although these plans can satisfy the victim's claim to compensation without reference to the economic means of the offender and can provide relief to those many victims of unknown and unapprehended offenders, they allow the offender to ignore the consequences of his harmful acts and are, as a consequence, of less penological value. Only restitution through pretrial diversion programs can avoid all these problems. To begin with, it forces the offender to come to terms with the harm his criminal actions have caused. By minimizing his penetration into the criminal justice system, it spares him of a conviction, which makes employment—so necessary for restitution—more difficult. If he is unemployed or has an alcohol or drug problem, pretrial diversion's guidance and assistance services can help him overcome these problems and become positively directed and productive.

These advantages of pretrial diversion must not be allowed to obscure its major shortcomings, of which there are several. To begin with, although pretrial diversion is proposed as a means by which to reduce the heavy volume of cases that the criminal justice system must process and that leads it to embrace plea bargaining and the crime control model, it is itself based on crime control principles. Thus, it involves the imposition of a correctional program without a conviction. It assumes but does not prove guilt. This, of course, is clearly contrary to the tenets of the due process model. This, however, is only the beginning. Program restrictions regarding which offenders are eligible for diversion may well violate the Equal Protection Clause of the Fourteenth Amendment. The offender's right to a speedy trial must be waived in order to have sentence withheld. And, as in presentence investigations, the issue of self-incrimination emerges when the offender, still presumed to be innocent, may be required to discuss the details of his alleged offense with his diversion counselor.[96] Finally, pretrial diversion may also dilute the deterrent effectiveness of punishment. Empirical studies of existing diversion programs generally show that pretrial diversion does not lead to higher recidivism rates among participating offenders. In fact, the data gathered by the Vera Institute's Manhattan Court Employment Project show that the rearrest rate over a 12-month period for offenders successfully completing diversion programs was 15.8 percent as compared with 46.1 percent for the control group.[97] However, deterrence can be either specific or general, and the effect of pretrial diversion programs on general deterrence is much more problematic. The same question of the impact on general deterrence is also raised by probation; however, with pretrial diversion, it is much more acute. After all, with probation, the offender is at least convicted, and as Herbert L. Packer points out, "The very fact of criminal conviction is itself a form of punishment, particularly to the relatively law-abiding citizen."[98] Pretrial diversion removes even the punishment of conviction, and the effect that this will have on general deterrence has yet to be ascertained.

Corrections: The Need for a New Definition

The shortcomings of pretrial diversion may well outweigh the advantages. Even so, it deserves our serious consideration. It does, after all, provide for the possible use of restitution and, thereby, permits corrections to be so redefined that it brings within its purview not only the correction of the offender but also the correction of the havoc he has played on his victims.

This is a critically important issue. Increasingly the public is becoming demoralized by a correctional enterprise and a criminal justice system that is more solicitous of providing due process for the offender than for the victim. Even such a traditional liberal as Professor Sidney Hook has confessed: "Since many crimes of violence are committed by repeaters, the likelihood of my becoming a victim of crime is much greater than the likelihood of my becoming a criminal. Therefore, the protection of my rights not to be mugged, assaulted, or murdered looms larger in my mind than my rights as a criminal defendant."[99] His argument is based wholly on calculative principles:

> I submit that at the present juncture of events because our American cities have become more dangerous to life and limb than the darkest jungle, we must give priority to the rights of potential victims. I am prepared to weaken the guarantees and privileges to which I am entitled as a potential criminal, or as a defendant, in order to strengthen my rights and safeguards as a potential victim. Purely on the basis of probabilities, I am convinced that I run a greater danger of suffering disaster as a potential victim than as a potential criminal or defendant. It is these probabilities that shift from one historical period to another that must be the guide of wise, prudent, and just administration of the law.[100]

The law is losing its normative hold even on Professor Hook, who is close to concluding with Mr. Pickwick that the law is an ass. If the public at large is not to follow suit and become calculative in its orientation toward, and obedience to, the law, its normative hold on the entire citizenry must be strengthened. One principal means by which this can be accomplished would be for the entire criminal justice system—and especially a more comprehensively defined correctional component—to demonstrate that the law is, in fact, concerned with not only protecting all citizens from criminal wrongdoing but also providing them with restitution once they have been victimized. Only at this juncture will the public recognize the legitimacy of the correctional enterprise and of the criminal justice system more generally.

Notes

1. James Q. Wilson, *Thinking About Crime* (New York: Basic Books, 1975), p. 209.
2. Chief Justice Warren E. Burger, "We Refuse to be Responsible for the People We Imprison," address at the 1972 Annual Dinner, National Conference of Christians and Jews, Philadelphia, November 1972.
3. Herbert L. Packer, *The Limits of the Criminal Sanction* (Stanford, Calif.: Stanford University Press, 1968), p. 39.
4. Henry Weihofen, "Retribution Is Obsolete," in *Responsibility,* ed. Karl Frederich (Englewood Cliffs, N.J.: Prentice-Hall, 1960), p. 120. Originally published in *Nomos* 3 (1960).

5. Morris R. Cohen, "Moral Aspects of the Criminal Law," in *Crime and Justice,* vol. 2, *The Criminal in the Arms of the Law,* ed. Leon Radzinowicz and Marvin E. Wolfgang (New York: Basic Books, 1971), p. 35. Originally published in *Yale Law Journal* 49 (April 1940).
6. C. S. Lewis, "The Humanitarian Theory of Punishment," *Res Judicatae* 6 (1953): 228. Frederick Douglass made much this same point when he rhetorically inquired, "Must I undertake to prove that this slave is a man? That point is conceded already. Nobody doubts it. The slaveholders themselves acknowledge it in the enactment of laws for their government. They acknowledge it when they punish disobedience on the part of the slave. There are 72 crimes in the State of Virginia, which, if committed by a black man (no matter how ignorant he be), subject him to the punishment of death; while only two of the same crimes will subject a white man to a like punishment. What is this but the acknowledgement that the slave is a moral, intellectual and responsible being. The manhood of the slave is conceded." Douglass, "Fourth of July Oration," in *What Country Have I? Political Writings by Black Americans,* ed. Herbert J. Storing (New York: St. Martin's Press, 1970), p. 33.
7. Lewis, "The Humanitarian Theory of Punishment," p. 226.
8. Jeffrey Murphy, "Three Mistakes About Retributivism," *Analysis* 31 (April 1971): 166.
9. Packer, *The Limits of the Criminal Sanction,* p. 49.
10. Isaac Ehrlich, "The Deterrent Effect of Criminal Law Enforcement," *The Journal of Legal Studies* 1, no. 2 (June 1971): 259-276.
11. See George E. Antunes and A. Lee Hunt, "The Impact of Certainty and Severity of Punishment on Levels of Crime in American States: An Extended Analysis" (Paper presented to the Annual Meeting of the American Political Science Association, Washington, D.C., September 1972). Antunes and Hunt found that the larger the proportion of recorded crimes resulting in imprisonment—that is, the greater the certainty of punishment—the lower the crime rates. However, they also found, contrary to Ehrlich, that increased severity in punishment has a significant deterrent effect only on murder. See also Robert Chauncey, "Deterrence: Certainty, Severity, and Skyjacking," *Criminology* 12, no. 4 (February 1975): 447-443, who concludes on the basis of his study of legal sanctions imposed on skyjackers that certainty of punishment does deter but that severity of punishment does not.
12. Ehrlich, "The Deterrent Effect of Criminal Law Enforcement," p. 275. Despite Ehrlich's assurances to the contrary, James Q. Wilson is correct in pointing out that "it is not entirely clear whether the crime reduction associated with lengthy prison terms, found by Ehrlich, is the result of the deterrent effect of those terms on would-be criminals who are contemplating imprisonment, or the incapacitating effect of those terms on would-be

13. Ehrlich, "The Deterrent Effect of Criminal Law Enforcement, p. 274.
14. Wilson, *Thinking About Crime*, p. 176.
15. Ibid., p. 177.
16. Steven Goldberg, "On Capital Punishment," *Ethics* 85, no. 1 (October 1974): 78.
17. As Gordon Tullock writes: "In discussing the concept of deterrence, I find that a great many people seem to feel that, although it would no doubt work with respect to burglary and other property crimes, it is unlikely to have much effect on crimes of impulse, such as rape and many murders. They reason that people who are about to kill their wives in a rage are totally incapable of making calculations at all. But this is far from obvious. The prisoners in Nazi concentration camps must frequently have been in a state of well-justified rage against some of their guards; yet this almost never led to their using violence against the guards, because punishment—which, if they were lucky, would be instant death, but was more likely to be death by torture—was so obvious and so certain. Even in highly emotional situations, we retain some ability to reason, albeit presumably not so well as normally." Tullock, "Does Punishment Deter Crime?" *Public Interest*, no. 36 (Summer 1974), p. 108. See also Edward C. Banfield, *The Unheavenly City Revisited* (Boston: Little, Brown, 1974): "' Crimes of passion' are rarely committed in the presence of policemen or against persons who are in a good position to defend themselves" (p. 181).
18. Wilson, *Thinking About Crime*, pp. 186, 200. See also William E. Cobb, "Theft and the Two Hypotheses," in *The Economics of Crime and Punishment*, ed. Simon Rottenberg (Washington, D.C.: American Enterprise Institute for Public Policy Research, 1973), pp. 19-30. Cobb examines the question of whether the crime of burglary pays and concludes, on the basis of the Norfolk, Virginia, experience, that most people who take up the profession of burglary have made a fairly rational career choice.
19. Goldberg, "On Capital Punishment," p. 69. It must be stressed that not every advocate of deterrence is also in favor of capital punishment.
20. Ibid., p. 70.
21. Ibid., p. 74. Indeed, see Isaac Ehrlich, "The Deterrent Effect of Capital Punishment: A Question of Life and Death," *The American Economic Review* 65, no. 3 (June 1975): 397-417, who concludes on the basis of his simultaneous regression analysis that "an additional execution per year over the period in question [1933-1969] may have resulted, on average, in 7 or 8 fewer murders" (p. 414). See also Ernest van den Haag, *Punishing Criminals: Concerning a Very Old and Painful Question* (New York: Basic Books, 1975), pp. 207-217. For a methodological evaluation of Ehrlich's research, see "Statistical Evidence on the Deterrent Effect of Capital

Punishment," *Yale Law Journal* 85, no. 2 (December 1975): 164-227.
22. Mark DeWolfe Howe, ed., *Holmes-Laski Letters, 1916-1935* (Cambridge, Mass.: Harvard University Press, 1953), p. 806.
23. As Gordon Tullock notes, "If we have the choice between preventing crime by training the criminal to be good—i.e., rehabilitating him—or deterring crime by imposing unpleasantness on criminals, the former is the one we would like to choose." "Does Punishment Deter Crime?" p. 110.
24. Francis A. Allen, "Criminal Justice, Legal Values and the Rehabilitative Ideal," *Journal of Criminal Law, Criminology and Police Science* 50 (1960): 229.
25. To many, this is the source of still another criticism of rehabilitation, namely, that it is fundamentally grounded on the principles of the "Therapeutic State, in which the citizen-patient's conduct is governed by the clinical judgment of the medical despot." Tomas S. Szasz, "Crime, Punishment, and Psychiatry," in *Current Perspectives on Criminal Behavior: Original Essays on Criminology,* ed. Abraham S. Blumberg (New York: Knopf, 1974), p. 278.
26. As Karl Menninger, founder of the famed Menninger Clinic and Foundation and former president of the American Psycho-Analytic Association, writes: "The very word *justice* irritates scientists. No surgeon expects to be asked if an operation for cancer is just or not. . . . Behavioral scientists regard it as equally absurd to invoke the question of justice in deciding what to do with a woman who cannot resist her propensity to shoplift, or with a man who cannot repress an impulse to assault somebody. This sort of behavior has to be controlled; it has to be discouraged; it has to be *stopped.* This (to the scientist) is a matter of public safety and amicable coexistence, not of justice." Menninger, *Man Against Himself* (New York: Harcourt, Brace, 1938), p. 69. Emphasis in the original. See also Menninger's *The Human Mind* (New York: Literary Guild of America, 1930): "The declaration continues about travesties upon *justice* that result from the introduction of psychiatric methods into courts. What science or scientist is interested in *justice?* Is pneumonia just? Or cancer? . . . The scientist is seeking the amelioration of an unhappy situation. This can be secured only if the scientific laws controlling the situation can be discovered and complied with, not by talking of 'justice'" (p. 428). Emphasis in the original.
27. C. S. Lewis, "The Humanitarian Theory of Punishment," p. 230.
28. See James Robison and Gerald Smith, "The Effectiveness of Correctional Programs," *Crime and Delinquency* 17, no. 1 (January 1971): 67-80: "Analysis of findings in a review of the major California correctional programs that permit relatively rigorous evaluation strongly suggests the following conclusion: *There is no evidence to support any program's claim of superior rehabilitative efficacy"* (p. 10). Emphasis in the original. Robison

and Smith summarize their discussion of the effectiveness of various correctional programs as follows: "The single answer, then, to each of the five questions originally posed—Will the clients act differently if we lock them up, or keep them locked up longer, or do something with them inside, or watch them more closely afterward, or cut them loose officially?'—is 'Probably not'" (p. 80). See also Robert Martinson, "What Works? Questions and Answers about Prison Reform," *Public Interest,* no. 35 (Spring 1974), pp. 22-54.
29. *Science* 179 (January 1973): 250-257.
30. Ibid., p. 253
31. Ibid.
32. Only two justifications seem at all compatible: retribution and specific deterrence. On this, however, more later.
33. National Advisory Commission on Criminal Justice Standards and Goals, *Report on Corrections* (Washington, D.C.: Government Printing Office, 1973), p. 2. It should be stressed that the whole thrust of the definition is toward the reformation or correction of the offender. It ignores altogether the need to correct the havoc the offender has played on the victim of his criminal wrongdoing.
34. James S. Campbell, Joseph R. Sahid, and David P. Stang, *Law and Order Reconsidered,* a staff report to the National Commission on the Causes and Prevention of Violence (Washington, D.C.: Government Printing Office, 1969), p. 572.
35. Ibid. See also Gerald Leinwand, *Prisons* (New York: Pocket Books, 1972).
36. Of that number, 181,534 were confined in state institutions and 22,815 were in prison in federal institutions. Male prisoners far outnumber female prisoners, accounting for about 97 percent of the entire inmate population. As of December 31, 1973, there were 197,665 male inmates and only 6,684 female inmates in state and federal correctional institutions in the United States. National Criminal Justice Information and Statistics Service, *Prisoners in State and Federal Institutions on December 31, 1971, 1972, and 1973,* Law Enforcement Assistance Administration, U.S. Department of Justice (Washington, D.C.: Government Printing Office, 1975), pp. 12, 14, 16.
37. *Crime in the United States—Uniform Crime Reports—1974,* U.S. Department of Justice (Washington, D.C.: Government Printing Office, 1975), p. 49.
38. Chief Justice Warren E. Burger, "No Man is an Island," an address at the Mid-Winter Meeting of the American Bar Association, Atlanta, February, 1970.
39. Martin A. Levin, "Urban Politics and Policy Outcomes: The Criminal Courts," in *Criminal Justice,* ed. George F. Cole (Belmont, Calif.: Duxbury Press, 1972), p. 335.

40. Dean V. Babst and John W. Mannering, "Probation Versus Imprisonment for Similar Types of Offenders," *Journal of Research in Crime and Delinquency* 2 (July 1965): 61.
41. Peter W. Greenwood et al., *Prosecution of Adult Felony Defendants in Los Angeles County: A Policy Perspective* (Santa Monica, Calif.: RAND, 1973), p. 109.
42. Wilson, *Thinking About Crime,* p. 165.
43. Murphy, "Three Mistakes About Retributivism," p. 166.
44. *Crime in the United States—Uniform Crime Reports—1974,* p. 55.
45. Wilson, *Thinking About Crime,* p. 173.
46. Ibid., p. 172.
47. Robert Martinson, "What Works? Questions and Answers About Prison Reform," *The Public Interest,* no. 35 (Spring 1974), p. 25. See also R. G. Hood, "Research on the Effectiveness of Punishments and Treatments," in *Crime and Justice,* vol. 3, *The Criminal in Confinement,* ed. Leon Radzinowicz and Marvin E. Wolfgang (New York: Basic Books, 1971), pp. 159-182; Walter C. Bailey, "Correctional Outcome: An Evaluation of One Hundred Reports," in *Crime and Justice,* vol. 3, *The Criminal in Confinement,* ed. Radzinowicz and Wolfgang, who declares: "Evidence supporting the efficacy of correctional treatment is slight, inconsistent, and of questionable reliability" (p. 190); and Leslie T. Wilkins, *Evaluation of Penal Measures* (New York: Random House, 1969), who concludes that "the major achievement of research in the field of social psychology and treatment has been negative and has resulted in the undermining of nearly all the current mythology regarding the effectiveness of treatment in any form" (p. 78).
48. See Wilson, *Thinking About Crime,* p. 201. This is not to minimize the importance of length of sentence. Too often a short stay in prison simply teaches the criminal new tricks and provides him with plenty of time to use them on the public. Moreover, because the rate of index crime begins to decrease after age 23 (see Table 6.5), longer sentences may be useful in confining those who have already been convicted of serious crimes during the very period in which they are most likely to commit additional offenses.

Table 6.5 Peak Arrest Rate Ages for Index Crimes

Offense	Peak arrest rate age
Nonnegligent homicide	23
Forcible rape	18
Robbery	18
Aggravated assault	22
Burglary	16
Larceny	16
Auto theft	16

CORRECTIONS

49. Shlomo Shinnar and Reuel Shinnar, "The Effects of the Criminal Justice System on the Control of Crime: A Quantitative Approach," *Law and Society Review* 9, no. 4 (Summer 1975): 581-611.
50. It must be stressed that the proposal to make incapacitation—that is, specific deterrence—and retribution the operative principles of the criminal justice system does not mean that efforts at rehabilitation must be scrapped. Abandoning the theory that the governing purpose of the correctional enterprise is rehabilitation does not mean abandoning efforts at rehabilitation itself.
51. Paul Eidelberg, *A Discourse on Statesmanship: The Design and Transformation of the American Polity* (Urbana: University of Illinois Press, 1974), p. 27.
52. Wilson, *Thinking About Crime,* p. 177.
53. *Report on Corrections,* p. 223.
54. Ibid., p. 221.
55. Ibid., pp. 231-232. See also National Council on Crime and Delinquency, *Policies and Background Information* (Hackensack, N.J.: NCCD, 1972), p. 15.
56. See *Report on Corrections,* p. 222.
57. "Life in prison is very dangerous. Many inmates' predatory instincts are not neutralized merely by incarceration. Their aggression is simply transferred from civil society to prison society. Although prisons have always been dangerous, they are becoming increasingly so, as judges continue to send to prison a lower and lower percentage of first offenders and nonviolent criminals." Alan E. Bent and Ralph A. Rossum, *Police, Criminal Justice, and the Community* (New York: Harper & Row, 1976), p. 152. See Allen J. Davis, "Report on Sexual Assaults in the Philadelphia Prison System and Sheriff's Vans," in *Crime and Justice,* vol. 3, *The Criminal in Confinement,* ed. Radzinowicz and Wolfgang, pp. 141-146.
58. The failure of rehabilitative efforts to reduce rates of recidivism has, of course, already been considered and will be addressed again below.
59. President's Commission on Law Enforcement and Administration of Justice, *The Challenge of Crime in a Free Society* (Washington, D.C.: Government Printing Office, 1967), pp. vii, 170.
60. Vernon Fox, *Introduction to Corrections* (Englewood Cliffs, N.J.: Prentice-Hall, 1972), p. 104.
61. There are two difficulties with this emphasis on normative power, however. To begin with, it must be granted that not every offender is capable of responding well simply to normative power. As Norval Morris, dean of the University of Chicago Law School, once rather bitterly commented, correctional success would be much easier to achieve "if we had a better class of people to deal with." Quoted by Chief Justice Warren E. Burger in "We Refuse to be Responsible for the People We Imprison." Secondly,

even community-based corrections may involve the simultaneous presence of especially remunerative and normative compliance structures. Thus, if offenders are treated in the community rather than incarcerated in prison because, as was discussed above, it is so much more economical, or because the prisons are filled to capacity, these prudential but altogether calculative considerations are likely to diminish the overall effectiveness of normative power in achieving the desired correctional objectives.

62. Some would even go so far as to seek to "minimize the penetration" of the offender into any stage of the entire criminal justice system through a liberal use of pretrial diversion. This will be taken up in some detail below.
63. Judges follow the probation officers' recommendations in presentence investigation reports about 95 percent of the time. Fox, *Introduction to Corrections*, p. 109.
64. Ibid., p. 106.
65. Because the enforcement functions of probation must obviously rely to some extent on the use or the threat of coercive power, probation must also deal with the problem of the simultaneous presence of mutually exclusive compliance structures.
66. Fox, *Introduction to Corrections*, p. 104.
67. Martinson, "What Works?" p. 47.
68. Ibid., p. 48. See also Thomas J. Cook and Frank P. Scioli, Jr., "Volunteer Program Effectiveness: The Reduction of Recidivism" (Paper delivered at the Southwest Political Science Association, San Antonio, Texas, March 1975), who are in general agreement with the findings of Martinson.
69. Robison and Smith, "The Effectiveness of Correctional Programs," p. 69.
70. Martinson, "What Works?" p. 44. Emphasis in the original. See Robison and Smith, "The Effectiveness of Correctional Programs," who stress that "the important point" of all this "is that an ideological belief in the effectiveness of community treatment apparently altered the experimental results" (p. 69).
71. Campbell et al., *Law and Order Reconsidered*, p. 573.
72. Ibid.
73. According to the President's Commission on Law Enforcement and Administration of Justice, probation officers with over 100 cases are responsible for approximately 76 percent of all misdemeanor cases and 67 percent of all felony cases. *The Challenge of Crime in a Free Society*, p. 169.
74. Ibid., p. 167. The National Advisory Commission stressed the importance of considering "work loads, not case loads," in determining staff requirements. Therefore, it proposed that specific tasks should be "identified, measured for time required to accomplish the task, and translated into numbers of staff members needed." *Report on Corrections*, p. 319.
75. Robison and Smith, "The Effectiveness of Correctional Programs," pp. 76-77; see also Stuart Adams, "Some Findings From Correctional Case

Load Research," *Federal Probation* 31, no. 4 (December 1967): 48-57.
76. Martinson, "What Works?" p. 47. Emphasis in the original.
77. Marvin E. Frankel, *Criminal Sentences: Law Without Order* (New York: Hill & Wang, 1973), p. 27.
78. 339 U.S. 56 (1950). Mr. Justice Frankfurter dissenting.
79. See Chapter 2.
80. Tullock, "Does Punishment Deter Crime?", p. 109.
81. Martinson, "What Works?" p. 23.
82. Ibid.
83. Ibid., pp. 37, 48.
84. *Attorney General's Survey of Release Procedures* (Washington, D.C.: Government Printing Office, 1939), 4: 4.
85. The percentage of offenders released by parole from federal prisons is considerably lower. In that same year, of the 12,380 persons released, only 6,974 or 56 percent were released by parole. *National Prisoner Statistics: Prisoners in State and Federal Institutions on December 31, 1971, 1972, and 1973,* Federal Bureau of Prisons, U.S. Department of Justice (Washington, D.C.: Government Printing Office, 1975), p. 25.
86. Edwin H. Sutherland and Donald R. Cressey, *Criminology,* 8th ed. (Philadelphia: Lippincott, 1970), pp. 584-585.
87. *California Prisoners,* 1967 (Sacramento: California Department of Corrections, 1968), p. 83.
88. Michael J. Hindelang et al., *Sourcebook of Criminal Justice Statistics, 1973,* Law Enforcement Assistance Administration, U.S. Department of Justice (Washington, D.C.: Government Printing Office, 1973), p. 428.
89. See Sheldon Glueck and Eleanor Glueck, *Five Hundred Criminal Careers* (Cambridge, Mass.: Harvard University Press, 1930); *Later Criminal Careers* (New York: Commonwealth Fund, 1937); and *Criminal Careers in Retrospect* (New York: Commonwealth Fund, 1943).
90. National Advisory Commission on Criminal Justice Standards and Goals, *Report on Courts* (Washington, D.C.: Government Printing Office, 1973), p. 27.
91. For a further discussion of the uses of pretrial diversion, see Roger Baron, Floyd Feeney, and Warren Thorton, "Preventing Delinquency Through Diversion: The Sacramento County 601 Diversion Project," *Federal Probation* 37, no. 1 (March 1973): 13-18.
92. See Robert M. Carter, "The Diversion of Offenders," *Federal Probation* 36, no. 4 (December 1972): 31-36.
93. See Arthur Niederhoffer, "Criminal Justice by Dossier: Law Enforcement, Labeling, and Liberty," in *Current Perspectives on Criminal Behavior: Original Essays on Criminology,* ed. Blumberg, pp. 47-67.
94. Bent and Rossum, *Police, Criminal Justice, and the Community,* pp. 151-154, 178-180.

95. Gerhard O. W. Mueller and H. H. A. Cooper, *The Criminal, Society, and the Victim,* Law Enforcement Assistance Administration, U.S. Department of Justice, Selected Topic Digest no. 2 (Washington, D.C.: Government Printing Office, 1973), p. 7.
96. See Donald M. McIntyre, *Criminal Justice in the United States,* rev. ed. (Chicago: American Bar Foundation, 1974), pp. 45-46. See also Joan Mullen, *The Dilemma of Diversion,* U.S. Department of Justice (Washington, D.C.: U.S. Government Printing Office, 1975), pp. 23-27.
97. *Report on Courts,* p. 29.
98. Packer, *The Limits of the Criminal Sanction,* p. 46.
99. Sidney Hook, "The Rights of the Victims: Thoughts on Crime and Compassion," *Encounter* 38, no. 4 (April 1972): 12.
100. Ibid., p. 13.

Bibliography

Allen, Francis A. *The Borderland of Criminal Justice.* Chicago: University of Chicago Press, 1964.

Chauncey, Robert. "Deterrence: Certainty, Severity, and Skyjacking." *Criminology* 12, no. 4 (February 1975): 447-473.

Cohen, Morris R. "Moral Aspects of the Criminal Law." *Yale Law Journal* 49 (April 1940): 1009-1026.

Ehrlich, Isaac. "The Deterrent Effect of Capital Punishment: A Question of Life and Death." *The American Economic Review* 65, no. 3 (June 1975): 397-417.

——. "The Deterrent Effect of Criminal Law Enforcement." *The Journal of Legal Studies* 1, no. 2 (June 1972): 259-276.

Fox, Vernon. *Introduction to Corrections.* Englewood Cliffs, N.J.: Prentice-Hall, 1972.

Goldberg, Steven. "On Capital Punishment." *Ethics* 85, no. 1 (October 1974): 67-74.

Hook, Sidney. "The Rights of the Victims: Thoughts on Crime and Compassion." *Encounter* 38, no. 4 (April 1972): 11-15.

Kaplan, John. *Criminal Justice: Introductory Cases and Materials.* Mineola, N.Y.: Foundation Press, 1973.

Leinwand, Gerald. *Prisons.* New York: Pocket Books, 1972.

Lewis, C. S. "The Humanitarian Theory of Punishment." *Res Judicatae* 6 (1953): 224-230.

Martinson, Robert. "What Works? Questions and Answers About Prison Reform." *The Public Interest,* no. 35 (Spring 1974), pp. 22-54.

Mueller, Gerhard O. W., and Cooper, H. H. A. *The Criminal, Society, and The Victim.* Washington, D.C.: Government Printing Office, 1973.

Mullen, Joan. *The Dilemma of Diversion.* Washington, D.C.: Government Printing Office, 1975.

Murphy, Jeffrey. "Three Mistakes About Retributivism." *Analysis 31* (April 1971).

National Advisory Commission on Criminal Justice Standards and Goals. *Report on Corrections.* Washington, D.C.: Government Printing Office, 1973.

Packer, Herbert. *The Limits of the Criminal Sanction.* Stanford, Calif.: Stanford University Press, 1968.

Plattner, Marc F. "The Rehabilitation of Punishment." *The Public Interest,* no. 44 (Summer 1976), pp. 104-116.

President's Commission on Law Enforcement and Administration of Justice. *The Challenge of Crime in a Free Society.* Washington, D.C.: Government Printing Office, 1967.

Radzinowicz, Leon, and Wolfgang, Marvin E., eds. *Crime and Justice,* vol. 2, *The Criminal in the Arms of the Law.* New York: Basic Books, 1971.

—— *Crime and Justice,* vol. 3, *The Criminal in Confinement.* New York: Basic Books, 1971.

Robison, James, and Smith, Gerald. "The Effectiveness of Correctional Programs," *Crime and Delinquency* 17, no. 1 (January 1971): 67-80.

Rosenhan, D. L. "On Being Sane in Insane Places." *Science,* 179 (January 1973): 250-257.

Rottenberg, Simon, ed. *The Economics of Crime and Punishment.* Washington, D.C.: American Enterprise Institute for Public Policy Research, 1973.

"Statistical Evidence on the Deterrent Effect of Capital Punishment," *Yale Law Journal* 85, no. 2 (December 1975): 164-227.

Szasz, Thomas S. "Crime, Punishment, and Psychiatry." In *Current Perspectives on Criminal Behavior: Original Essays on Criminology,* edited by Abraham S. Blumberg. New York: Knopf, 1974.

Tullock, Gordon. "Does Punishment Deter Crime?" *The Public Interest,* no. 36 (Summer 1974), pp. 103-111.

van den Haag, Ernest. *Punishing Criminals: Concerning a Very Old and Painful Question.* New York: Basic Books, 1975.

Wilson, James Q. *Thinking About Crime.* New York: Basic Books, 1975.

7
CRIMINAL JUSTICE IN THE AMERICAN "COMMERCIAL" REPUBLIC: AN ASSESSMENT

The preceding chapters have introduced compliance analysis to the study of the criminal justice system. They have explored not only the three kinds of power (coercive, remunerative, and normative) that an organization can employ to control its lower participants but also the three kinds of reaction (alienative, calculative, and moral) that these lower participants can have to the employment of this power. They have stressed the importance of congruent compliance relationships, so that the kind of power that is employed by an organization tends to coincide with the kind of involvement of its lower participants. Finally, they have employed this analytical framework to undertake a systematic examination to the entire criminal justice system.

To begin with, compliance analysis has been used to explain the many interface or interrelationship problems that exist among the components of the criminal justice system. Each of these components relies upon a different kind of power—the police upon coercion, the courts upon normative power, and corrections upon remuneration. When these components are required to interact with one another, as they must do, the dominant power of one component begins to compete with the dominant power of another, vitiates its strength, and, thereby, diminishes its ability to meet the challenges before it. Intense interface conflict is an inevitable consequence.

Second, compliance analysis has been utilized to help explain the overall failure of the criminal justice system. This has been accomplished in large part by shifting levels of analysis and focusing on each component individually. By so doing, it has been shown that all three components are finding it increasingly necessary to employ simultaneously more than one kind of power, thereby neutralizing the potency of each. Police, through their redefinition of police work to include social service and police advocacy roles; courts, through their embrace of plea bargaining and the calculative crime control model; and correctional personnel, through their contemporaneous efforts at retribution, deterrence, and rehabilitation; all are equally affected by this internal incongruence.

Third, compliance analysis has been used to help explain why the criminal justice system has come to operate almost exclusively on crime control principles. The intense positive (moral) involvement stimulated by the criminal justice system's use of normative power and the intense negative (alienative) involvement prompted by its contemporaneous reliance on coercive power end up cancelling out each other. The result is an orientation in many defendants that is either of low positive or low negative intensity—the very definition of calculative involvement. The entire criminal justice system comes to be viewed and to view itself as a commercial enterprise wherein remunerative compliance relationships supplant normative and coercive ones. At this juncture, plea bargaining, the calculative crime control model, and administrative efficiency emerge as crucial considerations. The tragic consequences of all of this have been powerfully described by James Q. Wilson: "We have trifled with the wicked, made sport of the innocent, and encouraged the calculators. Justice suffers, and so do we all."[1]

Finally, compliance analysis has been employed to help provide a realistic appraisal of the criminal justice system and the prospects for reform of each of its components. Thus, it has suggested that efforts by the police to generate greater moral involvement on the part of the community (that is, to enhance police-community relations) through the employment of normative power and the assumption of social service and police advocacy roles are likely to fail as long as the police must also employ coercive power in order to carry out their traditional law enforcement and order maintenance roles. Its assessment of the prospects for an elimination of plea bargaining in the criminal justice system is also to the point. It suggests that so long as the specter of "system overload" remains and so long as the politics of complicity continues unabated, shortcuts by judicial personnel will be taken, due process will be frustrated, and the substantial discrepancy that exists in the lower courts between what the Supreme Court says ought to occur and what in fact does occur will continue. The appraisal of the correctional enterprise is equally realistic. It suggests that until some agreement on the purpose of corrections and the kind of power it will employ is reached, correctional agencies will continue to be ineffectual, recidivism rates will remain at approximately 65 percent, and James Q. Wilson's proposal that criminals be simply isolated and punished may well be the most practical and appropriate way of reducing the crime rates.

Thus, compliance analysis suggests that the prospects for reform are remote and that incongruity and ineffectiveness will continue. Plea bargaining, the crime control model, administrative efficiency, and other remunerative-calculative compliance relationships will prevail. Two factors significantly contribute to this. The first has already been considered in this chapter and does not need to be elaborated upon here: It pertains to the manner in which the intense positive involvement stimulated by the criminal justice system's use of normative power and the intense negative involvement prompted by its simultaneous reliance on coercive power end up cancelling each other out, leaving only a calculative involvement in the lower participants, that is, an involvement of either low positive or low negative intensity. The second factor has not yet been taken up, but will be at this time: It pertains to the essentially "commercial" nature of the American regime. Stated in terms of compliance analysis, the likelihood of the criminal justice system breaking free from the use of remunerative-calculative compliance structures is remote, for the entire American system is fundamentally committed to the use of remunerative power.

America: The Commercial Republic

As noted in Chapter 2, the United States is essentially a "commercial" republic. It relies almost exclusively on calculation and what Tocqueville has called the "principle of self-interest rightly understood."[2] Instead of employing coercion or normative power to govern its citizens, it "checks one personal interest by another, and uses, to direct the passions, the very same instrument that excites them."[3] For the consequences of these arrangements on the criminal justice system to be fully appreciated, the foundations of this "commercial" republic must be briefly explored.[4]

When the founding generation surveyed the inhabitants of America, they found them to be "too proud for monarchy, yet too poor for nobility, and it is to be feared, too selfish and avaricious for a virtuous republic."[5] They faced a crucial problem: How could good and decent government be established and sustained by such men? The government would have to be a republic, the "genius" of the American people would permit nothing less.[6] But, how could a republican government composed of such "selfish and avaricious" men be rendered safe and secure? The answer of the framers of the U.S. Constitution was simple: They set about to establish a commercial, as opposed to a virtuous, republic.[7]

The founders of the American commercial republic regarded mankind as "ambitious, rapacious, and vindictive."[8] They understood men to be driven by self-interest[9] and consumed by the desire for distinction and the love of honor.[10] They considered men's passions for "power and advantage"[11] to be so powerful and basic that it would be unrealistic—nay, in fact, "folly"—to expect to control them adequately by traditional republican reliance on "pure patriotism,"[12] respect for character,[13] conscience or religion,[14] or even the not very lofty maxim that "honesty is the best policy."[15] For the founding generation, such "remote considerations of policy, utility, or justice" could never provide adequate control over man's monetary passions and immediate interests.[16] If these "weaker springs of the human character"[17] were to be relied upon, human nature's "lust for power"[18] and proclivity towards avarice[19] would prevail and divide mankind into parties, inflame them with mutual animosity, and render them much more disposed to oppose each other than to cooperate for their common good. As *The Federalist* observed, this propensity for mankind to fall into mutual animosities is so powerful "that where no substantial occasion presents itself, the most frivolous and fanciful distinctions have been sufficient to kindle their unfriendly passions and excite their most violent conflicts."[20] Thus, man is predictable in such matters: He will have his factions, whether or not there are readily apparent reasons for them. His passions will, as a consequence, often lead him in ways inconsistent with "the dictates of reason and justice."[21] In fact, his reason will often end up in the service of his passions, providing him with arguments for self-indulgence rather than with incentives to virtue.[22]

Given this view of human nature, the founders of the American commercial republic made little effort to improve mankind through moral reformation or regeneration.[23] They considered any government built upon the assumption of such improvement to be erected upon the sands.[24] Likewise, they placed little confidence in the continued presence of "enlightened statesmen."[25] Rather, they sought to design institutions that would depend upon "the ordinary depravity of human nature."[26] They followed the sage advice of Alexander Hamilton, when he declared in the New York State Constitutional Ratifying Convention: "Men will pursue their interests. It is as easy to change human nature as to oppose the strong current of selfish passions. A wise legislator will gently divert the channel, and direct it, if possible, to the public good."[27] Thus, they sought to design mechanical devices and institutional contrivances that would not attempt to block or dam these interests or transform them, but to direct and channel them through the process of mutual checking. As Gouverneur Morris insisted, "The vices as they exist, must be turned against each other."[28] In so doing, they established an essentially commercial republic, a republic that through mutual checking and a reliance on man's natural inclination to follow his own "sober second thoughts of self interest"[29] provided "Republican remed[ies] for the diseases most incident to Republican Government."[30]

The Need For Realism

The founding generation's establishment of a commercial republic has had pervasive and profound consequences for America and for its criminal justice system. Most significantly, it has subjected them to the mixed blessings that accompany commerce. Montesquieu perspicaciously captured this ambiguity when he declared: "Commercial laws, it may be said, improve manners for the same reason that they destroy them. They corrupt the purest morals . . . and we see every day that they polish and refine the most barbarous."[31]

Commerce can indeed "polish and refine the most barbarous" aspects of humanity. It requires that a man be disciplined in the habits of "frugality, economy, moderation, labor, prudence, tranquility, order and rule."[32] These habits, as Tocqueville has observed, "render men independent of one another, give them a lofty notion of their personal importance, lead them to seek to conduct their own affairs, and teach how to conduct them well." They may not be sufficient by themselves "to make men virtuous," but they are powerful enough to "draw them in that direction."[33] However, as Montesquieu went on to stress, commerce can also "corrupt the purest morals." It encourages men to seek only "those petty and paltry pleasures with which they glut their lives." And, although commerce may render men independent, it often renders them too independent, so that they become isolated, alienated, atomized. Tocqueville has explored the consequences for men preoccupied with self-interest:

> Each of them, living apart, is as a stranger to the fate of all the rest; his children and his private friends constitute to him the whole of mankind. As for the rest of his fellow citizens, he is close to them, but does not see them; he touches them, but does not feel them; he exists only in himself and for himself alone; and if his kindred still remain to him, he may be said at any rate to have lost his country.[34]

Thus, the founding generation's commitment to commercial principles has curiously suspended the American regime—its criminal justice system included—in a remunerative-calculative no-man's-land. Vibrating between purity and barbarity, between an attraction to normative power on the one hand and a necessary embrace of coercion on the other, the American commercial republic has managed to convert even matters of principle (or justice) into matters of interest that are subject to bargaining and negotiation.[35] Definite advantages have resulted from the operation of these commercial principles. Perhaps most importantly, the American regime has enjoyed an absence of strident and ideological politics.[36] Because compromise between competing interests is much easier than between opposing principles, American politics has been characterized by tolerance and an ungrudging acknowledgement of the right of opposing interests to exist and be pursued.[37] This advantage has also been present in the criminal justice system as well, which is noticeably free of inquisitorial zeal.

However, as one would expect when dealing with the question of commerce—especially in light of Montesquieu's observations— the advantages that have resulted from this interest-based politics have not been unqualified; they have been offset in part by a number of disadvantages. To begin with, in its contemporary manifestation,[38] it has led to an increase in the exercise of discretion—with problems for the American regime no less than for its criminal justice system. Because it is anxious to allow each person the greatest opportunity to pursue his own self-interest, it has been reluctant to formulate laws or programs with much detail or specificity. Rather, it has preferred delegation of power to definition by law. The exercise of this discretionary authority has in turn helped to destroy political responsibility, often with untoward consequences.[39] In the criminal justice system, for example, the vast discretionary authority of the police has led to efforts to impose greater community control and, in response, to further politicization and fraternalization of the police.

THE AMERICAN "COMMERCIAL" REPUBLIC 269

With the widespread discretion and the greater political independence that the principles of the American commercial republic have been instrumental in providing, the likelihood for substantial reform has been adversely affected. As Paul Robert Wolff has observed, these principles "systematically favor the interests of the stronger against the weaker parties . . . and tend to solidify the power of those who already hold it."[40] This is also apparent in the criminal justice system, where efforts to introduce in police departments criteria of effectiveness as well as efficiency have been frustrated by the dominant rewards structure that finds it easier to evaluate police performance on the basis of such quantitative data as arrest records than through an assessment of such qualitative evidence as citizen satisfaction and community support. The politics of complicity that exists in the lower courts also reflects this problem. The self-interest that has resulted in an abandonment of due process and an introduction of the techniques of the crime control model has subsequently sought to implicate the entire bureaucratic matrix in its operation; it has thereby effectively frustrated all efforts at reform, including those reforms designed to alleviate the need for such techniques in the first place. Corrections, too, is affected by this problem. Thus, despite growing evidence that rehabilitation does not work, correctional personnel remain committed to this dominant philosophy and to the use of community-based corrections. Moreover, as Robert Martinson has pointed out, on occasion they have even attempted to suppress this growing body of damaging evidence.[41]

Finally, this interest-based politics has still another disadvantage: When carried to extremes, it makes conflict of interest a principle of government rather than a criminal act.[42] As Tocqueville has indicated, a preoccupation with self-interest enervates the soul and weakens any commitment to the common good. It contributes to a certain narrowness, a certain moral and political myopia. In the criminal justice system, it exacerbates interface or interrelationship problems among police, courts, and corrections and renders cooperation among them all the more problematic.

As is apparent, the criminal justice system is by no means immune to the commercial spirit that flourishes in America; as a consequence, plea bargaining and the calculative crime control model, administrative efficiency as measured on a cost-per-unit basis, the politics of complicity, and interface conflict among police, courts, and corrections are perhaps inevitable. Those who would reform the criminal justice system must acknowledge this reality, if their proposals are not to be wrecked on the shoals of frustration and despair. They must recognize that it is a part of a regime in which there is operative in "the whole system of human affairs, private as well as public" a "policy of supplying by opposite and rival interests, the defect of better motives."[43] The dominant presence of remunerative-calculative compliance relationships within the criminal justice system is not likely to be fundamentally altered until the American commercial republic is.

Notes

1. James Q. Wilson, *Thinking About Crime* (New York: Basic Books, 1975), p. 209.
2. Alexis de Tocqueville, *Democracy in America*, ed. Phillips Bradley, 2 vols. (New York: Random House, 1945), 2: 130.
3. Ibid., p. 131.
4. For a fuller elaboration of these themes, see Ralph A. Rossum, "The Foundations of the American Commercial Republic," in *The Non-Lockean Roots of American Democratic Thought*, ed. J. Chaudhuri (Tucson: University of Arizona Press, 1977), pp. 30-43, 66-71.
5. Mercy Warren, *History of the Rise, Progress, and Termination of the American Revolution* (Boston: 1805), 3:370.
6. Thus, Edmund Randolph of Virginia declared: "We had, he said, no motive to be governed by the British government as our prototype. He did not mean however to throw censure on the Excellent fabric. If we were in a situation to copy it he did not know that he should be opposed to it; but the fixt genius of the people of America required a different form of government." Max Farrand, ed., *The Records of the Federal Convention of 1787* (New Haven, Conn.: Yale University Press, 1937), 1: 66 (hereafter cited as Farrand). See also John Dickinson of Delaware: "A limited Monarchy he considered as one of the best governments in the world. It was certain that equal blessings had never yet been derived from any of the republican form. A limited monarchy, however, was out of the question. The spirit of the time—the state of our affairs, forbade the experiment, if it were desirable." Farrand, 1: 87; and James Wilson of Pennsylvania: "The British government cannot be our model. We have no materials for a similar one. Our manners, our laws, the abolition of entails, and of primogeniture, the whole genius of the people are opposed to it." Farrand, 1: 153.
7. As Noah Webster declared: "The system of the great Montesquieu will ever be erroneous," until the words property and self-interest "are substituted for virtue, throughout his *Spirit of Laws.*" Noah Webster, "An Examination into the Leading Principles of the Federal Constitution," in *Pamphlets on the Constitution of the United States,* ed. Paul Leicester Ford (Brooklyn, N.Y.: Historical Printing Club, 1888), p. 59.
8. Alexander Hamilton, James Madison, and John Jay, *The Federalist,* ed. Jacob E. Cooke (New York: World, 1961), No. 6, p. 28. (All subsequent references to *The Federalist* are to this edition.)
9. Ibid., No. 10, p. 59.
10. See Gouverneur Morris's comments in the Federal Convention of 1787, Farrand 1: 53. See also Gordon S. Wood, *The Creation of the American Republic, 1776-1887* (Chapel Hill: The University of North Carolina Press, 1969), p. 574.

11. *Federalist* No. 15, p. 97.
12. See Alexander Hamilton, Farrand, 1: 276.
13. See James Madison, Farrand, 1: 134.
14. Ibid. See also *Federalist* No. 10, p. 61.
15. See Madison, Farrand, 1: 134.
16. *Federalist* No. 6, p. 31.
17. Ibid., No. 34, p. 212.
18. Ibid., No. 63, pp. 426-427.
19. Ibid., No. 30, p. 193.
20. Ibid., No. 10, p. 59.
21. Ibid., No. 15, p. 96.
22. Ibid., No. 42, p. 283; No. 48, p. 334. Yet, *The Federalist* continues, although reason "is timid and cautious when left alone," it is existent, nonetheless. *Federalist* No. 49, p. 340. With adequate institutional assistance, it can ensure that the "cool and deliberative sense" of the public will ultimately prevail. *Federalist* No. 63, p. 425. Perhaps the most unusual compliment the framers paid to the rationality of the public was in asking them to realize that all men are human, of limited capacity, and, consequently, prone to impulse and passion. See Benjamin F. Wright, *"The Federalist* on the Nature of Political Man," *Ethics* 59, no. 2 (January 1949): p. 28.
23. See Gottfried Dietze, *The Federalist: A Classic of Federalism in Free Government* (Baltimore: The Johns Hopkins University Press, 1960), p. 22; see also Wood, *The Creation of the American Republic*, pp. 428, 485.
24. See Wright, *"The Federalist* on the Nature of Political Man," p. 4.
25. *Federalist* No. 10, p. 60.
26. Ibid., No. 78, p. 530.
27. Jonathan Elliot, ed., *The Debates in the Several State Conventions on the Adoption of the Federal Constitution as Recommended by the General Convention at Philadelphia in 1787,* 2nd ed. (Philadelphia: Lippincott, 1863), 2: 320.
28. Farrand, 1: 512. *The Federalist* concurred: "Ambition must be made to counteract ambition." No. 51, p. 349.
29. The phrase is from Frederick Douglass, "Fourth of July Oration," in *What Country Have I? Political Writings by Black Americans,* ed. Herbert J. Storing (New York: St. Martin's Press, 1970), p. 40.
30. *Federalist* No. 10, p. 65.
31. Baron de Montesquieu, *The Spirit of the Laws,* trans. Thomas Nugent (New York: Hafner, 1949), bk. 10, chapt. 1, p. 316.
32. Ibid., bk. 5, chapt. 6, p. 46.
33. Tocqueville, *Democracy in America,* 2: 268, 131.
34. Ibid., 2: 336.

35. See Robert Paul Wolff, "Beyond Tolerance," in Robert Paul Wolff, Barrington Moore, Jr., and Herbert Marcuse, *A Critique of Pure Tolerance* (Boston: Beacon Press, 1969), p. 21.
36. For a further discussion of the advantages that have resulted from the operation of these commercial principles, see Alan E. Bent and Ralph A. Rossum, *Police, Criminal Justice, and the Community* (New York: Harper & Row, 1976), pp. 259-265.
37. The benefits that this more moderate politics provides are immediately apparent when one contrasts the stability of the American regime, with its willingness to treat even matters of principle as though they were conflicts of interest, with the instability of the French regime, with its penchant to regard conflicts of interest as matters of principle. See Wolff, "Beyond Tolerance," p. 21.
38. For a superb treatment of the contemporary manifestation of this interest-based politics, see Theodore J. Lowi's discussion of "interest group liberalism" in *The End of Liberalism: Ideology, Policy, and the Crisis of Public Authority* (New York: Norton, 1969). See also Grant McConnell, *Private Power and American Democracy* (New York: Knopf, 1967).
39. See Lowi, *The End of Liberalism*, pp. 85-93.
40. Wolff, "Beyond Tolerance," p. 46.
41. Robert Martinson, "What Works? Questions and Answers About Prison Reform," *The Public Interest*, no. 35 (Spring 1974), p. 23.
42. Lowi, *The End of Liberalism*, p. 86.
43. *Federalist* No. 51, p. 349.

Bibliography

Bent, Alan E., and Rossum, Ralph A. *Police, Criminal Justice, and the Community.* New York: Harper & Row, 1976.

Diamond, Martin, Fisk, Winston Mill, and Garfinkel, Herbert. *The Democratic Republic.* 2nd ed. Chicago: Rand McNally, 1970.

Elliot, Jonathan, ed. *The Debates in the Several State Conventions on the Adoption of the Federal Constitution.* 5 vols. 2nd ed. Philadelphia: Lippincott, 1863.

Farrand, Max, ed. *The Records of the Federal Convention of 1787.* 4 vols. New Haven, Conn.: Yale University Press, 1937.

Ford, Paul Leicester, ed. *Essays on the Constitution of the United States.* Brooklyn, N.Y.: Historical Printing Club, 1892.

——, ed. *Pamphlets on the Constitution of the United States.* Brooklyn, N.Y.: Historical Printing Club, 1888.

Hamilton, Alexander, Madison, James, and Jay, John. *The Federalist.* Edited by Jacob E. Cooke. New York: World, 1961.

Lowi, Theodore J. *The End of Liberalism: Ideology, Policy, and the Crisis of Public Authority.* New York: Norton, 1969.

McConnell, Grant. *Private Power and American Democracy.* New York: Knopf, 1967.

Rossum, Ralph A. "The Foundations of the American Commercial Republic." In *The Non-Lockean Roots of American Democratic Thought,* edited by J. Chaudhuri. Tucson: University of Arizona Press, 1977.

Tocqueville, Alexis de. *Democracy in America.* Edited by Phillips Bradley. 2 vols. New York: Random House, 1945.

Wolff, Robert Paul, Moore, Barrington, Jr., and Marcuse, Herbert. *A Critique of Pure Tolerance.* Boston: Beacon Press, 1969.

CASE INDEX

Abbate v. *United States,* 359 U.S. 187 (1959), 173n
Adams v. *Illinois,* 405 U.S. 278 (1972), 178n
Adamson v. *California,* 331 U.S. 46 (1947), 134, 165n
Aguilar v. *Texas,* 378 U.S. 108 (1964), 167n
Andreson v. *Maryland,* 96 S.Ct. 2737 (1976), 169n
Apodaca v. *Oregon,* 406 U.S. 404 (1972), 174n
Argersinger v. *Hamlin,* 407 U.S. 25 (1972), 124, 141
Ashe v. *Swenson,* 397 U.S. 436 (1970), 146
Associated General Contractors v. *Altshuler,* 490 F. 2d 9 (1973), 92
Atkins v. *Texas,* 325 U.S. 398 (1945), 148

Baldwin v. *New York,* 399 U.S. 66 (1970), 165n
Barber v. *Page,* 390 U.S. 719 (1968), 150
Barker v. *Wingo,* 407 U.S. 514 (1972), 147
Barron v. *Baltimore,* 7 Peters 243 (1833), 118, 119
Bartkus v. *Illinois,* 359 U.S. 121 (1959), 146
Baxter v. *Palmigiano,* 96 S.Ct. 1551 (1976), 63n
Benton v. *Maryland,* 395 U.S. 784 (1969), 124, 144, 146
Berch v. *Stahl,* 15 CrL 1022 (1974), 63n
Berger v. *United States,* 295 U.S. 78 (1935), 171n
Betts v. *Brady,* 316 U.S. 455 (1942), 140-141
Bivens v. *Six Unknown Named Agents,* 403 U.S. 388 (1971), 133
Blackledge v. *Perry,* 417 U.S. 21 (1974), 172n
Boykin v. *Alabama,* 395 U.S. 238 (1969), 213
Brady v. *United States,* 397 U.S. 742 (1970), 213
Breed v. *Jones,* 421 U.S. 519 (1975), 173n
Brinegar v. *United States,* 338 U.S. 160 (1949), 166n
Brown v. *Allen,* 344 U.S. 433 (1953), 158
Brown v. *Mississippi,* 297 U.S. 278 (1936), 135-136
Bruton v. *United States,* 391 U.S. 123 (1968), 150

Cardwell v. *Lewis,* 417 U.S. 583 (1974), 127, 166n
Carroll v. *United States,* 267 U.S. 132 (1925), 126-127

CASE INDEX

Chambers v. *Florida,* 309 U.S. 227 (1940), 136
Chambers v. *Maroney,* 399 U.S. 42 (1970), 126
Chimel v. *California,* 395 U.S. 752 (1969), 126, 129, 178n
Coffin v. *Reichard,* 143 F. 2d 443 (1944), 53
Cohen v. *Hurley,* 366 U.S. 117 (1961), 123, 165n
Cole v. *Arkansas,* 333 U.S. 196 (1948), 124
Coleman v. *Alabama,* 399 U.S. 1 (1970), 143, 178n
Cooper v. *California,* 386 U.S. 58 (1967), 166n
Coppedge v. *United States,* 369 U.S. 438 (1962), 162

Delli Paoli v. *United States,* 352 U.S. 232 (1957), 175n
Desist v. *United States,* 394 U.S. 244 (1969), 160-161, 178n
DeStefano v. *Woods,* 392 U.S. 631 (1968), 178n
Douglas v. *California,* 372 U.S. 353 (1963), 143, 157
Downey v. *Perini,* 17 CrL 2324 (1975), 175n
Doyle v. *Ohio,* 96 S. Ct. 2240 (1976), 170n
Duncan v. *Louisiana,* 391 U.S. 145 (1967), 120, 124, 164n, 173n, 178n

Ellison v. *United States,* 206 F. 2d 476 (1953), 166n
Escobedo v. *Illinois,* 378 U.S. 478 (1964), 136, 143, 161
Estes v. *Texas,* 381 U.S. 532 (1965), 119, 149, 164n
Eubanks v. *Louisiana,* 356 U.S. 584 (1958), 148

Faretta v. *California,* 422 U.S. 806 (1975), 142-143
Fay v. *New York,* 332 U.S. 261 (1947), 174n
Fay v. *Noia,* 372 U.S. 391 (1963), 158
Francis v. *Henderson,* 425 U.S. 536 (1976), 45n, 177n
Furman v. *Georgia,* 408 U.S. 238 (1972), 63n, 152-153, 155-156

Gates v. *Collier,* 16 CrL 2055 (1974), 54
Gideon v. *Wainwright,* 372 U.S. 335 (1963), 124, 141
Gilbert v. *California,* 388 U.S. 218 (1967), 143
Green v. *New Kent County,* 391 U.S. 430 (1968), 110n
Green v. *United States,* 335 U.S. 184 (1957), 172n
Gregg v. *Georgia,* 428 U.S. 153 (1976), 175-176n
Griffin v. *California,* 380 U.S. 609 (1965), 169n
Griffin v. *Illinois,* 351 U.S. 12 (1956), 157-158
Griggs v. *Duke Power Co.,* 401 U.S. 424 (1971), 91-92, 110n
Griswold v. *Connecticut,* 381 U.S. 479 (1965), 119, 122, 164n, 165n
Gustafson v. *Florida,* 414 U.S. 260 (1973), 128

Hamilton v. *Alabama,* 368 U.S. 52 (1961), 143
Harris v. *New York,* 401 U.S. 222 (1971), 138-139, 178n
Harris v. *United States,* 331 U.S. 145 (1947), 129
Harris v. *United States,* 390 U.S. 234 (1968), 126
Hoag v. *New Jersey,* 356 U.S. 464 (1958), 145
Holden v. *Hardy,* 169 U.S. 366 (1898), 119, 164n

CASE INDEX

Holt and *Sarver*, 309 F. Supp 362 (1970), 54
Hoyt v. *Florida*, 368 U.S. 57 (1961), 148, 174n
Hurtado v. *California*, 110 U.S. 516 (1884), 121, 124

Illinois v. *Allen*, 397 U.S. 337 (1970), 65n, 150
In re Gault, 387 U.S. 1 (1967), 162
In re Oliver, 333 U.S. 257 (1948), 124
In re Strum, 15 CrL 1030 (1974), 63n
Irvin v. *Dowd*, 366 U.S. 717 (1961), 149

Jackson v. *Indiana*, 406 U.S. 715 (1972), 54
James v. *United States*, 366 U.S. 213 (1961), 160
Johnson v. *Louisiana*, 406 U.S. 356 (1972), 150
Johnson v. *New Jersey*, 384 U.S. 719 (1966), 161
Johnson v. *Zerbst*, 304 U.S. 458 (1938), 140
Joint Anti-Fascist Refugee Committee v. *McGrath*, 341 U.S. 123 (1951), 164n
Jurek v. *Texas*, 428 U.S. 262 (1976), 175-176n

Katz v. *United States*, 389 U.S. 346 (1967), 126, 178n
Ker v. *California*, 374 U.S. 23 (1963), 167n
Klopfer v. *North Carolina*, 386 U.S. 213 (1967), 124
K.Q.E.D. v. *Houchins*, 18 CrL 2252 (1975), 63n

LeBatt v. *Twomey*, 16 CrL 2351 (1975), 63n
Lefkowitz v. *Newsome*, 420 U.S. 283 (1975), 215n, 217n
Linkletter v. *Walker*, 381 U.S. 618 (1965), 159-161, 219n
Lisemba v. *California*, 314 U.S. 219 (1941), 164n
Lynumn v. *Illinois*, 382 U.S. 528 (1963), 169n

McCarthy v. *United States*, 394 U.S. 459 (1969), 213
Mackey v. *United States*, 401 U.S. 667 (1971), 178n
Main Road v. *Aytch*, 17 CrL 2480 (1975), 63n
Malloy v. *Hogan*, 378 U.S. 1 (1964), 124, 135
Mapp v. *Ohio*, 361 U.S. 643 (1961), 51, 124, 130-132, 159, 160, 181, 182
Mempa v. *Rhay*, 389 U.S. 128 (1967), 143
Michigan v. *Payne*, 412 U.S. 47 (1973), 178n
Michigan v. *Tucker*, 417 U.S. 433 (1974), 138, 178n
Miranda v. *Arizona*, 384 U.S. 436 (1966), 51, 52, 135, 137, 139, 143, 161-162, 170n, 172n, 181-182
Morrissey v. *Brewer*, 408 U.S. 471 (1972), 54
Murray's Lessee v. *Hoboken Land and Improvement Co.*, 18 Howard 272 (1856), 120

Norris v. *Alabama*, 294 U.S. 587 (1935), 148
North Carolina v. *Pearce*, 395 U.S. 711 (1969), 144-145, 178n
Norwalk CORE v. *Norwalk Redevelopment Agency*, 395 F. 2d 920 (1968), 110n
Nunez v. *United States*, 370 F. 2d 538 (1967), 166n

On Lee v. *United States,* 343 U.S. 747 (1952), 166n
Oregon v. *Hass,* 420 U.S. 714 (1975), 138-139, 170n, 178n

P. v. *Wright,* 242 N.E. 2d 180 (1968), 166n
Paka v. *Manson,* 16 CrL 2256 (1974), 63n
Palko v. *Connecticut,* 302 U.S. 319 (1937), 119, 164n
People v. *Harmon,* 15 CrL 2425 (1974), 63n
People v. *Lovercamp,* 16 CrL 2375 (1975), 63n
Pointer v. *Texas,* 380 U.S. 400 (1965), 124, 150
Powell v. *Alabama,* 287 U.S. 45 (1932), 140-141, 143
Powell v. *Texas,* 392 U.S. 514 (1968), 152
Preston v. *United States,* 376 U.S. 364 (1964), 166n
Procunier v. *Martinez,* 416 U.S. 396 (1974), 54
Proffitt v. *Florida,* 428 U.S. 242 (1976), 175-176n

Rehm v. *Malcolm,* 14 CrL 1069 (1974), 63n
Rideau v. *Louisiana,* 373 U.S. 73 (1963), 149
Ristaino v. *Ross,* 96 S. Ct. 1017 (1976), 173n
Roberts v. *Louisiana,* 428 U.S. 325 (1976), 175-176n
Robinson v. *California,* 370 U.S. 660 (1962), 124, 151-152
Rochin v. *California,* 342 U.S. 165 (1952), 168n
Roe v. *Wade,* 410 U.S. 113 (1973), 19, 41
Rogers v. *Richmond,* 365 U.S. 532 (1961), 169n
Ross v. *Moffitt,* 417 U.S. 500 (1974), 157, 172n

Santo Bello v. *United States,* 404 U.S. 257 (1971), 213
Sheppard v. *Maxwell,* 384 U.S. 333 (1966), 149
Spano v. *New York,* 360 U.S. (1959), 169n
State ex rel Harvey v. *Knoxville,* 166 Tenn 550 (1933), 110n
Stone v. *Powell,* 428 U.S. 465 (1976), 45n, 168n, 177n
Stovall v. *Denno,* 388 U.S. 293 (1967), 178n
Strauder v. *West Virginia,* 100 U.S. 313 (1880), 148
Strunk v. *United States,* 412 U.S. 434 (1973), 173n
Swain v. *Alabama,* 380 U.S. 202 (1965), 148

Tate v. *Short,* 401 U.S. 395 (1971), 157, 176n, 207
Taylor v. *Louisiana,* 419 U.S. 522 (1974), 148, 174n
Terry v. *Ohio,* 392 U.S. 1 (1968), 127-128
Townsend v. *Sain,* 372 U.S. 293 (1963), 169n
Trop v. *Dulles,* 356 U.S. 86 (1958), 151, 165n
Twining v. *New Jersey,* 211 U.S. 78 (1908), 134-164n

United States v. *Calambra,* 414 U.S. 338 (1974), 134, 168n, 178n
United States v. *Edwards,* 415 U.S. 800 (1974), 128
United States v. *Hale,* 421 U.S. 171 (1975), 170n
United States v. *Jefferson County Board of Education,* 372 F. 2d 836 (1966), 110n

CASE INDEX

United States v. *Kim,* 19 CrL 2281 (1976), 166n
United States v. *Lanza,* 260 U.S. 377 (1922), 146
United States v. *Mandujano,* 96 S. Ct. 1768 (1976), 170n
United States v. *Marion,* 404 U.S. 307 (1971), 173n
United States v. *Rabinowitz,* 339 U.S. 56 (1950), 129, 247
United States v. *Robinson,* 414 U.S. 218 (1973), 128
United States v. *Swinton,* 18 CrL 2035 (1975), 171n
United States v. *Wade,* 388 U.S. 218 (1967), 143, 162, 178n
United States v. *Weir,* 15 CrL 2164 (1974), 168n
United States v. *Wilson,* 421 U.S. 309 (1975), 172n

Waller v. *Florida,* 397 U.S. 387 (1970), 146, 173n
Washington v. *Texas,* 388 U.S. 14 (1967), 124, 174n
Weeks v. *United States,* 232 U.S. 383 (1914), 130
Weems v. *United States,* 217 U.S. 349 (1910), 151
Wesberry v. *Sanders,* 376 U.S. 1 (1964), 122
Wilkerson v. *Utah,* 99 U.S. 130 (1879), 151
Williams v. *Florida,* 399 U.S. 78 (1970), 150
Williams v. *Illinois,* 399 U.S. 235 (1970), 157, 176n
Williams v. *United States,* 401 U.S. 646 (1971), 178n
Wolf v. *Colorado,* 338 U.S. 25 (1949), 130, 159-160
Wolff v. *McDonald,* 418 U.S. 539 (1974), 54
Woodson v. *North Carolina,* 428 U.S. 242 (1976), 175-176n

INDEX

A

Abernathy, M. Glenn, 139, 170n, 172n, 178
Abraham, Henry J., 164n, 166n, 170n, 174n, 179
Adams, Stuart, 260n
Aggravated assault, 7-10
Ahern, James F., 94, 108n, 111n, 113
Allen, Francis A., 231, 256n, 262
American "Commercial" republic, 61, 266-269
Amsterdam, Anthony, 168
Anderson, Stanley V., 107n
Ares, Charles E., 44n, 220n
Arraignment, 32
Arrest
    defined, 24
    police discretion in, 25-29
Atkins, Burton M., 193, 217n, 218n, 222
Austin, John, 199, 219n
Auto theft, 12-13

B

Babst, Dean V., 238, 258n
Bail
    bail bond, 30
    defined, 30
    reform, 203-210
Bailey, Walter C., 258n
Balch, Robert, 85, 108n, 113
Ball, Howard, 165n, 179

Ban, Michael, 181, 215n
Banfield, Edward C., 23, 42n, 46, 108n, 255n
Banton, Michael, 103n, 105n, 113
Barbour, George, 98, 112n, 113
Barnard, Chester I., 64n
Baron, Roger, 261n
Bayley, David H., 22-23, 42n, 46, 85, 102n, 108n, 113
Bazelon, David L., 220n
Becker, Theodore L., 60, 65n, 163, 178n, 179, 214-215n, 222
Bent, Alan E., 46, 65n, 66, 68, 83, 85, 101-106n, 108n, 112n, 113, 179, 218n, 220n, 222, 259n, 261n, 272n
Bentham, Jeremy, 199, 219n
Berger, Peter L., 22
Berns, Walter F., 20, 41n, 46
Bickel, Alexander, 183, 216n
Birkby, Robert H., 214n
Bish, Robert L., 96, 111n, 113
Black, Algernon D., 108n, 113
Black, Charles L., Jr., 179
Black, Justice Hugo, 120-123, 140, 144, 151, 160-161
Blackmore, Ray J., 72, 104n
Blackmun, Justice Harry A., 19, 127, 134, 139, 142-143, 155
Blackstone, Sir William, 198-199, 219n
Bloom, Allan, 41n
Blumberg, Abraham S., 3, 39n, 46, 187, 192, 195, 210-211, 213, 217n, 218n, 221n, 222
Booking, 29

Bordua, David, 74, 104-105n
Boyle, Emily W., 193, 217-218n, 222
Brannon, Bernard C., 94, 111n
Brennan, Justice William, 123, 135, 153-154, 156
Brown, Justrice Henry B., 119
Burger, Chief Justice Warren E., 48, 61n, 91, 131, 133, 134, 138, 142, 155, 157, 167n, 179, 186-187, 196, 212, 217-218n, 221n, 224, 226, 235-236, 253n, 257n, 259n
Burglary, 12

C

Campbell, James S., 45n, 45, 105-106n, 257n, 260n
Cannon, Mark W., 222
Canon, Bradley C., 168n
Cardozo, Justice Benjamin N., 119, 130, 199-200, 219n, 222
Carter, Robert M., 261n
Cash bond programs, 207-210
Casper, Jonathan D., 3, 39n, 46, 169n, 179, 182, 189, 214-215n, 217-218n, 222
Chase, Harold W., 175n, 179
Chauncey, Robert, 254n, 263
Citation in lieu of arrest, 207
Clark, Ramsey, 21-22, 41n, 68, 102n
Clark, Justice Tom, 130, 137, 149, 159-160, 199
Clor, Harry M., 20-21, 41n, 46
Cobb, William E., 255n
Cohen, Morris, 225, 254n, 262
Cole, George F., 220n, 222-223
Collateral attack, 35
Collateral estoppel, 146
Community-based corrections, 241-242
Community Treatment Project (CTP), 241, 243-244
Compliance analysis, 56-61, 264-266
Constraints on judicial administration, 197

Controlled discretion, 154-155
Cooper, H. H. A., 46n, 262-263n
Court administrators, 212
Cressy, Donald R., 41n, 45n, 47, 248, 261n
"Crime control model" of criminal justice, 58
Curtis, Justice Benjamin R., 120

D

Daniel, Clifton, 174n, 180
Dash, Samuel, 133, 167n
Davis, Allen J., 259n
Davis, Kenneth Culp, 40, 43n, 46, 103n, 114
Dawson, Robert O., 35, 45n, 46
Declaratory theory, 198-199
Deterrence, 58, 60, 224, 226-230, 234, 238
Diamond, Martin, 272
Dickinson, John, 270n
Dietze, Gottfried, 271n
Dolbeare, Kenneth M., 214n
Douglas, Justice William O., 127, 140
Douglass, Frederick, 271n
Downie, Leonard, Jr., 197-198, 218-219n, 222
Downing, Rondal G., 219n
Ducat, Craig R., 175n, 179

E

Edelhertz, Herbert, 40n, 47
Ehrlich, Isaac, 227-228, 254-255n, 262
Eidelberg, Paul, 240, 259n
Eisenstein, James, 217n, 222
Elliot, Jonathan, 271n, 272
Erskine, Hazel, 39n, 218n
Etchison, James C., 42n
Etzioni, Amatai, 56-57, 59, 64n, 103n, 111n

INDEX

F

Fairman, Charles, 165, 179
Farrand, Max, 270-271n
The Federalist, 23, 42n, 60, 65n, 116, 163n, 266, 270-272n
Feeley, Malcolm M., 60, 64-65n, 163, 178n, 179, 214-215n, 222
Feeney, Floyd, 261n
Fellman, David, 163n, 179
Fish, Peter Graham, 218-219n, 222
Fisk, Winston Mill, 272
Foote, Caleb, 204, 220n
Ford, Paul Leicester, 270n, 272
Fox, Vernon, 45n, 47, 259-260n, 263
Frank, Jerome, 219n
Frankel, Judge Marvin E., 34, 44n, 47, 176n, 179, 261n
Frankfurter, Justice Felix, 118, 120, 130, 146, 247
Friendly, Alfred, 174n, 179
Friesen, Ernest C., Jr., 196-197, 211, 218-221n, 222
"Fundamental rights" interpretation, 119-121

G

Gabor, Ivan, 103n, 113n
Garfinkel, Herbert, 272
Garmire, Bernard L., 70-71, 76, 81-82, 89, 94, 103-105n, 108n, 111n
Germann, A.C., 104n
Glaser, Daniel, 45n
Glueck, Eleanor, 249, 261n
Glueck, Sheldon, 249, 261n
Goldberg, Justice Arthur, 136
Goldberg, Steven, 179, 228-229, 255n, 262
Goldfarb, Ronald, 174n, 179
Greenwood, Peter, 238, 258n
Gusfield, Joseph, 102n
Gwyn, William B., 107n

H

Habeas corpus, 117, 158
Hahn, Harlan, 78, 107n, 114
Hamilton, Alexander, 267
Hammond, Phillip E., 214n
Hardy, Ben, 40n
Harlan, Justice John Marshall, 119, 122, 137-138, 161
Harris, Richard N., 78, 106n
Hawkins, Gordon, 18, 40n, 47
Hindelang, Michael J., 38, 40n, 101n, 107n, 216n, 261n
Holmes, Justice Oliver Wendell, 200, 219n, 230
Hood, R. G., 258n
Hook, Sidney, 253, 262n, 263
Hughes, Chief Justice Charles Evans, 135

I

Incarceration, 234, 241
Indeterminate sentencing, 188, 231-232
Index crimes, 5
Indictment, 31-32
Information, 31
Interface conflict
    courts and the police, 50-53
    courts and corrections, 53-54
    the police and corrections, 54-56
Israel, Jerold H., 51, 52n, 164n, 166n, 176n, 178n, 179

J

Jacob, Herbert, 39, 43n, 44n, 216n, 218n, 221n, 222
James, Howard, 181, 214n, 222
Johnson, Elmer H., 103-104n
Johnson, Richard M., 214n
Judge shopping, 188
Judicial impact studies, 181-183
Judicial unification, 211-212

K

Kamisar, Yale, 43-44n, 47
Kaplan, John, 18, 40n, 47, 133, 168n, 179, 263
Kirby, Michael P., 220-221n
Kirkham, George L., 55, 64n, 66
Kristol, Irving, 20, 20n, 41n
Kuykendall, Jack L., 107n, 114

L

"Labeling" process, 250
LaFave, Wayne R., 43n, 47, 51, 62n, 164n, 166n, 176n, 178n, 179
Larceny-theft, 12
Leinwand, Gerald, 257n, 263
"Least restrictive means" test, 53
Levin, Martin, 238, 257n
Lewis, Anthony, 171n, 179
Lewis, C. S., 226, 232, 254n, 256n, 262
"Lex talionis," 225
Lipsky, Michael, 67, 101-102n, 114
Low, Christopher, 103n, 113n
Lowi, Theodore, J., 272n, 273

M

McConnell, Grant, 272n, 273
McDonell, Gary L., 107n
McIntyre, Donald M., 43n, 47n, 61, 62n, 66, 262n
Mandatory capital punishment, 154-156
Manhattan Bail Project, 204
Mannering, John W., 238, 258
Manwaring, David, 215n
Marshall, Chief Justice John, 118
Marshall, Justice Thurgood, 152-154, 156
Martinson, Robert, 45n, 47, 65n, 239, 243, 247, 257-258n, 260-261n, 263, 269, 272n
Mather, Lynn, 218n

Mathews, Justice Stanley, 122
Medalie, Richard J., 215n
Mendelsohn, Harold, 85, 102n, 108n, 113
Mendelson, Wallace, 179
Menninger, Karl, 256n
Mill, John Stuart, 19, 41n
Miller, Frank W., 44n
Milner, Neal, 182, 215n, 222
Montesquieu, Baron de, 60, 65n, 267-268, 271n
Montreal police strike, 227
Morris, Gouverneur, 267
Morris, Norval, 18, 40n, 47, 259n
Mueller, Gerhard O. W., 46n, 262-263n
Muir, William K., Jr., 214n
Mulkey, Michael, 217-218n
Mullen, Joan, 46n, 262n, 263
Murder, 6-7
Murphy, Justice Frank, 140
Murphy, Jeffrey, 226, 254n, 258n, 263
Murphy, Michael J., 215n, 222
Murphy, Walter F., 214n

N

Nagel, Stuart S., 215n
Neubauer, David, 43-44n, 47, 61, 220n, 223
Newman, Donald J., 47
Niederhoffer, Arthur, 70, 103n, 106n, 108n, 261n
Norris, Donald F., 104n

O

Oaks, Dallin, 133, 167n, 179, 215n
Ostrom, Eleanor, 96, 112-113n, 114
Ostrom, Vincent, 96, 111n, 113
Overcharging
    vertical, 189, 192
    horizontal, 189, 192

INDEX

P

Packer, Herbert L., 40n, 47-48, 58-59, 61n, 65n, 66, 183-185, 216n, 223, 227, 252, 253-254n, 262n, 263
Parks, Roger B., 96, 112-113n, 114
Parole, 37, 247-249
Patric, Gordon, 214n
Paulsen, Monrad, 131, 167n
Peremptory challenge, 33, 148
Perry, David C., 114
"Plain view" doctrine, 126
Plattner, Marc F., 263
Plea bargaining
  abolition of, 201
  advantages of, 1-2, 48-49, 188-192
  defined, 1-2
  disadvantages, 3, 49, 192-194
  federal rules for regulation of, 213-214
  public opposition to, 194-195
Police advocacy, 59
Police-community relations
  negative reinforcements, 79-80
  problematic nature of, 99-101
  proposed reforms, 80-81
Police fraternalization, 77, 268
"Police perjury," 132
Police personality, 82-85
Police role
  law enforcement and order maintenance, 71-73
  police advocacy, 73-74
  role conflict, 76
  social service role, 73
Politics of complicity, 188, 195-196, 269
Positivist jurisprudence, 199-200
Powell, Justice Lewis, 134, 147, 154-155
Preliminary hearing, 31
Presentence investigation report, 242-243, 245-246
Presumption of guilt, 184
Presumption of innocence, 185

Pretrial diversion, 29, 37, 51, 201-202, 249-252
Pritchett, C. Herman, 62n, 169n, 180
Probation, 36, 242-247

R

Radelet, Louis A., 77, 106n, 114
Radzinowicz, Leon, 263
Randolph, Edmund, 270n
Rape, 11
Reardon, Paul C., 174n, 180
Rehabilitation, 58, 60, 224, 230-234, 238
Rehnquist, Justice William, 128, 134, 139, 142, 155, 157
Reiss, Albert J., 62n, 66, 69, 76, 103n, 105n, 107n, 112n, 114
Release on recognizance (ROR), 30, 207
Restitution, 250-252
Retribution, 58, 60, 224, 225-226, 234, 238
Retroactivity, 159-161
Robbery, 11
Roberts, Justice Owen J., 140
Robertson, John A., 223
Robison, James, 256-257n, 260n, 263
Rosenhan, D. L., 233, 263
Rossum, Ralph A., 45n, 45, 65n, 66, 105-106n, 108n, 111-112n, 113-114, 165n, 176n, 178-179n, 179-180, 217-218n, 220n, 222-223, 259n, 261n, 270n, 272n, 273
Rottenberg, Simon, 255n, 263
Rubin, Jesse, 71, 102n, 104-105n
Ruchelman, Leonard, 103n, 105n, 114

S

Santarelli, Donald, 14
Saunders, Charles, Jr., 86-87, 108-109n, 111n, 114
Schlesinger, Steven R., 180

Schwartz, Herman, 159, 177n
Scott, Robert, 48, 57, 61n, 64n, 111n
Screening, 50-51, 201-202
Seeburger, Richard H., 215n
Selective incorporation, 122-124
Self-representation, 142-143
Shinnar, Reuel, 239-240, 259n
Shinnar, Shlomo, 239-240, 259n
Sigler, Jay A., 172n, 180
Skogan, Wesley C., 39n
Skolnick, Jerome, 52, 62n, 65n, 66, 71, 103n, 108n, 114, 131, 132, 167n, 180, 216n
Smith, Gerald, 256-257n, 260n, 263
Sorouf, Frank J., 214n
Special Intensive Parole Unit (SIPU), 244-245
Speedy Trial Act of 1974, 187
Steinmetz, Suzanne, K., 43n, 104n
Stevens, Justice John Paul, 154-155
Stewart, Justice Potter, 126, 129, 134, 137, 142, 146, 149, 151, 153-155, 160
Storing, Herbert J., 271n
Street level bureaucrats, 67
Sutherland, Edwin H., 41n, 45n, 47, 248, 261n
Sutherland, Justice George, 140, 143
"System overload," 58
Szasz, Thomas S., 256n, 263

T

Tanenhaus, Joseph, 214n
Terris, Bruce J., 104n, 107n
Thomas, William R., 168n
Thorton, Warren, 261n
Tigar, Michael E., 215n, 223
Tocqueville, Alexis de, 60, 65n, 266-269, 270-271n, 273
Total incorporation, 121-122
Traynor, Robert J., 51
Tullock, Gordon, 247, 255n, 256n, 261n, 263
Tydings, Senator Joseph, 196

U

Uniform Crime Reports, 5

V

van den Haag, Ernest, 255n, 263
Vera Institute, 252
"Victimless crimes"
  arguments against, 17-20
  arguments for, 20-21
  number of, 16-17
Voir dire, 33

W

Wald, Michael, 215n, 223
Walnut Street Prison, 234
Wambaugh, Joseph, 77, 105n
Ward, Richard H., 70, 103n
Warren, Chief Justice Earl, 127, 135, 137, 151, 162
Warren, Mercy, 270n
Wasby, Stephen L., 45n, 168n, 180, 214n, 223
Wasserman, Robert, 74, 104-105n
Watson, Richard A., 219n
Way, H. Frank, Jr., 214n
Weber, Max, 99, 112n
Webster, Noah, 270n
Weihofen, Henry, 253n
Westley, William A., 71, 104n, 114
Wettick, R. Stanton, Jr., 215n
Whitaker, Gordon P., 96, 112-113n, 114
White, Justice Byron, 126, 128, 134, 137-138, 148, 150, 153, 155, 156
White collar crime
  cost of, 15-16
  kinds of, 14-15
Wice, Paul, 44n
Wickersham Commission, 92, 139
Wilkins, Leslie T., 258n
Wilson, James, 270n

Wilson, James Q., 22-23, 28, 42-43n, 47, 65n, 75, 78-79, 82, 100, 102-103n, 105-107n, 113n, 114-115, 224, 228, 238, 239, 253-255n, 258-259n, 263, 265, 270n
Wolff, Robert Paul, 65n, 269, 272n, 273
Wolfgang, Marvin E., 263
Wolfson, Stanley, 98, 112n, 113
Wood, Gordon S., 270n
Wright, Benjamin F., 271n

Z

Zimmerman, Joseph, 112n